The Modern Language Review

JULY 2014   VOLUME 109   PART 3

General Editor
PROFESSOR DEREK CONNON

English Editor
PROFESSOR ANDREW HISCOCK

French Editor
DR ALISON WILLIAMS

Italian Editor
PROFESSOR JANE EVERSON

Hispanic Editor
PROFESSOR DEREK FLITTER

Germanic Editor
PROFESSOR ROBERT VILAIN

Slavonic Editor
DR KATHARINE HODGSON

Assistant Editor
DR JOHN WAŚ

MODERN HUMANITIES RESEARCH ASSOCIATION

The Modern Humanities Research Association

was founded in Cambridge in 1918 and has become an international organization with members in all parts of the world. It is a registered charity number 1064670, and a company limited by guarantee, registered in England number 3446016. Its main object is to encourage advanced study and research in modern and medieval European languages, literatures, and cultures by its publication of journals, book series, and its Style Guide.

Further information about the activities of the Association and individual membership may be obtained from the Hon. Secretary, Dr Barbara Burns, School of Modern Languages and Cultures, University of Glasgow, Glasgow G12 8RS, UK, email membership@mhra.org.uk, or from the website at www.mhra.org.uk

The Association's publications, including most back volumes, are available in print or electronically. Full details are available from www.mhra.org.uk

The Modern Language Review

The *Modern Language Review* is one of five journals available to members of the Modern Humanities Research Association in return for a composite membership subscription payable in advance through the Assistant Treasurer. (Associate membership is open to graduates for four years after their first degree, and postgraduate membership is also available.) Some other publications of the MHRA are available to members at special rates.

The *Modern Language Review* and other journals published by the MHRA may be ordered from JSTOR (http://about.jstor.org/csp).

ISSN 0026–7937 (Print)
ISSN 2222–4319 (Online)
© 2014 The Modern Humanities Research Association

All rights reserved. No part of this publication may be reproduced in any material form (including photocopying or storing it in any medium by electronic means) without the prior written permission of the copyright owner, except in accordance with the provisions of the Copyright, Designs and Patents Act 1988, or under the terms of a licence permitting restricted copying issued in the UK by the Copyright Licensing Agency Ltd, Saffron House, 6–10 Kirby Street, London EC1N 8TS, England, or in the USA by the Copyright Clearance Center, 222 Rosewood Drive, Danvers, Mass. 01923. Application for the written permission of the copyright owner to reproduce any part of this publication must be made to the General Editor.

DISCLAIMER

Statements of fact and opinion in the content of the *Modern Language Review* are those of the respective authors and contributors and not of the journal editors or of the Modern Humanities Research Association (MHRA). MHRA makes no representation, express or implied, in respect of the accuracy of the material in this journal and cannot accept any legal responsibility or liability for any errors or omissions that may be made.

TYPESET BY JOHN WAŚ, OXFORD

Guidelines for Contributors to *MLR*

The *Modern Language Review* publishes articles and book reviews in English on any aspect of modern and medieval European (including English and Latin American) languages, literatures, and cultures (including cinema). The journal does not publish correspondence. We are glad to receive general and comparative articles as well as those on language-specific topics. We encourage submissions from postgraduates. Articles should be submitted to the appropriate section editor in one typescript copy together with an identical electronic copy sent as an email attachment. Articles should conform precisely to the conventions of the *MHRA Style Guide*, 3rd edn, 2013 (ISBN 978-1-78188-009-8), obtainable from www.style.mhra.org.uk, price £6.50, US$13, €8; an online version of the *Guide* is also available from the same address. Authors should provide an abstract of their articles with keywords highlighted in bold type. This abstract should not exceed 100 words. At the end of articles and reviews contributors should include, in this order, their affiliation or location; name as it is to be printed; name and postal address for correspondence; and email address. Simple references should be incorporated into the text (see *MHRA Style Guide*, 10.2). Double spacing should be used throughout, including quotations and footnotes, which should be in the same large size of type as the rest of the article. Articles are typically about 8000 words in length including footnotes, but longer and shorter ones are also welcome. Quotations and references should be carefully checked. Quotations from languages covered by the journal, and from Latin and Greek, should be given in the original language. Latin and Greek passages should normally be translated or at least paraphrased; usually this is not required in the case of modern languages, though it may be helpful where dialects or early forms of the language are cited. However, since the journal has a broad readership, please provide translations or paraphrases of quotations within comparative or general articles (except for modern French). If in doubt, consult the appropriate section editor.

The *Modern Language Review* regrets that it must charge contributors for the cost of corrections in proof which the Editor in his or her discretion thinks excessive. Contributors should keep a copy of their typescript. Typescripts not accepted for publication will not normally be returned. If your article is accepted, you will be asked to supply a definitive version of it both in hard copy and as an email attachment. Authors should ensure that there is no discrepancy between the computer file and the printout.

It is a condition of publication in this journal that authors of articles and reviews assign copyright, including electronic copyright, to the MHRA. *Inter alia*, this allows the General Editor to deal efficiently and consistently with requests from third parties for permission to reproduce material. The journal has been published simultaneously in printed and electronic form since January 2001. Permission, without fee, for authors to use their own material in other publications, after a reasonable period of time has elapsed, is not normally withheld.

On publication of each issue of the journal authors will receive, by email, the finalized PDF of their contribution as it appears in the printed volume. Physical offprints are not supplied. Authors of articles will also receive a complimentary copy of the printed issue in which the article appears.

Articles and books for review should be sent to the Editor concerned:

General and Comparative. Professor Derek Connon, Department of French, Swansea University, Swansea, SA2 8PP (d.f.connon@swansea.ac.uk).
English and American. Professor Andrew Hiscock, School of English, Bangor University, Bangor, LL57 2DG (mhraassistant@bangor.ac.uk).
French. Dr Alison Williams, Department of French, Swansea University, Swansea, SA2 8PP (a.j.williams@swansea.ac.uk).
Italian. Professor Guido Bonsaver, Pembroke College, Oxford OX1 1DW (guido.bonsaver@pmb.ox.ac.uk).
Hispanic. Professor Derek Flitter, School of Modern Languages, Queen's Building, University of Exeter, Exeter EX4 4QH (d.w.flitter@exeter.ac.uk).
German, Dutch, and Scandinavian. Professor Robert Vilain, School of Modern Languages, University of Bristol, 17 Woodland Road, Bristol, BS8 1TE (robert.vilain@bristol.ac.uk).
Slavonic and Eastern European. Dr Katharine Hodgson, School of Modern Languages, Queen's Building, University of Exeter, Exeter EX4 4QH (k.m.hodgson@exeter.ac.uk).

CONTENTS

ARTICLES

	PAGE
'Simplicité, clarté et précision': Grammars of Italian 'pour les Dames' and Other Learners in Eighteenth- and Early Nineteenth-Century France By HELENA SANSON	593
Filming the Silent (Br)Other: Levinasian Ethics and Aesthetic Faith in Patrick Drevet's *Les Gardiens des pierres* and Philip Gröning's *Die große Stille* By ERIN TREMBLAY PONNOU-DELAFFON	617
An Unthinkable *History of King Richard the Third*: Thomas More's Fragment and his Answer to Lucian's *Tyrannicide* By JÜRGEN MEYER	629
Lord Byron: Paratext and Poetics By OURANIA CHATSIOU	640
'Why don't you write a play?' Kipling the Poet in Full By JOHN BATCHELOR	663
Narratives of Child Sexual Abuse in Cristina Comencini's Novel *La bestia nel cuore* By LUCIANO PARISI	674
Vallejo and González Prada: A Note on *Trilce* XIX By DOMINIC MORAN	689
'Die Juden schießen!' Translations by Hermann Adler and Wolf Biermann of Yitzhak Katzenelson's Epic Poem of the Warsaw Ghetto By PETER DAVIES	708
Writers' Linguistic Observations and Creating Myths about Languages: Czesław Miłosz and Joseph Brodsky in Search of the 'Slavonic Genius of Language' By SHAMIL KHAIROV	726
Freedom and Captivity in the Works of Vladimir Sorokin and Vladimir Tuchkov By NICOLAS DREYER	749

REVIEWS

Stories and Minds: Cognitive Approaches to Literary Narrative, ed. by Lars Bernaerts and others (RICHARD WALSH)	775
Literary Studies and the Pursuits of Reading, ed. by Eric Downing and others (JOHANNES ENDRES)	776
Elizabeth B. Bearden, *The Emblematics of the Self: Ekphrasis and Identity in Renaissance Imitations of Greek Romance* (STEVEN MENTZ)	777
Patricia Eichel-Lojkine, *Contes en réseaux: l'émergence du conte sur la scène littéraire européenne* (MARIE-CLAUDE CANOVA-GREEN)	779
Monika Class, *Coleridge and Kantian Ideas in England, 1796–1817: Coleridge's Responses to German Philosophy* (PHILIPP HUNNEKUHL)	780
Adam Max Cohen, *Wonder in Shakespeare* (PETER SILLITOE)	781
Early African American Print Culture, ed. by Lara Langer Cohen and Jordan Alexander Stein (KATY L. CHILES)	783
Michael R. Page, *The Literary Imagination from Erasmus Darwin to H. G. Wells: Science, Evolution, and Ecology* (KEITH WILLIAMS)	784

Rosemary Ashton, *Victorian Bloomsbury* (ROSALIND CRONE) 786
Science in Modern Poetry: New Directions, ed. by John Holmes (PAUL WRIGHT) . . 787
Colin Hill, *Modern Realism in English-Canadian Fiction* (MICHELLE SMITH) . . . 789
Robert Fraser, *Night Thoughts: The Surreal Life of the Poet David Gascoyne* (NEIL ROBERTS) 790
The Oxford Handbook of Modern and Contemporary American Poetry, ed. by Cary Nelson (STEPHEN FREDMAN) 791
Julia Novak, *Live Poetry: An Integrated Approach to Poetry in Performance* (SAMUEL ROGERS) 794
The Song of Roland, trans. by John DuVal, intro. by David Staines (LUKE SUNDERLAND) 795
Wace, *The Hagiographical Works: The 'Conception Nostre Dame' and the Lives of St Margaret and St Nicholas*, ed. and trans. by Jean Blacker and others (HUW GRANGE) 796
Les Paroles Salomun, ed. by Tony Hunt (MAUREEN BOULTON) 798
Texte et contre-texte pour la période pré-moderne, ed. by Nelly Labère (JONATHAN PATTERSON) 799
Procès de Jacques d'Armagnac: édition critique du ms. 2000 de la Bibliothèque Sainte-Geneviève, ed. by Joël Blanchard (IRÈNE FABRY-TEHRANCHI) 800
Irit Ruth Kleiman, *Philippe de Commynes: Memory, Betrayal, Text* (CATHERINE EMERSON) 801
Corneille, Molière, Racine: Four French Plays. 'Cinna', 'The Misanthrope', 'Andromache', 'Phaedra', trans. by John Edmunds, intro. by Joseph Harris (TIM CHILCOTT) . . 802
Michel Jeanneret, *Versailles, ordre et chaos*; André Félibien, *Les Fêtes de Versailles*, ed. by Michel Jeanneret (MARIE-CLAUDE CANOVA-GREEN) 803
Correspondance de Pierre Bayle, vol. X: *Avril 1696–juillet 1697. Lettres 1100–1280*, ed. by Elisabeth Labrousse and Antony McKenna (JOHN CHRISTIAN LAURSEN) . . . 805
William F. Edmiston, *Sade: Queer Theorist* (PETER CRYLE) 806
Honoré de Balzac, *'The Girl with the Golden Eyes' and Other Stories*, trans. by Peter Collier, intro. by Patrick Coleman (ANDREW WATTS) 807
Francesco Manzini, *The Fevered Novel from Balzac to Bernanos: Frenetic Catholicism in Crisis, Delirium and Revolution* (OWEN HEATHCOTE) 808
Hannah Thompson, *Taboo: Corporeal Secrets in Nineteenth-Century France* (FRANÇOISE GRAUBY) 809
La Littérature symboliste et la Langue, ed. by Olivier Bivort (SAM BOOTLE) 810
Allen Thiher, *Understanding Marcel Proust* (JENNIFER RUSHWORTH) 812
Alfred Séguin, *Le Robinson noir*, ed. and intro. by Roger Little; Julie Gouraud, *Les Deux Enfants de Saint-Domingue*, and Michel Möring, *L'Esclave de Saint-Domingue*, ed. and intro. by Roger Little (JARROD HAYES) 813
Kate Griffiths and Andrew Watts, *Adapting Nineteenth-Century France: Literature in Film, Theatre, Television, Radio and Print* (BRADLEY STEPHENS) 815
Albert Camus au quotidien, ed. by André Benhaïm and Aymeric Glacet (MARK ORME) 816
Claire Gorrara, *French Crime Fiction and the Second World War: Past Crimes, Present Memories* (ANGELA KIMYONGÜR) 817
Christina Howells, *Mortal Subjects: Passions of the Soul in Late Twentieth-Century French Thought* (JAMES WILLIAMS) 818
Rebelles et criminelles chez les écrivaines d'expression française, ed. by Frédérique Chevillot and Colette Trout (NATHALIE MORELLO) 819
George Corbett, *Dante and Epicurus: A Dualist Vision of Secular and Spiritual Fulfilment* (JENNIFER RUSHWORTH) 821
Idee su Dante: esperimenti danteschi 2012. Atti del Convegno, Milano, 9-10 maggio 2012, ed. by Carlo Carù (PAOLO DE VENTURA) 822

Contents

The Printed Media in Fin-de-Siècle Italy: Publishers, Writers, and Readers, ed. by Ann Hallamore Caesar and others (URSULA J. FANNING)	824
Elizabeth Leake, *After Words: Suicide and Authorship in Twentieth-Century Italy* (ROBERT S. C. GORDON)	826
Deborah Amberson, *Giraffes in the Garden of Italian Literature: Modernist Embodiment in Italo Svevo, Federigo Tozzi and Carlo Emilio Gadda* (GIUSEPPE STELLARDI)	828
Nicola McLelland, *J. G. Schottelius's 'Ausführliche Arbeit von der Teutschen HaubtSprache' (1663) and its Place in Early Modern European Vernacular Language Study* (DAVID N. YEANDLE)	829
Felicity Rash, *German Images of the Self and the Other: Nationalist, Colonialist and Anti-Semitic Discourse, 1871–1918* (FLORIAN KROBB)	832
Burkhard Meyer-Sickendiek, *Lyrisches Gespür: Vom geheimen Sensorium moderner Poesie* (RÜDIGER GÖRNER)	834
Stephan Kraft, *Zum Ende der Komödie: Eine Theoriegeschichte des Happyends* (THOMAS MARTINEC)	836
Grenzen im Raum — Grenzen in der Literatur, ed. by Eva Geulen and Stephan Kraft (TOM CHEESMAN)	837
Sadness and Melancholy in German-Language Literature and Culture, ed. by Mary Cosgrove and Anna Richards (INGO CORNILS)	839
Barthold Heinrich Brockes, *Werke*, vol. I: *Selbstbiographie, Verdeutschter Bethlemitischer Kinder-Mord, Gelegenheitsgedichte, Aufsätze*, ed. by Jürgen Rathje (KEVIN HILLIARD)	840
Nadja Reinhard, *Moral und Ironie bei Gottlieb Wilhelm Rabener: Paratext und Palimpsest in den Satyrischen Schriften* (K. F. HILLIARD)	842
Tom Kindt, *Literatur und Komik: Zur Theorie literarischer Komik und zur deutschen Komödie im 18. Jahrhundert* (THOMAS MARTINEC)	844
Yvonne Joeres, *Die 'Don-Quijote'-Rezeption Friedrich Schlegels und Heinrich Heines im Kontext des europäischen Kulturtransfers: Ein Narr als Angelpunkt transnationaler Denkansätze* (CLAUDIA NITSCHKE)	845
Christian van der Steeg, *Wissenskunst: Adalbert Stifter und Naturforscher auf Weltreise* (MICHAEL MINDEN)	846
John Walker, *The Truth of Realism: A Reassessment of the German Novel 1830–1900* (DIRK GÖTTSCHE)	847
Matt ffytche, *The Foundation of the Unconscious: Schelling, Freud and the Birth of the Modern Psyche* (MARTIN LIEBSCHER)	848
Franz Richard Behrens, *Todlob: Feldtagebuchgedichte 1915/16*, ed. by Michael Lentz; *Mein bester Freund — Hamlet: Drehbücher, Kinotexte, Filmkritiken*, ed. by Gerhard Rühm and Monika Lichtenfeld (JEREMY ADLER)	850
Genese Grill, *The World as Metaphor in Robert Musil's 'The Man without Qualities': Possibility as Reality* (DANIEL STEUER)	851
Kafka, Prag und der Erste Weltkrieg/Kafka, Prague and the First World War, ed. by Manfred Engel and Ritchie Robertson; *Kafka und Prag: Literatur-, kultur-, sozial- und sprachhistorische Kontexte*, ed. by Peter Becher and others (JEREMY ADLER)	853
Paul Michael Lützeler, *Hermann Broch und die Moderne: Roman, Menschenrecht, Biografie* (DARIA SANTINI)	856
Andrew Barker, *Fictions from an Orphan State: Literary Reflections between Habsburg and Hitler* (DAVID MIDGLEY)	857
Robert K. Weninger, *The German Joyce* (DAVID MIDGLEY)	858
Anja Bischof, *Funktion und Bedeutung von Erinnerung im erzählerischen Werk Johannes Urzidils* (RITCHIE ROBERTSON)	860

'*Man will werden, nicht gewesen sein*': *Zur Aktualität Max Frischs*, ed. by Daniel Müller Nielaba and others (HANS J. HAHN) 861
Axel Englund, *Still Songs: Music in and around the Poetry of Paul Celan* (ANNJA NEUMANN) 862
Judith Schossböck, *Letzte Menschen: Postapokalyptische Narrative und Identitäten in der Neueren Literatur nach 1945* (ROBERT WENINGER) 863
A New History of German Cinema, ed. by Jennifer M. Kapczynski and Michael D. Richardson (MARTIN BRADY) 865
Anindita Banerjee, *We Modern People: Science Fiction and the Making of Russian Modernity* (ERIC LAURSEN) 867
Denis Kozlov, *The Readers of 'Novyi mir': Coming to Terms with the Stalinist Past* (CLAIRE SHAW) 868
Abstracts of Articles, Vol. 109, Part 3 (July 2014) 870

'SIMPLICITÉ, CLARTÉ ET PRÉCISION': GRAMMARS OF ITALIAN 'POUR LES DAMES' AND OTHER LEARNERS IN EIGHTEENTH- AND EARLY NINETEENTH-CENTURY FRANCE

Introduction

In 1748, in Berlin, the printing presses of Ambrosius Haude and Johannes Carl Spener published a 464-page grammar entitled *Introduction a la grammaire des Dames* [. . .] *A l'usage de toutes sortes de Commencans*.[1] The author of the text is not named on the title-page, but his name was David Estienne Choffin. In the unpaginated preface he explains his aims:

> J'espere que ce livre pourra servir à toutes sortes de Commencans, jeunes ou vieux, filles ou garcons, savans ou ignorans. [. . .] Elle peut enfin servir aux personnes les plus simples, à qui sans cela on ne peut rien faire comprendre. De sorte qu'à l'egard des commencans, on peut sans exageration appeler cette Methode La methode universelle.

Here the implication is that if a work claimed in its title that it was suitable for a lady, that it was a 'grammaire des Dames', a reader who picked it up from the shelves of a bookshop would implicitly know that it was in fact suitable for all types of beginner. To stress this point, Choffin explicitly deals with it in two interesting model dialogues at the end of his grammar, the first of which is an 'Entretien entre une jeune demoiselle, & une gouvernante francaise, touchant la Grammaire des Dames'. Here a governess and a young girl discuss the main features of the structure and layout of this type of grammar, such as the presence of tables, 'planches', of noun declensions and verb conjugations. More such explanations and descriptions of the adopted strategy follow, also in the second dialogue, where two unidentified speakers converse about how best to use these works to study and learn. The dialogue is also a sort of advertisement for the 'Grammaire des dames' texts in general, and in particular for another such grammar the same author had published:

Research for this article has been possible thanks to the generous support of the Leverhulme Trust, to which I express my sincerest gratitude.

[1] There is a parallel French/German text. The full French title is: *Introduction a la grammaire des Dames; renfermant 1 Une harmonie pratique des langues francoise & allemande 2 Un vocabulaire des mots les plus connus 3 Un recueil de frases les plus communes 4 Et une grammaire concentrée, accompagnée de la Pratique avec un avant-propos ou l'on indique la maniere de se servir de ce livre. A l'usage de toutes sortes de Commencans*. This was followed by other editions in 1757, 1763, and 1783, all with the same publisher, Haude and Spener. The spelling of titles and quotations here and passim has been preserved as in the original and has not been modernized. Inconsistencies are therefore part of the texts.

Quelle grammaire prenez-vous pour la meilleure?
Je n'en sache point qui reunisse d'abord toute la theorie a la pratique, ni qui convienne mieux aux jeunes demoiselles, & aux autres personnes qui ignorent le Latin, que celle qui est intitulée: La grammaire des Dames.[2]
C'est aussi en particulier pour ces personnes-là qu'elle a ete composée? [. . .] La peut-on avoir ici?
On peut l'avoir dans toutes les Villes, si l'on donne commission aux Librairies.
Ou est elle imprimée?
Si je ne me trompe pas, c'est a Berlin.
Je tacherai de me la procurer.
Vous ne vous en repentirez pas.[3]

This grammar by Choffin was far from an isolated case. Across eighteenth-century Europe, a number of authors composed grammars, of their own language or of foreign languages, which addressed a readership of 'ladies', but also at the same time, and more generally, of beginners.[4] Grammarians who indicated in the titles of their works that they had written 'for the Ladies', 'pour les Dames', 'per le Dame', 'für die Damen' (or 'für Frauenzimmer') often also further specified, either in the subtitle or in the body of the text, that they meant to address, more broadly, a readership that was not necessarily familiar with the Latin language—still considered the foundation for any serious study of languages and their grammar. On the contrary, they often insisted on having devised and adopted study methods that did not require any knowledge of the classical language nor any pedantic, boring, or taxing application. Their

---

[2] The reference is here most probably to Choffin's own *Nouvelle grammaire à l'usage des Dames, et des autres personnes qui ne savent pas de latin* (Berlin: Haude & Spener, 1747). In 1756-57 Choffin published also a *Grammaire françoise, réduite en tables, a l'usage des dames, et des autres personnes qui ne savent pas de latin*, 1: *Neue Französische Grammatik Auf eine besondere Art eingerichtet, und in Tabellen gebracht; zum Besten des Frauenzimmers und anderer Personen, die das Latein nicht verstehen*, 2 vols (Berlin: Haude & Spener). There was another edition in 1767-68.

[3] Choffin, *Introduction*, p. 456.

[4] For 'Grammars for the Ladies' as a European phenomenon see *La Grammaire des Dames*, ed. by Wendy Ayres-Bennett (=*Histoire épistémologie langage*, 16.2 (1994)), in particular Gabriele Beck-Busse, 'La Grammaire française dédiée à mes jeunes amies: bibliographie raisonnée de manuels de la langue française à l'usage de la jeunesse féminine (1564-1850)', pp. 35-53; Madeleine Reuillon-Blanquet, 'Les Grammaires des dames en France & l'apprentissage des langues à la fin du XVIIIe siècle', pp. 77-94; Susanne Staudinger and Edeltraud Dobnig-Jülch, 'Frauen+(viel) Grammatik=(viel) Frauengrammatik? Zur Verbreitung und Typologie spezieller Grammatiken im 18. Jahrhundert', pp. 169-90. Also useful, Madeleine Reuillon-Blanquet, 'Grammaires des Dames, ou comment rendre "instructive et amusante" une étude généralement considérée comme rébarbative', in *Langages de la Révolution (1770-1815): actes du 4ème Colloque international de lexicologie politique (1991)* (Paris: Klincksieck, 1995), pp. 163-75; Nadia Minerva, 'Le donne e la grammatica: su alcune "Grammaires des Dames" tra Sette e Ottocento', in *Dames, demoiselles, honnêtes femmes: studi di lingua e letteratura francese offerti a Carla Pellandra*, ed. by Nadia Minerva (Bologna: CLUEB, 2000), pp. 73-105; *Voix féminines: Ève et les langues dans l'Europe moderne. Actes du colloque organisé par la SIHFLES à Gargnano, les 6-8 juin 2011*, ed. by Irene Finotti and Nadia Minerva, Documents pour l'histoire du français langue étrangère ou seconde, 47-48, 2 vols (Saint-Cloud: SIHFLES, 2011-12).

grammars, they claimed, were quite the opposite of this, offering instead a light, engaging, and easy way of learning a new language.

This type of grammatical production is part of a wider European trend in book production at this period, which seemingly targets the same intended readership and which concerns works of science, literature, theology, botany, chemistry, astronomy, physics, and so on. A well-known example of this comes from Italy with Francesco Algarotti's *Newtonianismo per le dame, ovvero dialoghi sopra la luce e i colori*, published in 1737 and soon translated into French, English, and German.[5] A reference to the 'ladies' in the titles of these works can be interpreted as an indirect allusion to a readership which is not composed of scholars or more learned people in general, but, on the contrary, is made of the less learned, beginners even, and to a work that presents the content in a more accessible manner (for instance, as a collection of letters or as a dialogue), making use of a style that is accessible to everyone, with accessible language and accessible terminology.

France saw a good number of 'Grammaires pour les Dames/des Dames' throughout the century. Besides grammars of French, Italian was one of the languages that feature most among texts of this type.[6] Despite recent critical studies on the 'Grammaire des dames', there is a need for further work on the production of Italian grammars in France in the eighteenth and early nineteenth centuries. This article intends to offer a contribution to this topic, by focusing on a selection of grammars of Italian composed by Italian authors, presenting their main features, and analysing how they tried to cater for and adapt to a readership of 'ladies' and non-Latinate learners.

---

[5] For an outline of this type of literary and scientific production 'for the ladies' in the Italian context see Helena Sanson, *Women, Language and Grammar: Italy 1500-1900* (Oxford and London: Oxford University Press for the British Academy, 2011), pp. 188-200; for France, see Linda Timmermans, *L'Accès des femmes à la culture (1598-1715): un débat d'idées de Saint François de Sales à la Marquise de Lambert* (Paris: Champion, 1993), pp. 370-86, and Jeanne Peiffer, 'La Littérature scientifique pour les femmes au siècle des Lumières', in *Sexe et genre: de la hiérarchie entre les sexes*, ed. by Marie-Claude Hurtig and others (Paris: CNRS, 2002), pp. 137-46; for England, Geoffrey V. Sutton, *Science for a Polite Society: Gender, Culture, and the Demonstration of Enlightenment* (Boulder, CO: Westview Press, 1995), and Mary Terrall, 'Natural Philosophy for Fashionable Readers', in *Books and the Sciences in History*, ed. by Marina Frasca-Spada and Nick Jardine (Cambridge: Cambridge University Press, 2000), pp. 231-54; for Germany, Moira R. Rogers, *Newtonianism for the Ladies and Other Uneducated Souls: The Popularization of Science in Leipzig, 1687-1750* (New York: Peter Lang, 2003).

[6] Regarding numbers, based on the presence of the formula 'Grammaire des Dames/pour les Dames/à l'usage des Dames' (or the equivalent in translation) in the actual title, Gabriele Beck-Busse has quantified in a recent study this type of grammatical production, with reference to the French and Italian languages, to include, respectively, 22 and 15 grammars. Of these 37 titles, she specifies, only 15 and 10 respectively are physically extant, although another 13 grammars can be included in the corpus because they share common features with this kind of work, despite the fact that the title does not contain any specific phrase of this type. See Gabriele Beck-Busse, 'A propos d'une histoire des "Grammaires des Dames": réflexions théoriques et approches empiriques', in *Voix féminines*, ed. by Finotti and Minerva, pp. 13-43 (p. 13).

Grammars for French Ladies

Grammarians who wrote in their works that they targeted ladies among their readers often insisted in their prefaces or dedications on the fact that they had adopted special strategies to make sure their grammars were simple, pleasant, and not at all boring. They similarly explained that limited study effort was required. All these reassurances were of course based on long-standing common assumptions that women's weaker intellectual abilities or lack of academic experience made them less able than men to devote themselves to what were perceived as taxing subjects or to engage with abstract ideas. But these reassurances, as we shall see, would equally work for all those who were new to learning languages, or not too familiar with grammar, its terminology, and its categories: that is, a readership of 'commençants'.

Among grammars of French for French ladies, where the label 'pour les/des dames' is explicitly present in the title, we find, for instance, De Prunay's *Grammaire des dames* (1777), Antoine Tournon's *Les Promenades de Clarisse et du marquis de Valzé, ou nouvelle méthode [. . .] à l'usage des dames* (1784), Abbé Barthélemy's *Grammaire des dames* (1785), or Nicolas Adam's *La Vraie Manière d'apprendre une langue quelconque, vivante ou morte, par le moyen de la langue françoise [. . .]. Grammaire françoise universelle à l'usage des dames* (1779). It might seem somehow contradictory that eighteenth-century grammarians would target 'ladies' with their works and insist on the need to learn French well, when in the previous century Vaugelas, in his *Remarques* of 1647, considered women to be arbiters of *bon usage*. But there the focus was, to start with, on spoken French, and ladies' 'ignorance' and lack of formal education were an asset rather than a limitation, because it made them impartial judges on linguistic issues, free as they were from the pedantry and affectation that came with knowledge of the classical languages: ladies had 'un jugement "naïf" ou authentique sur les usages du français'.[7] And one should not forget, of course, that Vaugelas was referring to French as spoken by the elite, namely, to 'la façon de parler de la plus saine partie de la Cour'.[8] Still, despite his views on women's use of French, Vaugelas had thought it necessary

---

[7] Wendy Ayres-Bennett and Magali Seijido, *Remarques et observations sur la langue française: histoire et évolution d'un genre* (Paris: Garnier, 2011), p. 86. See also Wendy Ayres-Bennett, 'Women and Grammar in Seventeenth-Century France', *Seventeenth Century Studies*, 12 (1990), 5–25; 'Le Rôle des femmes dans l'élaboration des idées linguistiques au xviie siècle en France', in *La Grammaire des Dames*, ed. by Ayres-Bennett, pp. 35–53; and *Sociolinguistic Variation in Seventeenth-Century France: Methodology and Case Studies* (Cambridge: Cambridge University Press, 2004). On the influence of Vaugelas on French grammar writing and the tradition of *remarqueurs* see also Ayres-Bennett, *Vaugelas and the Development of French Language* (London: MHRA, 1987), pp. 201–22.

[8] Claude Favre de Vaugelas, *Remarques sur la langue françoise, utiles a ceux qui veulent bien parler et bien escrire* (Paris: Camusat et Le Petit, 1647), fol. a1[v]. He further specifies that the *bon usage* is defined by 'la façon d'escrire de la plus saine partie des Autheurs du temps' and that 'Quand je dis *la Cour*, i'y comprens les femmes comme les hommes, & plusieurs personnes de la

to adapt the presentation and content of his work—for instance by opting for short observations on doubtful points of usage rather than more traditional structures—so that women, and those with no familiarity with Latin, could profit more fully from it.⁹

When in the eighteenth century grammarians shifted their attention rather more to written French, with that came the insistence that les 'dames', and women more generally (so not only the ladies of the court), had to gain a proper knowledge of their mother tongue and its spelling.¹⁰ There could be no excuse for women who made grammatical and spelling mistakes in writing, as was so often the case with their sex. A remedy for this state of affairs had to be found. Yet, this did not mean, of course, that ladies should learn grammar 'par règle', as in the male, Latin-oriented Collèges and universities, as women should, of course, shun any form of affectation and even more so of pedantry. What was needed was a fine balance between both extremes: affectation of knowledge and affectation of ignorance were equally condemned.¹¹

If a sound knowledge of grammar and orthography was required, it was one that had to start from knowledge of French itself rather than from knowledge of Latin (as had traditionally been the case until then), thus reflecting the wider contemporary move away from Latin, and towards French autarchy, in the production of grammars in this period. In this respect, for instance, de Prunay wrote in his *Grammaire des dames*,¹² published in Paris in 1777, that 'les jeunes Demoiselles' had better *not* know Latin, 'la lecture de cette langue etant inutile et meme contraire à la nôtre'. In other words, he continued, 'c'est dans le francais meme qu'il faut apprendre le francais', and by so doing, 'les Dames, désabusées du prejugé qu'il fallait necessairement savoir le latin pour bien ortographier le francais [. . .] se feront un plaisir d'etre en etat d'ecrire

---

ville où le Prince reside, qui par la communication qu'elles ont avec les gens de la Cour participent à sa politesse' (fol. a1ᵛ).

⁹ The same approach was followed by Marguerite Buffet, who, in her *Nouvelles observations sur la langue françoise* (Paris: Cusson, 1668), explicitly aimed to present her material in a simplified and abbreviated manner, so as to avoid boring her female readers. For the association between women and those who did not know Latin see Gabriele Beck-Busse, 'Les "femmes" et les "illitterati"; ou, la question du latin et de la langue vulgaire', in *La Grammaire des Dames*, ed. by Ayres-Bennet, pp. 95–119.

¹⁰ See Reuillon-Blanquet, 'Les Grammaires des Dames en France'; Deena Goodman, '*L'Ortografe des dames*: Gender and Language in the Old Regime', *French Historical Studies*, 25 (2002), 191–223. General accusations against women's faulty written usage were not absent in the seventeenth century either, of course, but in the metalinguistic texts there are few comments on this point. See Ayres-Bennett, *Sociolinguistic Variation*, pp. 128–29, 165.

¹¹ The linguistic usage of the Précieuses was seen as an extreme case of affectation and was often the object of satirical attacks. See on this Ayres-Bennett, *Sociolinguistic Variation*, pp. 133–43.

¹² De Prunay, *Grammaire des dames, ou l'on trouvera des principes surs & faciles, pour apprendre à ortographier correctement la Langue francaise, avec les moyens de connaitre les expressions provinciales, de les eviter, & de prevenir, chez les jeunes demoiselles, l'habitude d'une prononciation vicieuse* (Paris: Lottin l'aîné, 1777).

aussi correctement qu'elles parlent'.[13] Two years later, along the same lines, Nicolas Adam proposed a series of grammars that were based first of all on systematic and sound knowledge of French, as expounded in his *Grammaire françoise universelle à l'usage des dames* (1779).[14] Clearly finding his inspiration in the new approach of the Port-Royal grammarians, according to whom it was possible to identify some universal foundations that lay at the basis of all languages, Adam insisted that only once French ladies knew their mother tongue well could they then successfully proceed to study Latin, as well as other foreign languages. Wanting to offer his readers the means to do so, he embarked on publishing grammars of Latin (1780), Italian (1783), English (1786), and German (1787),[15] all of which required a prior sound knowledge of his 1779 French grammar. More broadly, then, grammars 'pour les Dames' could also commonly indicate works which proposed a learning method that turned on its head the hierarchical order between Latin and the vernaculars, and one which did not require (or at least this was the claim) any previous knowledge of the classical language.[16]

This type of claim and learning method was applied also to the acquisition of foreign languages, very useful ornaments for refined ladies, 'une perfection sans laquelle il n'est presque pas possible, qu'une Dame soit bien élevée'.[17] Among the languages that would adorn 'les Dames', Italian played an important role. Despite its prestige having slowly decreased on an international

---

[13] Ibid., pp. xxiii–xxxi.

[14] Nicolas Adam, *La Vraie Manière d'apprendre une langue quelconque, vivante ou morte, par le moyen de la langue françoise; ouvrage divisé en plusieurs parties. 1 Grammaire françoise à l'usage des dames, servant de base à toutes les autres Langues. 2 Grammaire italienne. 3 Grammaire latine. 4 Grammaire angloise. 5 Grammaire allemande. 6 Grammaire, &c. &c &c. Ière partie* (Paris: Benoît Morin, 1779).

[15] Nicolas Adam, *La Vraie Manière d'apprendre une langue quelconque, vivante ou morte, par le moyen de la langue françoise, ou démonstration et pratique de la nouvelle méthode d'enseignement. Grammaire latine* (Paris: Benoît Morin, 1780); *Grammaire italienne, à l'usage des dames, ou la vraie maniere d'apprendre aisément, et le plus promptement qu'il est possible, la langue italienne, par le moyen de la Grammaire françoise universelle, à l'usage des dames* (Paris: Benoît Morin, 1783); *La Vraie Manière d'apprendre une langue quelconque, vivante ou morte, par le moyen de la langue françoise, ou démonstration et pratique de la nouvelle méthode d'enseignement. Grammaire anglaise* (Paris: Benoît Morin, 1786); *La Vraie Manière d'apprendre une langue quelconque, vivante ou morte, par le moyen de la langue françoise. Cinquième partie. Grammaire allemande* (Paris: Benoît Morin, 1787).

[16] Adam's production of grammatical works calls to mind that which followed Claude Lancelot's *Nouvelle méthode pour apprendre facilement et en peu de temps la langue latine* (Paris: Antoine Vitré, 1644), composed for the Petites Écoles of Port-Royal, with his subsequent grammars to learn Greek (1655), Spanish (1660), and Italian (1660). Adam starts from French, though, and then moves on to other languages.

[17] *Bibliothèque des Dames, contenant Des Règles générales pour leur conduite, dans toutes les circonstances de la Vie. Écrite par une Dame, & publiée par Mr Le Chev. R. Steele. Traduite de l'Anglois* (Amsterdam: Emanuel du Villard, 1716), p. 22. The considerations expressed in the text, which is usually attributed to Mary Harrison, Lady Wray, and translated into French by François Michel Janiçon, apply equally well to French ladies at the time.

level compared with previous centuries, in the eighteenth century it continued to be widely appreciated throughout Europe within the traditional contexts of music and theatre.[18] Besides being fashionable in elegant conversation, it was also used, for instance, by intellectuals and artists. A case in point is Voltaire,[19] whose interest in and experience of the Italian language were certainly influenced by two important women in his life, both of them *italianisantes*, namely his beloved Émilie du Châtelet (1706–1749) and Madame Denis (Marie Louise Mignot, 1712–1790), his niece and companion in the years spent at the Château de Ferney.

Showing knowledge of Italian was a way for Parisian ladies to dazzle in society. Some writers felt obliged to warn women of the potential dangers that learning the language could entail, though, given that Italian was often perceived across Europe as the language of love:[20] 'Les femmes apprennent volontiers l'Italien qui me paroît dangereux'—we read in the Marquise de Lambert's *Lettres sur la véritable éducation* (1729) addressed to her daughter—'c'est la langue de l'amour, les Auteurs Italiens sont peu chatiez: il regne dans leurs ouvrages un jeu de mots, une imagination sans regle qui s'oppose à la justesse de l'esprit'.[21] Potential temptations and dangers aside, ladies loved it and they could count on help in learning it coming from Italian teachers, or Italianized French teachers, who were plentiful, especially in the capital. To learn Italian, ladies could also avail themselves of a rich production of Italian grammars,[22] as well as of grammars meant specifically 'pour les Dames'.

Some of these texts might not present specifically the label 'pour les Dames/ des Dames' in the title, but were still meant for ladies, as well as for those, men

---

[18] On the question of teaching and learning Italian in France in earlier periods, namely between 1500 and 1650, see, for a general discussion, Nicole Bingen, 'L'insegnamento dell'italiano nei paesi di lingua francese dal 1500 al 1650', in *Italia ed Europa nella linguistica del Rinascimento: confronti e relazioni. Atti del Convegno internazionale Ferrara Palazzo Paradiso 20–24 marzo 1991*, ed. by Mirko Tavoni, 2 vols (Modena: Panini, 1996), I, 419–41; for a bibliography of texts to learn Italian see Bingen, *Le Maître italien (1510–1660): bibliographie des ouvrages d'enseignement de la langue italienne destinés au public de langue française, suivie d'un répertoire des ouvrages bilingues imprimés dans les pays de langue française* (Brussels: Van Balberghe, 1987); and for a bibliography of Italian works published in French-speaking countries in the sixteenth and seventeenth centuries see Bingen, *Philausone (1500–1660): répertoire des ouvrages en langue italienne publiés dans les pays de langue française de 1500 à 1660* (Geneva: Droz, 1994).

[19] See Gianfranco Folena, 'Divagazioni sull'italiano di Voltaire', in his *L'italiano in Europa: esperienze linguistiche del Settecento* (Turin: Einaudi, 1983), pp. 397–431.

[20] On linguistic commonplaces see Harro Stammerjohann, 'L'immagine della lingua italiana in Europa', in *Linguistica italiana fuori d'Italia: studi, istituzioni*, ed. by Lorenzo Renzi and Michele A. Cortelazzo (Rome: Bulzoni, 1997), pp. 27–51. And of course Bouhours recalls, in his *Entretiens d'Ariste et d'Eugène* (Paris: Sebastien Mabre-Cramoisy, 1671), two anecdotes, attributed respectively to Charles V and a Spanish 'cavalier', claiming that Italian was the language of the 'Dames', and that in the Earthly Paradise Eve spoke Italian (and Adam French) (p. 90).

[21] *Lettres sur la véritable éducation* (Amsterdam: Bernard, 1729), p. 144.

[22] On the very first grammars of Italian for French-speakers see Giada Mattarucco, *Prime grammatiche d'italiano per francesi: secoli 16–17* (Florence: Accademia della Crusca, 2003).

and women, who, the author explains, did not know Latin. Placido Catanusi, for instance, a man of letters from Messina living in Paris, professor of civil and canon law, published his *Instruction a la langue italienne* in 1667, dedicating it 'A Son Altesse Royale Madame la Duchesse de Guyse' and more generally to the 'Dames délicates', to whom 'la méthode pedantesque fait horreur, & qui cherchent pour apprendre l'Italien des voyes plus douces, & plus aisées'.[23] This is why in his short text (120 pages) he avoids grammatical terminology and offers, in a discursive structure and tone, linguistic suggestions rather than rules ('sans les Règles de Grammaire'), believing as he does that Italian should rather be learnt by reading good authors. He also advises his pupils to learn by heart the Italian lyrics he has adapted to contemporary French arias.[24] Similarly, Claudio Borgesi wanted to assist the 'personnes sans étude' in learning Italian: in 1673 he published his *Nouvelle methode ou Grammaire italienne pour apprendre facilement & en peu de temps la Langue*, specifically, we learn from the title-page, 'en faveur de ceux & celles qui n'entendent point la Langue Latine' and 'commode aussi aux Etrangers, pour sçavoir les difficultez Françoises'.[25] The emphasis is, right from the title, on readers being able to learn in a short time with limited effort, thus echoing very closely, as we saw earlier, the formulation in Lancelot's grammar and other seventeenth-century *Méthodes*.[26]

---

[23] Catanusi, *Instruction a la langue italienne pour l'apprendre sans les Regles de la Grammaire. Avec un Recueil de Chansons accommodées aux Airs François, & un Traité de la Poësie Italienne pour les plus Curieux* (Paris: Mettayer et chez l'Auteur, 1667), p. 3. The following year Catanusi published another text, which, despite its similar title (*Instruction a la langue italienne, contenant deux parties, dans la premiere il est traitté de tout ce qui regarde la parfaite connoissance de cette Langue. Et la seconde est un Recueil de Chansons Italiennes, accommodées aux Airs François de ce temps* (Paris: Estienne Loyson, 1668)), is in fact altogether a different grammar (much more detailed and systematic), dedicated this time to Madame Le Maistre, one of his pupils, as we understand from the dedicatory letter. Catanusi must be remembered also for his *Œuvres amoureuses de Pétrarque, traduites en françois, avec l'italien à costé* (Paris: Loyson, 1667; also 1669 and 1707), a translation of a selection of Petrarch's sonnets and of his *Trionfi*, preceded by a life of the poet.

[24] Catanusi, *Instruction a la langue italienne*, p. 9.

[25] *Nouvelle methode ou Grammaire italienne, pour apprendre facilement & en peu de temps la Langue* (Paris: chez la Veuve de la Coste, à la petite porte du Palais, qui regarde le Quay des Augustins, à l'Ecu de Bretagne et chez l'Auteur, au coin de la rue S. Christophle, proche Nôtre Dame, chez un Apoticaire, à l'Etoille, 1673). In his preface Borgesi claims he is addressing 'les personnes sans étude que la curiosité ou la necessité oblige à aprendre & entendre cette agreable Langue' (fol. 2ᵛ). He points out (fol. 2ʳ⁻ᵛ), among the distinguishing features of his work, that verbs are conjugated in both Italian and French and that he offers the conjugation of all irregular verbs (see pp. 48–128), contrary to other works. On Borgesi's grammar see Mario Mormile, *L'italiano in Francia* (Turin: Meynier, 1989), pp. 92–93.

[26] See on this, for instance, Simone Delesalle and Francine Mazière, 'Grammaire générale et grammaire particulière: les Méthodes de Claude Irson', in *History of Linguistics 2002: Selected Papers from the Ninth International Conference on the History of the Language Sciences, 27–30 August 2002, São Paulo-Campinas*, ed. by Eduardo R. J. Guimarães and Diana Luz Pessoa de Barros (Amsterdam and Philadelphia: Benjamins, 2007), pp. 41–63, and, by the same authors, 'Les Méthodes au XVIIᵉ siècle: un outil composite. Irson, Lancelot, Nicole', in *History of Linguistics*

Italian is also the target language of one of the first extant grammars to have the label 'des Dames' in its title, namely Louis de Pelenis's *Galerie francoise, et italienne* of 1688,[27] which aims to present at the same time the grammar of both French and Italian, something which was not unusual at the time.[28] The reference to ladies is to be found on the second title-page of the *Première chambre*, which reads *La Grammaire des dames ou l'Introduction à la grammaire françoise et italienne, divisée en 28 leçons. La grammatica delle dame o Introduzione alla grammatica Francese e Italiana, divisa in 28 lezioni*. The 'Première chambre' and the 'Cinquième chambre' have two different dedicatees ('Mademoiselle Cecile de Lezze' and 'Messieurs Loüis et Marc Antoine Mocenigo'), and the aim of the text is to provide an easy introduction to grammar for the less learned. We read in the former: 'je vous dédie La Grammaire des dames, qui t'enseignera les moyens d'entendre en peu de tems & sans grande difficulté les règles necessaires pour l'intelligence des mes deux Grammaires' (p. 3), and in the latter, in the address 'Au lecteur', Pelenis specifies that his work is meant to teach 'la Grammaire à ceux qui n'ont pas étudié' and 'pour la commodité des étrangers' (p. 8).

Antonini's 'Traité' (1726) and 'Grammaire italienne à l'usage des Dames' (1728)

In France, in the course of the eighteenth century, 'les Dames' progressively feature more openly in the titles of grammars of Italian, and a well-known example was the work of the Italian Abbé Annibale Antonini. Originally from near Salerno (perhaps Biagiosa or Cuccaro or Centola, where his family owned some land), in Campania, Antonini (1702–1755) had studied in Naples and, after living in Germany, Holland, and England, had moved to Paris in 1726, where he was a (very successful) language teacher of young girls of the

---

2008: Selected Papers from the Eleventh International Conference on the History of the Language Sciences, 28 August–2 September 2008, Potsdam, ed. by Gerda Hassler (Amsterdam and Philadelphia: Benjamins, 2011), pp. 251–63.

[27] Louis de Pelenis, *La Galerie francoise, et italienne* [. . .]. *Cinquieme chambre. La galleria francese, et italiana di Lodovico di Pelenis. Quinta stanza* (Venice: Andrea Poletti, 1688). The text is preserved in very few copies; the one in the Bibliothèque Universitaire in Tours, from which I quote, contains only the first and fifth 'chambres', bound together.

[28] See, for instance, the first grammar of French for Italians, the *Grammatica italiana per imparare la lingua francese* (Rome: Francesco Corbelletti, 1625) by the Frenchman Pierre Durand (Pietro Durante), Jean Alexandre (Giovanni Alessandro) Lonchamps's *Trattato della Lingua Francese e Italiana* (Rome: Andrea Fei, 1638), Robert Paris's *Nuova grammatica francese, e italiana* (Messina: Bisagni, 1675), or Michele Berti's *L'arte d'insegnare la lingua francese per mezzo dell'italiana o' vero la lingua italiana per mezzo della Francese* (Florence: alla Condotta, 1677). We also find trilingual grammars, such as Antoine Fabre's *Grammatica per imparare la lingua italiana, francese e spagnola* (Rome: Francesco Corbelletti, 1626).

aristocracy and the high bourgeoisie for the following twenty-five years. He returned to Naples towards the end of his life, and died there in 1755.[29]

His first grammatical work, in 1726, the *Traité de la grammaire italienne, dedié a la Reine* was meant for Maria Leszczyńska, one of the daughters of King Stanisław Leszczyński of Poland, and wife of Louis XV.[30] Maria had been studying Italian, and this fact, as Antonini explains in the 'Epistre dedicatoire', was encouraging other ladies at the Parisian court to follow her example. The *Traité* is quite a dense grammar, with its 482 pages, in a portable and manageable duodecimo, full of remarks, even on minute points, and examples. Antonini, we read in the preface, is aware of this fact and it is a conscious choice: 'J'ai tâché de dire sur chacune d'elles [les parties d'Oraison] tout ce qui s'en peut dire, ou pour le moins tout ce que j'en sai',[31] and to those who objected to the number of examples he had included, he replied that he considered them useful to his readers as they would clarify rules and make them more intelligible. They are, it is worth mentioning, all literary examples, the vast majority taken from Dante, Petrarch, and Boccaccio. In this Antonini follows, of course, the tradition of Italian grammars, from the sixteenth century onwards, which usually privilege this kind of choice (as Italian was codified in the Renaissance on the basis of the great fourteenth-century authors, it would then remain for centuries essentially a literary language). By way of these examples, Antonini explains, his readers will fill 'l'esprit & la memoire de leurs plus beaux morceaux, & de leurs meilleures pensées'.[32] So this is very much a work on Italian grammar with a 'literary' approach to language. After a preface (pp. i–xxii) on the origin and the main features of the Italian language, the *Traité de la grammaire italienne* starts with a section 'De la prononciation' (pp. 1–64), followed by others on articles (pp. 65–108); nouns (and adjectives) (pp. 109–51); pronouns (pp. 152–92); verbs (pp. 193–377); adverbs (pp. 378–418); prepositions (pp. 419–62); conjunctions (pp. 463–78); interjections (pp. 479–82 [but 422 erroneously in the text]). The preface is interesting for its remarks on the specificity of Italian if compared with other languages. A foreign language, we read, must be learnt not only thanks to the good works of the great authors, but also by means of 'le commerce & la

---

[29] On his life and work see Anna Buiatti, 'Antonini, Annibale', in *Dizionario biografico degli italiani* (Rome: Istituto della Enciclopedia Italiana, 1960–), III, 517–18, and Maria Luisa Cappello, 'Les Ouvrages grammaticaux et lexicographiques d'Annibale Antonini et leurs échos en Italie au XVIIIe siècle', in *L'Universalité du français et sa présence dans la Péninsule Ibérique: actes du Colloque de la SIHFLES tenu à Tarragone (Université Rovira i Virgili) du 28 au 30 septembre 1995*, ed. by Juan García-Bascuñana and others, Documents pour l'histoire du français langue étrangère ou seconde, 18 (Saint-Cloud: SIHFLES, 1996), pp. 261–68.

[30] Antonini, *Traité de la grammaire italienne, dedié à la Reine* (Paris: Philippe-Nicolas Lottin, 1726).

[31] Ibid., p. xviii.

[32] Ibid.

conversation des gens qui parlent bien',³³ this being even more the case for Italian, because:

notre Langue se peut considerer, & comme une Langue vivante, & comme une Langue morte. C'est une Langue morte, en ce que nous tirons ses regles, & même tous les mots qui la composent, d'Auteurs anciens; elle est vivante, en ce que nous la parlons encore aujourd'hui, & que nous la parlons de la même manière qu'on la parloit autrefois: & certainement c'est le plus grand avantage de la Langue Italienne. [. . .] La première chose qui la doit faire estimer, est sans doute [. . .] sa constance & son invariabilité.³⁴

Antonini draws attention, therefore, to the literariness and conservatism of Italian, even when spoken. He then goes on to stress how the fact that the rules of Italian grammar had been 'constantes & invariables' in time meant that the language was free from the 'tirannie & [. . .] caprices de l'usage'. This, he explained:

ne dépend point des gens de la Cour, [. . .] ce ne sont point eux qui l'établissent, ni qui le font, mais les Gens de Lettres; & parmi les Gens de Lettres, ceux qui sont recommandables, & accrédités par leurs Ouvrages. Et bien que l'on porte en Italie les egards & le respect pour les Dames au-delà de ce qu'on fait par tout ailleurs; la complaisance pour elles ne va pourtant point jusqu'à leur donner aucun droit sur la Langue.³⁵

It is this literary rather than spoken nature of Italian that meant that 'usage' was not a determining factor in dictating its rules: Italy's 'dame' were therefore not in the position to be arbiters of language as they had been in Vaugelas's France. This is one of the reasons why eighteenth-century Italian grammatical production did not specifically target ladies among its potential readers and why we do not find a subgroup of grammars of Italian *per le dame*.³⁶ But in France things were different, and French ladies were indeed in a position to stimulate the composition of Italian grammars for their benefit, Italian being abroad much more alive as a spoken language than it was in the peninsula itself (where the everyday language was the local dialect).³⁷ This is perhaps why Antonini decided to publish, two years later, in 1728, a text which explicitly

³³ Ibid., pp. viii–ix.
³⁴ Ibid., pp. viii–xii.
³⁵ Ibid., pp. xvi–xvii. Antonini's text here reads almost like a direct challenge to the claim made by Vaugelas, mentioned earlier, that he will follow for French 'la façon de parler de la plus saine partie de la Cour'. It also recalls what Lancelot wrote in his *Nouvelle méthode pour apprendre facilement et en peu de temps la langue italienne*, when he remarked that: 'Cette Langue a cela de particulier; qu'au lieu que les autres Langues sont ou mortes ou vivantes, celle-cy doit estre considerée tout ensemble & comme morte, & comme vivante: ce qui en rend l'exacte connoissance un peu plus difficile' (I quote from the 1676 edition (Brussels: Eugène Henry Fricx), p. 11).
³⁶ See Sanson, *Women, Language and Grammar*, pp. 209–17.
³⁷ In the vast and varied production of French grammars for Italian-speakers in the Settecento, we find a number of texts dedicated specifically to Italian ladies. Given the prestige French enjoyed in Italy at the time, particularly among the 'dame' in their conversation (theorists and moralists acknowledged this fact with regret, as a damaging trend at the expense of the Italian language

bears the title 'pour les Dames': his *Grammaire italienne à l'usage des Dames* (Paris: Rollin & Bordelet), in duodecimo. Dedicated to the Princess de Bouillon, this work also contains thirteen dialogues—to respond to the criticisms of those who complained about their absence in the *Traité*. The *Grammaire italienne*, writes Folena, 'godette subito dei favori del pubblico, non solo femminile, e l'"Antonini" finí per indicare quasi per antonomasia il manuale d'italiano' ('immediately proved popular with a readership comprised of both men and women, and the "Antonini" became the Italian language handbook par excellence').[38] When in 1762 Goldoni arrived in Paris from Venice to spend the last years of his life there (working also as a teacher of Italian for the daughter of Louis XV and then the sisters of Louis XVI), this still seemed to be very much the case, as he pointed out in his *Piccola Venezia* in 1765:

> El linguaggio italian, con mio contento,
> Caro deventa alla nazion francese,
> E tutti i cortigiani e i parigini
> Cerca maestri e compra l'Antonini.[39]

The Italian language, to my delight, is dear to the French nation, and all courtiers and Parisians seek out teachers and buy the Antonini.

To be fair, Antonini's work had attracted detractors too: his grammar was criticized by Monsieur de La Lande, interpreter to the king and professor of Italian, French, history, and geography, in his *Refutation des faux principes repandus dans la grammaire italienne à l'usage des Dames par l'Abbé Antonini Napolitain* (1729).[40] La Lande proceeded to point out all the mistakes—the

---

and of Italian customs and morals), this is not surprising. Using French in conversation implied a touch of exoticism which Italian lacked. On this point see Sanson, *Women, Language and Grammar*, pp. 217–32.

[38] Folena, 'Divagazioni sull'italiano di Voltaire', p. 405. All translations are my own unless otherwise indicated.

[39] Cited ibid., pp. 406–07.

[40] *Refutation des faux principes repandus dans la grammaire italienne à l'usage des Dames par l'Abbé Antonini Napolitain* (Paris: Vve Pissot, 1729), p. 29. Grammarians and dictionary compilers often either expressed their debts to other authors or did not spare them from criticisms: Antonini himself had attacked in the preface to his *Dictionnaire italien, latin et françois* (I quote from the 1743 edition in 2 volumes (Paris: Prault)) the dictionary of the renowned French grammarian and lexicographer Jean Vigneron (Italianized as Veneroni) (*Dittionario italiano, e francese. Dictionaire italien, et francois, del signor Giovanni Veneroni. Arricchito piu nobilmente, e da notabili errori con diligenza ricorretto* [. . .] *Messo in ordine espressamente all'uso de' signori italiani* [. . .] *dal signor Filippo Neretti parigino* (Venice: Lorenzo Basegio, 1698, with several subsequent editions)), in which, he explained, there were a number of mistakes: 'ce livre n'est ni Italien, ni François, quoique en le publiant, celui qui s'en dit Auteur, ait prétendu enseigner l'une et l'autre Langue'. Many words, he continued, had been 'mal entendus, & par conséquent mal traduits' to the point that 'les trois quarts sont nouveaux pour moi & inconnus. Je ne les ai jamais entendu prononcer, & ne les ai lûs que dans son Livre' (p. vi). After more than a page of criticisms on specific points of Veneroni's dictionary, Antonini concludes: 'Si, après ce que je viens de dire, quelqu'un est satisfait de cet Ouvrage, je l'avertis d'avance que le mien ne peut manquer de lui déplaire. Tous deux sont diamétralement opposés' (p. vii).

'principes erronés' that made up a 'cahos tenebreux de regles'—that he had found in Antonini's work, accusing him of teaching Neapolitan or Sicilian rather than Tuscan, 'le langage de l'un, ne valant pas mieux que l'autre' (although, it must be said, Lalande's remarks are not devoid of errors either).[41]

Yet, despite these attacks, in 1731, Antonini brought out a new edition of his *Grammaire italienne à l'usage des Dames*,[42] dedicating it this time to a Madame Knight ('l'Angleterre, redevable à votre Famille, du progrès des Arts & des Sciences, ne pourra desaprouver l'usage d'une Langue, dont votre recommandation lui fera sentir toute l'utilité'),[43] and which went on to be reprinted by four different Parisian printers in the same year.[44] In the preface, dated 25 October 1730, Antonini explains that he made no changes compared with previous editions, but he makes a point of explaining that Bembo, Castelvetro, Buommattei, Cinonio, and the *Vocabolario della Crusca* 'sont les garands de ce que j'ai avancé dans mon Ouvrage'.[45] What he changed compared with his previous work is that, previously, he had assumed that his readers 'outre la connoissance du Latin, avoient du moins une legere teinture de la Langue Italienne'. Unfortunately this 'ne devoit pas être du goût de tout le monde: Aussi la plûpart l'ont-ils négligé comme trop chargé de Regles & de recherches'. Taking this criticism on board, he made a clear declaration of intent as to his work: 'Je ne les blâme pas; à quoi bon faire une étude sérieuse & régulière d'une langue que l'on n'aprend que pour s'amuser?'[46] His grammar is deliberately composed with a non-Latinate readership in mind:

J'ai composé cette nouvelle Grammaire pour ceux qui ne sçavent pas le Latin, & qui n'ont pas la moindre connoissance de la Langue Italienne. [...] On n'y trouvera que les Règles les plus nécessaires & les plus simples, énoncées avec toute la clarté, la précision & la brieveté, dont je suis capable. [...] Car j'ai travaillé pour ceux qui veulent aprendre sans peine, ou du moins avec une mediocre application. Une simplicité méthodique, & dénuée de toute érudition, leur plaît, les amuse & les instruit: Une Méthode trop sçavante & trop étudiée les étonne, les rebute, & ne les instruit point.[47]

This must have sounded very reassuring: results guaranteed with minimum effort, especially given that no Latin was required. Clearly, women fitted this description of intended readers really well and were the perfect audience for a simple, clear, and straightforward learning method: they had no Latin and were usually deemed to have limited abilities for intense intellectual work.

---

[41] La Lande, *Refutation*, p. 70. La Lande did not spare Antonini's 1726 Italian grammar either and branded it as one of the worst to have dealt with the subject.

[42] *Grammaire italienne à l'usage des Dames, avec des dialogues et un traité de la Poësie.* [...] *Nouvelle édition* (Paris: Jean-Luc Nyon, 1731).

[43] Antonini, *Grammaire italienne*, 1731, fol. a3^r.

[44] C. Robustel, F. Didot, J.-L. Noyon, and Jean Musier, all in 12°.

[45] Antonini, *Grammaire italienne*, 1731, fol. a4^r.

[46] Ibid., fol. a4^v.

[47] Ibid., fols a4^v–a5^r.

Antonini points out that there are ladies who are just as capable of learning as men (if not more so), and particularly of learning languages; nonetheless, he sets out to facilitate their task:

> Au reste, cette grammaire sera principalement à l'usage des Dames, quoique je sçache qu'il y en a parmi elles qui sont plus capables d'aplication que la plûpart des hommes, & qu'en particulier elles ont beaucoup de penetration pour apprendre les Langues.[48] Cependant je crus d'ailleurs qu'il falloit soulager leur peine, & leur adoucir un travail, dont le succès peut m'être si glorieux. Rien ne seroit plus flatteur pour moi, que de leur inspirer le goût d'une langue qui semble faite pour elles.[49]

Despite openly targeting a female readership, he then promotes the qualities of his grammar also for male readers:

> J'ose appeler l'Italien, le Langage des Dames, soit parce qu'il exprime mieux toute la délicatesse de leurs sentimens, & toute la finesse de leurs pensées, soit parce qu'il est le plus propre à menager la modestie & la pudeur, qui caracterise leur Sexe. Aussi je ne vois guéres de Dames d'un certain esprit qui ne veuille sçavoir un peu d'Italien, ainsi qu'autrefois les Dames Hetruriennes vouloient sçavoir un peu de Grec, au rapport d'un de nos Poëtes. Quoiqu'il en soit, si des hommes cherchoient aussi une Méthode aisée pour apprendre d'eux-mêmes l'Italien, & sans beaucoup de fatigue, je crois qu'ils pourroient en toute assurance préferer la mienne à celle de Veneroni:[50] car outre que j'ai sçû éviter quantité de fautes, où il est tombé, on trouvera dans ma Grammaire plusieurs Regles fort utiles, dont il ne fait aucune mention.[51]

Given, as we saw earlier, the actual, literary nature of the Italian language, it is legitimate to wonder which kind of Italian was illustrated in Antonini's grammar. Grammarians of the past might have been, as he claimed, his 'garands', but as Gianfranco Folena remarks: 'L'italiano che l'Antonini propone nella sua grammatica manuale è una lingua di conversazione galante. [. . .] L'indirizzo vuol essere tutto pratico, colloquiale, rivolto a metter l'italiano alla portata di questo ambiente salottiero e a rendere minima la fatica'[52] ('The Italian that Antonini proposes in his grammar handbook is a language of elegant conversation. [. . .] The emphasis is on practical, colloquial usage, with the intention of making Italian available to the salons, and reducing exertion'). Whereas these grammars of Italian for foreign learners aimed, above

---

[48] Other authors, like Antonini here, also claimed women were quite adept at learning languages, although this was due rather to their gift for imitation than real intellectual skills.
[49] Antonini, *Grammaire italienne*, 1731, fol. a5^r.
[50] The *Maître italien* (Paris: Loyson, 1678), by Veneroni, was one of the most successful grammars of Italian in France throughout the eighteenth century, with numerous subsequent editions and adaptations of various kinds. It enjoyed also translations into English (with the title *Italian Master* or *Complete Italian Master*) and into German (as *Grammatica, oder Sprach-Meister*), and was still popular in the nineteenth century (an *Italiänischer Sprachmeister* was printed in Frankfurt in 1811, a *Complete Italian Master* in London in 1840, and a *Nouveau Veneroni, ou Grammaire italienne* in Paris as late as 1844).
[51] Antonini, *Grammaire italienne*, 1731, fol. a5^{r-v}.
[52] Folena, 'Divagazioni sull'italiano di Voltaire', p. 406.

all, to teach how to use Italian in conversation, in Italy in the eighteenth century, it is well known, Italian as a language of conversation in everyday life did not really exist.[53] It is therefore no surprise that the grammatical forms that Antonini sets out in his work are hybrid ones that mix archaizing and dialectal elements: 'quest'italiano [...] equivaleva in sostanza all'italiano dell'*opéra italien*, alla lingua dei melodrammi seri o giocosi, dei balletti e delle farse'[54] ('this Italian [...] corresponded in essence to the Italian of the *opéra italien*, the language of serious or comic melodramas, of ballets and farces'). The dialogues he includes testify to the artificiality that permeates the language, 'una lingua tutta spropositata, tutta intessuta di complimenti e cerimonie, la lingua squisitamente settecentesca delle convenzioni di salotto o di camerino'[55] ('a high-flown language, full of compliments and ceremonial formulas, the quintessentially eighteenth-century language of salon culture or dressing-room conventions'). The following extracts are a clear illustration of these features:

Dialogo primo. Un cavaliere, ed una Dama
Mel'inchino divotamente, mia Signora.
Serva sua, Serva sua divotissima.
E lunga pezza, che non l'abbiamo veduta: ci ha scordato tutto affatto.
E una novità il vederla. Qual vento l'ha condotta!
Vengo, Signora, a far le parti del mio debito. Vengo per adempire le parti del mio debito. Non ardisco venirla ad infastidire così spesso.
Effettivamente l'avviene di rado: e pure non saprebbe nulla farci di più grato.[56]

Dialogue one. A gentleman, and a Lady
Devotedly, I bow down before you, my Lady.
Your Servant, your most devoted Servant.
We have not seen you in so long: you have forgotten us altogether.
It is a pleasant surprise to see you. What brought you here!
I come, my Lady, to pay my respects. I come to present my respects. I do not dare come and disturb you so often.
True, it does not happen often: yet, nothing could be more pleasant to us.

Dialogo secondo. Due cavalieri
[...]
Prendo da lei commiato: ho un Amico, che mi aspetta al Palazzo Reale. A rivederci. Quando sarà de' nostri? Non trascuri cotanto i suoi servidori.[57]

Dialogue two. Two gentlemen
[...]
I bid you farewell: I have a Friend, who awaits me at the Royal Palace. Goodbye. When will you join us? Do not neglect your friends so.

[53] See Sanson, *Women, Language and Grammar*, pp. 130–36.
[54] Folena, 'Divagazioni sull'italiano di Voltaire', p. 407.
[55] Ibid.
[56] Antonini, *Grammaire italienne*, 1731, p. 236.
[57] Ibid., p. 240.

Dialogo quinto. Una Dama colla sua Cameriera
  Dov'è la mia Cameriera?
  Eccomi Signora; che comanda?
  Che mi si dia da vestire.
  Qual'abito vuol porsi quest'oggi?
  Datemi la Robba di velluto nero; colla gonnella di broccato.
  Comanda la Cuffia di merletti?
  No: ne voglio una nuova, con una fettuccia di color di fuoco.
  [. . .] Arrecatemi la pasta per lavarmi le mani; e l'acqua di nanse (l'eau de senteur).
  [. . .] Allentatemi un poco il busto. Datemi una spilla.
  Vedete Sciocca i belli guanti, che mi date! Anderò a far visite coi guanti di ieri.
  Vi chieggo perdono, Signora: eccone altri. Sono non so come quest'oggi. Ho gli occhi pesti. Sono tutta pallida. Come sono sparuta![58]

Dialogue five. A Lady with her Chamber-Maid
  Where is my chamber-maid?
  Here I am, my Lady; what do you wish of me?
  That you should help me to dress.
  Which dress would it please my Lady to wear today?
  Give me the black velvet dress; with the brocade skirt.
  Would my Lady like the lace bonnet?
  No, I should like a new one, with a bright red ribbon.
  [. . .] Bring me the paste to wash my hands; and the *eau de senteur*.
  [. . .] Loosen my corset a little. Bring me a brooch.
  Look, foolish girl, which gloves you have brought me! I shall go and pay my visits wearing the gloves I had on yesterday.
  I beg your pardon, my Lady: here are some others. I am not quite myself today. My eyes have dark circles beneath them. See how pale I am, how gaunt I look!

It is, to borrow once again Folena's words, 'Un italiano bastardo, di fondo galante e colloquiale, ma di questa colloquialità ipotetica dei manuali di conversazione; un italiano ridotto in fondo al comune denominatore col francese, ma con tutti i pittoreschi attributi di lingua di lusso e di corte'[59] ('A spurious Italian, colloquial and elegant in its essence, the artificially colloquial language of conversational manuals; an Italian which becomes one with French, but with all the picturesque qualities of a language of luxury and of the court').

In 1742 Antonini published in Paris a revised version of his grammar. There is no reference here to 'les Dames' in the title, which seems now more scholarly and to be targeting a wider public: *Grammaire italienne pratique et raisonnée* (then reprinted in 1746, and then also in Paris, 1758, edited by G. Conti, followed by two editions in Lyon in 1759 and 1763; a German translation, *Das Hannibal Antonini gründliche und practische italiänische Grammatik*, was published in Dresden in 1771).[60] But this is in essence exactly the same text

---

[58] Ibid., pp. 252–54.
[59] Folena, 'Divagazioni sull'italiano di Voltaire', p. 407.
[60] He also extended his attention to French grammar with his *Principes de la grammaire*

as the *Grammaire des Dames* as regards the presentation of the different parts of speech. There are only a few differences, such as the 'Préface' (pp. 3–24) (although this is in fact the same as the preface, discussed earlier, that opens the *Traité de la grammaire italienne dediée à la Reine*), the 'Introduction générale à l'étude des Langues' (pp. 25–84), and the section on pronunciation ('Grammaire italienne. De la prononciation'), which deals with the subject in a more detailed manner by making use also of a more discursive style (pp. 85–111).[61] Once again, then, the reference to 'ladies' in the title seeks to signal accessibility, rather than really introducing a 'revolutionary' method of learning, and no doubt responded to commercial strategies, as did his expansion of his language-teaching activity. Alongside his grammar production, for instance, Antonini aimed to make Italian more accessible to those who studied it by engaging in other activities, for instance as lexicographer[62] and

---

françoise, pratique et raisonnée (Paris: Duchesne, 1753), which was then translated, annotated, and published by the Abbé Marchioni in 1760, after Antonini's death, as *Grammatica francese dell'abbate Antonini, tradotta, ed aumentata dall'abbate Marchioni. Vi s'aggiungono più di mille frasi che si desiderano nel celebre dizionario dell'autore di questa gramatica* (Venice: Francesco Pitteri). The text contains some interesting references to women's use of language. Antonini dedicates his *Principes* to the members of the Académie Française, who had been, he claims, his advisers ('qui m'ont donné des conseils, & m'ont éclairé sur mes doutes' (fol. π2^v)) and admits also, in his preface, to the particular effort devoted to the section on pronunciation, the *Traité de la prononciation*. For this section, he writes, he had not only consulted the best texts available on the subject, but also: 'J'ai cru devoir y ajouter les avis de ceux qui parlent le plus purement; de Gens de Lettres sans accent; de Dames de la Cour & de Paris le mieux élevées' (p. ii). In doing so, he continued, he followed the view of Cicero, 'qui croyait la prononciation des Dames toujours la plus sûre, comme n'étant point corrompue par l'usage des autres Langues, & par le commerce fréquent des Étrangers' (p. ii). And as for 'la maniere de les consulter [les Dames de la Cour], j'ai pratiqué ce que Vaugelas conseille en pareil cas; c'est-à-dire, qu'au lieu de chercher à s'instruire par des questions, on doit se contenter d'observer comme les mots se prononcent dans l'occasion, & dans la conversation commune' (p. ii). It is worth noticing the presence in the titles of both Antonini's *Grammaire italienne* and his *Principes* of the term 'raisonnée', another buzz word, like 'méthode', that echoes Port-Royal and its grammatical production, but this time the *Grammaire générale et raisonnée* (1660) by Arnauld and Lancelot. Commercial strategies dictated both that authors placed themselves in the line of tradition, to gain authority, and that they claimed innovation, to gain an edge on their competitors.

[61] I consulted the 1763 edition published in Lyon by Pierre Duplain.

[62] The first edition of his *Dictionnaire Italien, Latin et François, contenant non seulement un Abrégé du Dictionnaire de La Crusca, mais encore tout ce qu'il y a de plus remarquable dans les meilleurs lexicographes, Etymologistes, et Glossaires* (Paris: Vincent, 1735) was followed by a further two Parisian editions in 1738 and 1743, another three in Lyon in 1760, 1762, and 1770, six in Venice between 1745 and 1793, as well as one in Amsterdam and Leipzig in 1760. (See Andrea Dardi, 'Uso e diffusione del francese', in *Teorie e pratiche linguistiche nell'Italia del Settecento*, ed. by Lia Formigari (Bologna: Il Mulino, 1984), pp. 347–72 (p. 355).) Antonini's *Nuovo Dizzionario italiano-tedesco e tedesco-italiano* (translated into German by G. A. Lehninger) was published in Leipzig in 1762, with further editions, and in Vienna in 1793. For foreigners keen to learn Italian, Antonini put together also an anthology of poetry, *Rime de' più illustri poeti italiani* (Paris: Muzier, 1731, with further subsequent editions), which collects examples from the Italian lyrical tradition ranging from Petrarchism to Arcadia (including Antonini's own verse, II, 293–300). His *Recueil de lettres françoises et italiennes de bienséance et marchandes pour ceux qui souhaitent d'aprendre à bien écrire en Italien* (Basel: Emanuel Thurneysen, 1761) has a similar didactic aim. An interesting

translator,[63] as well as by editing Italian classical texts,[64] with which he aimed to target a wider public of less learned readers.

Abbé Bencirechi's Weekly Lessons

Antonini was not the only Italian grammarian to target 'les Dames' explicitly with his works in eighteenth-century Paris. The capital was a pole of attraction that offered a wealth of opportunities for those who were willing and determined to try their luck at teaching Italian, among other things. Among these Italian tutors and grammarians we find the Tuscan Abbé Bencirechi, who spent eight years teaching ladies at the court of Vienna before moving to Paris in 1771, where he continued tutoring the *beau monde*.[65] While still in Austria he had published *L'Art d'apprendre la langue italienne dédié à Mademoiselle* [. . .] *La Comtesse Josephe de Wilzek* (1764),[66] the dedicatee being an aristocratic lady who had been one of his pupils for some time.[67] Bencirechi claims (a common claim in works of this type at the time) that he has come up with an innovative method, so complete and exact that it was better than any edition of Veneroni's grammar that had been published until then,[68] to the point that 'les Italiens mêmes trouveront dedans plusieurs choses, qui pourront leur être utiles'.[69] The first of the four parts of Bencirechi's 384-page work is preceded by an 'Explication succinte de termes de grammaire pour servir d'Introduction à la langue Italienne pour ceux, qui ne savent pas le Latin',[70] precisely along the lines of what Veneroni had done in his *Maître*

---

and successful text, also for the practical and historical information it contains, is his *Mémorial de Paris et de ses environs. A l'usage des Voyageurs* (Paris: Saugrain, 1732; also 1734, 1744 and 1749, enlarged and ed. by G. T. Raynal), which is a guide to the city for travellers.

[63] For instance, see his translations of Fontenelle's *Entretiens sur la Pluralité des mondes* (*Ragionamenti su la pluralità de' mondi* (Paris: Brunet, 1748)), of Paolo Rolli's 1728 *Remarks upon M. Voltaire's Essay on the Epick Poetry of the European Nations* (*Examen de l'essai de M. de Voltaire sur la Poésie épique* (Paris: Rollin, 1728)), and of Andrew Michael Ramsay's *Voyages de Cyrus* (1727) (*I viaggi di Ciro* (Naples: [n. pub.], 1753)).

[64] Among these, for instance: Giovanni Della Casa, *Prose e rime* (Paris: Cristoforo Davitte 1727); Giovanni Battista Guarini, *Il pastor fido* (Paris: Jean François Knapen, 1729); Tasso's *Aminta* (Paris: Rollin, 1729, with further subsequent editions) and *La Gierusalemme liberata* (Paris: Prault, 1744); Giovan Giorgio Trissino, *L'Italia liberata da' Goti* (Paris: Guillaume Cavelier, 1729); Ludovico Ariosto, *Orlando furioso* (Paris: Prault, 1746, and London, 1783, both in 4 volumes).

[65] On Bencirechi's life and works see Mormile, *L'italiano in Francia*, pp. 151–54; Reuillon-Blanquet, 'Les Grammaires des Dames en France'.

[66] *L'Art d'apprendre la langue italienne dédiée à Mademoiselle* [. . .] *La Comtesse Josephe de Wilzek* (Vienna: George Louis Schulz, 1764). [67] Ibid., fol. 2ʳ.

[68] As we saw earlier for Antonini, Bencirechi too criticized Veneroni's work: 'Quoiqu'il ait paru jusqu'ici plusieurs Editions de la Grammaire Italienne de Mr Veneroni, j'ai cependant remarqué, qu'aucune de ces Éditions n'a suffisamment rempli son objet, outre qu'on y trouve bien des choses, qui méritent d'être corrigées tant en matière de Langue, que d'Ortographe' (ibid., fol. 4ʳ).

[69] Ibid., fol. 4ᵛ.

[70] Ibid., pp. 1–9. Definitions refer, among others, to 'syllabes, monosyllabes, voyelles, consonnes, genre, nombre, cas, article, nom, pronom, verbe, participe, adverbe, préposition, conjonction, interjection'.

italien, first published in 1678, where a similar introduction 'pour les Dames et ceux qui ne sçavent pas le Latin' opens the text.[71]

The intent is clear: once 'les nouveaux Amateurs de la Langue Italienne, qui ne savent pas le Latin, auront bien conçu ces termes Grammaticals, ils n'auront plus qu'à s'y familiariser par l'usage, & par l'application, que le Maître doit leur en faire faire dans les rencontres, qui se présenteront'.[72] After a very short first part on pronunciation (pp. 9–30), the proper grammatical exposition begins (Parts II and III, pp. 30–162), followed by a vocabulary list (pp. 163–214) of Italian nouns and verbs (with parallel text), divided into semantic fields, followed in turn by a 'Recueil de manières de parler Italiennes, qui font la délicatesse de la Langue' (pp. 214–23), again in parallel text, and a collection of twenty-one dialogues (pp. 223–70) on a variety of topics, which is in turn followed by a collection of proverbs, of Italian synonyms, of personal letters (also by renowned authors, such as Bembo, Tolomei, Aretino, Magalotti, and Apostolo Zeno), abbreviations of titles in letter-writing, and a list of well-known Italian academies and well-known modern and ancient authors. This is all for the benefit of a reader who, besides studying the language, might want to extend her (or his) knowledge of Italian culture and literature further.

Bencirechi's next work was the *Leçons hébdomadaires de la langue italienne à l'usage des Dames*, published in 1772,[73] by which time he was living in Paris. The text is dedicated 'Aux Dames Françaises' (pp. iii–vii): there are far too many grammars, Bencirechi explains, which are either 'trop volumineuses & qui effrayent, ou trop abrégées [...] ou trop diffuses & qui fatiguent par les détails [...] ou trop arides' (p. iv), which is why his own *Leçons* will instead be 'simples dans l'Exposé des Principes de la Langue Italienne, leur clarté dans les détails en facilite l'étude, & en augmente l'intérêt'. Most important is the fact that, since they are '[r]édigées d'une manière concise', they require nothing of that 'contention d'esprit qui enfante le degoût, ni ce tissu de réflexions grammaticales, dont les personnes de votre sexe en sont pas ordinairement susceptibles, & qui les éloignent du travail' (pp. iv–v). Bencirechi's method is

[71] I consulted the 1691 edition (Amsterdam: Pierre Brunel), where this introduction occupies pp. 1–22. In subsequent editions of the *Maître* (e.g. 1699; 1709), the reference to the 'dames' in the title of the 'Introduction' is removed, but it is kept in the body of the text.

[72] Bencirechi, *L'Art d'apprendre la langue italienne*, p. 9.

[73] Abbé Bencirechi, *Leçons hébdomadaires de la langue italienne à l'usage des Dames, suivies de deux Vocabulaires; d'un Recueil des Synonymes Français de l'Abbé Girard, appliqués à cette langue; d'un Discours sur les Lettres Familieres; d'un Précis des Regles de la versification Italienne: dédiées aux Dames Françaises* (Paris: Veuve Ravenel; Fétil, 1772). Bencirechi presents himself as an 'auteur [...] connu & protégé par plusieurs personnes d'un rang distingué, tant à Paris qu'à Vienne en Autriche, où il a eu l'honneur d'enseigner la Langue Italienne aux Dames de la Cour' (p. ix). There was a further edition in 1778, *Leçons hebdomadaires de la langue italienne a l'usage des Dames, [...] dédiées aux Dames Françaises [...]. Nouvelle édition avec des additions faites par l'auteur* (Paris: chez l'auteur; Fétil). In 1783 a revised version of the *Leçons hébdomadaires* was published with the title *Étrennes italiennes présentées aux Dames qui désirent d'apprendre l'italien* (Paris: Dénos).

quite straightforward and consists in offering weekly lessons (with rules to be learnt by heart) over a period of eight months, so as to allow ladies to carry on with their many other different activities.[74] He adopts a pragmatic approach, and specific grammatical terminology is used only when necessary:[75] in his first weekly lesson of the month of January he writes that, being fully aware that grammatical terminology might bore ladies, he chose to 'la donner insensiblement, en l'adaptant aux endroits où elle doit trouver place' (p. 1), a further declaration of intent. Mixing theory and practice, each lesson (of three pages each) consists of a first part specifically on grammar, followed by a vocabulary section that pertains to everyday life and feminine topics, such as 'Ce qu'il faut pour l'habillement & la parure d'une Dame', 'Service de Toilette', 'Service de Table', 'Meubles de la Maison', and so on.

From the first week of May, ladies should then also start translating texts (that a teacher needs to check) and subsequently also devote themselves to Italian orthography (from August) and Italian proverbial sayings (from October). A vocabulary list, French–Italian and Italian–French (pp. 133–82 and 183–216), completes the grammar and is then followed by a 'Raccolta de' Sinonimi francesi dell'Ab. Girard,[76] applicati alla lingua italiana' ('Collection of French Synonyms by the Abbé Girard, applied to the Italian language') (pp. 217–68), a 'Discorso sulle lettere famigliari' ('Discourse on letters to family and friends') (pp. 269–86), the main Italian 'Abbreviature' ('Abbreviations') (p. 287), and a 'Compendio delle regole della poesia italiana' ('Compendium of Italian poetry rules') (pp. 293–324), again, as we saw for *L'Art*, all useful instruments for speakers who wanted to show (or show off) a general knowledge of Italian culture in their conversation in society or, if necessary, in their writing.

Antonio Scoppa: 'pour les Dames' or 'pour la jeunesse'?

Between the end of the eighteenth century and the beginning of the nineteenth Antonio Scoppa, another Sicilian, a noble from Messina, member of several learned academies and university teacher in Paris, published several texts on Italian grammar: among these we find his 1808 *Grammaire italienne pour les Dames*.[77] With this work, Scoppa explains in the preface, he was targeting

---

[74] Ladies are addressed throughout the text, which is composed as a conversation of the author with his readers. See, for instance: 'Il est nécessaire, Mesdames, de vous observer ici que nous avons bien [. . .]' (p. 9); 'C'est à présent, Mesdames, que vous pourrez commencer à traduire' (p. 52).

[75] Bencirechi keeps only eight parts of speech (the participle is dealt with under the heading of the verb), modifying the order by discussing adverbs, conjunctions, and prepositions before the verb.

[76] The reference is to Gabriel Girard's *La Justesse de la langue françoise, ou les différentes significations des mots qui passent pour synonimes* (Paris: d'Houry, 1718), which had numerous subsequent editions.

[77] Antonio Scoppa, *Grammaire italienne pour les Dames, dans laquelle, par la simplification et la*

an undefined readership of 'Français amateurs de la langue italienne en leur donnant les principes avec netteté et précision' and making use of 'la même méthode que j'ai adoptée à Rome lorsque j'ai voulu donner aux Italiens les élémens de la langue française'.[78] The grammar is divided into fourteen lessons in three parts, dealing respectively with pronunciation (pp. 10–39),[79] the ten parts of speech ('article, nom, adjectif, pronom, verbe, participe, préposition, adverbe, conjonction, interjection', pp. 40–88), and syntax and orthography (pp. 89–122).

His readers, Scoppa declares, will see for themselves that none of the rules, principles, or observations that can be found in more voluminous grammars has been omitted and that, on the contrary, his Italian grammar contains 'plusieurs notions nouvelles, et [. . .] un traité complet de la véritable prononciation': nevertheless, his 'grammaire' is 'dégagée de toutes les inutilités dont est remplie celle de Veneroni; inutilités qui grossissent des volumes à l'aspect desquels la jeunesse la plus zélée s'effraie et se décourage'.[80] The reference here to 'la jeunesse' is of course an intriguing one in a grammar that targets the 'dames' in its very title, especially since Scoppa, at the very end of the

précision des règles, exposées avec une nouvelle méthode, ainsi que par un traité tout nouveau sur la véritable prononciation, et par un meilleur choix de dialogues et d'expressions italiennes, on peut apprendre cette langue facilement et en peu de temps (Paris: Gérard, 1808). This had been preceded by his *Traité sur la prononciation de la langue italienne [. . .] suivi d'un recueil des meilleurs morceaux des plus célèbres auteurs italiens* (Versailles: Blaizot, 1801; also 1803). Another edition of 1802 presents an inverted title *Recueil des meilleurs morceaux des plus célèbres auteurs italiens, en prose et en poësie, qui sert à faire connoître le génie [. . .] précédé d'un traité sur la prononciation italienne* (Paris: Moutardier, 1802). He then published separately, the following year, the *Traité de la Poésie italienne, rapportée à la poésie française, dans lequel on fait voir la parfaite analogie entre ces deux langues, et leur versification très-ressemblante* (Paris: Veuve Devaux; Sallior; Renouard, 1803) and a few years later a comparative work on prosody, *Les Vrais Principes de la versification développés par un examen comparatif entre les langues italienne et française*, 3 vols (Paris: Veuve Courcier, 1811–14), on which see Alexandre Choron, *Rapport fait à la Classe des Beaux-Arts de l'Institut Impérial de France sur l'ouvrage de M. Ant. Scoppa, intitulé: Les Vrais Principes de la versification, développés par un examen comparatif entre les langues italienne et française, etc.* (Paris: Didot, 1812).
[78] Scoppa, *Grammaire italienne*, p. 5. The reference is here to his *Elementi della gramatica francese per uso degl'italiani, ossia Compendio della gramatica dell'abate d. Antonio Scoppa ridotta in ventiquattro lezioni per opera dello stesso autore. Coll'aggiunta in fine di alcuni dialoghi, lettere, racconti, e massime in francese* (Rome: Carlo Mordacchini ai Cesarini, 1807). Among his other works on French grammar, we find also the *Nuovo metodo sulla grammatica francese ridotta a 34. lezioni ciascuna delle quali è seguita da alcuni scelti temi per l'esercizio delle traduzioni, e delle versioni [. . .]. Coll'aggiunta in fine d'un breve trattato della versificazione francese paragonata coll'italiana* (Rome: Fulgoni, 1805), which had further editions in 1808 and 1826. The model for this grammar is the very successful, despite its brevity, *Éléments de la grammaire française* (1780) by Charles-François Lhomond. In 1836 Scoppa published his *Nuovo metodo pratico, e ragionato sulla gramatica francese per uso degl'italiani: coll'aggiunta in fine d'un breve trattato della versificazione francese paragonata coll'italiana* (Messina: Fiumara). On Scoppa see the bibliographical information in Michele Basile, *Ricordi biografici di Antonio Scoppa [letterato e filologo]: con giunte ed Appendice* (Messina: Nicastro, 1904).
[79] Scoppa gives a series of remarks on the pronunciation of Italian across the peninsula and specific phonological features of different parts of Italy. See on this pp. 13 ff.
[80] Scoppa, *Grammaire italienne*, p. 7.

preface, eloquently summarizes the main features of grammars 'for ladies' by indicating that he follows 'Simplicité, clarté et précision, trois objets que je me propose dans ce petit ouvrage qui par ces raisons peut bien mériter le titre de *Grammaire italienne pour les Dames*'.[81] Because his work, he openly states, is simple, clear, and precise it well deserves, and falls under, the general label 'pour les Dames' that encompasses all beginners. Hence the earlier reference to 'la jeunesse', which, at a closer reading, is then followed by further ones to 'les jeunes étudiants',[82] the 'écoliers', and the 'écoliers zélés'—that is, to less learned readers defined by their age, as we just saw, instead of their sex.[83]

Once again, the label 'pour les Dames' emerges as one devoid of its full semantic value. As we saw earlier, texts of this type seem to be more than anything else introductions to grammar, means to acquire in the space of a few months a working knowledge of a foreign language, in terms of reading, speaking, and pronunciation, as well as being texts that include a readership of young beginners.[84] And after this first course of study, Scoppa's readers can aim for more, such as learning how to use Alberti's dictionary,[85] reading Goldoni's comedies to appreciate the beauty of Italian dialogues (and thus also shunning Veneroni's dialogues), letting Annibal Caro and Francesco Redi guide them in composing letters and Boccaccio entertain them with the best *novelle* that the Italian tradition has to offer.[86] Not to mention the benefit they can reap, Scoppa explains, from the *Vocabolario della Crusca*, but also from Dante, Petrarch, and modern authors.[87]

Some grammatical features are of particular interest. For instance, even though Scoppa is writing for beginners, whether ladies or young pupils, we find no attempt to explain what a declension is (and these are commonly used in the text), nor what a noun is. Scoppa prefers to offer his readers

---

[81] Ibid., p. 9.
[82] Ibid., p. 7.
[83] Ibid., pp. 77, 78, 122.
[84] Among Scoppa's other works, we find the *Élémens de la grammaire italienne, mis à la portée des enfans de cinq ou six ans; ouvrage en Dialogues, divisé en XXXVI Leçons [. . .] nécessaires à tous les Commençans, pour parler la langue d'usage* (Paris: Courcier, 1811), dedicated to two of his pupils, a girl and a boy, Mlle Caroline and Monsieur Eugène Guenoux, with the aim of making the study of Italian more pleasant for children.
[85] Here the reference is to Francesco Alberti di Villanuova's *Nouveau Dictionnaire françois-italien, composé sur les Dictionnaires de l'Académie de France et de la Crusca, enrichi de tous les termes propres des sciences et des arts, qui forment une augmentation de plus de trente mille Articles, sur tous les autres Dictionnaires qui ont paru jusqu'à présent*, 2 vols (Bassano: Remondini, 1777) (the date refers to the first Italian edition: the first French edition was published in Marseille in 1771).
[86] Scoppa, *Grammaire italienne*, pp. 7–8.
[87] Similarly, Scoppa points out in a footnote (p. 100, n. 1), Italian learners of French should not limit themselves to Goudar or Lhomond: 'C'est l'étude de trois mois au plus.' They should rather use the dictionary of the Académie and carefully reflect on the works by the Abbé Olivet, Dumarsais, Fénelon, Bossuet, and the grammar by the Abbé Sicard, useful tools to reach perfection in conversation with the French.

practical criteria to help distinguish, on the basis of the suffix, a masculine from a feminine form. Presenting his content as 'observations' on the Italian language, he also attempts to reproduce phonosyntactic doubling (even when not actually used in Italian), in cases such as 'a me, a te, a ciascuno' ('to me, to you, to everyone') (as 'a-mme, a-ttè, a-cciascuno', p. 23), or offer a note on what he calls the 'ripieno' ('filling') particles.[88] The final lesson, no. 14 (pp. 104–22), deals with Italian orthography, one of the last elements Scoppa sees as indispensable in his grammar, and the text closes with a vocabulary list (pp. 123–32), including everyday nouns, verbs from various semantic fields, a list of prepositions and of conjunctions accompanied by examples, as well as some dialogues (pp. 138–49) between friends and equals (using the 'tu' form), and between people who use more formal registers in their conversation (using instead either the 'voi' or the 'lei' forms of address).

We find no other explicit reference to a readership of 'dames', besides the initial one in the title. But that in itself would have been enough for Scoppa's potential readers to know that once they opened the text, they would be faced with a study method and a presentation of grammar that shunned pedantry in favour of accessibility, at least in its intentions.

Conclusions

The formula 'Grammaire des Dames' or 'pour les Dames' in the title of grammatical works points on the one hand to a commercial intent by authors and publishers and on the other to a demand for a certain kind of text coming from readers. The formula can be used on its own, or as a primary part of the title, followed by a subtitle that acts as explanation or, vice versa, just as part of the subtitle. In all cases, a closer look at the contents indicates that the formula has a more general meaning, besides its stricter semantic connotations. Specifically in terms of grammars, the 'dames' become the representatives of a non-Latinate type of reader, often expanded to include also young people and complete beginners.

[88] 'Les grammairiens italiens appellent *ripieno*, tout ce qu'on emploie dans les phrases, sans que cela soit nécessaire au tissu grammatical, mais ce qui néanmoins sert à donner de l'énergie, de l'évidence, et de l'ornement au discours, et qui caractérise le Génie de la langue: *già mai forse ecco pure via mica punto egli ella bene ne tutto.* Non dico già che mi sia vero. Credete, ch'io sia *forse* uno sciocco! Ecco già, ch'io son disposto ad ubbidirvi' (Scoppa, *Grammaire italienne*, pp. 96–97, my italics). There is a large bibliography on the 'génie de la langue': on the rise of this concept in France see, for instance, the recent *Traduire en français à l'âge classique: génie national et génie des langues*, ed. by Yen-Mai Tran-Gervat (Paris: Presses de la Sorbonne Nouvelle, 2013). For Italy, see the reflections in Raffaele Simone, 'Esiste il genio delle lingue? Riflessioni di un linguista con l'aiuto di Cesarotti e Leopardi', in *La parola al testo: scritti per Bice Mortara Garavelli*, ed. by Gian Luigi Beccaria and Carla Marello, 2 vols (Alessandria: Edizioni dell'Orso, 2002), I, 415–29. On the origin and background of the concept see Toon Van Hal, '*Génie de la langue*: The Genesis and Early Career of a Key Notion in Early Modern European Learning', in *Language & History*, 56 (2013), 81–97.

At the opposite pole of the 'dames' one would then have to place scholars and learned people, who knew Latin well, had a more institutionalized type of educational background, and therefore represented a more formal and dry method of learning, the epitome of this type of reader and learner being the scholar. The association of a certain work with the 'dames' also had implications for the all-important questions of 'sociabilité', 'honnêteté', and 'bon goût', all qualities which were, again, naturally associated with ladies.[89] Buyers who went for this type of work would then ultimately be made to feel that their choice indicated they shared these same qualities. They would study a grammar that explicitly renounced boring, erudite presentations in favour of a style and a language that reflected the amiable conversation of the 'dames'. They would learn a foreign language, or their own mother tongue, by means of a text that adopted

> une élaboration, une composition qui soit agréable, divertissante, variée; qui soit claire et compréhensible que l'ouvrage puisse être étudié sans le secours d'un maître; qui soit plutôt élémentaire, c'est-à-dire qui se limite à l'essentiel afin d'être brève, concise, pertinente; qui préfère le pratique au théorique, le concret à l'abstrait, en mettant l'accent sur l'application et l'applicabilité (exercices, dialogues, vocabulaires, textes etc.) au lieu d'enseigner un système de règles stériles et arides et, par conséquent, peu utiles.[90]

Choosing a 'Grammaire pour les Dames' from the shelves of a bookshop was ultimately a sign of distinction rather than an acknowledgement of one's limitations. Their readers might have been regarded as 'commençans' with respect to grammatical terminology and knowledge, but they also represented a more 'modern' type of learner, one that in shunning pedantry and stuffiness embodied a certain grace and lack of affectation, in the manner of Castiglione's courtier. The eighteenth-century 'gentilhommes' and 'dames' who opted for a 'Grammaire pour les Dames' continued the long-standing tradition that had seen, centuries earlier, the perfect 'cortegiano' and 'donna di palazzo' react, in their display of linguistic 'sprezzatura', against 'arte o regula alcuna'.[91]

CLARE COLLEGE, CAMBRIDGE   HELENA SANSON

[89] Beck-Busse, 'A propos d'une histoire', pp. 20–21.
[90] Ibid., p. 21.
[91] 'La bona consuetudine adunque del parlare credo io che nasca dagli omini che hanno ingegno e che con la dottrina ed esperienzia s'hanno guadagnato il bon giudicio, e con quello concorrono e consentono ad accettar le parole che lor paion bone, le quali si conoscono per un certo giudicio naturale e non per arte o regula alcuna' (Baldassar Castiglione, *Il libro del Cortegiano*, Book I, Chapter 35, ed. by Amedeo Quondam and Nicola Longo (Milan: Garzanti, 2003), p. 78) ('Hence I believe that good custom in speech springs from men who have talent and who have gained good judgment from study and experience, and who therefore agree and consent to accept the words that to them seem good, which are recognized by a certain innate judgment and not by any art or rule' (*The Book of the Courtier by Count Baldesar Castiglione*, trans. by Leonard Eckstein Opdycke (New York: Charles Scribner's Sons, 1903), p. 48)).

FILMING THE SILENT (BR)OTHER: LEVINASIAN ETHICS AND AESTHETIC FAITH IN PATRICK DREVET'S *LES GARDIENS DES PIERRES* AND PHILIP GRÖNING'S *DIE GROSSE STILLE*

Throughout his writings, especially his seminal *Totalité et infini: essai sur l'extériorité* and *Autrement qu'être ou au-delà de l'essence*, Emmanuel Levinas turned traditional Western philosophy on its head, making ethics—rather than ontology—a first philosophy.[1] Reflecting back on his works, the philosopher explains: 'L'éthique, ici, ne vient pas en supplément à une base existentielle préalable; c'est dans l'éthique entendue comme responsabilité que se noue le nœud même du subjectif.'[2] Yet Levinas wrote relatively little about literature and referred only briefly to cinema, two art forms that regularly narrate, depict, and examine subjects engaged in ethical encounters. When the philosopher did treat aesthetics directly in his 1948 essay 'La Réalité et son ombre', his assessment was generally negative. He dismissed artwork as a 'plastic' 'image' or 'idol' fixed in time.[3] Since, in Levinas's view, the aesthetic experience effects 'une passivité foncière' in both creator and spectator,[4] it implies abdicating responsibility for and before the Other,[5] that is, the ethical imperative at the core of what it means to be human. Despite the philosopher's misgivings, recent scholarship has called attention to the literariness of his work, as well as the possible relationship of his ethical thinking to literature and cinema.[6]

The present article builds on this scholarship by pairing ethics and aesthetics, as well as narrative and audiovisual works. Though of different genres, contemporary French author Patrick Drevet's novel *Les Gardiens des pierres* and German film-maker Philip Gröning's documentary *Die große*

---

[1] *Totalité et infini: essai sur l'extériorité* (The Hague: Nijhoff, 1961) and *Autrement qu'être ou au-delà de l'essence* (The Hague: Nijoff, 1974).

[2] *Éthique et infini: dialogues avec Philippe Nemo* (Paris: Fayard, 1982), p. 101.

[3] 'La Réalité et son ombre', *Les Temps Modernes*, 38 (November 1948), 771–89 (pp. 782, 781).

[4] Ibid., p. 774; see also Patrick Drevet, *Huit petites études sur le désir de voir* (Paris: Gallimard, 1991), p. 27.

[5] Levinas does not use the terms *autre*, *Autre*, *autrui*, and *Autrui* systematically. On this question see Adriaan T. Peperzak, 'Preface', in *Emmanuel Levinas: Basic Philosophical Writings*, ed. by Adriaan T. Peperzak and others (Bloomington: Indiana University Press, 1996), pp. vii–xv (pp. xiv–xv). For clarity, 'Other' refers here to the human Other, while references to the wholly Other, God, are specified as such.

[6] Notable examples include Jacques Aumont, *Du visage au cinéma* (Paris: L'Étoile, 1992); Sarah Cooper, *Selfless Cinema? Ethics and French Documentary* (London: Legenda, 2005); Colin Davis, *Ethical Issues in Twentieth-Century French Fiction: Killing the Other* (Basingstoke: Macmillan, 2000); Robert Eaglestone, *Ethical Criticism: Reading after Levinas* (Edinburgh: Edinburgh University Press, 1997); Sam B. Girgus, *Levinas and the Cinema of Redemption: Time, Ethics, and the Feminine* (New York: Columbia University Press, 2010); and Jill Robbins, *Altered Reading: Levinas and Literature* (Chicago: University of Chicago Press, 1999).

Stille (*Into Great Silence*) invite a comparative approach.[7] Drevet's vivid prose aspires to cinema or painting's visual immediacy: 'mon idéal est effectivement l'expérience visuelle immédiate', Drevet notes in a rare interview.[8] Conversely, while purportedly non-fictional, even a documentary 'contains any number of "fictive" elements', as Michael Renov compellingly advances in *Theorizing Documentary*.[9] With striking thematic and stylistic similarities, the novel and documentary attempt to communicate a (fictional or real) cinematographic encounter between a cloistered community of French monks and a crew setting out to film the monastic experience. While both works successfully depict external motions, time and again they come up against the impossibility of fully accessing and subsequently representing—whether on the page or on screen—their subjects' interior lives. With their rich imagery and images, the two stunning, understudied pieces thus offer a lens through which to explore representations of the Levinasian asymmetrical self–Other relationship that attempt to 'articulat[e] a non-reductive relation to alterity'.[10] Indeed, as I maintain, by confronting the very limits of personal encounter and aesthetic representation, Drevet's novel and Gröning's documentary paradoxically uncover art's communicative potential and reveal their own faith therein. In so doing, these works shed new light on Levinasian-inspired approaches to literature and cinema.

Drevet's richly descriptive novel relates a film crew's travels to an isolated Provençal valley to document the closing of a sparsely populated abbey. The novel crystallizes this broader encounter of cultures and communities (secular and sacred) in the meeting of individuals (film-maker and monk), namely the crew's sound technician, Hans, and Abel, one of the monastics. A third party, the narrator, observes the two men's often silent interactions. Through his memoirs, the narrator, a lighting engineer, seeks figuratively to illuminate an ambiguous relationship that fascinates him: 'J'ai entrepris ce récit pour épouser au plus près sa démarche [celle de Hans], m'éduquer à sa sensibilité, sentir ce qu'il sentit' (*GP*, p. 40). Such lexical choices—*épouser, sensibilité, sentir*—establish straightaway a desire for encounter on a deep, intimate, visceral level.

Similarly, Gröning's camera seeks to bring to light intimate spaces, rituals, and relations. *Die große Stille* is the first—and thus far only—documentary

---

[7] Patrick Drevet, *Les Gardiens des pierres* (Paris: Gallimard, 1980) and *Die große Stille* (*Into Great Silence*), dir. by Philip Gröning (New York: Zeitgeist, 2007). Further references to Drevet's novel, abbreviated as *GP*, appear after quotations in the text.

[8] Gervais Reed, 'Rencontre avec Patrick Drevet', *New Novel Review*, 1.2 (April 1994), 62–78 (p. 69).

[9] 'Introduction: The Truth about Non-Fiction', in *Theorizing Documentary*, ed. by Michael Renov (New York: Routledge, 1993), pp. 1–11 (p. 2). See also Drevet, *Huit petites études*, pp. 30–31.

[10] Sarah Cooper, 'Looking Back, Looking Onwards: Selflessness, Ethics, and French Documentary', *Studies in French Cinema*, 10 (2010), 57–68 (p. 58).

shot in the Grande Chartreuse, the famous Carthusian charterhouse tucked away in the French Alps and closed even to pilgrims and retreatants. As in Drevet's novel, the subject of Gröning's documentary initially seems to be the monastic site and community as a whole. Yet in an analogous way, individual subjects soon come into focus. Two in particular recur more frequently than the rest: a young black novitiate who appears in a variety of contexts, and a second young monk who opens and closes the film, prays in solitude, and sounds the chapel's bell.[11] Given these recurrent presences, the figures appear as intriguing to Gröning the documentarian as Abel and Hans are to Drevet's fictional narrator/film-maker. *Die große Stille*'s scenes delineated by repeated intertitles, biblical quotations in white text on a black screen, such as Jeremiah 20. 7's 'Tu m'as séduit, o [sic] Seigneur, et moi je me suis laissé séduire', further suggest a double seduction in play here. In this context, the quotation evokes the monastic seduced by his God *and* the director aesthetically attracted to a veiled way of life and its mysterious characters.

In works featuring relatively little plot action, Drevet's and Gröning's choices focus the attention of the reader or spectator and create what Paul Arthur calls in his analysis of *Die große Stille* a 'semblance of narrative continuity'.[12] For instance, as we follow the film's postulant preparing his vows and the community planning its welcome, we detect a hint of storyline in a monastic and filmic world otherwise characterized by slowness, contemplation, seasonal cycles, and daily material and liturgical repetition. Such attention advances Drevet's novel, too, which 'se déroule avec la remarquable lenteur d'un film', as the book's back cover cautions its would-be reader. Moreover, these narrative and aesthetic preferences gesture towards all that, literally or figuratively, did not make the cut. By zooming in on certain characters and dynamics, Drevet and Gröning turn the gaze of the narrator or camera away from other details, subjects, and potential encounters, implicitly acknowledging the impossibility of their projects attaining exhaustiveness.

In spite of close attention to particular subjects, the Other thwarts attempts at total representation, and this most acutely in Drevet's retrospectively narrated text.[13] The novel's incipit sets the tone: 'L'horizon de la route disparut au bas du pare-brise' (*GP*, p. 9). This detail establishes the cinematographic gaze straightaway and emphasizes all that escapes from the windshield's 'lens'. Arriving at the monastery, the crew's frustrated director, Paco, senses with 'certitude' that the abbey 'lui avait d'ores et déjà échappé' (*GP*, p. 27). The

[11] Given the monks' anonymity, silence, and fairly uniform garments, physical traits such as facial features, hair, or bits of distinctive fabric peeking out from under a habit help the viewer identify characters until they have appeared more regularly.

[12] 'Into Great Silence', *Cineaste*, 32.3 (Summer 2007), 71–73 (p. 72).

[13] Gervais Reed identifies this 'hope of expressing a totalizing vision' in Drevet's other works, too. See 'Patrick Drevet', in *The Contemporary Novel in France*, ed. by William Thompson (Gainesville: University Press of Florida, 1995), pp. 352–68 (p. 362).

very first shot that he envisions proves impossible, as even the narrator admits: 'Nous n'aurions jamais pu, en effet, enregistrer sur la pellicule les effets d'une telle lumière' (*GP*, p. 15). The spectre of parting and loss hangs over the novel more generally, as well. Like the soon-to-be-closed abbey, Hans and Abel's encounter eludes the narrator, 'déjà effacée, irrévocablement révolue' (*GP*, p. 55). Indeed, all presence is predicated upon absence in the novel. The abbey's closing catalyses the film project, as underscored by the abbot's abrupt response to Paco's disbelief that the monks would 'abandon' their stunning setting: 'Vous ne l'auriez pas vu [. . .] s'il n'y avait eu notre départ' (*GP*, p. 34). Similarly, Hans's death prompts the narrator's memoirs: 'moi-même, [. . .] je n'aurais pas davantage revu tout cela ni écrit le récit de ce tournage si Hans ne s'était, voici désormais combien de jours, combien de mois, tué dans un accident de la route' (*GP*, p. 293). Written partly in the Proustian tradition,[14] Drevet's self-reflexive novel crafts a narrator keenly cognizant of memory's lacunae, limits, and artifice and of the temporal and psychological distance separating him from Hans and the latter's encounter with Abel. To compensate, the narrator relies on intuitions and suppositions: 'Qu'éprouvait-il [Hans] à ce moment-là?', 'Il est probable qu'il était resté un moment en arrière', etc. (*GP*, pp. 13, 34). At times, he calls attention to his own subjectivity: 'Cependant suis-je sûr d'avoir bien vu? N'est-ce pas moi qui interprète?' (*GP*, p. 223). At other times he dismisses outright an impression as the product of his imaginative excesses: 'sans doute n'était-elle que l'effet de mon imagination romanesque' (*GP*, p. 247). As the accumulation of such doubts exposes the Other as an elusive presence, so too the added adjective *romanesque* casts a shadow over the ambitions of the greater literary project.

By consciously exposing one's creation as a mise-en-scène and questioning the very possibility of a seamless account, Drevet's novel and its fictional embedded film take up the challenge of authentically relating to the Other and, in turn, relating that Other to a third-party reader or audience. Using narration, how does one translate the many-textured, dense silence that reigns over the monastery and Abel? How cinematographically might a camera that focuses on objects capture the monks' 'interior' life or way of loving 'sans objet' (*GP*, pp. 32, 152)? *Les Gardiens des pierres* evokes the focus of the monks' contemplation by describing a static film shot of an empty place setting in the refectory: 'au bout de la table, cette place vacante à laquelle on avait donné un couvert, dont le vide rayonnait d'une présence à venir' (*GP*, p. 164). This ritual element of the meal signals hospitality towards a stranger to come. A worldly hungry guest, or the ultimate Guest from whom the former cannot be separated in the Jewish and Christian traditions, *l'étranger* metaphorically

---

[14] On this influence see John Taylor, 'From Sense Impressions to Sensibility (Patrick Drevet)', in *Paths to Contemporary French Literature*, 3 vols (New Brunswick: Transaction, 2004), I, 69–74 (pp. 69–70).

designates the human and divine Other in both Drevet's novel and Levinas's work. The philosopher maintains: 'Poser le transcendant comme étranger et pauvre, c'est interdire à la relation métaphysique avec Dieu de s'accomplir dans l'ignorance des hommes et des choses.'[15] In the context of Drevet's novel, the inseparability of the worldly and the transcendent suggests that material and ethical attention to objects and Others provides a way—perhaps the only way—for the film-makers and narrator to gesture towards 'une présence qui pourtant se dérob[e]' (GP, p. 156). Hence, the empty place setting captured by the camera speaks to a desire for the (wholly) Other encounterable only as trace: 'l'imagination voulait aussitôt deviner [cette présence], entraînant la pensée et les sens à se la figurer, à la cerner dans les limites mêmes de l'espace vierge que le couvert lui aménageait comme une empreinte' (GP, p. 164).

Similarly, though with different technical possibilities and challenges, Gröning's documentary confronts the difficulty of representing the invisible presence at the heart of monastic contemplation. In his commentary on the film Paul Arthur goes so far as to maintain that 'many of the repeated scenes, regardless of their esthetic appeal, are fundamentally empty, "meaningless", insofar as what they signify—the internal aura or meaning of prayer—is essentially beyond filmic representation'.[16] I would nonetheless contend that the documentary wordlessly gestures towards this 'beyond' and struggles against non-representability by exploiting sound, light, and scenic transitions. Concerning sound, *Die große Stille* takes its auditory cues from its subjects, whose rule urges them to practise 'a tranquil listening of the heart, that allows God to enter through all its doors and passages'. This practice, in the Carthusian view, 'draw[s] us on to still greater silence'.[17] So too the film's lack of incidental music and voice-over (two of the Carthusians' conditions for filming the documentary) draws the viewer 'into' the silence, as Gröning's own English translation of the title, *Into Great Silence*, stresses.[18] This quiet attunes the spectator's ear to the silences between and beneath the film's numerous sounds—bells ringing, feet shuffling, hands chopping celery or firewood, snow melting, and voices chanting, calling a cat, occasionally speaking, even laughing. Silence enables hearing, as in Drevet's estimation: 'Le silence, on ne l'entend pas, par définition, et pourtant, c'est ce qui nous permet d'entendre.'[19]

Visually, too, the documentary calls attention to that which is not normally perceived, for instance by playing with natural light and focus to create

[15] *Totalité et infini*, p. 50.
[16] 'Into Great Silence', p. 72.
[17] 'Texts: Statutes', The Carthusian Order <http://www.chartreux.org/en> [accessed 15 November 2013] (chs 4.2, 4.3).
[18] Steven D. Greydanus, 'Into Great Silence: Director Philip Gröning Discusses Life at the Grande Chartreuse Monastery, the Presence of God in the World, and his Award-Winning Film', *Decent Films Guide* <http://www.decentfilms.com/articles/groning> [accessed 15 November 2013].
[19] Reed, 'Rencontre', p. 70.

a grainy, fuzzy texture that reveals dust particles suspended in the air. Two scenes involving the Eucharist further call to mind a subtle divine presence. In the first, the aforementioned anonymous young monk keeps watch until dawn before the exposed sacrament—the real presence of Christ's body in Roman Catholicism. In the second, the community encircles the altar, as the distant, elevated camera captures light streaming from on high through a window above, illuminating and seemingly participating in the monks' communion. Finally, the film's scenes shift from darkness to light, silence to sound, stillness to motion, and inside to outside. These transitions draw the viewer nearer to the monks' interior world only to pull back again and focus on their more easily visualized material lives and quotidian tasks. These transitions, however, need not signal cinema's failure to access the 'aura or meaning of prayer'; instead, these shifts stylistically perform the conscious and careful integration of work and prayer at the heart of monastic life.[20] As with Drevet's film-makers' focus on the empty place setting or Levinas's concept of the transcendent as stranger, these transitions suggest that the worldly *is* the site of the spiritual. If so, Drevet's and Gröning's works seem to suggest, then why not art, too? By such aesthetic and technical choices, a film like Gröning's aspires 'to become a monastery, rather than depict one'.[21]

Yet, despite the novel's and film's responses to the challenges of representation through aesthetic beauty and efforts to distil presence, both necessarily confront their temporal and material limits. Drevet's text underscores the monks' 'sempiternel' rituals, rhythms, and faith that will live on after the closing of the monastery and the filming (*GP*, p. 118). Even with its slow-paced 162-minute running time, long enough to invite the viewer into a sensory retreat from fast-paced, stimuli-filled modern life,[22] *Die große Stille* tacitly acknowledges its ephemeral nature dwarfed by the millennial duration of the Carthusian order and Christian faith. Time-lapse photography seemingly accelerates the passage of days, nights, and even seasons over and around the monastery and its finite, mortal inhabitants, emphasizing eternity and continuity. In this way, Gröning's documentary subtly raises a question posed explicitly by Drevet's novel, whose characters acknowledge, 'Il faut bien que ce film se termine. L'art est-il donc condamné à cette vision de mort?' (*GP*,

---

[20] Like the Rule of St Benedict's dual focus on *ora et labora*, the Statutes of the Carthusian Order stress the importance of manual labour for contemplatives.

[21] 'Ein Film, selbst mehr Kloster als Abbild.' See 'Über den Film: Synopsis, *Die Große Stille*' <http://www.diegrossestille.de/deutsch/>, and 'About the Film: Synopsis', *Into Great Silence* <http://www.diegrossestille.de/english/> [accessed 15 November 2013].

[22] The final product's length and rhythm recall the film's own slow genesis; its press kit notes: 'In 1984 [. . .] Gröning wrote to the Carthusian order for permission to make a documentary about them. They said they would get back to him. Sixteen years later, they were ready.' See '*Into Great Silence*: Philip Gröning', *Zeitgeist Film* <http://www.zeitgeistfilms.com> [accessed 15 November 2013].

p. 237). Moreover, while the documentary and the difficult prose about a fictional art-house film may not aspire to reach mass audiences, both nonetheless circulate as discrete objects in a marketplace, consumed and critiqued by countless others. As a production and a publication, they differ fundamentally from the lived spirituality of their subjects, which has no concern for utility, profit, or even intelligibility in a modern, more secular world.

In *Les Gardiens des pierres* and *Die große Stille* the challenge of ethical encounter and aesthetic representation culminates in reconfigurations of the 'epiphany' of the face of the Other. Witnessing to an asymmetrical ethical relationship for Levinas, the face of the Other troubles the onlooker. Its gaze 'supplie et exige'.[23] In Drevet's novel the initial experience of the monastery foreshadows such a human encounter, the building's façade and interior 'nudité' striking its visitors (*GP*, p. 29). Later, the narrator sees in 'le poli impénétrable' of Hans's face an evocation of the monastery itself (*GP*, p. 67). The face's opacity likewise causes Hans to feel puzzled by Abel's gaze: 'Il y sentit une question qu'il ne comprenait pas [. . .]. Et leurs regards semblèrent tantôt se saisir en ce que tout regard a d'invisible tantôt s'arrêter sur les contours matériels des yeux' (*GP*, p. 77). The crewman eventually confesses to the narrator, '[Abel] me renvoie plus à moi-même qu'il ne me permet de le comprendre' (*GP*, p. 281). In one particularly developed passage the narrator himself senses the fraternity and 'altérité radicale' inscribed on the monk he 'faces' during the final liturgical office (*GP*, pp. 260, 253). He goes to great lengths—descriptive and syntactical—to communicate this duality:

Mes yeux de nouveau sur Père Abel s'acharnaient alors à en décortiquer les traits. A la limite extrême de mon regard, je distinguais ces deux êtres qui pourtant n'en faisaient qu'un en lui: la personne infinie, immuable, inaccessible, non pas cachée sous son visage et dans son corps, bien évidente au contraire, celle qui imprimait à la chair ces traits, ce teint, cette physionomie unique, ce pâle front bombé, ce nez à peine busqué, ces lèvres au dessin souligné par la suture de la muqueuse à la peau, cet ovale du visage, et ces sourcils noirs effilés vers les tempes, et ces yeux immenses dont les paupières contenaient les globes entre leurs courbes douces, les cercles noirs des iris enfin, investis tout entiers par le regard brûlant comme s'ils n'avaient été que pupille, bref: l'autre; et la personne limitée, non pas dérisoire mais vulnérable, celle qu'en vérité je ne voyais pas avec mes yeux mais que je captais de tout mon être, connaissant ses pensées, comprenant son émotion, ses illusions, ses erreurs, devinant son désir, parce qu'en fin de compte je les avais moi-même, et à l'égard de qui je ne pouvais éprouver, confusément mêlé de jalousie et de compassion, qu'un sentiment d'infinie fraternité: mon prochain. (*GP*, pp. 261–62)

This passage paradoxically conjoins strangeness and familiarity in an encounter that mirrors the 'déchirante différence' and 'affinités secrètes' that the narrator imagines Hans experienced (*GP*, p. 171). The Other's irreducibility

---

[23] *Totalité et infini*, p. 48.

to self-sameness and yet proximity are equally readable on a face that here, as for Levinas, proves both veiled and vulnerably exposed. An accumulation of clauses strives to describe exhaustively the narrator's vis-à-vis, but an excess defies his efforts. With two colons, the narrator stops to summarize descriptions we sense could continue: 'bref: l'autre' and ': mon prochain'. Whereas Gervais Reed interprets Abel as 'what in Lacanian theory is called totality',[24] a more Levinasian understanding of alterity foregrounds the ethical and spiritual underpinnings of such an encounter. Just as in the philosopher's estimation the face is not 'seen', 'il est l'incontenable, il vous mène au-delà',[25] so Abel's resists the narrator's efforts to capture it in thought and on the page, pointing instead beyond to 'la personne infinie' (*GP*, p. 261). The face's 'simultaneous' presence and absence, communicated by the passage's double accent on materiality and inscrutability, echoes Levinas's notion of 'l'Autre dont la présence est discrètement une absence'.[26] Drevet would concur: 'je crois que les objets de nos désirs, qu'ils soient des choses, des êtres, qu'ils soient des hommes, des femmes, ce n'est qu'un reflet du Tout Autre auquel finalement nous aspirons'.[27]

In *Die große Stille*'s own reworking of the face-to-face encounter, five facial scenes break up the normal progression of sequences every fifteen to thirty minutes. In each, a medium close-up shot features an individual monk, who holds the camera's gaze more or less firmly for about ten seconds. The screen blackens, and a second then a third monk appear in turn. Whereas the narrator's gaze and description mediate our access to Hans and Abel's encounters in Drevet's novel, the camera mediates those between Gröning and the individual Carthusians. These portraits, particularly the first set, are all the more striking given the camera's positioning up to this point. While the project necessitates intrusion into a cloistered life not normally accessible to visitors, discretion prevails up to and between these scenes. The camera rarely angles straight on, privileging side or back views or keeping a respectful distance; the subjects often lower their gaze, focusing elsewhere, their heads sometimes covered. The frontality and duration of these shots offer the monks' faces up to Gröning's camera and the film's viewer, in the same way that Abel's is offered to the narrator's gaze and Drevet's reader. The monastics react differently to the camera—with timidity/aversion, humour/complicity, or directness/provocation—as glimpses of their personalities come across despite their silence. Notwithstanding this sudden candour and seeming closeness, the viewer senses that there is so much more to these individuals and the

---

[24] 'Patrick Drevet', p. 361.
[25] *Éthique et infini*, p. 91; see also *Totalité et infini*, p. 168, and Drevet, *Petites études sur le désir de voir II* (Paris: Gallimard, 1996), e.g. pp. 16, 24, 162.
[26] *Totalité et infini*, p. 128.
[27] Reed, 'Rencontre', p. 76.

community as a whole that he/she will never access. Similarly, Drevet, himself an amateur film-maker who has penned essays on cinema and other visual arts, acknowledges the 'gêne' of the spectator when a subject in a documentary fixes the camera, and 'la résistance du réel devant le piège insidieux qui voudrait le capter à son insu'. Ashamed, in the author's assessment, 'de le voir se donner à voir alors que nous ne nous donnons pas à voir nous-mêmes', we desire to 'address' this (image of the) Other before us in a true unmediated face-to-face encounter, just as we feel uncomfortably targeted by his gaze: 'Son regard semble nous connaître: il ne nous voit pas mais nous *envisage* quand même. Nous sommes interrogés [. . .]. Plus que lui en vérité, c'est nous qui sommes "pris sur le vif."'[28]

With these cinematic and narrative variations and glosses on the face-to-face encounter, as with other aesthetic, stylistic, and technical choices we have explored, Drevet and Gröning remain conscious of the limits of their chosen means of artistic expression.[29] Attempts to create a totalizing representation, while seductive, ultimately meet with frustration: It is impossible to capture 'le phénomène pur' (Drevet's term), produce a 'synthèse' of the self and Other (Levinas's), or reduce the Other to aesthetic frames (imposed by Gröning as documentarian).[30] Uncovering traces of Levinasian thought in *Les Gardiens des pierres* and *Die große Stille* allows us to discern how, in attempting to capture the (br)Other on the page or screen, each project confronts not only artistic, but human limits. Quoting and glossing Louis-René des Forêts, Drevet writes:

'Ce que nous cherchons à atteindre se trouve toujours détourné et modifié par l'acte médiateur qu'il nous faut accomplir pour l'atteindre.' *Ceci est vrai de l'art comme de la vie*, et le cinéma se révèle, d'une façon peut-être plus évidente que les autres formes de l'art en raison de son affrontement plus direct avec le réel, l'expression d'un désir qu'il ne parvient pas à assouvir.[31]

From this perspective, cinema's thwarted aspirations lay bare our own limited efforts to relate to and understand others.

Yet in their perseverance, both *Les Gardiens des pierres* and *Die große Stille* by the same gesture incarnate hope, however fragile and limited, in human creation. In the novel, the narrator confirms this faith at the monk's final office. Overwhelmed by harmonic beauty as the psalmody is chanted back

---

[28] 'L'Art de la nuit', in *Huit petites études*, pp. 24–49 (pp. 40–41, emphasis added). 'Pris sur le vif' alludes here to André Bazin's description of the photographic object's illusion of unmediated, captured reality. This article is of fundamental importance for Drevet's views on cinema.

[29] Having reflected extensively on both writing and film-making, Drevet is also aware of the aims and means that at times link, at times distinguish these two creative practices. See, for instance, his essay 'Le Papillon et la fleur', in *Le Vœu d'écriture: petites études* (Paris: Gallimard, 1998), pp. 85–102.

[30] Drevet, *GP*, p. 51; Levinas, *Éthique et infini*, p. 82.

[31] Drevet, *Huit petites études*, p. 45 (emphasis added); see also p. 38.

and forth, he explains: 'Dans la même rencontre du langage et de l'autre je connaissais cette adéquation illuminante de la parole et de l'être' (*GP*, p. 260). When the abbot asks Paco if he is satisfied with his images, the director, who earlier lamented the incommensurability of art and prayer and the former's inability to achieve a real presence ('une œuvre, ce ne sera jamais l'eucharistie!'), responds, 'Je crois que dans notre domaine aussi il faut savoir se confier à la Grâce' (*GP*, pp. 237, 274). It may not produce the film they imagined, Paco suggests, but the one 'qui voulait se faire' (*GP*, p. 274). With his surprising construction (the relative pronoun *qui* and verbs that follow), the director ascribes intention and agency to the film itself and hints at his own faith therein. While never explicitly, given the uncommented nature of the documentary, *Die große Stille* also suggests faith in the medium's ability to communicate beauty, peace, even eventual presence. The film's tone, rhythm, and techniques—marked strikingly by silence, stillness, slowness, sparseness, and attention, as in the novel—remain faithful to the subject at hand. In this way, as Catherine Lupton writes, the film project succeeds in communicating the monks' faith: 'It imbues the everyday material world of the monastery with the intensity of faith; a vividness of being that comes through in a vividness of seeing and hearing, in the way the film reproduces within itself the minute care and steadfast attention that the monks devote to every activity they undertake.'[32]

In their exploration of the limits but also the communicative powers of language and image, Drevet's novel and Gröning's film marry aesthetics and ethics and meditate on a respectful, authentic way of relating to others that proves neither possessive nor reductive. These works' creators 'wager' that it is possible to '[t]raduire l'invisible dans le visible', in the words of the director of *Les Gardiens*'s fictional film, and the visible into imagery (*GP*, p. 32). In this way, *Les Gardiens des pierres* and *Die große Stille* compellingly suggest that the very things that separate us (language, the camera, time, the body, otherness) can in fact connect us. Drevet's and Gröning's approaches to art hence resonate with Simone Weil's gloss on the Greek concept *metaxu*: 'Deux prisonniers, dans des cachots voisins, qui communiquent par des coups frappés contre le mur. Le mur est ce qui les sépare, mais aussi ce qui leur permet de communiquer. [...] Toute séparation est un lien.'[33] This paradox, and even the metaphor of the cell, hark back to the very subjects of the novel and film, who live out their lives in radical solitude yet also community. In this way, *Les*

[32] 'Faith in the Audiovisible: *Into Great Silence* and Devotional Cinema', in *Vertigo*, 3.6 (Summer 2007) <http://www.closeupfilmcentre.com/> [accessed 15 November 2013]. Lupton relates the film to Nathaniel Dorsky's concept of devotional cinema, which according to the film-maker 'is the opening or the interruption that allows us to experience what is hidden', and that 'opens us to a fuller sense of ourselves and our world'. See *Devotional Cinema*, 2nd edn (Berkeley: Tuumba, 2005), p. 18.

[33] *La Pesanteur et la grâce* (Paris: Plon, 1988), p. 228.

Gardiens des pierres and *Die große Stille* can be construed as religious works, not primarily because of their themes or subjects, but as Levinas understood the term. Both aim to re-link, *re-lier*, that which is necessarily separated. Levinas writes: 'Nous proposons d'appeler religion le lien qui s'établit entre le Même et l'Autre, sans constituer une totalité.'[34]

If, as the philosopher maintains in 'La Réalité et son ombre', an art form 'réalise le paradoxe d'un instant qui dure sans avenir', hopelessly condemned to repetition,[35] Drevet's novel and Gröning's film struggle against that limitation. By self-reflexively calling attention to the creative process and to the viewing subject, these works intimate the possibility of an encounter that exceeds those within the diegesis. For two artists who invest their very selves in their work, that relationship encompasses creator and reader or spectator. On the artist's perspective, Drevet writes: 'Autant que toute discipline artistique, l'écriture inscrit nos souffles, nos gestes, et tout ce qu'ils supposent, en amont, de charnel, dans une énigmatique projection de notre corps';[36] and Gröning himself admits of the film that 'ich darin natürlich auch Parallelen zum Leben als Künstler sehe. Und zu meinem Alltag als Filmemacher' ('I also see parallels here to the life of an artist. And to my everyday life as a film-maker').[37] Far from being condemned to passivity, the receptive reader or spectator engages with the 'repli', 'recueillement', and 'retraite' that reading, in Drevet's view, invites much as does Gröning's film.[38] Such a receptivity enables a 'rencontre avec l'unique, le limité, le prochain', with the artist in 'cette médiation curieuse qui place face à face': 'par-dessus le temps et l'espace, la découverte d'une infinie fraternité'.[39]

If one conceives of the work of art as the real, and not merely the shadow thereof, such a relationship potentially extends to one's self and the work. Drevet concludes his essay on cinema, 'L'Art de la nuit', with a quotation from Bernard de Clairvaux, and with language reminiscent of his own fictional director, Paco:

mais nous pouvons demander à ces objets mêmes d'avoir une présence, ou du moins d'être des traces et des repères capables de re-susciter en nous l'essentiel. Nous pouvons demander aux films [. . .] qu'ils nous regardent: un film, aussi évanescent que soit son passage, n'est une œuvre authentique que s'il est une matière, que s'il possède son propre corps dont est nécessaire la rencontre effective, c'est-à-dire si le film lui-même est réel.

[34] *Totalité et infini*, p. 10.
[35] 'La Réalité et son ombre', p. 782.
[36] *Le Vœu d'écriture*, pp. 20–21.
[37] 'Über den Film: Gespräch mit Philip Gröning, *Die Große Stille*' <http://www.diegrossestille.de/deutsch/>, and 'About the film: Interview with Philip Gröning, *Into Great Silence*' <http://www.diegrossestille.de/english/> [accessed 15 November 2013].
[38] *Huit petites études*, pp. 11.
[39] Drevet, *Le Vœu d'écriture*, p. 47; *Huit petites études*, pp. 12, 15.

[...] Les grands films sont ceux qui nous habitent comme des personnes, des visages intérieurs [...]. Mais alors le bonheur qu'on en retire ne tient en rien à l'habileté technique: 'Ici, c'est la Grâce et non la langue qui enseigne.'[40]

In an essay on movement in time in Levinas's work as related to film, Sarah Cooper similarly suggests in more scholarly, secular terms the 'enabling possibility' of asking 'how we live a relation to the interval' and '[w]hat is born through this encounter' with a work of art.[41] Drevet's suggestion and Cooper's question are fruitful ones, opening up the possibility of an aesthetic *and* ethical encounter with a work of art and with others through that work. *Les Gardiens des pierres* and *Die große Stille* perform those relations masterfully, inviting us readers and spectators to partake in the experience.

ILLINOIS STATE UNIVERSITY   ERIN TREMBLAY PONNOU-DELAFFON

[40] *Huit petites études*, pp. 48–49.
[41] 'Emmanuel Levinas', *Film, Theory and Philosophy: The Key Thinkers*, ed. by Felicity Colman (Durham: Acumen, 2009), 91–99 (pp. 97, 98).

AN UNTHINKABLE *HISTORY OF KING RICHARD THE THIRD*: THOMAS MORE'S FRAGMENT AND HIS ANSWER TO LUCIAN'S *TYRANNICIDE*

> Hic igitur quid faciam? quo me potissimum uertam?
>
> (Thomas More)[1]

A Critical Conundrum: Mapping More's Historiographical Project

Five hundred years ago, in 1513, Thomas More began to compose a history of King Richard III. The narrative was never finished. However, More did not destroy the text, and from the time of its first obscure publication thirty years after the initial stages of its composition in John Harding's *Chronicle from the Beginning of England to the Reigne of Kind Edward the Fourth*, together with its continuation into the reign of Henry VIII (publ. 1543, STC² 12767), as compiled by Richard Grafton, a printer, it continued to wield a sustained political influence. Together with William Rastell's edition of *The Workes of Sir Thomas More, Knight* (1557, STC² 18076) and the edition of More's *Opera Latina* (printed in Louvain, 1568), the *History* appeared in one Latin and two separate English versions. As they were circulated in other historiographical compilations, including Raphael Holinshed's *Chronicles* (1577, STC² 13568), all three versions secured the lasting image of a tyrannous King Richard III who was eventually defeated and superseded by the Earl of Richmond, Henry Tudor. What started as rumour and later became Tudor propaganda charged Richard with being the agent responsible for various crimes offending the law of nature: he was suspected of being the murderer of a former king, Henry VI (regicide), of his elder brother George (fratricide), of his wife Anne (uxoricide), and, most importantly in the eyes of successive generations, of plotting the mysterious disappearance and probably violent death of his two nephews, Prince Edward of York and his younger brother Richard (infanticide). Thus, there was no difficulty in presenting Henry Tudor literally as a godsend; or, in other words, as a providential liberator who put an end to a tyrant.

As I shall argue in this article, More did not produce such a simple and

---

[1] 'So then, what am I to do? Where can I possibly turn?': *Declamatio Thomae Mori Lvcianicae Respondens*, in *The Complete Works of St. Thomas More*, ed. by Richard Sylvester and others, 15 vols (New Haven: Yale University Press, 1963–97), III.1: *Translations of Lucian*, ed. by Craig R. Thompson (1974), pp. 94–127 (p. 113); hereafter referred to as *Response*, with page numbers given parenthetically. More's rhetorical exercise (its modern English translation printed parallel to the Latin) was written as a reply to his own translation of Lucian's Greek original Τυραννοκτόνος into Latin as *Lvciani Declamatio pro Tyrannicida* (hereafter *Declamation*: ibid., pp. 78–93). A modern English translation of this *Declamation* is provided in the Appendix (ibid., pp. 197–204), to which I will refer parenthetically hereafter. The *Complete Works* will be referred to as *CW*. All texts originally composed in Latin or Greek will be quoted in their English translation.

one-sided narrative as in later examples, although he leaves no doubt about his negative attitude towards Richard. However, as the author of this historiographical text, he faced a number of crucial legal and moral problems, especially in relation to the future implications of events he recorded, evaluated, and narrated. This is particularly linked to the fact that Richard's tyranny was not the only government to be presented in the narrative: a larger textual compilation, originally designed and still recognizable in the English version, becomes evident in More's vague announcement 'to write the time of the late noble prince of famous memory king Henry ye seuent'—this proved to be a project that he had never even begun.[2] However, this allusion, together with the reference to a notorious false pretender called Perkin Warbeck in one and the same sentence, points towards a work of larger scale in which the Richard biography would have found its due place. In spite of its fragmentary status, the material More left to posterity provided an important basis for the notorious Tudor myth. In view of an almost complete absence of authorial statements on the project, the multiplicity of different textual versions suggests that More repeatedly struggled with his difficult subject matter, but also that he never arrived at a conclusive narrative bridge that might have led him to Henry Tudor. At the moment at which the Richard narrative terminates, a 'blank' space is created, and this provides an almost tangible manifestation of More's representational problems.

The fact that he must have kept the drafts of his project under lock and key may indicate that More harboured serious doubts regarding Henry VII's regal status. Possibly to protect himself or his scribes from any enquiries or even potential charges (e.g. of high treason),[3] a note on the Latin 'Paris' manuscript suggests that its contents were actually a stylistic and rhetorical exercise: 'propriae exercitationis gratia, nec ita magno studio conscriptam' ('written for private practice, with no particularly serious intent').[4] Even though this manuscript is not autographed by More himself, such a note with its focus on formal rehearsal, rather than studious erudition, would be enough to explain the manuscript's fragmentary status. Nonetheless, particularly on account of this fragmentary nature, recent literary criticism has considered More's Richard project a conundrum, in terms of both its literary significance and its ideological value.[5]

[2] *CW*, II: *The History of King Richard the Third*, ed. by Richard S. Sylvester (1963), pp. 82–83.

[3] See John Bellamy, *The Tudor Law of Treason: An Introduction* (London: Routledge & Kegan Paul, 1979), p. 9.

[4] *CW*, xv: *In Defence of Humanism: Letter to Martin Dorp, Letter to the University of Oxford, Letter to Edward Lee, Letter to a Monk. With a New Text and Translation of 'Historia Richardi Tertii'*, ed. by Daniel Kinney (1986), p. 314.

[5] Editorial remarks on the sheer quantity of 'daunting textual problems' (Richard S. Sylvester, 'Introduction', in More, *CW*, II, p. xix) stand in contrast to Elizabeth Story Donno's critical judgement regarding a 'baffling work', likely 'to perplex and tease the reader' ('Thomas More and

Arguing on a discursive rather than a textual level, George M. Logan points out that

> More's account of Richard breaks off in the events of September 1483—that is, only a couple of months after the usurpation—the subject of the *History* as it stands is, of necessity, primarily the means of *gaining* a tyranny rather than [. . .] the means of *preserving* one—which in fact Richard wasn't very good at.[6]

This is persuasive, and yet Logan identifies the problem which More had already solved in his written text as the main objective: that of presenting Richard as the epitome of evil. Nevertheless, the greater challenge lies in the text which was not (or ever to be) written.

In the present article I shall argue that a brief examination of two other texts and their engagement with Henrician constitutional and legal issues will help to establish a strategic, intertextual link with the *History* project. Firstly, we must take account of More's earlier argument developed for the *Response to a tyrant's assassin*, which was presumably composed in 1506. This text is framed by More's and Erasmus of Rotterdam's efforts to translate the Greek satires by Lucian of Samosata (120–180 CE) into Humanist Latin. Secondly, we will consider John Fortescue's treatise on *The Governance of England* (1471), which has its origin in the reign of King Edward VI, and which makes the distinction between good and bad kingship, providing convincing criteria for the present context. Both these writings shed new light on More's historiographical ambitions, and particularly on his failure to present the young Earl of Richmond as a providential liberator from the yoke of tyranny. The common denominator in each of the three texts (More's *History*, More's *Response*, and Fortescue's treatise) is the problem of deciding how a state (whether a smaller '*polis*' or a larger 'commonwealth') should respond to one who aspires to liberate those around him from the yoke of tyranny. However, the issue at hand concerns less the question of victory over a tyrant than the underlying consequences that reach far beyond this given situation, affecting economic and constitutional as well as theological factors. In the *Response* More's persona as a legal adviser in the imaginary republic expresses concern regarding the sheer magnitude of the liberator's expected reward:

> What sum is large enough if it means recovery of fields, homes, fortunes, children, wives, the liberty and safety of all people and finally the very altars and temples of the gods? The more burdensome this sum is to the city, the more care we must take lest it be awarded rashly. The vast expenditures with which we are threatened [. . .] are enough to empty our treasury. (p. 99)

Richard III', *Renaissance Quarterly*, 35 (1982), 401–47 (p. 401)). There are even expressions of utter frustration in dealing with one of the 'most untamed texts ever written by a humanist', as Hanan Yoran puts it in 'Thomas More's *Richard III*: Probing the Limits of Humanism', *Renaissance Studies*, 15 (2001), 514–37 (p. 514).

[6] George M. Logan, 'More on Tyranny', *Thomas More Studies*, 2 (2007), 19–32 (p. 26).

Cool reasoning supporting matters of state, rather than irrational enthusiasm for a charismatic individual, is the strategy recommended by More's orator in his advice to the judges. Unfortunately, the former option was far more problematic in composing the Richard *History*. This was particularly the case in view of Henry VIII's commissioning of Polydore Vergil to compose his *Anglica historia* in 1514 (first printed in 1534)—a commission that was intended actively to support the formation of a providential Tudor myth in order to vindicate his own father's accession to the throne.[7] In short, while the *Response* symbolized More's legal views on tyranny in a scenario safely located in the realm of imagination, the narrator of the Richard *History* was restricted by bare constitutional realities.

The second section of this article will briefly revise the dialectical strategies pursued by More's persona in his *Response* to the Lucianic liberator's claims for reward. It will then point to the concept of 'divine providence' as the true reason for the assassin's success, rather than his bravery. The final section will focus on the link to Fortescue's treatise *On the Governance of England*, with its distinction between tyranny and 'sound' state rulership together with an assessment of the means of oppression as practised by tyrants in contrast to the politics of a king and his council. On the basis of these considerations, the article will ultimately suggest that More's problems over the representation of Henry VII as an uncontested ruler of England were grounded in his spiritual conviction of the supremacy of divine providence, and in qualms caused by the legal situation dating back to pre-Tudor constitutional legislation.

A Reward for the Assassin? More's Lucianic Writings and the Richard 'History'

One key to the understanding of the political and pragmatic dilemma that arose for More may be found in his early career as a lawyer at the time he was composing the *History* in about 1513. A particularly popular task in the education of future lawyers was the composition of so-called *controversiae*, a genre well known in Roman law.[8] In these brief and highly ambiguous case scenarios the law student was obliged to adopt a standpoint either pro or contra a given proposition, no matter how absurd it might be. The very absurdity of such an item would have been recognized by educated readers

---

[7] See Patrick Collinson, 'Truth, Lies, and Fiction in Sixteenth-Century Protestant Historiography', in *The Historical Imagination in Early Modern Britain: History, Rhetoric, and Fiction, 1500–1800*, ed. by Donald R. Kelley and David Harris Sacks (Cambridge: Cambridge University Press, 1997), pp. 37–68.

[8] See Arthur F. Kinney, *Humanist Poetics: Thought, Rhetoric and Fiction in Sixteenth Century England* (Amherst: University of Massachusetts Press, 1986), pp. 19–22. See also Kinney's more recent article 'Inhabiting Time: Sir Thomas More's *Historia Richardi Tertii*', in *A Companion to Thomas More*, ed. by A. D. Cousins and Damian Grace (Madison, NJ: Fairleigh Dickinson University Press, 2009), pp. 114–26.

as a marker of the case's fictional status. However, these *controversiae* would foster a re-examination of existing laws, and would actually be seen as a means to avoid potential conflicts caused by legal loopholes.

For an understanding of More's *Response*, the argumentative exercise in such legal *controversiae* seems to be of the highest significance: here, the persona defends the city council's decision to deny the assassin his reward. According to the brief narrative introduction to the *Declamation*, the assassin had overwhelmed the guards of the palace, but on entering it he failed to confront the tyrant in person. Instead, he met the tyrant's son, killed him, and left. The tyrant, eventually finding his son dead, drew the sword from the corpse and committed suicide. Denied his reward, the assassin takes the city to court: he argues that by slaying the tyrant's son, he killed the worse man of the two, because the father only acted as a tool in his son's hands. In order to be sure of the father's seemingly predictable suicide, the assassin mutilated the dead son's corpse and stuck his sword into it before he left the scene. Referring to both the tyrant's and his son's deaths, the assassin insists in his *Declamation* on the long-term benefits of his actions and confidently concludes: 'It is I, to be sure, who overthrew the entire tyranny' (p. 204).

In the *Response* More's possession of the necessary rhetorical, logical, and forensic skills in the field of *controversiae* is seen in the way he has his mouthpiece act as legal adviser. He has him step forward because he is 'only defending the city, which is summoned to the bar by him [the assassin]' (p. 99). In the account which follows, he deconstructs the argument presented by the Lucianic claimant of the award, drawing attention to the degree of pride, 'impuden[ce]' (p. 107), 'cowardice' (p. 155, passim), and 'insan[ity]' (p. 121) in the tyrant-slayer's character, rather than identifying any positive virtues, such as charity and chivalry. The deed might have caused disaster:

What if the tyrant had been disposed to do what you yourself would doubtless have done, and what it is far more likely he would have done than what he actually did— summon his guard, call his ruffians together, arm his scoundrels; and, when the body of his son was brought before him, his cruel nature and his rage at so horrid a sight would have caused him to vent his wrath and fury first of all on you, by whom his son was slain, and then on the entire city for which he was slain? (p. 121)

More's persona sees the ultimate cause for the liberation in divine providence rather than in foolish violence and manslaughter. He refutes the assassin's view that the city was, in fact, ruled by the son. For if the old man had been a tyrant in the first place, his proud, greedy, and ambitious nature would not have allowed him to share his power (p. 101). Conversely, if the son was not in power, 'assuredly he is not one against whom tyrannicide could be committed' (p. 103). Both assumptions leave the assassin potentially as a profane killer:

nevertheless, More's persona is 'inclin[ed] to the more lenient interpretation', and grants the assassin an exculpating 'patriotic motive' (p. 107).

One of the most important subjects discussed in the *Response* is the assassin's claim to have foreseen the tyrant's reaction at seeing his dead son, and to have acted accordingly. Considering this gift of foresight, the persona argues sarcastically that there was no point in running away from the scene after slaying the son: with his power of anticipation, the assassin should have known that the tyrant would return unarmed in the first place, and kill himself in the second. However, the city was in fact very lucky because the tyrant would have had the means to take revenge upon everyone. Thanks must thus be given to the gods, who 'remembered our prayers and entreaties; the gods took pity on the miseries of our enslavement; the gods came to our aid in our worst, most extreme peril' (p. 121). Ultimately, therefore, 'it was the gods who caused the tyrant's death' (p. 125). In other words, More's orator invokes the grand design of divine providence which becomes evident only on account of the final outcome, rather than in the psychological motivations of an individual's actions.

As in his *Response*, so in the Richard *History* More alludes to providence in his presentation of rulers and their decline—and thus he inscribes his text within a theological and eschatological frame rather than in a secular, historiographical paradigm. The internal dilemma in the task which he had set himself was the need to place the material world of human experience within a providential grand design; or, in other words, to reconcile eternal divine law with transient human legislation. The course of providence seemed indeed to be severely disturbed: after all, the Tudors had been debarred from regal dignity since the time of King Edward III; and, as such, Henry Tudor was not under any circumstances to be respected as a legitimate pretender to the throne.[9] By taking the crown, he therefore had to be considered as just another tyrant.

Undoubtedly, the *History* fragment displays More as a narrator who clearly sides with the opposition against Richard. He ascribes a leading part in this to his friend and supporter John Morton, in 'the conspiracy or rather good confederacion, between ye Duke of Buckingham and many other gentlemen against him [Richard III]' (p. 87). The qualification of the negative term 'conspiracy' by means of an exculpating phrase 'good confederacion', as well as the unreservedly positive connotation of 'gentlemen', provides enough evidence for More's position in favour of the opposition. In Rastell's 1557 version of the text it is therefore the Duke of Buckingham who features, according to the final words of Bishop Morton (and of the text), as the most impressive living pretender to the throne at that time:

---

[9] See Mortimer Levine, *Tudor Dynastic Problems, 1460–1571* (London: Allen & Unwin, 1973), p. 35.

It might yet haue pleased Godde for the better store, to haue geuen him [the present king, Richard III] *some of suche other excellente vertues mete for the rule of a realm, as our lorde hath planted in the parsone of your* [Buckingham's] *grace*. (p. 93, emphasis added)

These considerations widen our perspective of the role of divine providence in this *History*. Morton (and with him, More's narrator) implicitly suggests that the Duke of Buckingham, thanks to the diplomatic talent and power of persuasion demonstrated throughout the narrative, had cleared the way for Richard's seizure of power. Moreover, it becomes evident that More, hiding behind Bishop Morton, may even have regarded Buckingham himself as a potentially legitimate, if not providential, pretender. Before arriving at this surprising conclusion, Morton/More refers to various other manifestations of divine providence in recent matters of the royal succession, even attending to the minor role Morton has played in the political power game:

If the world woold haue gone as I would haue wished, king Henryes sonne [the Lancastrian King, Henry VI] had had the crown & not king Edward [the Yorkist King, Edward IV]. But after that god had ordered hym to lese it, and king Edwarde to reigne, I was neuer soo mad, that I would with a dead man striue against the quicke. So was I to king Edward faithfull chapleyn, & glad wold haue bene y^t his childe [Prince Edward] had succeded him. Howbeit if ye secrete iudgement of god haue otherwyse prouided: I purpose not to spurne against a prick, nor to labor to set vp that god pulleth down. (p. 92)

The fallible human mind, despite maintaining faith in the grand providential design, has no access to the ultimate reason for historical changes it witnesses. The seemingly pointless fate of the two princes must, nevertheless, have at least some meaning in this scheme, for (as More's narrator points out) 'god neuer gaue this world a more notable example, neither in what vnsuretie standeth this worldly wel, or what mischief worketh the prowde enterprise of an hyghe heart, or finally what wretched end ensueth such dispiteous crueltie' (p. 86). Although he suggests more than one possibility of royal succession (with Richard of York and Henry, Duke of Buckingham, as the two most legitimate pretenders), nowhere in his statements do we find the slightest hint that the Earl of Richmond, Henry Tudor, could be part of this providential scheme. As in his *Response* to Lucian's *Declamation*, More suggests here that providence is an agent in the course of events, but cannot sufficiently explain why someone illegitimate should be awarded the prize of the commonwealth.

All this points to an extremely precarious conclusion: if Richard must be considered an evil tyrant, as More invariably insists,[10] then his successor has

---

[10] See the phrases 'traitorous tyranny' (p. 86), '[t]he out & inward troubles of tyrauntes' (p. 87), and 'tirant' (p. 91). As a general verdict on Richard's government, More's narrator states: 'And as the thinge euill gotten is neuer well kept: through all the time of his reygne, neuer ceased there cruel death & slaughter, till his own destruccion ended it' (p. 82).

equally to be regarded as a usurper. Following this line of argument, the present king, who had been in power for four years in 1513, was also implicated. Under a tyranny, More's *Response* suggests, there *is* no lawful inheritance of government, since all just laws are suspended and ineffective: 'a tyrant always dies intestate, since the laws, which alone can make a will valid, are held captive by him', and 'he who succeeds to the place of a deceased tyrant is not an heir but a new tyrant, for he does not succeed but usurps' (p. 105). In a nutshell, the main representational problem for More appears to have been Henry VII's actual usurpation of the throne, along with the continuation of this lawless state under his son Henry VIII. More needed to find a way out of this dilemma either by using prevarications in favour of Henry VII or by keeping his reservations private. With his decision not to publish, let alone to continue his project, he obviously opted for the latter alternative. Unlike the fictitious legal adviser of 1506, who does not feel 'bound to the reasons for others' silence, whatever they are' (p. 99), More did not raise his historiographical voice again, either in 1513 or at any later time. Instead, he kept the road clear towards a career at a court whose legitimacy he might have severely shaken if he had chosen to.

Tyranny or Kingship? Fortescue's Models of Good and Bad Power

In his *Response* to the Lucianic assassin More's orator illustrates a few of the defining criteria of what constitutes a tyrant, and tyranny: that he must rule alone; that he executes his own will only; that he defends his power by cruelty and violence; and that the natural law is suspended in a tyranny. Logan points out that More largely followed 'Aristotle's simple, economical definition of tyranny' with its Christian, scholastic interpretation.[11] In the present context it is pertinent to recall the pre-eminent political thinker of fifteenth-century England, Sir John Fortescue, Chief Justice of the Court of King's Bench. Indeed, Fortescue was *the* most eminent theorist of contemporary constitutional law in the period, and despite his political conformism, which had secured him first a high position at the Lancastrian court of Henry VI and later at that of the Yorkist Edward IV, he was to be considered a legal and political authority principally for his dialogues entitled *In Praise of the Laws of England* (first printed in 1545) and *On the Governance of England* (MS 1471). In the latter he provides a definition of a tyrant which again follows the scholastic understanding of this term. Fortescue expresses his ideas in *Governance* in the following manner: 'For, as Saint Thomas [of Aquinas] says, when a king rules his realm only to his own profit, and not to the good of his subjects, he

---

[11] Logan, 'More on Tyranny', p. 20.

is a tyrant.'[12] He emphasizes the supremacy of God's natural law over human royal legislation, and, by referring to the biblical cases of Nimrod (Genesis 10) and Herod (Matthew 2), he demonstrates how state law may degenerate into tyrannical oppression. Although Herod's will to have the children of Israel killed was one communicated 'by royal dominion', the order was both against God's will and against the social obligation to achieve the best for the king's subjects by obeying the Golden Rule:

> Wherefore as often as such a king does anything against the law of God, or against the law of nature, he does wrong, notwithstanding the said law declared by the prophet. And it is so, what the law of nature wills in this case, that the king should do to his subjects, as he would have done to himself, if he were a subject.[13]

In contrast to this example of 'royal dominion', Fortescue promotes government by *'dominium politicum et regale'* ('political and royal dominion'), which implies a strong contractual link between the king and his subjects: the king must seek the consent of his subjects, represented by the nobility in the state. He 'may not rule his people by other laws than such as they assent to and therefore he may set upon them no impositions without their own assent'.[14]

In More's *History* this contractual nature of government is perverted first and foremost by Richard himself and his kingmaker, the Duke of Buckingham. Richard's personal failings (driven by ambition and paranoia) were covered up by Buckingham's oration in the Guildhall, which artificially constructed a political (and social) legitimacy out of Richard's claim for power, based upon a casuistic interpretation of the citizens' 'consent'. In fact, according to More's narrative, only a handful of his own supporters applauded Richard after a 'maruelouse obstinate silence' among the majority of the magistrates. Finally, a rather low noise could be understood by the Duke of Buckingham as public cheering and thus taken as the popular assent so desperately needed for Richard's subsequent acclamation (p. 76). A more enthusiastic but no less theatrical response is triggered in a scene located at Baynard's Castle in which Richard first turns down the crown and thus prompts a vocal encouragement from his bystanders, before he condescends to accept it (pp. 77–80). In the continuation of the *History* beyond the coronation (which itself is nowhere described in the fragment) Richard rewards Buckingham with no favours for his previous services: he could not tolerate a powerful man beside him, and certainly would never have shared his power. These fundamental shortcomings in Richard's kingship notwithstanding, the concept of legitimate state power was violated no less by Henry Tudor who claimed his eligibility on

---

[12] John Fortescue, *On the Laws and Governance of England*, ed. by Shelley Lockwood (Cambridge: Cambridge University Press, 1997), p. 91.
[13] Ibid.
[14] All quotations ibid., p. 83 (emphasis original).

extremely weak constitutional grounds, and then, after manipulating the political facts, proclaimed himself king the night before the Battle of Bosworth, and was officially invested as king only by a belated parliamentary act, dated September 1485.

Fortescue's text, in discussing good and bad rulership, raises another topic which becomes pertinent when considering the retrospective viewpoint More adopts towards the events in and following the year 1487. As Fortescue points out, a clear indication of a tyrannous disposition is a ruler's arbitrary setting of excruciatingly high 'taxes or other impositions upon the people of that land without the assent of the three estates'.[15] Fortescue quotes the *casus* provided by the high medieval French king Louis IX, who had ruled in the thirteenth century: Louis had also caused his 'commons [to be] so impoverished and destroyed, that they can barely live'.[16] The flattering counter-image is that of Edward IV's Yorkist England, which 'is ruled under a better law; and therefore the people thereof are not in such penury, nor thereby hurt in their persons, but they are wealthy, and have all things necessary to the sustenance of nature'.[17]

In the light of such comments on state finance, it was easy for More to see in Henry VII's rulership a new tyranny:[18] John More in the 1490s, as well as his son Thomas in the first decade of the sixteenth century, strongly opposed the tax measures which had been implemented by Henry and deployed to secure his power. Richard Marius, a historian, held the opinion that, because of More's significant lapse into silence, he must have produced more than simple 'evidence in a genuine effort to find the truth'. Without drawing the obvious parallels to More's *Response*, Marius claims that this text 'is polemical of course—a polemic both against Richard and against tyranny'.[19] Yet, Marius does not recognize the full force of the attack, which would also have delegitimized the current ruler at that time. Following this line of argument, the question is not, as Charles Ross has suggested, '[h]ow More may have developed his treatment of Richard's character had he continued his work',[20] but how he might have related the crucial moment when Henry Tudor, the liberator about to appear in the story, defeated Richard and seized power immediately though illegitimately after his victory at Bosworth.

It now seems feasible to conclude that in the *Response* to Lucian's assassin

---

[15] *On the Laws and Governance of England*, p. 87.
[16] Ibid. p. 88.
[17] Ibid., p. 90. In a note to this edition of Fortescue, a quotation included by Lockwood shows King Edward in a distinctly anti-tyrannical light: 'I purpose to live upon mine own and not to charge my subjects except in great and urgent causes, concerning more the weal of themselves, and also the defence of them and of this realm, rather than mine own' (p. 94, n. 54).
[18] See Sean Cunningham, *Henry VII* (New York: Routledge, 2007), p. 127.
[19] Richard Marius, *Thomas More: A Biography* (New York: Knopf, 1984), p. 100.
[20] Charles Ross, *Richard III*, 2nd edn (New Haven: Yale University Press, 1999), p. xli.

and in the narrative known as *The History of King Richard the Third*, the underlying problem was not the plan, and execution, of killing a tyrant. Much more pressing was the problem of the representation of a person who was not naturally entitled to receive the reward for such a deed. In the *Response* it is suggested that the stakes were high enough to threaten the national economy—implying that the liberator could easily turn into a new tyrant by blackmailing the whole commonwealth. In like fashion, it might be argued that, from More's conservative legal point of view, Henry had wrongly been given the crown as the highest prize a commonwealth could offer, and had thus held his nation hostage in the years after his success. This, however, would have been an outrageous charge, and that, I would argue, is why the *History* remained unfinished, quite simply because its contents were not meant for anybody's eyes or ears, least of all those of the 'uneducated'. Far from being a text for the simple 'folke' written by a 'Tudor apologetic',[21] More's project failed in what may ironically have been designed as the author's early attempt to find favour at Henry VIII's court.

MARTIN LUTHER UNIVERSITY HALLE-WITTENBERG/ERFURT UNIVERSITY
JÜRGEN MEYER

[21] James Simpson, *Reform and Cultural Revolution, 1350–1547* (Oxford: Oxford University Press, 2002), p. 193.

LORD BYRON: PARATEXT AND POETICS

> But then the fact's a fact—and 'tis the part
>   Of a true poet to escape from fiction
> Whene'er he can; for there is little art
>   In leaving verse more free from the restriction
> Of Truth than prose, unless to suit the mart
>   For what is sometimes called poetic diction,
> And that outrageous appetite for lies
> Which Satan angles with for souls, like flies.
>   (Lord Byron)[1]

In his *Poetics*, Aristotle famously argued that 'poetry is more philosophical and more serious than history' because 'poetry tends to express universals, and history particulars'.[2] However, what happens to a text's poetics when the 'particulars' become an integral part of the 'universals'? For, during the Enlightenment, a period which reinvented classicism, poetry and history, or fiction and fact, were subtly coupled in the hybrid form of annotated poetry.

Taking their cue from the Augustan satirists' subversive paratext, Gibbon's ironic scholarly footnotes, and the eighteenth-century ballad collectors' extensive scholarly apparatus, Romantic-period poets too began using paratext in various forms, including mainly annotation, prefaces, introductory epistles, headnotes, dedications, epigrams, and appendices. I use the term 'paratext' with reference to one of its components, the 'peritext' or the 'more typical paratext', which, as explained by Gerard Genette, includes elements that 'necessarily [have] a *location* that can be situated in relation to the location of the text itself'.[3] I would like to focus here on annotation and, specifically, the annotated verse romance, which in the Romantic period Sir Walter Scott, Robert Southey, and Lord Byron developed into a distinct form. In the Romantic period the division between 'letters' or literature and factual writing was not securely in place—the former might include travel and biography, for instance—and that is partly why footnotes and/or endnotes could be and were used in such writing. Romantic writers thus imaginatively exploited this liminal moment before the genres were more precisely defined and annotated fiction became an oddity.

Stuart Curran interpreted the 'Romance of the Regency' as a 'liminal genre',

---

[1] George Gordon Byron, *Don Juan: Cantos VI, VII, and VIII* (London: Hunt and Clarke, 1825), VIII. 86.
[2] Aristotle, *Poetics*, trans. by Malcolm Heath (Harmondsworth: Penguin, 1996), p. 16.
[3] Gerard Genette, *Paratexts: Thresholds of Interpretation*, trans. by Jane E. Lewin and Richard Macksey (Cambridge: Cambridge University Press, 1997), pp. 4–5. Originally *Seuils* (Paris: Éditions du Seuil, 1987).

where 'fiction is in balance with fact'.⁴ However, the fiction–fact dynamics in Romantic annotated poetry are far more subtle and complex, and cannot simply be defined as 'in balance'. The symbiosis of poetic text and paratext is very often latently antagonistic, generating a tense, dissonant hybridity that has a direct impact on Romantic-period poetics, and requires, therefore, further exploration and a much more detailed theorization. In our attempt to better illustrate and appreciate the liminal nature of poetic form in the Romantic period, it is important to consider certain new parameters, such as the degree to which paratextual particulars interrupt or interact with the universals of the sublime Romantic poem, and whether they make it less philosophical, or less serious. Equally, we need to explore the extent to which annotation determines the reading process of a Romantic poetic text and how fiction and fact interact in the creative, imaginative process of a Romantic poet.

In his *Grammar of the English Language* (1823) William Cobbett fervently denounced literary notes, criticizing, in particular, the authorial practice of interrupting the main narrative and diverting the reader's attention to the notes:

> As to stars [*] and the other marks which are used for the purpose of leading the eye of the reader to *Notes*, in the same page, or at the end of the book, they are perfectly arbitrary. You may use for this purpose any marks that you please. But, let me observe to you here, that *Notes* ought seldom to be resorted to. Like parentheses, they are *interrupters*, and much more troublesome interrupters, because they generally tell a much longer story. The employing of them arises, in almost all cases, from confusion in the mind of the writer. He finds the matter *too much for him*. He has not the talent to work it all up into one lucid whole; and, therefore, he puts part of it into *Notes*. Notes are seldom *read*.⁵

Contemporary readers disliked the interruptions, and, this is certainly still a contentious issue, as even modern critics, such as Alice Levine, see the hybridity of poem and prose paratext as bad art. Levine specifically observes of the notes to *The Giaour* that 'by their very existence, they pull the reader away from the story and the poetry, and, in both their content and style, work overtime to dispel the atmosphere and emotion built up in the poem'.⁶

Other contemporaries, however, read notes with avidity. One of Byron's European counterparts, Madame de Staël, responded on 30 November 1813 to his brief praise of her *De L'Allemagne*⁷ in one of his notes to *The Bride of*

---

⁴ Stuart Curran, *Poetic Form and British Romanticism* (Oxford: Oxford University Press, 1986), p. 145.
⁵ William Cobbett, *Grammar of the English Language* (London: John M. Cobbett, 1823), p. 143.
⁶ Alice Levine, 'Byronic Annotations', *Byron Journal*, 35.2 (2007), 125–36 (p. 131). Subsequent references will be given parenthetically in the text.
⁷ Madame Germaine De Staël, *De L'Allemagne* (Paris: H. Nicolle, 1810; in translation, London: John Murray, 1813).

Abydos by claiming that her inclusion in one of Byron's notes would ensure her 'remembrance by posterity':

> I do not know how to express to you, my lord, how honoured I feel to be in a note to your poem, and in what a poem! For the first time it seems I am certain to be remembered by posterity, and you have placed at my disposal that realm of esteem which will be yours more and more every day.[8]

Are Byron's notes 'troublesome interrupters' that 'are seldom read', or desired interactions with a committed readership? Byron's notes certainly present themselves as the key to the charismatic author's 'real' voice and personality. In many ways, his notes resemble an intertextual window for fellow authors to be approved or mocked, or a peep-hole through which the general public would voyeuristically satiate its thirst for celebrity news, catching glimpses of Byron's relationships to his literary circle, experiencing him as a public persona, and becoming a co-traveller on his exotic journeys. Tom Mole has persuasively observed that 'Byron splits himself between text and footnote [...] providing a number of approaches to an imagined pre-textual Byron'. As Mole adds, 'the slow revelation of more and more of the supposed "original" arouses and sustains desire for the whole'.[9]

Byron's notes, however, are not merely an undisciplined or calculated authorial self-projection. More significantly, they are integral to his poetics of Romantic irony, part of a total 'macro-text' in which everything matters and productively interplays. They are not generated from 'confusion in [Byron's] mind', but from his calculated objective to construct a hybrid, ironic narrative combining sublime poetic fiction with antiquarian prosaic fact and personal polemic. Byron takes on Cobbett's point about the notes interrupting the narrative force, and even at the beginning of his career, the emotions he evoked through poetic lyricism were subject to the interrupting and dispelling force of the notes—a deliberated effect through which Byron disrupts temporal and spatial order, and in some ways anticipates the workings of modernist poetics. Byron does enhance his celebrity status through his notes, but this is not his ultimate objective. He certainly dominates and seduces his readers through direct address, but, more importantly, he disrupts the reading process in order to bring his ironic hybrid construction to life.

This article seeks to shed new light on the widely researched subject of Byronic irony by approaching it from a paratextual perspective, focusing specifically on annotation in the form of footnotes and endnotes. *Don Juan* has long been celebrated as the *locus classicus* of English Romantic irony and the

---

[8] *Madame de Staël: Selected Correspondence*, ed. by George Solovieff, trans. by Kathleen Jameson Cemper (New York: Springer, 2000), p. 329.

[9] Tom Mole, 'Narrative Desire and the Body in *The Giaour*', in *Byron: A Poet for All Seasons. Proceedings of the 25th International Byron Conference*, ed. by Marios Byron Raizis (Athens: Messolonghi Byron Society, 2000), pp. 90–97 (pp. 90, 93).

dualistic Greek τέλος—both end and perfection—of Byronic digressive irony. If *Don Juan* is the summation of Byron's irony, which work constitutes its beginning? Considering the aesthetic and stylistic affinity between paratext and digression, I will briefly indicate a trajectory of the aesthetic development of Byron's annotation. I suggest that the famed digressive structure of *Don Juan* develops not solely from the example of Pulci and Berni but out of the paratextual play of the Oriental tales, where Byron's notes deviate from and interrupt the romance, constructing a hybrid narrative which interweaves the performance of the poem with personal conversation. My argument is that *Don Juan* is a proactive assimilation of paratextual commentary that had characterized Byron's poetics ever since *English Bards and Scotch Reviewers* (1809)[10] and that, retrospectively, reveals that this seeming 'paratextual' commentary has been integral to a totalized, hybrid text all along. The discussion which follows explores for the first time Byron's writing and annotating practices in select draft manuscripts, proofs, and fair copies and suggests how further consideration of his writing practice might illustrate how Byron's use of notes enabled and embedded hybridity at the heart of his poetic creation.

A first significant point in relation to the evolution of the poetics of Byron's paratext is that, before this paratext became a powerful agent of disruptive irony in the Oriental tales, it started as an 'echo', or a continuation and further elaboration, of the main poetic text to which it was appended. In the early works paratext was, to a large extent, subordinate to the poetic narrative, supporting and justifying its purposes and objectives. *English Bards and Scotch Reviewers*, Byron's first satire, hosts a relatively extensive paratext, as we might expect with an aggressive genre whose *ad hominem* attacks on rival poets need to be substantiated. Ranking Byron's works according to their note-to-line ratio, this text comes first: in the fourth edition of 1810/11, 1050 lines are accompanied by ninety footnotes. In the first edition of 1809 there were fifty-six footnotes to 696 lines. The extensive paratext provides a verification and explanation of the poem's satire. It constitutes an instructive parallel to the main body of the text, absolutely necessary to the common reader, and at the same time demonstrates specialized knowledge of the contemporary inner circle of publishers and writers, most of whom Byron exposes in the main text. For instance, the main poetic text includes blatantly abusive satire against Robert Southey:

> Behold the ballad-monger Southey rise!
> (l. 196)

---

[10] George Gordon Byron, *English Bards and Scotch Reviewers: A Satire*, 2nd edn (London: James Cawthorn, 1809). References to this edition will be given parenthetically in the text.

> Oh, Southey! Southey! cease thy varied song!
> A bard may chant too often and too long:
> As thou art strong in verse, in mercy, spare!
> (ll. 219–21)
>
> 'God help thee', Southey, and thy readers too.
> (l. 228)

This is then complemented by the footnote's humiliating satire:

'Thalaba', Mr Southey's second poem, is written in open defiance of precedent and poetry. Mr S. wished to produce something novel, and succeeded to a miracle. 'Joan of Arc,' was marvellous enough, but 'Thalaba,' was one of those poems 'which,' in the words of Porson, 'will be read when Homer and Virgil are forgotten, but—*not till then*'. (p. 16)

These three little words at the end superbly conclude the sentence, and *Thalaba* is excoriated by a footnote. It is very much a palpable hit, a rapier thrust of wit the effect of which dramatically intensifies the poetic extract's ultimate objective of ridiculing Southey.

The first quarto edition of another satire, the *Waltz*—published in March 1813 under Byron's pseudonym 'Horace Hornem'—was printed privately by S. Gosnell for Sherwood, Neely, and Jones with eleven footnotes in 257 lines. Like *English Bards and Scotch Reviewers*, its footnotes offer a significant enhancement of the main text's satiric tone and political aims. They continue the main text's allegorical critique against the first four Georges, and especially the Prince Regent, for the cultural and political influence Germany increasingly exerted upon England during their reigns. In the following note Byron engages the reader in the actual composition of his poem, and also in his criticism of the Regent, by asking him to complete a blank, disyllabic space in one of his lines, which, according to Jerome McGann, alludes to Lord Moira, Francis Rawdon, first Marquis of Hastings (1754–1826), one of the Regent's ardent supporters:[11]

The gentle, or ferocious, reader may fill up the blank as he pleases—there are several disyllabic names at his service (being already in the Regent's).[12]

The footnote replies to the main text's ridiculing of the Regent's supporters:

> Blest was the time Waltz chose for her debut;
> The court, the Regent, like herself were new;
> [...]

---

[11] *Lord Byron: The Complete Poetical Works*, ed. by Jerome J. McGann, 7 vols (Oxford: Clarendon Press, 1980–93), III, 402, 396. Cited hereafter as *CPW*.

[12] Horace Hornem, Esq. [pseudonym of Lord Byron], *Waltz: An Apostrophic Hymn* (London: S. Gosnell for Sherwood, Neely, and Jones, 1813), p. 21. Subsequent references will be given parenthetically in the text.

> New white-sticks, gold-sticks, broom-sticks, all new sticks!
> With vests or ribands—deck'd alike in hue,
> New troopers strut, new turncoats blush in blue:
> So saith the muse: my ____, what say you?
>
> (pp. 21–22)

Childe Harold's Pilgrimage presents a similar text–paratext symbiosis and synergy, although here paratext has a much more dominant presence than in any of Byron's earlier works. It is highly intricate, including footnotes and endnotes, a selection of Poems (twenty in the third edition and twenty-nine in the seventh (1814)), and a long Appendix, with topographical and historiographical information about Spain, Albania, Greece, and Turkey, as well as specimens of poetry in modern Greek. In *Childe Harold* II, which hosts the most extensive and complex paratext of all the Cantos, the paratext is essentially a systematic enlargement of Byron's philhellenic ethno-political ideas introduced during the course of the poem: a further emphasis on his passionate longing that Greece should be freed from Turkish dominion. Byron in the notes, and the Childe in the poem, are both 'peripatetic readers', 'dispossessed and displaced, [trying to repossess themselves] through their cosmopolitan travels; through a reading of place'.[13] There is an aesthetic resemblance between the inherently factual and realistic main travelogue and the antiquarian notes that provide topographical and cultural information. Despite its imaginary or fictional elements, the main poetic text also involves a significant historical, topographical, and chronological materiality that binds it with its paratext. Indeed, according to Alice Levine, 'while the notes allow the poet to speak *in propria persona* and outside the poem, as it were, the continuity between the narrator of the poem and the speaker of the notes is fairly seamless'.[14]

This thematological and aesthetic homogeneity and collaborations between *Childe Harold*'s text and paratext do not help Byron to manifest the poem's systematic, ironic vacillation between Romantic idealism and melancholic realism, or the constant process of self-creation and self-destruction that the Byronic narrator and the Childe are involved in. However, in the Oriental tales—a milestone in the aesthetic development of Byron's paratext—Byron achieves an ingenious dramatization of philosophical, Romantic irony by allowing paratext to break its previous bonds of servitude to the dominant poetic text and turn into a rebellious slave that aggressively interrupts and subverts the poem's world of serious, sublime imagination.

In *The Bride of Abydos* (1814) Byron extols Zuleika's unique oriental beauty:

---

[13] Frederick Garber, *Self, Text, and Romantic Irony: The Example of Byron* (Princeton: Princeton University Press, 1988), pp. 4, 21.

[14] Levine, pp. 130–31.

> Such was Zuleika—such around her shone
> The nameless charms unmark'd by her alone;
> The light of love, the purity of grace,
> The mind, the Music breathing from her face,
> The heart whose softness harmonized the whole—
> And, oh! That eye was in itself a Soul![15]

To the phrase 'the Music breathing from her face', he appends the following endnote:

> This expression has met with objections. I will not refer to 'Him who hath not Music in his soul,' *but merely request the reader to recollect, for ten seconds*, the features of the woman whom he believes to be the most beautiful; and, if he then does not comprehend fully what is feebly expressed in the above line, I shall be sorry for us both. (p. 62, emphasis added)

By inserting the note ostensibly to anticipate potential criticism, Byron privileges his reader as enlightened and encourages a lingering contemplation upon the reader's—necessarily and essentially—individual ideal of beauty, briefly halting the poetic narrative. The Byronic note urges a ten-second break with its reader. It wants to capture and control the reader's attention. According to an 1813 draft of *The Bride of Abydos* held at the National Library of Scotland, in the first form of this note the suspension of thought that Byron demanded from the reader constituted 'one minute'.[16] The same draft includes Byron's revised and extended version of this note, in which the 'one minute' is diminished to '30 seconds'; the latter is then crossed out and replaced by the final 'ten seconds'. Byron presumably tested out and timed a reasonable attention span and settled on the last of these. This reveals something very important about his authorial intentions: that he was very consciously interrupting his main poetic narrative by attempting to appeal to the reader's own life experience in validating the metaphor. Thomas Moore suggested that the relevant line (and thus the paratextual interaction) was the product of much thought and revision, which further corroborates the idea of Byron deliberately controlling his text's reading process and experience:

> Of one of the most popular lines in this latter passage, it is not only curious, but instructive, to trace the progress to its present state of finish. Having at first written—
>
> 'Mind on her lip and music In her face,' he afterwards altered it to—
>
> 'The mind of music breathing in her face.'

---

[15] George Gordon Byron, *The Bride of Abydos: A Turkish Tale* (London: John Murray, 1813), I. 176–81. Subsequent references will be given parenthetically in the text.

[16] Edinburgh, National Library of Scotland (NLS), Acc. 12604/04026, 'MS, 1813, of "The Bride of Abydos" by Lord Byron, with dedication and addenda'. Subsequent references will be given parenthetically in the text.

But, this not satisfying him, the next step of correction brought the line to what it is at present—
'The mind, the music breathing from her face'.[17]

The Byronic notes puncture sentiment and the illusion of fiction, upsetting the reader's bond with the main poetic text. In attempting to appreciate how destructive, or subtly creative, Byronic annotation is, we will focus on the footnote, which, compared with the endnote, has more immediate power to interrupt and ironize the poetic narrative, and, specifically, on *The Giaour*'s footnotes, which are the most playful and intricate in Byron's œuvre.

Within the poetical text of *The Giaour*, at some point towards the middle of the poem, there is a simile that represents the climax of a Turkish fisherman's meditations on the psychological pressure a guilty mind experiences:

> The Mind, that broods o'er guilty woes,
> Is like the Scorpion girt by fire,
> In circle narrowing as it glows,
> The flames around their captive close,
> Till inly search'd by thousand throes,
> And maddening in her ire,
> One sad and sole relief she knows,
> The sting she nourish'd for her foes,
> Whose venom never yet was vain,
> Gives but one pang, and cures all pain,
> And darts into her desperate brain;
> So do the dark in soul expire,
> Or live like Scorpion girt by fire.[18]

At this point, an orthodox reader might interrupt the perusal of the poem and read the footnote:[19]

Alluding to the dubious suicide of the scorpion, so placed for experiment by gentle philosophers. Some maintain that the position of the sting, when turned towards the head, is merely a convulsive movement; but others have actually brought in the verdict 'Felo de se.' The scorpions are surely interested in a speedy decision of the question; as, if once fairly established as insect Catos, they will probably be allowed to live as long as they think proper, without being martyred for the sake of an hypothesis. (pp. 8–9)

The reader might then continue reading the poem:

> So writhes the mind Remorse hath riven,
> Unfit for earth, undoom'd for heaven,

---

[17] *The Life, Letters and Journals of Lord Byron*, ed. by Thomas Moore (London: John Murray, 1839), p. 218.

[18] George Gordon Byron, *The Giaour: A Fragment of a Turkish Tale* (London: John Murray, 1813), p. 8. Subsequent references will be given parenthetically in the text.

[19] Only the first six editions of *The Giaour* had the notes printed as footnotes.

> Darkness above, despair beneath,
> Around it flame, within it death!
>
> (p. 9)

As mentioned above, that might be the reading practice and experience of the ideal reader who obeys the guidance of the paratext in shaping the reading experience. A more independent reader might defer reading the footnote until the image of the scorpion has been completed. An enraptured reader might—initially, at least—omit reading the footnote. The paratext here offers food for thought after the excitement of the first reading: elucidation of the metaphor for the ignorant spiced with ironic wit for the knowing.

The metaphor and note associate self-harm with the Byronic hero. The image of the scorpion trapped between the threatening light of fire and the darkness of the soul arouses the reader's curiosity as it alludes to the mysterious, demonic Giaour. A climax has been built up by the previous image of sexual desire as a Sisyphean chase of hopes through a child's attempt to capture the fabled butterfly of Kashmeer, 'the most rare and beautiful of the species' (p. 6)—a chase that must end in either frustration and failure or ruin of the object sought. This climactic chain of associative images, however, is aggressively interrupted only four lines before the completion of the scorpion image. The footnote forcibly replaces fictional imagination by the realm of scientific experiment, an experiment that the footnote-writer treats humorously, reducing his own heroizing of suicide to insect proportions in an almost Swiftian way. The footnote turns into a burlesque, a sarcastic mockery and parody of the poem: a comic interlude appended to it. The philosophers, the characters of the footnote's stage, look like caricatures when compared with the Giaour, yet endow his agony in their own turn with a sense of insignificance and a sort of comical lightness.

The undermining of the power of the poetic narrative is done surreptitiously. Byron manipulates the action of the narrative from the margins. He hardly inhabits the principal text as the storyteller. He mainly ascribes this task to the four narrators: the ballad singer; the Turkish fisherman; the Christian monk; and the Giaour. The authorial role he assumes in the principal text is that of antiquarian translator and Western philhellenist editor of a Romaic ballad, as he claims in his final note:

> The story in the text is one told of a young Venetian many years ago, and now nearly forgotten. I heard it by accident recited by one of the coffee-house story-tellers who abound in the Levant, and sing or recite their narratives. The additions and interpolations by the *translator* will be easily distinguished from the rest by the want of Eastern imagery. (p. 41, emphasis added)

He may lack the authority of the poem-narrator, but Byron fully manipulates the potentials of the footnote-narrator, subtly controlling the poetic narrative by interrupting it. There is, thus, a continuous, Schlegelian, palindromic movement between establishment and re-establishment, enhanced by *The Giaour*'s complex structure of 'disjointed fragments' presented through the perspective of four different narrators, each one being of a distinct cultural background (p. 1). The text–paratext dynamics are never balanced or static, but always exist in an almost Heraclitean flux.

The Giaour's footnotes often host Byron's ironic, comical commentary against both Christianity and Islam. They thereby deconstruct the orientalist romance, which traditionally took seriously and rendered sublime an Ottoman culture that, if not chivalric in the Western sense, certainly manifested a strict patriarchal code of honour. Marilyn Butler argues that, with 'an urbane Voltairean detachment', Byron mocks the Muslim 'conception of the afterlife',[20] and Nigel Leask adds that Byron '[debases] Islamic religion [. . .] to superstition',[21] portraying its dogmas as savage and completely arbitrary. Thus, Byron writes:

The Koran allots at least a third of Paradise to well-behaved women; but by far the greater number of Mussulmans interpret the text their own way, and exclude their moieties from heaven. Being enemies to Platonics, they cannot discern 'any fitness of things' in the souls of the other sex, conceiving them to be superseded by the Houris. (p. 12)

Byron's irony and anti-religious sentiments, however, are also extended against Greek Orthodox Christianity. Although his sarcasm against Islam 'proves Turkish rule ethically unacceptable' and enhances his philhellenic intentions, 'the story never [shows] the Christian church in a more favourable light'.[22] Byron stresses the Giaour's indifference towards the monk's urges for penitence that would secure him eternal salvation, and actually omits the monk's sermon, portraying thus Christian religion as hollow and unable to offer what it claims, namely, forgiveness, salvation, and eternal peace of the soul:

The monk's sermon is omitted. It seems to have had so little effect upon the patient, that it could have no hopes from the reader. It may be sufficient to say, that it was of a customary length (as may be perceived from the interruptions and uneasiness of the patient), and was delivered in the usual tone of all orthodox preachers.[23]

This systematic, ironic interchange between poetry and prose, sublime Ro-

---

[20] Marilyn Butler, 'The Orientalism of Byron's *Giaour*', in *Byron and the Limits of Fiction*, ed. by Bernard Beatty and Vincent Newey (Liverpool: Liverpool University Press, 1988), pp. 78–96 (p. 87).

[21] Nigel Leask, *British Romanticism and the East: Anxieties of Empire* (Cambridge: Cambridge University Press, 1992), p. 30.

[22] Butler, p. 91.

[23] George Gordon Byron, *The Giaour: A Fragment of a Turkish Tale*, 7th edn (London: John Murray, 1814), p. 74. The note originally appeared as an endnote in this edition.

manticism and sceptical qualification, fiction and fact, qualifies the Byronic footnote as an efficacious means of 'artistic manifestation of the English romantic irony'.[24] Reading poetry with the paratext constitutes another form of arabesque: 'an artfully ordered confusion, a wonderfully perennial alternation of enthusiasm and irony which lives even in the smallest parts of the whole'.[25] The Byronic footnote is the Schlegelian 'smallest [part]' in which Romantic confusion and irony find an 'artful' host. In Derrida's terms, it is a 'Persephone' crossing between a sublime, Romantic kingdom, and a 'subterranean', paratextual one. It is a 'Tympan', a knell, which when played reverberates its repressed realistic qualities back onto the sentimental text.[26]

The Giaour was the only one of Byron's tales that in its original and first six editions appeared with footnotes. The Bride of Abydos (1813), The Corsair (1814), and The Siege of Corinth (1816), along with The Giaour's seventh and later editions, were published with endnotes, despite the evidence in Byron's draft manuscripts that he composed the Oriental tales predominantly with footnotes. Lara (1814) is the only tale to which Byron wrote neither footnotes nor endnotes. I have not yet discovered any specific directions that Byron gave to Murray to publish The Giaour's notes as footnotes in the first six editions or as endnotes in the following editions. Charles Robinson suggests that 'Byron's frequent additions to The Giaour as it went through various editions, necessitating new proofs and revises may have exasperated both publisher and printer, who may have changed to endnotes to make resetting the poem less expensive'.[27] Although I agree that this was probably a factor, Murray may also have done this as a strategy to mitigate the jarring mixture of modes and registers on the page; to distance the reader and allow him to defer reading the notes.

Although Murray later wrote to say he considered Byron's interweaving of prose and poetry in his works as '*bene-mixtura*', or 'well-blended',[28] he had been all too well aware that Byron's first readers reported a strong sense of disruption at the tales' 'mixture' of fact and fiction, pathos and humour. The British Review for instance, focused on the instance of the comical anecdote on Hassan's 'curling whiskers' in its criticism of The Giaour's bathetic variations and the footnotes' disruption of narrative:

[24] Anne K. Mellor, *English Romantic Irony* (Cambridge, MA: Harvard University Press, 1980), p. 18.

[25] Friedrich Schlegel, *Dialogue on Poetry and Literary Aphorisms*, trans. by Ernst Behler and Roman Struc (University Park: Pennsylvania State University Press, 1968), pp. 53–54.

[26] Jacques Derrida, *Margins of Philosophy*, trans. by Alan Bass (Sussex: Harvester Press, 1982), pp. ix–xxix.

[27] Charles E. Robinson, 'Byron's Footnotes', in *Byron: A Poet for All Seasons*, ed. by Byron Raizis, pp. 110–19 (p. 116).

[28] Letter sent to Byron on Tuesday, 18 February 1817, in *The Letters of John Murray to Lord Byron*, ed. by Andrew Nicholson (Liverpool: Liverpool University Press, 2007), p. 197.

Some [notes] call our attention from the midst of tumult and slaughter to some ridiculous story, or fable of superstition. We will not say that the inimitable satirist of the Scottish bards and reviewers is without the talent of humour; but we must say that the attempts at humour in these notes are very far below the standard of his lordship's undoubted taste and spirit. The note upon the phenomenon of the captain pasha's whiskers is a specimen of this ill-placed drollery. Indeed the curling of the angry Mussulman's beard when beset with foes which threaten him with instant death, was a circumstance very ill suited to the horror of the scene which it was the poet's purpose and duty to describe with that dignity which the most obvious of poetical proprieties demanded.[29]

On the other hand, we could argue that the endnote is actually far more disruptive than the footnote, since it would force the readers' eyes to move from the centre of the page not just to the bottom of it, but to the end of the whole tale, or even, perhaps, the end of the book. The strategy may have backfired by encouraging Byron's scholarly side and leading him, with Scott and Southey, down the path of combining romance with didactic prose. The *Eclectic Review*, for instance, claimed that in *The Bride of Abydos*, Byron's numerous topographical and cultural descriptions, which he characteristically called 'costume',[30] often detract from the main narrative. After using the word's literal meaning to mock Byron's 'muse', who is far too often dressed in oriental clothes, the review argues that in comparison with *The Giaour*, *The Bride of Abydos* is far more annoying and disruptive to the reader:

In poems so perfectly in *costume*, the imagination has frequently to stop for the understanding; and woe to the passage which requires a note for its explication! And again we must observe that all the learning which serves to deck out the muse in such exquisite costume, which brings her necklace out of one dusty tome, her dead dress out of another, her slippers from a third, and so on,—all this learning is utterly lost upon the majority of readers. [. . .] We make these observations, because this custom of disfiguring his pages with words that are not English, seems growing upon Lord Byron. There was something of it in the Giaour, but there is hardly a page in the present poem, but forces us to the notes at the end, for the explication of two or three outlandish terms.[31]

---

[29] *British Review*, 9 (October 1813), 132–45 (p. 141). For the relevant passage see *The Giaour*, p. 17: 'A phenomenon not uncommon with the angry Mussulman. In 1809, the Capitan Pacha's whiskers at a diplomatic audience were no less lively with indignation than a tiger cat's, to the horror of all the dragomans; the portentous mustachios twisted, they stood erect of their own accord, and were expected every moment to change their colour, but at last condescended to subside, which, probably, saved more heads than they contained hairs.'

[30] It is obvious from a number of Byron's letters to John Murray that he was proud of his oriental authenticity and that he took extra care to make sure that details regarding his oriental 'costume' were correct. For example, on 13 November 1813 he wrote to Murray: 'I don't care one lump of Sugar for my poetry—but for my costume—and my correctness on those points [. . .] I will combat lustily' (*Byron's Letters and Journals*, ed. by Leslie A. Marchand, 12 vols (London: John Murray, 1973–82), III (1974), 164–65).

[31] *Eclectic Review*, 11 (February 1814), 187–93 (p. 188).

For Byron, however, this 'disfiguring of [the] pages' and the 'imagination's [stopping] for the understanding' were important rhetorical techniques, and a dynamic way of relating to a readership as varied as the texts themselves.

Text and notes do not interact in Byron's printed texts only. What is easily disregarded is that their dynamic symbiosis and ironic interplay begin at the composition stage. Modern Byron scholars have not hitherto examined the question of aesthetic and stylistic (dis)continuity between the printed pages of Byron's texts on the one hand, and their draft pages on the other. The scope of this article does not allow me to do more than indicate briefly how central Byron's annotating practice was to composition. However, it will be clear that the composition of paratext interrupted and regulated the writing of poetry and that the reading of poetry and paratext would have mirrored the composition in this respect. In examining Byron's writing process to establish the order of composition of text and notes, even a close examination and comparison of ink consistency between text and notes cannot provide conclusive evidence about whether Byron wrote the notes as he went along, or after composing the whole poem. A bottle of ink lasts some time, after all, and so he might have completed the text of the poem before going back to write the notes in the same ink. However, by looking for pages where the ink significantly lightens between dips of his pen, it is certainly possible to identify places where Byron moved from text to note without pausing to dip his pen. Although it is extremely difficult to identify individual dips of the pen, in the cases mentioned below the darkness of the ink in the note markers seems consistent with that of the line in which they occur, which implies that Byron is likely to have inserted the notes while composing the poem.

Thus, in an 1808 draft manuscript of *English Bards and Scotch Reviewers* it appears probable that Byron adds all his notes as footnotes as he goes along, signalling them in the verse by using the mark 'X' next to the relevant lines, and separating them from the verse by drawing a long line, which he often defines as 'white line'—this definition being written and highlighted in a circle primarily on the left-hand side of the page just before the point where the line starts; or, occasionally, towards the right-hand side of the page, immediately above the line.[32] The volume of the notes is such that many of the manuscript's pages look as if they consist of two parallel, almost equal, conversant texts.[33] Similarly, in the fair copy of *Hints from Horace*, 'intended as a sequel to *English Bards and Scotch Reviewers*', dated 14 June and 3 May 1811, Byron seems to

---

[32] NLS, Acc. 12604/04007, 'MS, circa 1808, of loose inserts with annotations for Byron's "English Bards and Scotch Reviewers"'.

[33] The first edition of *English Bards and Scotch Reviewers* printed all its notes as footnotes, thus reflecting Byron's writing practice.

write most of the notes to his satires as footnotes as he composes the poem.[34] Again, he separates them from the main text by drawing the same 'white line', by using the indicative word 'note' next to the majority of them, and by using the same signalling mark 'X' in the verse section. Some notes are also written in the margins, and there are a few interlinear notes as well. The paratext, thus, is constantly interacting with the main poetic text, and is constantly in Byron's creative mind, as much as it is in the reader's.

Two of the manuscripts of the Oriental tales will be considered: the first draft and first fair copy of *The Bride of Abydos*, which will be referred to as MS A and MS B respectively,[35] following McGann's *CPW*. MS A includes six marginal brief notes that Byron seems to write as he goes along, adding them primarily in the right-hand margin. Therefore, it is apparent that in the first stage of the tale's composition Byron focused primarily on the poetry, rather than on the paratext. In MS B he clearly focuses on the notes. Unlike the two previous manuscripts, where he mostly used footnotes, here he employs a very different technique. Thus, in Canto I he writes the verse on the recto, adding the notes on the verso. In fact, many verso pages are blank: either Byron wrote the whole poem first on the recto sides, leaving all the verso pages blank for the subsequent addition of the notes; or else he wrote the poem and the notes at the same time, but left verso pages blank in case he decided to append notes at a later stage. However, judging by the ink consistency between the verso and recto pages, it seems most likely that he wrote the notes during the composition of the poem, rather than after its completion.

In Canto II Byron changes his practice slightly, by writing the verse on verso pages and the notes mostly on the recto, though some are given as footnotes. Thus, although in MS A the paratext and the main text were not really integrated, in MS B they are created concurrently and exist, literally, in parallel to each other. In another draft manuscript of *The Bride of Abydos*, dated 'November 11, 1813', we see the same technique as in MS B, Canto I, with the verse written on recto pages and the notes on versos.[36] There are very few notes here, though, possibly because Byron composed this at an earlier stage than MSS A and B. Moreover, exactly the same technique is employed in a draft manuscript of *The Corsair*,[37] and in Lady Byron's fair copy of *The Siege of Corinth*.[38]

One case where Byron certainly kept text and notes completely separate

---

[34] NLS, Acc. 12604/04018, 'MS, 1811, of Byron's "Hints from Horace", with preface and notes on separate sheets'.

[35] NLS, Acc. 12604/04027, 'MS, 1813, of Byron's "The Bride of Abydos"'. This includes both the draft and the fair copy.

[36] NLS, Acc. 12604/04026.

[37] NLS, Acc. 12604/04028, 'MS of "The Corsair", with copies of ? letters, 1814, of Byron to Lord Moore'.

[38] NLS, Acc. 12604/04034, 'MS, 1815, of Byron's "Siege of Corinth" in Lady Byron's hand'.

from each other is *Childe Harold* IV. An undated draft manuscript of this Canto includes no notes whatsoever, not even signals to indicate the intention to append a note subsequently.[39] It is a very heavily worked manuscript consisting entirely of poetry, with one stanza directly followed by the next, and no blank pages or spaces in between. The fact that Byron composed the poem either separately from or indeed before writing any notes is confirmed by a letter he wrote to Murray on 20 July 1817, while he was in Venice:

> I write to give you notice that I have completed the fourth and ultimate canto of Childe Harold. It consists of 126 stanzas, and is consequently the longest of the four. It is yet to be copied and polished; and the notes are to come of which it will require more than the third canto, as it necessarily treats more of works of art than nature.[40]

In a later, revised version of this manuscript, which is very probably the 'copied' and 'polished' version mentioned above, Byron writes one stanza on the recto, leaving the remainder (and reverse) of the leaf blank.[41] The reason for this is presumably that he intended to pass the manuscript on to Hobhouse who would add the notes in the spaces provided.[42]

With regard to *Childe Harold* I and II, there are no extant draft manuscripts, so we cannot tell what Byron's writing practice was when he began the poem. There have survived, though, the first fair copy[43] and a printer's copy 'in the hand of R. C. Dallas with Byron's own corrections and additions',[44] which will henceforth be referred to as MS M and MS D respectively, again following McGann's sigla. In MS M Byron writes all notes as footnotes, except for the few long prose notes which are added at the end of the manuscript. By comparing again the ink consistency between the main text and the paratext, we may infer that he probably composed poem and notes at the same time. More specifically, it seems likely that he often wrote a note directly after finishing writing the stanza which included the line to which he wanted to append the note. The earliest drafts of *Childe Harold* I and II were composed 'on location'.

---

[39] NLS, Acc. 12604/04048, 'MS, ? 1818, of Byron's "Childe Harold, Canto IV"'.

[40] *Byron's Letters and Journals*, V (1976), 362–63.

[41] NLS, Acc. 12604/04044, 'MS, 1817, of Byron's "Childe Harold Canto IV", and letter to Hobhouse, 1818'.

[42] Although Byron did write a few notes to the poem, the great majority of them were written by Hobhouse. In the fairly extended period from mid-August 1817 to early January 1818, Hobhouse has numerous accounts in his personal diary of spending a considerable amount of time writing notes for *Childe Harold* IV. See *Hobhouse's Diary*, ed. by Peter Cochran <http://petercochran. wordpress.com/hobhouses-diary/> [accessed 2 May 2013]. Relevant letters include those of 18, 19, and 23 August 1817.

[43] London, The John Murray Collection, MS M (the original fair copy of First and Second Cantos of *Childe Harold's Pilgrimage*, in Byron's handwriting).

[44] London, British Library, MS Eg. 2,027: '*Childe Harold's Pilgrimage: A Romaunt* by [George Gordon] Lord Byron; the first, and second cantos, as copied for the press for the first edition [London, 1812, 4to. with corrections and extensive notes in the handwriting, of the author, f. 4]'. The description used here follows McGann's wording from *CPW*, II, 266.

The landscapes, the nature, and the people Byron was elaborating on in his notes were all around him; they were an immediate presence, and were so vivid in his mind and thoughts that, while composing the poem, it was presumably easy to divert from the imagination and the Romantic contemplations to the reality of the landscape and the culture around him, and then return again to the imaginative creative process. While he was writing the Oriental tales, though, Greece, Turkey, and the Levant changed from presences to memories. This perhaps resulted in separate stages of the composition of *The Bride of Abydos*: initially he focused primarily on the poetry, leaving the addition of the majority of the notes for a later stage.

In MS D the notes that are copied in Dallas's hand and those written in Byron's hand, apart from the long prose notes added at the end, are all footnotes. MS D is particularly revealing because it demonstrates that Byron was interested in the position of the notes in his poems, and therefore that he was conscious of the reading experience his notes would produce; or, more importantly, that he considered his notes as an integral part of his texts and their reading process. In a letter to Murray of 16 September 1811, however, Byron expressed great frustration over the preparation of the notes for a *Childe Harold* proof that he wanted to pass on to Dallas; and this 'proof' must be the one from which Dallas made his own copy. Perhaps in a moment of pique, he claimed he wanted to forget about the notes completely, and he actually granted his printer absolute freedom with regard to their position:

I return the proof, which I should wish to be shown to Mr. Dallas, who understands typographical arrangements much better than I can pretend to do. The printer may place the notes in his *own way*, or *any way*, so that they are out of my way; I care nothing about types or margins.[45]

By contrast, MS D contains specific instructions for certain notes to be printed as footnotes. In the top right-hand corner of the beginning of Canto II there is a note in Byron's hand: 'The notes that are to appear at the bottom of the pages are so specified by a "(" line of the word page'. Accordingly, to nineteen notes in Canto II Byron prefixes the phrase 'on the page'. Most of these notes are fairly short, providing primarily translations of lexical items and topographical information. The fact that Byron did not want these to be printed as endnotes suggests that he was quite conscious of the volume and diversity of the *Childe Harold* II paratext, and that he wanted to make it as little disruptive as possible for his readers. In MS D of Canto I Byron gave no such instructions. In the first quarto edition of *Childe Harold* I and II this specific group of notes were all indeed published as footnotes, apart from two notes that were dropped. However, unlike the first edition, which employed footnotes and endnotes, the second edition had no footnotes in Canto I and

[45] *Byron's Letters and Journals*, II (1973), 100.

none in Canto II apart from the notes appended to the war song. The rest of the notes that Byron originally asked to be printed as footnotes were thus eventually printed as endnotes instead. We have no evidence showing that Byron complained about Murray's rejection of his guidelines about the position of the notes, or about Murray's randomness and inconsistency in editing them.

The semiotic rhetoric and positioning of Byron's notes on the printed page are integral to his poetics, rendering the proper editing of his notes an issue of great importance. The majority of the nineteenth-century editions of Byron's poetry retain his annotations in full. Throughout the Victorian period Byron was a very controversial figure in regard to matters of ethical and sexual propriety—especially after the publication of Thomas Moore's biography, *Letters and Journals of Lord Byron: With Notices of his Life* (1830), which revealed details of the infamous saga of his marriage and separation. Perhaps partly as a result of this, the public was still very much attracted by his bohemian and scandalous life and personality, and continued to be interested in his prefaces, which often recount his personal thoughts or incidents from his private life, as well as his notes, which constitute in many ways a fragmented autobiography. This continuing interest is reflected in Murray's 1845 collective edition of *The Poetical Works of Lord Byron*, which, along with the 1859 and 1869 reprints, have all the notes printed as footnotes. For the sake of space and homogeneity, these printings modified the original reading experiences of certain works, which in their early editions had all or some of their notes printed as endnotes (such as the Oriental tales, *Childe Harold* I and II, and *Don Juan*); but it is still very significant that they incorporate all Byron's notes. Similarly, modern popular editions of Byron's poetry, such as the Penguin Classics volume, follow the same format in printing all Byron's notes as footnotes.[46]

The majority of the Victorian editions tend either to print abridged versions of Byron's Appendix and Poems added to *Childe Harold* I and II, or else leave them out completely. Apart from very few cases, such as the 1905 Carlton Classics edition, which included no notes whatsoever,[47] the majority of *Childe Harold* editions, such as the 1860 and 1870 editions by Murray,[48] had all notes printed as endnotes after each canto. Even Murray, Byron's major publisher, changed his editorial practice and hence the original structure of some of Byron's poetic texts. In Murray's editions there are usually no editorial prefaces, so it is hard to tell whether there was a rationale behind this change. As

---

[46] *Lord Byron: Selected Poems*, ed. by Susan J. Wolfson and Peter J. Manning (Harmondsworth: Penguin, 1996). Although the editors handle the footnotes better than McGann, they do not collate all relevant texts.

[47] Byron, *Childe Harold's Pilgrimage*, Carlton Classics (London: John Long, 1905).

[48] *Childe Harold's Pilgrimage: A Romaunt by Lord Byron* (London: John Murray, 1860); *Childe Harold's Pilgrimage: A Romaunt by Lord Byron* (London: John Murray, 1870).

for the Oriental tales, the 1859 collective edition by David Bogue, for instance, and the 1848 edition of *The Giaour* and *The Bride of Abydos* by H. G. Clarke have all the notes printed as endnotes.[49] This means that apart from the case of *The Giaour*—which was originally published with footnotes—the Victorian editions tended to be faithful to the original editions of the tales. However, when *The Giaour* was published on its own, as in the 1842 edition by Murray, the notes tended to be printed as footnotes.[50]

When it comes to modern editions of Byron's works, Jerome McGann's *Complete Poetical Works* generated a great deal of controversy among literary critics, at the centre of which was McGann's presentation of Byron's paratext. According to Roger Poole, McGann fell into an important error of execution by 'including the Poems as separate lyrics in two totally different volumes of *CPW*; including only a part of the Appendix, and providing a mere summary of the Greek materials', thereby depriving *Childe Harold* II of its highly significant original political context, and ultimately, changing its original mode of perception.[51] In addition, McGann's edition had all of Byron's notes printed as endnotes at the back of each volume, in amongst his own commentary, a practice which complicated the perusal of the notes, occluding how these were actually set for the first readers and, more importantly, distorting Byron's authorial intentions and considerably mitigating the paratext's subversive effects. Byron's texts should not be 'mutilated', and his paratext should remain as it was originally: 'scatter'd through the pages'.[52] The semiotic of the page is crucial in studying Byron's paratext and establishing its impact on his poetics of ironic hybridity. In the manuscript editions under Donald H. Reiman's general editorship,[53] the page is historicized and Byron's paratextual hand is visibly involved in the creative compositional drama, in a way not apparent in McGann's *Complete Poetical Works*. The field of paratextual studies adds a whole new value to an edition such as Reiman's, which offers extremely

---

[49] *Byron's Eastern Tales*, ed. by David Bogue (London: 86 Fleet Street, 1859); George Gordon Byron, Baron Byron, *'The Giaour', and 'The Bride of Abydos'*, ed. by H. G. Clarke & Co. (London: 278 Strand, 1848).

[50] George Gordon Byron, Baron Byron, *The Giaour, A Fragment of a Turkish Tale*, 13th edn (London: John Murray, 1842).

[51] Roger Poole, 'What Constitutes, and What is External to, the "Real" Text of Byron's *Childe Harold's Pilgrimage, A Romaunt: and Other Poems* (1812)?', in *Lord Byron the European: Essays from the International Byron Society*, ed. by Richard A. Cardwell (Lewiston, NY: Mellen, 1997), pp. 149–208 (p. 160). McGann reprints the 'List of Romaic Authors'; 'two extracts of the Romaic with B's translation of the first'; 'a scene from a Goldoni comedy translated into the Romaic by Spiridion Vlanti along with B's English translation'; and 'a conclusion to the Appendix' (*CPW*, II, 212–17).

[52] *Don Juan*, I. 44–45.

[53] *The Manuscripts of the Younger Romantics: A Facsimile Edition. Lord Byron*, III: *Poems 1819–1822* and IV: *Miscellaneous Poems*, ed. by Alice Levine and Jerome J. McGann (New York: Garland, 1988).

useful insights into the evolution of paratextual rhetoric and poetics from composition to printing.

Byron's manuscripts reveal that the way his notes interrupt and determine the reading process of his poetic texts mirrors his own creative process. His poetic authorial persona was itself multifaceted, and the use of prose notes allowed the irruption of factual, antiquarian, comic, personal, and satiric elements. When he was in constant contact with the Murray circle, paratext was a constant presence in his works throughout their journey from manuscripts and drafts to fair copies and printed copies, and finally to publication and then further editions. When he was abroad, however, this paratextual presence began to fade or to be taken over by Hobhouse. This did not signal more unified centripetal poetry. On the contrary, Byronic hybridity became more radical, not conforming to a text–paratext split at all, and intensifying the amalgamation of Romantic imagination with Enlightenment scepticism.

Beppo (1818)[54] presents minimal annotation when compared with the noticeable paratextual presence in Byron's earlier poetry and especially the satires. It has only four footnotes in 792 lines. Where has the paratext gone? This question is fundamental to understanding Byron's change of style, his invention of a form of satire which incorporates the Romantic, of a Romanticism whose comic interruptions subvert its own reading process. The footnotes are still joined to the main text. They are changing hypostasis, becoming the chameleon narrator's asides that digress constantly from the main narrative, creating thus a conversational, burlesque tone. Consider the following italicized intertextual playful explanations of the terms 'Gondolier' and 'Cavalier Servente':

> Dids't ever see a gondola? For fear
>   You should not, I'll describe it you exactly:
> *'Tis long covered boat that's common here,*
>   *Carved at the prow, built lightly, but compactly,*
> *Rowed by two rowers, each called 'Gondolier,'*
>   *It glides along the water looking blackly,*
> Just like a coffin clapt in a canoe,
> Where none can make out what you say or do.
>   (st. 19)

> *The word was formerly a 'Cicisbeo,'*
>   *But that is now grown vulgar and indecent;*
> *The Spaniards call the person a 'Cortejo,'*
>   *For the same mode subsists in Spain, though recent;*
> *In short it reaches from Porto Teio,*
>   And many perhaps at least be o'er the sea sent.

---

[54] George Gordon Byron, *Beppo*, 6th edn (London: John Murray, 1818). References will be given parenthetically in the text.

> But Heaven preserve Old England from such courses!
> Or what becomes of damage and divorces?
> (st. 38, emphasis added)

The traveller's paratext is no longer relegated to the margins. The most perfect exemplification of the amalgamation of textual and paratextual poetics in *Beppo* is Byron's note to stanza 46, the only note he wrote in verse:

> In talking thus, the writer, more especially
>   Of women, would be understood to say,
> He speaks as a spectator, not officially,
>   And always, reader, in a modest way;
> Perhaps, too, in no very great degree shall he
>   Appear to have offended in this lay,
> Since, as all know, without the sex, our sonnets
> Would seem unfinish'd like their untrimm'd bonnets.
>   (Signed): PRINTER'S DEVIL.

The note glosses stanza 46, where Byron extols the beauty of Italian women. Byron's signature as 'PRINTER'S DEVIL' anticipates Murray's objections by playfully incorporating a note in verse, which acknowledges and pretends to apologize for the poet's scandalous reputation. The *OED* defines 'printer's devil' as 'an errand boy or apprentice in a printing office' (3rd edn, 2007). Byron masquerades as lowly 'printer's 'prentice', an ingenious sarcastic allusion to his often stated—yet unconvincing—lack of interest in the finicky processes of note positioning in particular and book production in general.

In *Beppo* Byron rehearsed the intimate colloquial poetic form and style that he would very soon perfect in *Don Juan*. *Beppo* was published on 28 February 1818, and as early as 3 July of that year Byron started composing the first Canto of his 'magnum opus', which incorporated into its main text all the opportunities for qualification, enlargement, glossing, self-mockery, and defensiveness that marginalia had previously afforded him. *Don Juan* became the apogee of a poem ingesting and digesting its own paratext, constructing thereby an appearance of spontaneity which cunningly demystified both the compositional and the reading processes, and inverted Coleridge's and Wordsworth's paratextual poetics, that had focused on projecting the elaborateness or mysticism of poetic composition. Like *Beppo*, *Don Juan* also presents quite minimal annotation. In Canto III, for instance, there are only seven notes for 984 lines, in Canto IV, five notes for 936 lines, and in Canto V, nine notes for 1272 lines.

Don Juan's text is haunted by digressions, most of which can justifiably be defined as an incorporated digressive paratext: a refinement and development of the annotation of the tales. *Don Juan*'s main text has swallowed its digressive and mocking paratext, and numerous stanzas are microcosmic dramatizations of this balanced symbiosis of oppositional dynamics. Paradoxically enough, both are generated by a single, Janus-faced poet-narrator who manages the narration of the epic romance and the editorial function of commentary at the same time. The content and style of digression change as the poem progresses. The culturally oriented, orientalist footnotes of the tales give way to satiric, reflective, mock-antiquarian, footnote-like asides—most often accommodated in the concluding couplet of *Don Juan*'s *ottava rima* stanzas—which, nevertheless, echo the tales' notes by also interrupting the reading process, giving personal information on the author, and making satiric or sceptical comments on religious or political idealism. More specifically, they can take the form of exclamatory feminine rhyme:[55]

> 'Tis pity learn'd virgins ever wed
>   With persons of no sort of education,
> Or gentlemen, who, though well born and bred,
>   Grow tired of scientific conversation:
> I don't choose to say much upon this head,
>   I'm a plain man, and in a single station,
> *But—Oh! ye lords of ladies intellectual,*
> *Inform us truly, have they not hen-pecked you all?*
>   (st. 22)

They can also accommodate the narrator's random personal confessions:

> Her eye (*I'm very fond of handsome eyes*)
> Was large and dark, suppressing half its fire.
>   (1. 60. 1–2, emphasis added)
>
>   [. . .] she, in sooth,
> Possessed an air and grace by no means common:
> Her stature tall—*I hate a dumpy woman.*
>   (1. 61. 6–8, emphasis added)

These asides may also take the form of a ventriloquized voice imitating moral cant:

> I knew his father well, and have some skill
>   In character—but it would not be fair
> From sire to son to augur good or ill:
>   He and his wife were an ill-sorted pair—
> *But scandal's my aversion—I protest*
> *Against all evil speaking, even in jest.*
>   (1. 51. 3–8, emphasis added)
>
> The darkness of her oriental eye
>   Accorded with her Moorish origin;

---

[55] References, given parenthetically in the text, will be to George Gordon Byron, *Don Juan: Canto I* (London: Thomas Davison, 1819).

> (Her blood was not all Spanish; by the by,
> *In Spain, you know, this is a sort of sin*[)].
> (I. 56. 1-4, emphasis added)

Finally, in some cases they expose a cynical religious scepticism and criticism of the metaphysical or supernatural through the medium of rhetorical questions that Byron addresses to his confused reader, who has no choice but slavishly to follow Byron's zigzag movements in his 'muddy' 'canals of contradiction',[56] hanging anxiously and desperately from his temperamental strings of words that oscillate between truth and fiction:

> *Grim reader! did you ever see a ghost?*
>   *No; but you've heard—I understand—be dumb*
> *And don't regret the time you may have lost,*
>   *For you have got that pleasure still to come:*
> *And do not think I mean to sneer at most*
>   *Of those things, or by ridicule benumb*
> *That source of the sublime and the mysterious:—*
> *For certain reasons my belief is serious.*
> (xv. 95, emphasis added)

Don Juan's parodic encyclopedic view of the world has essentially evolved from the footnote's poetics of informative antiquarianism. Therefore, the essence and aesthetics of the footnote are still present, but much has changed. In placing amusing, ironic material within the poem—instead of relegating it to a footnote or endnote—Byron is not diverting one's attention, but incorporating another source of humour into the body of the poem itself. In *Don Juan* he realized paratext's full potential in framing his poetics of Romantic irony. He takes to the next level his exploration, begun in the Oriental tales, of the paratext's capacity to deflate the illusions of fiction, constructing compulsory digressions and changes of tone which exist regardless of whether the reader reads a footnote/endnote or not. The reader is no longer in control of the reading process and choice of which parts of a miscellaneous text to peruse or in which order. Instead, the text is now in full control of the reader, obliging him to read the digressions it has assimilated. The supplement has now become compulsory. The hybridity of discourse has been embraced and the former hierarchy of text and paratext abandoned. Apart from these brief asides, there is also the large, well-known group of more lengthy digressions, which, in *Don Juan* I at least, extend for up to twenty stanzas. The poetic paratextual space becomes more discursive, '[wielding] a despotic control over a reader's attention'.[57] These extended digressions offer a freer and more radical

---

[56] George Gordon Byron, *Don Juan: Cantos XV and XVI* (London: John and H. L. Hunt, 1824), st. 88. 6-7. Subsequent references will be given parenthetically in the text.

[57] Truman Guy Steffan, *Byron's 'Don Juan': The Making of a Masterpiece*, 2 vols (Austin: University of Texas Press, 1957), I, 130.

conception of the asides we encounter elsewhere: a sort of discursive note, minimally relevant to the plot; an intertextual, aggressive, and ostentatious agent of textual interruption.

In *Don Juan* Byron achieves a Romantic irony by incorporating directly into his fiction the Enlightenment heritage of authorial paratextual presence associated both with antiquarian and with satiric genres. The multifaceted narrator see-saws between realistic scepticism and Romantic inhabiting of cultural Others. In the Oriental tales Byron demanded from his reader an occasional enforced detachment from the subjective engagement with the emotional and imaginative sublimity of his poetic text. In *Don Juan* he dominated the reader by swallowing all the paratextual claims to authorial authority into the narrative itself, turning the footnote's digressive irony into a mainstream Romantic poetic element.

Paratext is an integral, formative aspect of the Romantic period's poetics, fragmenting narrative by interweaving fiction with fact, or *muthos* with *historia*, and providing evidence for a more nuanced understanding of Romantic-period literature and its hybridity. The Romantic-period (foot)note, resembling the chorus of Greek classical drama, or an Arlecchino, disrupts the main poetic action, demanding the reader's attention. This aggressive intrusion of the antiquarian prose note into sublime, Romantic poetry is analogous to a Derridean *débordement*,[58] a transgression of the textual borders and boundaries which separate the margins from the centred text, and constitutes a crucial rhetorical means towards the manifestation of philosophical Romantic irony. The diverse and hybrid nature of Romantic poetic creation adds a very significant, under-researched variant to the already extremely diverse nature of what we call Romanticism, and paratext is at the very centre of it.

> I quite forget this poem's merely quizzical
>   And deviate into matters rather dry.
> I ne'er decide what I shall say, and this I call
>   Much too poetical. Men should know why
> They write, and for what end; but, note or text,
> I never know the word which will come next.
>   (IX. 41)

SWANSEA UNIVERSITY   OURANIA CHATSIOU

[58] *Deconstruction and Criticism*, ed. by Geoffrey Hartman (London and New York: Continuum, 1979; repr. 2004), p. 69.

'WHY DON'T YOU WRITE A PLAY?' KIPLING THE POET IN FULL

The Cambridge Edition of the Poems of Rudyard Kipling. Ed. by THOMAS PINNEY. 3 vols. Cambridge: Cambridge University Press. 2013. xlviii+2349 pp. £200. ISBN 978–1–107–01917–1 (set).

'Amazing' is the word that immediately springs to mind when I contemplate the scale of this project. Patience, focus, slow and systematic international searching of archives, and a cool-headed and meticulous devotion to textual accuracy are all evidenced in this massive new edition of Kipling's poems. The number of hitherto unpublished poems in the collection is the most headline-grabbing and immediately exciting feature of this edition. It should be recognized at the same time, though, that there is an equally impressive haul of poems which were hitherto 'published' only in the sense of having once appeared in print in some fugitive or marginal source. Among the wholly unpublished poems is 'The Press' (II, 2051–52), an assault on vulgar and intrusive journalists:

> Why don't you write a play—
>   Why don't you cut your hair?
> Do you trim your toe-nails round
>   Or do you trim them square?
> Tell it to the papers,
>   Tell it every day.
> But en passant, may I ask
>   Why don't you write a play?

The poem gets progressively closer to the bone and ends with excoriating contempt:

> Have you any morals?
>   Does your genius burn?
> Was your wife a what's its name?
>   How much does she earn?
> Had your friend a secret
>   Sorrow, shame or vice—
> Have you promised not to tell
>   What's your lowest price?
> All the housemaid fancied
>   All the butler guessed
> Tell it to the public press
>   And we will do the rest.
> Why don't you write a play?

Contempt for journalists was matched by contempt for government control of the arts in a pungent piece, 'Laudatores Actoris Empti' (III, 1971–72), about the London County Council's draft theatre bill of 1890. This was just as powerful as 'The Press'. It was effectively another 'unpublished' finding; the copy-text is an unattributed clipping in one of Kipling's scrapbooks. This piece of fuming indignation displays Kipling's obstinacy, his violent individualism, and his resistance to social norms. Those who have brought in this new legislation are despicably 'middle class':

> Fly to the villas whence ye came
>   And that best room the Sabbath knows,
> Where on the woollen mat aflame,
>   The weird wax flower, bell glassèd, glows;
> And 'neath the ceiling's aching eye
>   The few lean books in patterns lie.
>
> (p. 1972)

He wrote poetry from his early schooldays. His ear for the manner of established poets was precocious. A sequence of episodes by the schoolboy Kipling called 'Told in the Dormitory' is given in the heroic blank verse of Tennyson's *Idylls of the King* (III, 1595–96; 1637–38), and smaller comic verses are skilful pastiches—instantly recognizable—of major Romantic lyrics. Take this adaptation of Keats, entitled 'Tobacco' (II, 1226), written when Kipling was aged fourteen or fifteen (and already smoking a pipe):

> Sweet is the Rose's scent—Tobacco's smell
>   Is sweeter; wherefore let me charge again.
> Old blackened meerschaum, I have loved thee well
>   From youth, when smoke brought sickness in its train.

The Kipling who became world-famous is also the Kipling whose verse can haunt the memories of men in their seventies who first heard them when they were schoolboys. I say 'men' because Kipling's poetry is on the whole spoken by a male voice and assumes a male audience. Kipling's rhythms and sonorities are typically for those familiar with the music hall and the military band, and often it is the male perspective on human experience that is assumed and validated. This is particularly true, obviously, of the substantial body of poetry which he wrote during the Great War, though there are also some striking exceptions. Two out of the sequence called 'Epitaphs of the War' are imagined as spoken by raped, mutilated, and murdered women (II, 1140–47). The other forty or so epitaphs are spoken by dead men, some of whom are as utterly innocent as 'The Beginner' (II, 1142):

> On the first hour of my first day
>   In the front trench I fell.
> (Children in boxes at a play
>   Stand up to watch it well.)

Others have the pain of those who loved them to add to the anguish, as does 'The Bridegroom' (II, 1146):

> Call me not false, beloved,
>   If, from thy scarce-known breast
> So little time removed,
>   In other arms I rest.

Two of these tiny poems ('An Only Son' and 'A Son', both on p. 1140) sparsely present two deaths in one:

> I have slain none except my Mother. She
> (Blessing her slayer) died of grief for me.

And—this is clearly personal for Kipling—

> My son was killed while laughing at some jest. I would I knew
> What it was, and it might serve me in a time when jests are few.

Most personal of all is the lyric 'My Boy Jack', published in 1916. This is ostensibly about a sailor, not a soldier, but it clearly reflects Kipling's own feelings. Kipling's son John should have been disqualified for military service because of his poor eyesight, but Kipling used his fame and connections to ensure that his son should not be denied the honour of serving his country. John Kipling was just seventeen when he joined up as a young officer and eighteen when he was killed at the battle of Loos in September 1915. (He was not 'laughing at some jest'—the consensus based on surviving records is that half his head was shot away and he died in agony.) Like so much of Kipling's poetry, 'My Boy Jack' makes its full impact when performed by a skilled reader. A recent television drama based on the death of John Kipling includes an excellent reading of the poem by the actor David Haig, as Kipling (with Daniel Radcliffe as his son).

In 'My Boy Jack' the spoken lines are as brief as is compatible with moving the sense and the dramatic situation forward. Meanwhile, the unspoken and italicized lines, with their refrain, carry the full weight of the speaker's massive grief:

> "Have you news of my boy Jack?"
>   *Not this tide.*
> "When d'you think that he'll come back?"
>   *Not with this wind blowing, and this tide.*
> "Has any one else had word of him?"
>   *Not this tide.*
> *For what is sunk will hardly swim,*
>   *Not with this wind blowing, and this tide.*
> "Oh, dear, what comfort can I find?"
>   *None this tide,*

> *Nor any tide,*
> *Except he did not shame his kind—*
> *Not even with that wind blowing, and that tide.*
>
> *Then hold your head up all the more,*
>   *This tide,*
>   *And every tide;*
> *Because he was the son you bore,*
>   *And gave to that wind blowing and that tide!*
>
>   (II, 1098)

It is presumably this same son, John Kipling, who modelled for the addressee of the verses which comprise what is regularly cited as 'Britain's favourite poem'. This poem merits its phenomenally wide reach. It is about courage and is full of masculine strength, self-reliance, stoicism, and so on, yet every other line has a feminine ending. The utterance throughout is marked by confidence and authority, the speech rhythms lending themselves as naturally to the lines as though they had grown there of their own accord without any help from the writer. It looks and sounds effortless, and technically it is a masterpiece. I refer, of course, to 'If—' (II, 756–57). In technical terms, the third stanza is the most ingenious:

> If you can make one heap of all your winnings
> And risk it on one turn of pitch-and-toss,
> And lose, and start again at your beginnings
> And never breathe a word about your loss;
> If you can force your heart and nerve and sinew
> To serve your turn long after they are gone,
> And so hold on when there is nothing in you
> Except the Will which says to them: "Hold on!"

We don't stop here, obviously; the four stanzas flow continuously from the first 'If', and the last four lines move the poem into a universal rule for life which reflects Kipling's Methodist antecedents' faith in the preciousness of God-given time. Thus, although the triumphalism of the final lines sounds blood-stirring and military, what are actually commended here are narrowly focused, lower middle-class, early Victorian virtues. Kipling's heritage from his grandfather and father is now passed on to his son:

> If you can fill the unforgiving minute
> With sixty seconds' worth of distance run,
> Yours is the Earth and everything that's in it,
> And—which is more—you'll be a Man, my son!

Despite the claims made nearly thirty years ago in a biography by Martin Seymour-Smith[1] (a book described by one reviewer as 'incorrigible guess-

---

[1] Martin Seymour-Smith, *Rudyard Kipling* (London: MacDonald, 1989).

work'),[2] there is no evidence that Kipling was homosexual. What clearly are aspects of him, though, are his sensitivity to male bonding and his capacity to respond emotionally to other men. The personalities that he found among British serving soldiers were rich material for his writings, with their stoicism, their limited horizons and expectations, their intense solidarity with each other, and above all their speech. 'Danny Deever', emerging from this material, first published in 1890 as number 1 of the *Barrack Room Ballads*, is an unchallengeable masterpiece (I, 176–77). Danny himself is the only figure given a name; his comrades are identified by their rank. The stark pattern created by the ballad form and the military titles is subverted and ruptured by the emotions seething among the young men forced to witness Danny's punishment:

> "What are the bugles blowin' for?" said Files-on-Parade.
> "To turn you out, to turn you out," the Colour-Sergeant said.
> "What makes you look so white, so white?" said Files-on-Parade.
> "I'm dreadin' what I've got to watch," the Colour-Sergeant said.
>   For they're hangin' Danny Deever, you can hear the Dead March play,
>   The Regiment's in 'ollow square—they're hangin' 'im today;
>   They've taken of 'is buttons off an' cut 'is stripes away,
>   An' they're hangin' Danny Deever in the morning.

The ballad forces the reader's attention to the reality of death by hanging and then startlingly follows this with a supernatural event. There is no shift of tone or metre, just another plain answer to the final question asked by 'Files-on-Parade':

> "What's that so black agin the sun?" said Files-on-Parade.
> "It's Danny fightin' 'ard for life," the Colour-Sergeant said.
> "What's that that whimpers over'ead?" said Files-on-Parade.
> "It's Danny's soul that's passin' now," the Colour-Sergeant said.
>   For they're done with Danny Deever, you can 'ear the quick-step play,
>   The Regiment's in column, and they're marchin' us away;
>   Ho! The young recruits are shakin', and they'll want their beer today,
>   After hangin' Danny Deever in the mornin'!

The artist who could write this has the virtuosity to write anything.

One of the most beautiful of Kipling's lyrics has nothing to do with soldiers, or India, or male bonding; but it has a great deal to do with steadiness of purpose, self-reliance, and self-confidence. It is a ballad about a seventh-century monk in Sussex, celebrating on Christmas Day. 'Eddi's Service' is a small, quiet Sussex poem which has a metrical balance and certainty of voice which place it among the finest of Kipling's achievements (II, 689–90):

---

[2] Harry Ricketts, 'Beastliness', *London Review of Books*, 11.6 (March 1989), 13–14 (p. 13).

> Eddi, priest of St. Wilfrid
>   In his chapel at Manhood End,
> Ordered a midnight service
>   For such as cared to attend.
>
> But the Saxons were keeping Christmas,
>   And the night was stormy as well.
> Nobody came to service,
>   Though Eddi rang the bell.
>
>   (p. 689)

An 'old marsh-donkey' and a 'wet, yoke-weary bullock' come into the chapel. Eddi welcomes them, and the man and the two animals celebrate Christmas:

> "But—three are gathered together—
>   Listen to me and attend.
> I bring good news, my brethren!"
>   Said Eddi of Manhood End.
>
>   (p. 690)

The Chapel is always open, Christianity is universal:

> And when the Saxons mocked him,
>   Said Eddi of Manhood End,
> "I dare not shut His chapel
>   On such as care to attend."
>
>   (p. 690)

'Manhood End' sounds like a teasing invention, a name which could signify either the destruction or the purpose of manhood. The simple reality, though, is that it is the actual name of a village in Sussex close to his house, Batemans.

Manhood did preoccupy him, of course, and he confronted the challenge to it posed by strong women in 'The Female of the Species' (III, 1137–39), written in 1910 and described by his wife Carrie as 'his suffragette verses'.[3] They caused him difficulty; they were 'put aside for a long time' before being taken up again and completed (III, 1519). Those who want to see Kipling as misogynist can root for some ammunition here:

> Man's timid heart is bursting with the things he must not say,
> For the Woman that God gave him isn't his to give away;
> But when hunter meets with husband, each confirms the other's tale—
> The female of the species is more deadly than the male.
>
>   (p. 1137)

But as with other instances of apparent prejudice, the burden of meaning is not as it seems at first sight. 'Fuzzy-Wuzzy' salutes the courage of the tribe

---

[3] Quoted in Andrew Lycett, *Rudyard Kipling* (London: Weidenfeld & Nicholson, 1999), p. 419.

that the Soudan Expeditionary Force was seeking to subdue in 1885: 'So 'ere's *to you, Fuzzy-Wuzzy, at your 'ome in the Soudan; | You're a pore benighted 'eathen but a first-class fighting man'* (I, 181). 'The Ballad of East and West' (I, 225–29) takes this much further: it is about courage, honour, and close resemblance within profound differences. The Colonel's son and the young Indian warrior who would kill him recognize each other's courage. The verse celebrates a simple and overwhelming mutuality:

> They have looked each other between the eyes, and there they found no fault.
> They have taken the Oath of Brother-in-Blood on leavened bread and salt.
> They have taken the Oath of Brother-in-Blood on fire and fresh-cut sod.
> On the hilt and the haft of the Khyber knife, and the Wondrous Names of God.
>
> (p. 228)

There was never in Kipling's mind a simple power hierarchy either of the sexes or of the races. His interest is in exploring their differences and the many negotiations both parties conduct in order to find common ground, as in this instance where personal valour transcends all other barriers.

> *But there is neither East nor West, Border, nor Breed, nor Birth,*
> *When two strong men stand face to face, though they come from the ends of the earth!*
>
> (p. 229)

On his visit to Rangoon, Burma, in 1889, Kipling was dazzled by the brilliant colours of this Buddhist country and by the beauty of its young women: 'I love the Burman with the blind favouritism born of first impression. When I die I will be a Burman.'[4] He recalled Burma in 'Mandalay', published the following year, where the mutuality between cultures is embodied in a memory of a brief love affair (I, 207–09). The speaker is a demobbed soldier, now trapped in a dull job in London, whose memories are of release, consolation, mystery, and heady sensual excitement:

> Ship me somewhere east of Suez, where the best is like the worst,
> Where there aren't no Ten Commandments an' a man can raise a thirst;
> For the temple-bells are callin', and it's there that I would be—
> By the old Moulmein Pagoda, looking lazy at the sea;
> On the road to Mandalay,
> Where the old Flotilla lay,
> With our sick beneath the awnings when we went to Mandalay!
> Oh, the road to Mandalay,
> Where the flyin'-fishes play,
> An' the dawn comes up like thunder outer China 'crost the Bay!
>
> (pp. 208–09)

The poem became very widely known, partly because of its currency as a popular song set by the American composer Oley Speaks in 1907; the sheet

[4] Quoted ibid., p. 173.

music of this ballad for male voice sold over a million copies. (This was before the days of copyright; Kipling had differences with the publisher and later put an embargo on the song's distribution.) Sound recordings had been marketed in the United States since the 1890s, and this ballad was first recorded in 1912 (by the baritone Earl Cartwright); the recording, like the sheet music, was a commercial success. As a popular concert item, it was firmly embedded in the repertoire of great tenors and baritones until the 1960s; there are striking recordings of it by Peter Dawson and Lawrence Tibbett.

The impact and popularity of this ballad recall the questions raised by T. S. Eliot in his 1941 essay on Kipling's verse. Eliot's premiss is that 'we expect to have to defend a poet against the charge of obscurity' (as Eliot's own work had to be defended). But Kipling's case is different: 'we have to defend Kipling against the charge of excessive lucidity'.[5] From this viewpoint, Eliot warmly and effectively defended Kipling's choice of the ballad form (though it remains surprising that Eliot did not cite the great precedent of Wordsworth and Coleridge's *Lyrical Ballads* here). Eliot was writing from within the stronghold of coterie art—that narrowly defended high ground which he shared with Woolf, Joyce, Pound, Dorothy Richardson, and the young William Empson. He praised 'Danny Deever' as a barrack-room ballad which 'somehow attains the intensity of poetry', and he moved from this position to the generous claim that 'with Kipling you cannot draw a line beyond which some of the verse becomes "poetry"'.[6] Yet Eliot himself did draw the line: 'Mandalay' was omitted from his *Choice of Kipling's Verse*. Does this poem then become a test case over the question of what is admissible in Kipling and what is not?

> 'Er petticoat was yaller an' 'er little cap was green,
> An' 'er name was Supi-yaw-lat—jes' the same as Theebaw's Queen,
> An' I seed 'er first a-smokin' of a whackin' white cheroot,
> An' a wastin' Christian kisses on an 'eathen idol's foot.
>
> (p. 207)

The speaker uses his own language and his own limited set of references to recall the pleasure and wonder of the setting in which the romance was acted out:

> But that's all shove be'ind me—long ago an' fur away,
> An there ain't no 'busses runnin' from the Bank to Mandalay;
> An' I'm learnin' 'ere in London wot the ten-year soldier tells:
> "If you've 'eard the East a-callin', you won't never 'eed naught else".
>
> (p. 208)

When Shakespeare's Antony, another rough soldier, recalled that 'the beds i'

---

[5] *A Choice of Kipling's Verse: Made by T. S. Eliot, with an Essay on Rudyard Kipling* (London: Faber, 1941), p. 6.
[6] Ibid., p. 13.

the East are soft' (*Antony and Cleopatra*, II. 6. 50), he was sharing a similarly ineradicable memory.

Kipling's feeling for his soldiers is often sharply political, as in 'Tommy' (I, 178-79):

> I went into a theatre as sober as could be,
> They gave a drunk civilian room, but 'adn't none for me;
> They sent me to the gallery or round the music-'alls,
> But when it comes to fightin', Lord! they'll shove me in the stalls!
>
> (p. 178)

His attachment is also based on a profound respect for the common soldier's own attachments, priorities, and language. The men he presents can display a simple love for the work that they do and for the instruments that they use. In 'Screw-guns' (I, 184-86), first published in W. E. Henley's *Scots Observer* in 1890, the subject is a lethal machine designed to kill. To Kipling's soldier this weapon is a source of pride and a trusted companion:

Smokin' my pipe on the mountings, sniffin' the mornin'-cool,
I walks in my old brown gaiters along o' my old brown mule,
With seventy gunners be'ind me, an' never a beggar forgets
It's only the pick of the Army that handles the dear little pets—'Tss 'Tss!
For you all love the Screw-guns—the Screw-guns they all love you!
So when we call round with a few guns, o' course you will know what to do— hoo! hoo!
Jest send in your Chief an' surrender—it's worse if you fights or you runs:
You can go where you please, you can skip up the trees, but you don't get away from the guns!

(p. 184)

Pride, masculinity, solidarity, and a sense of belonging to an elite are all caught here. It is probably not a coincidence that the words can be sung to the tune of the Eton Boating Song, which was composed by Captain Algernon H. Drummond, Rifle Brigade (1844-1932); Drummond was stationed at Lahore during the 1870s.[7]

His love for those who do their work well was not restricted to English soldiers. 'Gunga Din' (I, 189-92) was based on a water-carrier called Juma, a servant of the Frontier Force regiment of the guides at the siege of Delhi in July 1857, the violent year of the Indian Mutiny. Kipling saw this water-carrier as a man of extraordinary courage. In this ballad Gunga Din saves the life of a British soldier at the cost of his own life:

> 'E carried me away
> To where a *dooli** lay,   *=litter

---

[7] Roger Ayers, notes on 'Screw-Guns' <http://www.kipling.org.uk/rg_screwguns1.htm> [accessed 31 October 2013] (the current notes were last edited 24 January 2010).

> An' a bullet come an' drilled the beggar clean.
> 'E put me safe inside,
> An' just before 'e died,
> "I 'ope you liked your drink," sez Gunga Din.
> (p. 191)

Part of the poem reads as follows:

> With 'is *mussick** on 'is back,   *=water-skin
> 'E would skip with our attack,
> An' watch us till the bugles made "Retire,"
> An' for all 'is dirty 'ide
> 'E was white, clear white, inside
> When 'e went to tend the wounded under fire!
> (p. 190)

On the vexed question of political correctness in Kipling, Daniel Karlin, in the notes to his exemplary Oxford Authors selection, provides a balanced and fair-minded discussion of 'Gunga Din'. Of lines 5–6 in the above quotation he wrote: 'the lines in this poem which caused the most offence [. . .] are the finest tribute the speaker can imagine; the connotations of "white" as "courageous, honourable, manly, upright" were ingrained in English (and American) popular culture in this period, and the verisimilitude of the phrase is matched by Kipling's honesty in using it'.[8]

Kipling constantly negotiated his own writerly identity. He was socially unplaced: his father was the descendant of Yorkshire Methodists, and as a journalist in India he was never a 'Sahib' (he was neither an officer nor an administrator). Kipling's parents did not 'belong'; neither did their son. The United Services College, where Kipling was at school, could never rank with Marlborough or Wellington, and as a young journalist who arrived to work with his father in India aged seventeen and had never been to a university or seen active service, he was an outsider among the British. This social marginalization gave him an invaluable perspective as a writer. Verses written in India have a devil-may-care energy. They are sharply observant about British bad behaviour: the scramble for status and appointments, greed, patronage, scandal-mongering, and heat-fuelled adultery are recurrent themes. His best stories and the supreme masterpiece among his novels—*Kim*—draw strength from this same non-aligned and unassimilated authorial perspective.

Talk of 'authorial perspective' inevitably takes one into the circumstances in which Kipling was writing, and it is worth noting here that this Cambridge edition could have given more context to the poems. It is less user-friendly in its presentation of the poems than were Daniel Karlin's selection from the

---

[8] *Rudyard Kipling: A Critical Edition of the Major Works*, ed. by Daniel Karlin, Oxford Authors (Oxford: Oxford University Press, 1999), p. 654.

poetry in his 1999 edition, quoted above, or Andrew Rutherford's excellent edition of Kipling's early verse (1986).[9] Rutherford's edition makes for comfortable reading. In that volume most of the poems have a headnote with some biographical information as well as explanatory footnotes on the page, whereas in the Cambridge edition the notes are concise and are all gathered together into the endnotes section in Volume III.

It is important to recognize that Kipling transcends categories. The received view of him can still be hostile and uninformed: overenthusiastic laureate of empire, politically insensitive racist, sentimental celebrant of the life of the common soldier, and so forth. Some of that is true, but none of it was ever the whole story. This new edition of the poems is a towering achievement, and a major contribution to the full picture of this complex, brilliant, and controversial writer.

NEWCASTLE UNIVERSITY   JOHN BATCHELOR

[9] *Early Verse by Rudyard Kipling, 1879-1886: Unpublished, Uncollected, and Rarely Collected Poems*, ed. by Andrew Rutherford (Oxford: Clarendon Press, 1986).

NARRATIVES OF CHILD SEXUAL ABUSE IN CRISTINA COMENCINI'S NOVEL *LA BESTIA NEL CUORE*

La bestia nel cuore, a novel published by Cristina Comencini in 2004, is one of the most interesting literary texts written in Italy about child sexual abuse. After providing some context for my research, I will analyse the narrative patterns developed in it by Comencini, highlight the tension that exists between them, and explain their significance in contemporary Italian culture.

The Italian Ministry of Justice logs approximately one thousand cases of child sexual abuse each year. Their real number is likely to be higher because the abused and their relatives are still reluctant to come forward: they regard exposure as embarrassing or shameful, are afraid of further violence, and find it difficult to break ties with abusers, who are often close to (or part of) their families.[1] In 2004 Alberto Pellai surveyed 3000 students in Milan high schools: 14.6% of them turned out to have been victims of abuse, which was severe for 0.8% of boys and 3.4% of girls. Pellai is convinced that his findings reveal an underestimated epidemic, that the victims of sexual abuse constitute approximately 5% of the child population, and that the Italian situation is therefore similar to that of twenty other countries studied by David Finkelhor in 1994.[2]

While it is difficult to determine the number of abused children more precisely, it is clear that a serious challenge is faced by families, committed citizens, and professionals of various kinds. In some areas their action has been effective. Italy has ratified the 1989 UN Convention on the Rights of the Child and EU Council framework decision 2004/68/JHA combating the sexual exploitation of children. The 1996 law 'Norme contro la violenza sessuale' (no. 66) and the 1998 law 'Norme contro lo sfruttamento della prostituzione, della pornografia, del turismo sessuale in danno di minore' (no. 269), both updated in 2006 and 2012, have removed controversial aspects of previous norms and established an advanced framework.[3] Italian child psychiatrists deal with their most difficult cases in interdisciplinary teams, often linked to

---

[1] Teresa Bertolotti and Paolo Scotti, 'Le violenze sessuali sui bambini: alcuni dati', *Maltrattamento e abuso all'infanzia*, 4.2 (2002), 85–105; Alberto Pellai and others, 'Quanti sono i minori vittime di abuso sessuale?', ibid., 6.3 (2004), 79–96; and Roberto Volpi, *I bambini inventati* (Florence: La nuova Italia, 2001).

[2] David Finkelhor, 'The International Epidemiology of Child Sexual Abuse', *Child Abuse and Neglect*, 18 (1994), 409–17.

[3] A victimized child is now considered abused regardless of her/his sexual maturity or presumed morality; the sexual abuse is seen as a crime against the person and not against family honour or public morality. The various forms of child sexual abuse are covered by the articles 600-04 and 609 of the Italian penal code. One can find useful comments in Franco Coppi, 'I reati sessuali nella legislazione penale italiana', in *I reati sessuali*, ed. by Franco Coppi (Turin: Giappichelli, 2007), pp. 1–31, and Ilaria Alfonso, *Violenza sessuale, pedofilia e corruzione* (Padua: Cedam, 2004), pp. 18–37 and 199.

well-known centres for the cure of the abused, such as the Centro per il bambino maltrattato in Milan, the Synergia Centro Trauma in Turin, and the Istituto degli innocenti in Florence. They have their scholarly journal (*Maltrattamento e abuso all'infanzia*), and have written excellent books on their work.[4]

Action in other areas has been less impressive. A child psychiatrist and a consultant for the Tribunale dei Minori in Milan (a 'solido contesto giudiziario per l'intervento' (*Trauma*, p. 17)), Marinella Malacrea complains about the media coverage and the kind of public opinion that that coverage implies:

se per dieci processi conclusisi con la condanna dell'imputato neppure una riga compare sulla stampa (a meno che il caso non contenga particolari tanto truci e insoliti da meritar un accenno, che a quel punto mette sotto i riflettori il 'mostro'), per un processo esitato nell'assoluzione, specie se l'accusato appare insospettabile, come troppo spesso accade, sei sicuro di finire sul giornale [. . .] Si scatena quello che gli americani elegantemente definiscono *backlash*, colpo di frusta: cioè un'onda culturale contraria alla triste consapevolezza della realtà, nonostante l'ormai crescente opera d'informazione sull'argomento. Tale onda continua a voler coltivare la rassicurante opinione che questo problema può sì riguardare disdicevoli eccezioni, depravati o psicolabili, ma non persone per bene; il contrario, ci rendiamo ben conto, è troppo destabilizzante.[5]

While US psychiatrists curing their abused patients can count on supportive communities and describe their work as restoring connections 'between the public and private worlds' and 'between survivors and their community',[6] Malacrea is cautious about these connections. She refers to 'variabili umane' which one needs to 'saper governare se non si [vuole] vederli trasformare rapidamente in labirinti senza uscita' (*Trauma*, p. 2). Rather than being a deliberate attitude, the hesitation of many Italians to confront child sexual abuse is the result of unexamined assumptions and traditions passively received.[7] The study of court discussions, media reports, and the ways in which children, violence, and sexual abuse have been portrayed in literature and films would reveal those untested assumptions and raise awareness of them at the same

---

[4] See in particular *Segreti di famiglia: l'intervento nei casi d'incesto*, ed. by Marinella Malacrea and Alessandro Vassalli (Milan: Cortina, 1990); Cristina Roccia and Claudio Foti, *L'abuso sessuale sui minori* (Milan: Unicopli, 1994); and Marinella Malacrea, *Trauma e riparazione: la cura nell'abuso sessuale all'infanzia* (Milan: Cortina, 1998).

[5] Marinella Malacrea, 'Abuso sessuale all'infanzia: esigenze cliniche e giudiziarie', *Cittadini in crescita*, 2.1 (2001), 33–63 (p. 48).

[6] Judith Lewis Herman, *Trauma and Recovery* (London: Pandora, 1992), pp. 2–3.

[7] David I. Kertzer, *Sacrificed for Honour: Italian Infant Abandonment and the Politics of Reproductive Control* (Boston: Beacon Press, 1993), and Victoria De Grazia, *How Fascism Ruled Women* (Berkeley: University of California Press, 1992), show that some forms of state control of family played a negative role in nineteenth- and twentieth-century Italian history. That might have contributed to the creation of an aversion to any public interference in family life even though it is now clear that child sexual abuse often takes place within the family.

time,[8] but cultural and literary studies on this topic are only half-developed in Italy. Social historians have discussed cases of child sexual abuse only in the context of projects focused on other issues.[9] Novelists, playwrights, and poets such as Verga, Svevo, Deledda, Pirandello, Tozzi, Drigo, Moravia, Morante, Saba, Tobino, Maraini, Bellezza, Comencini, Ferrante, Sanvitale, Ramondino, Conte, Cardella, Tamaro, and Vinci have devoted interesting texts to child sexual abuse, but literary scholars have seldom considered that theme in their work. There are also specific reasons for this critical neglect: narrative patterns are difficult to identify; the research carried out in French, German, and North American literatures is small;[10] and such research in any case helps only partially because the same narrative can have different shapes and meanings in different cultures.

My research is based on textual and comparative analyses, supported from findings in other disciplines, and it is in its early stages. I have identified three main narratives in the literature of the period considered. The works of Grazia Deledda (1871–1936), Alberto Moravia (1907–1990), and Dacia Maraini (born in 1936) provide their most recognizable expressions. Deledda started her literary career when many girls of poor origin were sexually abused in their workplaces (workrooms, factories, houses of employing families).[11] When she claimed that 'non esiste forse uomo che non commetta adulterio, e in migliaia di famiglie il fatto avviene nella stessa casa e a volte prende anche [. . .] il sapore dell'incesto',[12] she was referring to very young housemaids, forced into early employment by the death of their parents, lack of relatives, or extreme poverty, who were molested and sometimes seduced by their employers. She told their stories using a distinctive mixture of compassion, indignation, and fatalism: the girls were compared to doves, their seducers to hawks, savage warriors, vampires, and devils; for Deledda, though, there was no way this aspect of Italian life could be changed—laws did not seem to apply to these victims, and human beings are inevitably born to suffer ('l'antica

---

[8] This point is repeatedly made by Georges Vigarello, *A History of Rape* (Cambridge: Polity, 2001). See in particular pp. 3, 38, 161, 186, and 215.

[9] Michela De Giorgio, *Le italiane dall'unità a oggi* (Rome and Bari: Laterza, 1992); Bruno P. F. Wanrooij, *Storia del pudore: la questione sessuale in Italia 1860–1940* (Venice: Marsilio, 1990).

[10] Although small in size, that research can be extremely interesting, as the following examples all show: Janice Doane and Devon Hodges, *Telling Incest* (Ann Arbor: University of Michigan Press, 2001); Margaret-Anne Hutton, 'Assuming Responsibility: Christiane Rochefort's Exploration of Child Sexual Abuse in La Porte du fond', *MLR*, 90 (1995), 333–44; and Audrone Willeke, '"Father wants to tear out my tongue": Daughters Confront Incestuous Fathers in Postwar German Literature', *German Life and Letters*, 55 (2002) 100–16.

[11] Edoardo Majno, *I reati sessuali contro i fanciulli* (Milan: Ramperti, 1907), p. 6. See also De Giorgio, pp. 59–67.

[12] Grazia Deledda, *Opere e novelle*, 5 vols with an introduction by Emilio Cecchi (Milan: Mondadori, 1941–69), IV, 720.

colpa dei primi padri [...] attirò nel mondo il dolore e ricade indistintamente su tutti' (III, 968)).[13]

Taking place in Fascist and post-Fascist Italy, the stories told by Alberto Moravia are different for social, psychological, and aesthetic reasons. Moravia's abused adolescents (both girls and boys) live in Rome and are the children of well-off parents, and most abusers come from the same milieu. Moravia's psychological insights were surprisingly advanced for his time: he showed how deceitfully abusers act and justify themselves, described the emotional detachment with which the abused relinquish all initiative,[14] and revealed how tragically the victims of abuse may depend on their abusers. In *Le ambizioni sbagliate*, a novel published in 1935, Andreina loathes Stefano and yet, ten years after being raped by him as a child, she is still unable to reject him: her hatred contains, if not a remnant of love, at least an element of horrified and impotent subservience (I, 813). Moravia did not use words such as 'rape' or 'sexual abuse': he thought that good literature is ambiguous;[15] and his abused children are often perceived by most other characters (and some scholars) as independent, sexually free young men and women, fully responsible for their lives.[16]

The narrative exemplified by Maraini's work starting in the 1990s (after an early period in which she followed Moravia's approach) reintroduces clarity, compassion, and indignation. Writing, for Maraini, means giving things a name,[17] and her descriptions can be very direct.[18] Like Deledda, she uses metaphors to express her compassion for the victims of abuse, whom she compares to orange groves torn down to make room for horrendous new buildings or deer killed by poachers.[19] Unlike Deledda's, Maraini's indignation is not essentially aimed at individual abusers (whose shards of humanity she highlights), but at social habits and structures, at a phase in history in which men consider the domination of the opposite sex as essential (*Romanzi*, p. 835). Child sexual abuse is an example of violence against women in a patriarchal society.[20] Maraini's work is pessimistic, but there is no fatalism in it. Patriarchs can be opposed. The struggles for gender equality, for a just

---

[13] Neria De Giovanni, 'Introduzione', in *Religiosità, fatalismo e magia di Grazia Deledda*, ed. by Neria De Giovanni (Cinisello Balsamo: San Paolo, 1999), pp. 5–53, repeatedly exemplifies Deledda's fatalism.

[14] Rosetta, in *La ciociara*, becomes so apathetic that she seems almost like a puppet. See Alberto Moravia, *Opere: romanzi e racconti*, 14 vols (Milan: Bompiani, 2000–), III, 1439.

[15] Alberto Moravia, 'Schiocca la frusta', *L'espresso*, 21 September 1980, pp. 134–35.

[16] Bernard Henri Levy, 'I miei tre Moravia', *Corriere della sera*, 4 January 2008, p. 47.

[17] Dacia Maraini, *Amata scrittura* (Milan: Rizzoli, 2008), p. 55.

[18] Carol Lazzaro-Weis, 'Dacia Maraini', in *Italian Women Writers*, ed. by Rinaldina Russell (Westport: Greenwood Press, 1994), pp. 216–25 (p. 218).

[19] Dacia Maraini, *Romanzi* (Milan: Rizzoli, 2006), pp. 651 and 1317.

[20] The main character of Maraini's novel *Voci*, for example, is killed when and because she denounces the harmful power her stepfather has over her and her sister.

society, and against child abuse to some extent overlap, and strengthen each other. Maraini's attitude is widely admired because it gives hope, courage, and strength, but some of its aspects are slightly puzzling. Abused boys are rare in her fiction (there are some in *Buio*), and abusing women do not appear: the only sexual rapport she describes between an adult woman and a boy is portrayed as based on genuine feelings.[21]

The chronological order used to summarize these narratives may give the impression of an evolving awareness: the focus shifts from one social class to many, the understanding of abuse gains first a psychological and then a socio-historical dimension. But this impression can be easily questioned. 'Children' and 'sexual abuse' are unstable concepts, social constructs in which different assumptions, beliefs, and ideas merge or collide. Novels such as Deledda's *Il nostro padrone*—where two or three contrasting points of view (and complementary behaviours) compete for the reader's attention—show clashes between different, sometimes irreconcilable, sensitivities. These clashes have often remained hidden because Italy exemplifies at times what Sam Warner describes in relation to the UK medical system's understanding of child sexual abuse, with people relying on a 'grand narrative' and losing 'critical reflexivity'.[22] A way of telling stories has generally dominated the national culture (or crucial subcultures) for decades, making it difficult for alternative or complementary ways to emerge and find an outlet. The narrative exemplified here with Deledda's work prevailed in the first thirty years of the twentieth century: other writers selected similar plots, situations, characters, and tones.[23] Authors such as Dario Bellezza (*Storia di Nino*), the young Dacia Maraini (*La vacanza*, *L'età del malessere*), and Francesca Sanvitale (*Madre e figlia*) wrote about abuse from the 1950s to the 1970s, in texts that instantly reminded readers of the Moravian narrative.[24] The anti-patriarchal narrative

---

[21] Dacia Maraini, *Donna in guerra* (Milan: Rizzoli, 1998), pp. 97–103. Less common but still interesting narratives—mainly used by other authors—tell stories in which both child and adult are fully satisfied with their sexual relationship, or describe seductive children who maliciously tempt adults. Adults act as narrators in both cases.

[22] Sam Warner, *Understanding the Effects of Child Sexual Abuse* (London, 2009), p. 3. It is also puzzling that, as far as I know, no Italian author has published memoirs involving child sexual abuse. Doane and Hodges, pp. 98–112, Warner, p. 62, and Victoria Bates, '"Misery Loves Company": Sexual Trauma, Psychoanalysis and the Market for Misery', *Journal of Medical Humanities*, 33 (2012), 61–81, show that memoirs have played a decisive role in the denunciation and understanding of domestic violence elsewhere.

[23] Federigo Tozzi, *Novelle* (Florence: Barbès, 2009), for example, echoes both Deledda's powerless indignation and its ultimately religious connotation at the beginning of 'Il crocifisso'. Before telling the story of a twelve-year-old girl forced by poverty into prostitution, he remarks that God's creation has been left unfinished: 'ho pensato esista un mondo che Dio non ha finito di creare. La materia non è morta e non è viva [. . .] l'Adamo resta così a mezzo, cieco com'è, crede che le sue tenebre siano la luce; e quando il vento dei temporali passa sopra la sua pelle egli crede di camminare' (p. 160).

[24] Grazia Sumeli-Weinberg, *Invito alla lettura di Dacia Maraini* (Pretoria: University of South

later used by Maraini is now adopted by most younger writers, including Comencini.

This convergence of many writers of roughly the same age over a similar narrative pattern is partly inevitable, a sign of the *Zeitgeist*; but it is also related to the reluctance of Italians to think freely and critically about child abuse. The anti-patriarchal contextualization employed by Maraini and Comencini fits the denunciation of child sexual abuse. Victims are predominantly girls,[25] and abusers mostly men.[26] The activities of the feminist movements and child sexual abuse becoming a subject of open discussion are related phenomena: the former created the social openness that allowed the latter to take place.[27] Maraini's and Comencini's literary productions have consistently dealt with the interests of women; it would have been difficult and inconsistent for them to tackle this theme differently. However, by constantly linking the sexual abuse of minors to the denunciation of patriarchal societies, a dominant narrative is being created and something is lost in the process. The analysis of Comencini's *La bestia nel cuore* will help me prove that more narratives are needed today, and are probably in the making.

The Anti-Patriarchal Narrative

Cristina Comencini (born in 1956) is a writer and film director. She has written ten novels and two plays so far.[28] Her most successful novels show how couples or families tackle disturbing events which involve at least one of them. In *Le pagine strappate* the university student Federica witnesses two murders and removes them from her mind, in the same way in which pages of a diary can be torn out. She spends her time locked in her room, refuses to talk, and her relatives struggle to find a way to help her deal with her problems. Marina and Manfred, the main characters of *Quando la notte*, have troubled pasts: she has never been able to assert herself as a person; he was abandoned by his

---

Africa, 1993), shows that reviews of Maraini's early novels had titles such as 'Vacanza con Moravia', 'Una figlia della noia moraviana', 'Una Lolita moraviana', 'La quattordicenne di Moravia' (p. 246).

[25] Anna C. Salter, *Treating Child Sex Offenders and Victims* (Newbury Park: Sage, 1988), p. 17. For Rebecca Bolen and Maria Scannapieco, 'Prevalence of Child Sexual Abuse', *Social Service Review*, 73 (1999), 281–313, the difference is even more pronounced.

[26] 'Less than 5% of sex offences against children are known to have been committed by women, often in association with men, but population surveys suggest higher rates of offending by females' (Don Grubin, *Sex Offending against Children: Understanding the Risk* (London: Home Office, 1998)). Myriam S. Denov, 'To a Safer Place? Victims of Sexual Abuse by Females and their Disclosures to Professionals', *Child Abuse and Neglect*, 27 (2003), 47–61, suggests that sexual abuse by women is rarely reported or recorded as such.

[27] Nancy Whittier, *The Politics of Child Sexual Abuse* (Oxford: Oxford University Press, 2011).

[28] The texts by Comencini quoted in this article are: *Le pagine strappate* (Milan: Feltrinelli, 1991), *Passioni di famiglia* (Milan: Feltrinelli, 1994), *La bestia nel cuore* (Milan: Feltrinelli, 2004), and *Quando la notte* (Milan: Feltrinelli, 2009).

mother when he was a small child and has been raised to be autonomous in the extreme. Comencini recreates the testing but helpful forms of communication that take place in these contexts: 'quest'uomo, Marina, ti fa la guerra dall'inizio, ma nessuno, da quando sei nata, sa di te come lui' (p. 144). It takes a heart attack for Federica's father to be able to speak to his daughter. Key relationships among Comencini's characters are generally 'fatt[e] di forti dissidi, ma anche di grandi riavvicinamenti'.[29] Being a film director helps Comencini to be a better writer: her characters are well defined, dialogues are crisp, plots have a steady pace, and her dramatic imagination creates scenes of unusual strength in contemporary Italian fiction. Like her film-making, on the other hand, Comencini's writing favours melodramatic endings in which action overcomes, and may contradict, psychological analysis.

While Deledda, Moravia, and Maraini spoke of child sexual abuse many times, Comencini has dealt with this subject only once so far, in the novel *La bestia nel cuore* (of which she also directed a cinematic version in 2005).[30] The novel has received limited critical attention because its topic is emotionally charged, and reviewers and scholars have once again been unwilling to discuss it.[31] A detailed summary might be helpful. Sabina is a young woman living in Rome, where she dubs foreign films; her mother died eight years earlier, and her father five; her only brother has moved to the United States and works at the University of Virginia. She has a vague memory of her family: 'sembra che qualcuno abbia cancellato con la gomma i ricordi, la casa e i suoi abitanti, tutto distrutto. Come Cartagine. *Carthago delenda est*' (p. 27). Sabina lives with Franco, an actor, and has a few good friends, including Emilia, a former classmate, and Maria, who works with her. She dubs a film in which a woman of her age who, like her, enjoys jogging in the morning is raped in a park. The film causes Sabina an anxiety that she hesitates to understand or discuss (p. 53). That night she dreams of being in bed with her father, close to him and wet (p. 48). While still trying to dismiss the contents of her dream as accidental, Sabina flies to Virginia to ask her brother Daniele for enlightenment: what family was theirs? Why does she have so few memories? Does her dream have any particular meaning? Reluctantly, Daniele tells her that their father was a paedophile. He made him stop, and did his best to protect his younger sister, but could not prevent her from being abused twice (p. 168). Sabina is shocked, confused, and wants to know why Daniele has never raised the issue with her: 'sapessi quanto ci ho pensato! Non ti ricordavi niente, non me ne

---

[29] Flavia Laviosa quotes these words by Comencini in 'Cristina Comencini: scrittrice, scenografa e regista. Intervista', *Italica*, 86 (2009), 539–54 (p. 543).

[30] A short episode of child sexual abuse in *Passioni di famiglia* (pp. 23 and 157) has few developments.

[31] All recent novels by Comencini have been discussed in the yearly reviews of contemporary fiction published by Roberto Carnero in *The Italianist*. *La bestia nel cuore* is the only exception.

avevi mai parlato. Ho pensato che eri piccola, che era accaduto solo due volte [...] perché noi dobbiamo sempre saldare il conto con la verità? Perché non potevi essere lasciata in pace almeno tu?' (p. 169).

Being in an advanced state of pregnancy, Sabina also has the irrational fear that her child will resemble her father and almost wishes it not to be born: she does not feel ready to accept the similarities. She does not want to inform Franco and her friends of the abuse suffered, both because she feels sullied by guilt (p. 181) and because she does not want to be pitied (p. 182). After a few rows caused by her nervous tension, which Franco struggles to understand, she tells him but then runs away, convinced that she will never recapture the way Franco looked at her before her confession: 'distratto, innamorato, talvolta duro. Ora la fissava con stupore e pietà, ammutolito, annientato' (p. 194). While Franco and her friends look frantically for her, Sabina gives birth to her child on a train, with the help of a puzzled railway worker. Another dream (of a purifying seaquake) later reconciles Sabina with life: she welcomes her child, and is happy to see Franco again.

In the literature on child sexual abuse, this is an unusual, rather consoling, and ultimately optimistic story. The abuser is dead; Daniele has a supportive wife; Sabina is surrounded by helpful figures; both victims overcome their trauma and move on with their lives. As often in Comencini's fiction, tragic events hurt the victims and leave them wounded, but are confined to the past. The present, in her books, is a time for recovery. Maraini's and Moravia's texts are darker. In their works scars do not usually heal. Recovery and trust are impossible (in Moravia) or extremely difficult (in Maraini).

La bestia nel cuore confirms the role that memory (the lack or the reawakening of it) plays in the narratives of child sexual abuse. It also confirms, in at least two ways, what Doane and Hodges say about the difficulties of finding a workable framework for such stories. Those difficulties are firstly faced by Comencini's characters. Sabina is pushed by a film to rediscover the sexual abuse she suffered (p. 13), and takes key decisions imitating the behaviour of the protagonist of a novel she reads (p. 18). It is easier for her to analyse her life when she can compare it to those of other women or fictional characters (p. 73). Sabina's father also looked for narratives that could explain and perhaps, in his opinion, justify his abusive behaviour. He favoured the narrative of seductive girls who tempt old men, leaving on his desk a novel he wrote with 'la storia della relazione tra un professore e una sua allieva. Un misto di *Lolita* e dell'*Angelo azzurro*, scritto con uno stile ottocentesco. Un uomo maturo trascinato nel gorgo del peccato da una ragazza sfrontata e corrotta' (p. 118). In the society Comencini describes, people need narratives to make sense of what they do or what happens to them, and the narratives available to them matter. With this in mind, we can better understand another reason why Sabina does not want to reveal the abuse suffered. Children are inspiring figures and symbols of hope in recent Italian culture. Childhood is said by many to be the best time of their life.[32] Sabina believes her friends expect a similar account from her. If she revealed the abuse, she fears, either they would not believe her or, worse still, they would think Sabina herself to blame. It is an irrational but repeatedly recorded fear.[33]

The difficulty of finding a workable framework for a story of child sexual abuse is also faced by Comencini. The one she picks is one of male violence against young and very young women. The director of the dubbing company gives jobs only to women who sleep with him: 'gli piace sentire che le ragazze sono nelle sue mani, le scopa tutte prima di farle lavorare [. . .]. Cosa ridi? porco' (p. 15). The word *ragazze* (girls) has an added ambiguity in a novel on child sexual abuse. Maria's husband abandoned her to go and live with a classmate of their daughter, uncared for by her parents and thirty years his junior (pp. 55–57): 'gli uomini', Maria concludes, 'sono attratti dall'ingenuità, o dalla sopraffazione, che in fondo è la stessa cosa' (p. 57). Sabina's partner, Franco, seems to be different. He is a considerate man, teased by his mates for his kindness to women. 'A Franco pareva di appartenere a un terzo sesso, né uomo né donna, ma un misto fra i due. Gli piaceva possedere una donna, ma anche esserne posseduto' (p. 29). Sex for him must be a form of communication: 'quando vieni e la ragazza ti segue e tu segui lei, allora è un concerto con un gran finale. Ma altrimenti che senso ha? Se sei teso, masturbati e basta, senza farla tanto lunga!' (p. 29). He cares for Sabina, and helps her. When she is in Virginia, however, he has an affair with a colleague, an actress in a TV series in which he also has a role. Anita attracts him mainly because, in a production some years previously, she was still a girl and played the role of his daughter (p. 61). There is something incestuous in his passion for her:

> Franco sente il potere che ha su di lei, non riesce a controllare l'eccitazione, non può rifiutarsi. Lei lo vuole, lo desidera, non c'è niente di male, è un'adulta libera. Eppure è la bambina con cui ha recitato tanto tempo fa che all'improvviso gli passa davanti agli occhi, *buonanotte mamma, buonanotte papà*. E non inorridisce a quel pensiero. Cerca anzi le sue labbra, le apre e immagina come aprirà allo stesso modo la zona calda tra le gambe in cui affonda la mano. Non inorridisce, anzi. (p. 134)

Men are all like this, then, and women are dangerously attracted to the power

---

[32] Gilbert Bosetti, *L'Enfant-dieu et le poète: culte et poétiques de l'enfance dans le roman italien du XXe siècle* (Grenoble: Ellug, 1997).

[33] Katherine Brady, *Father's Days: A True Story of Incest* (New York: Seaview, 1979), pp. 58–59; David Finkelhor, *Sexually Victimized Children* (New York: Free Press, 1979), pp. 30–33, 105–06; Florence Rush, *The Best Kept Secret. Sexual Abuse of Children* (Englewood Cliffs: Prentice-Hall, 1980), pp. 46 and 146. Although Sigmund Freud later recanted his theses, his 'On the Aetiology of Hysteria', in *The Standard Edition of the Complete Psychological Works of Sigmund Freud*, 24 vols (London: Hogarth Press and the Institute of Psycho-Analysis, 1953–74), III: *Early Psycho-Analytic Publications (1893–1899)* (1962), pp. 187–221, is also clear on this subject (p. 204).

that men inevitably have in a traditional society. Maria acknowledges 'il desiderio di stargli sotto, in senso fisico e spirituale' (p. 147). Anita is attracted to Franco because 'quando ti ho incontrato ho sentito l'emozione che mi suscitavi da piccola' (p. 130). Like Maraini in *Voci*, therefore, Comencini constantly refers to a pervasive context of gender exploitation: 'una persona intelligente, sensibile, diciamo un genio' (Woody Allen) takes pornographic photographs of his stepdaughter (p. 55); 'il nostro probo e amato Thomas Jefferson [. . .] ha avuto una lunga relazione con una schiava mulatta, una ragazzina di quattordici anni — lui ne aveva quarantaquattro — a cui ha fatto fare cinque figli' (p. 118); a language teacher in an Oxford college had sex with Sabina when she was fifteen, in a summer school for foreign students (p. 118); TV executives do not hesitate to include in the afternoon schedule a cartoon in which some boys almost rape a girl (pp. 123–24); 'milioni di bambine' suffer Sabina's fate without having a chance to complain (p. 120).

Even in Maraini's *Voci*, this framework is not fully consistent with the story told. Maraini balances denunciation of patriarchal societies with attention to the dangerous forms of trust that children have for unreliable adults. Scholars of her work have sometimes overstressed the former and neglected the latter.[34] The same framework has a few extra inconsistencies in *La bestia nel cuore*. The abuser in this novel is not a strong patriarchal figure such as the war veteran depicted by Elisabeth Reichart in *La Valse*, the powerful, scheming, self-centred Iowa farmer described by Jane Smiley in *One Thousand Acres*, or the disciplinarian stepfather portrayed by Maraini in *Voci*. A teacher of Latin and Greek at a Rome high school, Sabina and Daniele's father was an unremarkable and isolated man (p. 154): Mr Conte 'non parlava altro che di scuola, di cultura, di libri [. . .] sembrava un marziano' (p. 68). His family seems to have depended more on his wife (also a high-school teacher) than on him. Mrs Conte liked 'certe sue forme d'immaturità, le piaceva fargli da mamma, accudirlo, perdonarlo' (p. 166) and sent her son the implicit message that 'papà ha queste manie, non ti fa male, sei suo figlio, siamo una famiglia, non lo saprà nessuno, lui è debole, tu devi essere forte come me' (p. 166).[35]

---

[34] See Judith Bryce, 'The Perfect Crime? Paternal Perpetrators in Dacia Maraini's *Voci*', in *Crime Scenes: Detective Narratives in European Culture since 1945*, ed. by Anne Mullen and Emer O'Beirne (Amsterdam: Rodopi, 2000), pp. 207–18; JoAnn Cannon, *The Novel as Investigation* (Toronto: University of Toronto Press, 2006), pp. 59–71; Stefania Lucamante, *A Multitude of Women* (Toronto: University of Toronto Press, 2008), pp. 186–206; Christina Siggers Manson, 'In Love with Cecchino: Opening the Door to Violence in Dacia Maraini's *Colomba* and *Voci*', *Journal of Romance Studies*, 5.2 (2005), 91–102; Grazia Sumeli Weinberg, 'Dacia Maraini's *Voci*', *Studi d'Italianistica nell'Africa Australe*, 12.2 (1999), 20–36; and Ada Testaferri, 'De-tecting *Voci*', in *The Pleasure of Writing: Critical Essays on Dacia Maraini*, ed. by Rodica Diaconescu-Blumenfeld and Ada Testaferri (West Lafayette: Purdue University Press, 2000), pp. 41–60.

[35] Emilia hesitantly explains Mrs Conte's behaviour by partly sticking to the patriarchal perversion of family life as a cause of abuse: 'penso che la madre abbia potuto coprire il padre. Lo adorava, faceva di tutto perché non litigasse con il figlio. Penso che si sia convinta che quello che

Margaux Fragoso has outlined in *Tiger, Tiger* a weak abusive character who is vaguely reminiscent of Mr Conte, and uses more tricks than power to satisfy his sexual needs with children. Mr Conte, though, is even weaker than Fragoso's character. After abusing Daniele for three years, from the time his son is five to the time he is eight, he stops the first time Daniele finds the energy to rebel: 'gli ho gettato contro il posacenere di marmo, lo avevo nascosto sotto le lenzuola. Gli ho fatto uscire sangue dalla testa. Gli ho gridato che l'avrei ammazzato se fosse venuto un'altra volta e se ti avesse toccato' (p. 166). Later, dying of cancer in a hospital, Mr Conte tells his son 'che dovevo occuparmi di te, che anche a te era accaduta la stessa cosa, due volte. Ne parlava come un padre amoroso che si preoccupa del trauma inflitto al figlio da un altro' (p. 168). Daniele follows up on his old threat and kills him off:

ho detto all'infermiere di preparare il doppio della morfina, che aveva sofferto come un cane tutta la notte. Era previsto che sarebbe accaduto. Ma non era vero, aveva dormito tranquillamente. Io invece ero stato sveglio a pensare a quelle due volte. È andato in coma subito, è morto in poche ore. (p. 169).

Other Narratives

Daniele's life has been difficult: he spent years in therapy; when he talks about the abuse he suffered as a child, he cries and his voice becomes unbearably thin (p. 165). He is unable to kiss, hug, or touch his children because of the memories and the concerns that the physical contact with them would raise. If his father's weak personality does not match the patriarchal framework, Daniele's story fits in even less. He was neither intimidated nor forced to have sex with his father. The teacher's voice 'di notte era quella di un bambino lamentoso, tremante di paura, per questo..., per questo...' (p. 165). Daniele's weakness was his trust in an unreliable adult, which Comencini defines as a 'fiducia sconsiderata nel prossimo' (p. 167).[36] Daniele was kind: 'la cosa più difficile da vincere con la terapia', he says, was the idea of his meekness (p. 164); 'vedo quel bambino. Non sono più io, ho dovuto ucciderlo. Ho dovuto far fuori la sua bontà, la tenerezza per lo stronzo, l'accondiscendenza per uno sguardo d'amore' (p. 165). Sabina agrees:

che fortuna che i bambini crescano, spariscano, diventino uomini, che la debolezza si trasformi in forza. Nessuno può più toccarli. Perdono la fiducia sconsiderata nel

accadeva di notte non era poi così terribile. Una donna si può convincere di questo per l'uomo che ama, per la famiglia. Può sacrificare un figlio perché tutto rimanga al suo posto, per alzarsi con la certezza che anche quel mattino penserà a cosa si mangia a pranzo, a cena, alla spesa da fare, alla cura dei figli, del marito. La perdita di queste certezze le è intollerabile' (p. 198).

[36] In another novel on child sexual abuse, *Volevo i pantaloni* (Milan: Mondadori, 1989), Lara Cardella similarly speaks of 'quello stupido istinto infantile che ti porta a consegnare la tua vita nelle mani della prima persona che ti lusinga con quattro moine e due bacetti' (p. 72).

prossimo, non si affidano con quel pericoloso sguardo inconsapevole, sanno come difendersi. Non si mettono più nelle mani di nessuno. (p. 167)

The word 'uomini' has in Italian the same ambiguity that 'men' has in English. It can mean adult males and it can mean people in general. Suddenly, in this novel, the victims of abuse are men (like Daniele) or 'men' (like Daniele and Sabina). The focus is no longer on gender but on age difference, on the trust that children may indiscriminately place in everyone, and on the ruthlessness with which abusers exploit it. Daniele's story is told in six pages. Comencini seems to have sensed that it involves a narrative different from the one she has privileged in the rest of her book and to have deliberately limited its length. A similar shift takes place in a few other passages of *La bestia nel cuore*. After her key conversation with Daniele, Sabina thinks:

se il pene di un uomo può rizzarsi davanti a una ragazzina perché è inerme, per via del suo sguardo incredulo soprattutto [. . .], e questo sguardo inconsapevole è la ragione stessa dell'eccitazione, allora qualcosa di questo deve appartenere a tutti gli esseri umani, a ogni rapporto erotico, anche al più normale. (p. 120)

The new emerging narrative has a more ethical than political connotation. It has to do with good and evil, with a potentially sadistic component that is shared by all human beings, accepted by some, and rejected or transformed by others (p. 130). Franco and Anita discuss it one evening in a rather confused passage (pp. 128–32). That component is *la bestia* human beings have *nel cuore*. This narrative has obvious historical precedents, particularly in Fedor Dostoevskii's *Crime and Punishment, Netochka Nezvanova, The Adolescent*, and *The Demons*, but it is new in the context of recent Italian literature on child sexual abuse. It neither replaces nor opposes the old narratives, but is generally a useful complement to them, facilitating more varied treatment of the subject and hence more open discussion of it.

Interestingly, the anti-patriarchal framework is looser in the film based on *La bestia nel cuore* (and bearing the same title), which Comencini made the year after publishing her novel. Most references to a pervasive pattern of gender exploitation are gone. Crucially, in the film Anita is just a young and tempting actress with whom Franco has a short affair. He is not seduced by the memory of her previous fragility. Not all men, it now seems, are attracted to bullying naive young girls. The message that Daniele thought to have implicitly received from his mother is explicit in the film: she tells him 'lui è debole, tu sei forte come me'.[37]

Another detail of the film deserves consideration. Its penultimate scene

[37] Cristina Comencini, *La bestia nel cuore* (Rai Cinema and Cattleya, 2006), XIV, 01:20:26. My two quotations from the film derive directly from it, and not from the published script (Marciano and others, pp. 15–127), which is different. For a detailed analysis of the novel's development into a film, one can profitably read Flavia Laviosa, 'Cristina Comencini, Novelist and Filmmaker:

ends with a short dialogue which is not in the novel. Negri, the director of the TV series in which Franco and Anita star, is a friend of both Franco and Sabina. A hospital nurse reproaches him for holding their child a few hours after its birth:

> — Soltanto i genitori possono toccare i bambini.
> — Chi lo dice?
> — È la regola.
> — Bella regola (XIX, 01:48:17–40)

There is nothing comic in child sexual abuse, and yet it would be difficult to describe this dialogue without using a comedy-related word. At the end of a film in which a father abuses his son and that son, once grown-up, is dramatically unable to touch his own children, spectators are invited to smile at the assumption that only parents are good at touching their children. This dialogue could be an expedient, a clumsy way to provide comic relief, but it could also be (and I believe it is) a further attempt by Comencini at rethinking narratives of child sexual abuse.

Negri, a film director like Comencini, speaks in the novel—to which we return—about the great love of his life, 'una donna [...] dura e passionale': 'se rispondeva male, voleva una carezza; se mi aggrediva, voleva far l'amore; se piangeva, voleva essere sgridata'. They broke up because 'non si può sempre interpretare, azzuffarsi ogni volta prima di far l'amore, insultarsi per avere una carezza' (p. 204). Comencini's characters are generally like that: wounded, aggressive, difficult to deal with, but also friendly. Sabina's child, Negri says, is lucky 'anche se è figlio di gente incasinata come loro' (p. 205). *La bestia nel cuore* has ugly characters (Sabina's father, Maria's husband, perhaps Sabina's mother), but they are not centre stage in the novel. Their wicked deeds take place before it starts. Readers spend their time with couples (Daniele and his wife, Sabina and Franco, Emilia and Maria) who make mistakes of all sorts and endanger their relationships, but love each other and stick together, with the help of good friends such as Negri. In this context of kind gestures, refined forms of communication, and unselfish acts, some comedy is perhaps inevitable. Friends ironically complain about the bad-tasting pistachio tea that Emilia keeps serving (pp. 21, 32, and 82). Franco makes jokes about the work he does for TV (pp. 41–42). The Italian Daniele's wife speaks is at the same time amusing (for the mistakes it contains) and admirable (for the way in which she revitalizes a language weakened by conventional expressions (pp. 116 and 161)). Negri is the target of his friends' jokes. Comedy is not linked to cases of child abuse directly: it surrounds them, like the kindness of relatives and friends.

The presence of comedic elements in Comencini's novel of child sexual abuse is also interesting as an attempt to reclaim something that can traditionally be found in accounts told by some (real or fictional) abusers. Humour, comedy, creative and elegant witticisms characterize, for example, the style of Humbert Humbert, the first-person narrator and abusing character in Vladimir Nabokov's *Lolita*. Can comedic elements sometimes complement the tragic tone that is almost inevitably present in the words of the abused or of those who take their side?[38]

One could say that this new narrative misrepresents child sexual abuse. The abused are much more difficult characters than Daniele and Sabina:[39] they are seldom surrounded by so many benevolent friends;[40] the absence of friends is one of the reasons why abusers are so successful in their seduction of children and adolescents. One could say, instead, that a narrative of this kind is welcome: it brings helpful optimism to those who must face a thoroughly depressing problem; *La bestia nel cuore* (and Comencini's entire literary work) may ultimately be the confident expression of a society strong enough to help *gente incasinata* to sort out their (and its own) *casini*, however serious they are. Of course, one might ask if such confidence is compatible with *La bestia nel cuore*'s denunciation of pervasive patriarchal power. And one might also say that current Italian society has no confidence in itself, that Comencini's representation is an updated version of the endearing but widely imagined communities of the cinematic comedies Italian-style of the 1960s. A debate in this vein could go on for a long time.

In any case, my original hypothesis turns out to be correct. New narratives on child sexual abuse are taking shape in Italian culture. One has highly respectable examples outside Italy and is compatible with the country's Christian tradition.[41] The other is more original, may seem irresponsible, but is perhaps intelligently sensitive. We should follow the development of both

[38] There are traces of humour also in Cardella's *Volevo i pantaloni*. The first-person narrator, Anna, says she was molested by her uncle Vincenzino at the age of ten, and wonders about his motives: 'ero appena una mocciosetta, una vavà da minna, come si dice qui da noi. Se a quasi sedici anni il mio seno era di una piattezza impressionante, figurarsi cosa doveva essere a dieci anni: la Pianura Padana personificata! E per quanto riguarda il resto, il resto non c'era proprio...' (p. 71). Humour is rather contrived here. The character uses it to try and distance herself from an event that troubled her. It is an awkward attempt to partially empower oneself in a context where humour and power are connected.

[39] See the perceptive remarks made by Deborah Gould, prosecutor at Stafford Crown Court, during a trial for child sexual abuse reported by the *The Times*, 15 June 2011, p. 6.

[40] Finkelhor, pp. 23–28; Salter, *Treating Child Sex Offenders and Victims*, pp. 223–45.

[41] Child sexual abuse has embarrassed Italian Catholics for some, probably non-essential, reasons. One is the large number of cases involving priests as abusers. Another is that the traumatic effects of the abuse seem to deny free will. On the latter, see in particular Domenico Mondrone, *Scrittori al traguardo*, 4 vols (Rome: La civiltà cattolica, 1943–47), II, 298; III, 246–47.

with attention. At times the different narratives that coexist in *La bestia nel cuore* may contradict rather than complement each other. That, in my opinion, makes them even more interesting and shows how serious and difficult Comencini's attempt is to innovate the ways in which these stories are told.

Comencini has an additional conclusion. At the end of the novel Negri goes to a police station and explains why Sabina was alone in an almost empty train when her son was born. His explanation is clumsy, and yet, before going home, Negri wants to make a final point with the chief officer who has questioned him:

io firmo il verbale, va bene, caso archiviato. Quanto all'affermazione del commissario: *Oggi il mondo è popolato di mascalzoni*, a quella devo replicare con forza. Prima il mondo brulicava di mascalzoni, signor commissario, molto più di oggi, si nascondevano nelle pieghe della morale, della famiglia, dei valori, ma erano mascalzoni veri, e in più non coscienti di esserlo, superbi del loro teatrino! I bambini venivano abbandonati, massacrati molto più di oggi, e nell'indifferenza generale! (pp. 213–14)

The key difference between the past, that Negri dislikes, and the present is a now widely accepted (he claims) principle, which he summarizes in his own, terribly emphatic way: '*non tacere mai*, a costo della vita, della reputazione, dello scandalo, del dolore' (p. 214). Negri's exaggeration does not prevent Comencini from highlighting these words by putting them at the very end of the novel. Readers will consider this invitation to speak out. They will have to reshape, contextualize, and rephrase it, but they will probably accept it. Comencini's thoughtful approach to such a complex issue encourages most to agree with the conclusion of her novel.

UNIVERSITY OF EXETER   LUCIANO PARISI

VALLEJO AND GONZÁLEZ PRADA: A NOTE ON *TRILCE* XIX

A number of commentators have suggested that César Vallejo's *Trilce* XIX ('A trastear, Hélpide dulce, escampas') may owe something to the thought of Manuel González Prada. Jean Franco merely includes the latter's name in a list of atheist/anticlerical philosophers (Max Müller and Feuerbach are the others) with whose work Vallejo was or may have been acquainted, but Xavier Abril is more specific, claiming that the poem is 'la consecuencia superior, poética y estilística, de "Los dados eternos"', which Vallejo had dedicated to 'el gran maestro', who had apparently read it 'con entusiasmo'.[1] As I aim to show in this article, neither critic explores the alleged link in sufficient detail, since further investigation reveals that almost every element of the poem, whether thematic or stylistic, is in some way indebted to both González Prada's prose writings and his poetry, which Vallejo glosses, paraphrases, and imaginatively transforms at various points. The particular links are significant enough in themselves but, as we shall see, they may also reveal something more general about the origin, nature, and purpose of a number of the more radical expressive innovations found throughout the collection.

Like 'Los dados eternos' and a number of other poems from *Los heraldos negros*, not least 'Espergesia', *Trilce* XIX focuses on the question of man's place and prospects in a godless world stripped of consoling myths, one which also obsessed González Prada. Yet much more significant than this sharing of core thematic material are the concrete ways in which that material is articulated and addressed throughout the poem, and I shall consider each of these in turn.

THE POEM

A trastear, Hélpide dulce, escampas,
cómo quedamos de tan quedarnos.

Hoy vienes apenas me he levantado.
El establo está divinamente meado
y excrementido por la vaca inocente   5
y el inocente asno y el gallo inocente.

Penetra en la maría ecuménica.
Oh sangabriel, has que conciba el alma,
el sin luz amor, el sin cielo,
lo más piedra, lo más nada,   10
    hasta la ilusión monarca.

---

[1] Jean Franco, *César Vallejo: The Dialectics of Poetry and Silence* (Cambridge: Cambridge University Press, 1976), p. 83; Xavier Abril, *Exégesis trílcica* (Lima: Editorial Gráfica Labor, 1980), p. 35. 'Los dados eternos', first published in *La Semana* (Trujillo), 1 (23 March 1918), was later included in *Los heraldos negros* (1919).

> Quemaremos todas las naves!
> Quemaremos la última esencia!
> Mas si se ha de sufrir de mito en mito,
> y a hablarme llegas masticando hielo, 15
> mastiquemos brasas,
> ya no hay donde bajar,
> ya no hay donde subir.
>   Se ha puesto el gallo incierto, hombre.

As all its exegetes note, the poem opens with a curious (from both a semantic and syntactic point of view) apostrophe to an invented muse or deity who embodies or represents the principle of Hope, derived from the Greek word ἐλπίς.[2] Now, although hope is treated with some ambiguity and even irony in the poem, Vallejo's Hélpide is initially invoked as a possible substitute for the false hope offered by the New Testament stories (described in the poem as mere 'mitos') of the Annunciation and Incarnation, which are brutally debunked in stanzas 2 and 3; Vallejo, as so often in *Trilce*, was clearly out to shock. In other words, a Hellenic, or rather Neo-Hellenic, world-view is pitted against the Christian vision deemed responsible for the spiritual malaise in which man has been languishing for so long ('cómo quedamos de tan quedarnos'). We find the same opposition everywhere in González Prada, whose own Hellenism was inherited principally from the English and German Romantics (he translated Shelley, Goethe, Heine, and Schiller, among others), the French Parnassians, and Nietzsche. In 'Prelusión', for example, the poetic foreword to *Exóticas* (1911), he exalts the sunlit 'paganismo inmortal' of the 'buenos Dioses de Hélade' over the 'grotescos Dioses inhumanos' and the 'noche del horror cristiano' which have replaced them, while in the prose poem 'Mi muerte', from the same collection, he spurns Christian funeral rites—'sagradas preces', 'rituales pompas', 'macabros cirios verdes', and the 'siniestra y hosca faz de bonzo ignaro'—preferring to die 'mirando el Sol' on a 'pira griega' so that his body will return to the earth, becoming 'fragancia, polen, nube, ritmo, luz, idea'.[3] In 'Musa helénica', meanwhile (a suggestive title in the present context), he turns his attention to poetry itself, berating the 'atronadora y rimbombante Poesía castellana' (see below for more on his views of Spanish poetry) and yearning for 'un nuevo y glorioso renacer del Paganismo' which will place 'la clámide ateniense' on the shoulders of '[la] moderna Poesía' (*Exóticas*, p. 303). Similar examples abound in his speeches and prose writings. In his famous address to the Athenaeum in Lima of 1886, for instance, he argued that 'La Literatura y el Arte claman *por que venga un soplo del antiguo mundo helénico* a perfumar de ambrosía el Universo, *a desva-*

---

[2] See Franco, *César Vallejo*, pp. 84–85.
[3] *Exóticas*, in *Obras*, ed. by Luis Alberto Sánchez, 7 vols (Lima: Ediciones COPÉ, 1986), v, 257–353 (pp. 263, 265–66, 346).

necer las místicas alucinaciones del fanatismo católico', while in the trenchant 'Instrucción católica' he angrily dismisses Christianity as a 'reacción judía y oriental contra la sana y hermosa civilización helénica'.[4] In a revealing interview with González Prada which took place shortly before the latter's death, it seems clear that Vallejo had taken on board the master's message, since he describes him reverentially as a latter-day Hellene: 'Su vigoroso dinamismo sentimental que subyuga y arrastra, la fresca expresión de eterna primavera de su continente venerable tiene algo de mármol alado y suave en que la Hélade pagana solía encarnar el gesto divino, la energía sobrehumana de sus dioses'.[5]

I should add that González Prada's may not be the only influence detectable in the opening lines of *Trilce* XIX. There also seems to be an echo of Baudelaire's 'La Muse malade', which opens: 'Ma pauvre muse, hélas!, qu'as-tú donc ce matin?' The matutine setting is the same and the tone similarly colloquial, though Vallejo takes his new-fangled demotic much further, and whereas Baudelaire begins by painting a sorry picture of the contemporary muse and ends by imagining a return to an idealized Greek antiquity which will reinvigorate her 'sang chrétien', Vallejo practically reverses the process, beginning with neo-pagan hope and ending amidst the uncertainties of the present. It was not, of course, uncommon for him to cannibalize rather than politely mimic his poetic sources, especially if they were French.[6]

Vallejo's choices of the Annunciation and the Nativity as targets for his critique of religious myth-making are self-suggesting, given their centrality to the Christian world-view which his poem is seeking to undermine.[7] Yet here too he may be drawing on specific sources, perhaps the most important of which is González Prada's essay on Renan, which Vallejo had evidently read, since in the interview cited above he refers to its author as the 'gran comentador de Renán'.[8] In that essay González Prada says of Renan's *Vie de*

---

[4] 'Conferencia en el Ateneo de Lima' and 'Instrucción católica', in *Páginas libres* (1894), in *Obras*, I, 25–287 (pp. 35–59, 123–48 (pp. 55, 139)).

[5] 'Desde Lima: con Manuel González Prada', in *Obras*, VII, 547–55 (p. 552). The interview was first published in *La Reforma* (Trujillo), 9 March 1918.

[6] The two most obvious examples are Verlaine and Samain, whose 'Art poétique' and 'Automne' Vallejo violently and in the second instance mockingly rehashes in *Trilce* XXXVI and LV respectively. Another possible source for Vallejo's invented Grecian muse might be Ernst Haeckel's *The Riddle of the Universe* (1899), which he had certainly read: see Franco, *César Vallejo*, pp. 9–11. Throughout that work, Haeckel champions ancient Greek learning over benighted Christianity, says of Hellenic polytheism that it 'still furnish[es] the finest images to the modern poet and artist', and argues that just as 'the classic poetry of the ancient Greeks incarnated their ideals of virtue in divine shapes', so should his own age 'lend the character of noble goddesses to our three rational ideals' (of truth, beauty, and virtue, all underpinned by scientific reason). See Ernst Haeckel, *The Riddle of the Universe*, trans. by Joseph McCabe (New York: Prometheus, 1992), pp. 277, 336.

[7] Some critics have seen in the cock a proleptic allusion to Peter's betrayal of Christ, though it is difficult to see how such a reference might make sense or function within the Nativity scene in the way that, say, Lorca's foretokening of the Passion in poems such as 'San Gabriel, Sevilla' (from the *Romancero gitano*) or 'Nacimiento de Cristo' (from *Poeta en Nueva York*) so clearly does.

[8] 'Desde Lima: con Manuel González Prada', p. 553.

Jésus (1863) (which, incidentally, he describes as having a distinctive 'sabor helénico'):

> Si por muchos de sus libros marcha Renan con los tímidos y conservadores, por su *Vida de Jesús* va con los avanzados zapadores de viejas teogonías. Mide muy bien la magnitud de su demolición, sabe que basta despojar a Cristo del barniz divino para derrumbar el edificio inmenso del Catolicismo.[9]

For González Prada, that act of demystification is wholly salutary, since it humanizes a Jesus long since reduced to bloodless doctrinal abstraction: 'Al terminar su lectura, se ve que el hijo de María gana inmensamente con perder la divinidad, pues de sombra mítica y legendaria se transforma en personaje real e histórico.'[10] All of this is surely echoed in Vallejo's poem. The Nativity scene in stanza 2 is one of animalian innocence (the unnecessary threefold repetition of the adjective 'inocente', bolstered by the chiasmus in line 6, lends the passage a naive, childlike air), with the only overtly religious term ('divinamente') being immediately and savagely undercut by the messy, distinctly earthbound adjectives 'meado' and 'excrementido', while in the following stanza the traditionally chaste Annunciation is aggressively sexualized and the importance and uniqueness of the protagonists diminished by the use of lower-case lettering (in marked contrast to the capital 'H' of 'Hélpide'), the formation of a single, compound noun from St Gabriel's name, and the addition of the generalizing adjective 'ecuménica'.[11] The jarring incongruities here, and in particular the crude 'somatization' of spiritual qualities, push a step further a similar series of deliberately mismatched noun–adjective pairings from 'Espergesia', another sardonically agnostic poem surely inspired by González Prada:

> Todos saben ... y no saben
> que la Luz es tísica,
> y la Sombra gorda ....
> y no saben que el Misterio sintetiza ....
> que él es la joroba
> musical y triste que a distancia denuncia
> el paso meridiano de las lindes a las Lindes.[12]

[9] González Prada, 'Renán', in *Páginas libres*, pp. 191–208 (p. 194).
[10] Ibid., p. 195.
[11] In his edition of *Trilce* (Madrid: Cátedra, 1991) Julio Ortega suggests that the misspelling 'excrementido', 'corrected' to 'excrementado' by Américo Ferrari in his edition of the *Obra poética* (Nanterre: Colección Archivos, 1988), p. 161, should stand, since 'tiene una resonancia más idiomática y lleva, quizás, una ligera ironía por asociación fónica a cultismos y arcaísmos' (p. 111). However, as Ricardo Silva-Santisteban points out in *Poesía completa II* (Lima: Pontífica Universidad Católica del Perú, 1997), Vallejo used the same spelling in his 1923 novella *Fabla salvaje* (p. 60). One possible, if perhaps unintended, 'resonance' of Vallejo's choice of term is the inclusion within it of the adjective 'mentido', since he is in the process of smothering a sublime lie in dung.
[12] See *Los heraldos negros*, ed. by Marta Ortiz Canseco (Madrid: Castalia, 2009), p. 147.

Such oxymoronic juxtapositions and underminings would become a staple of Vallejo's mature verse. Once more, however, there may be an additional poetic source for his pointedly vulgarized recasting of the stable scene. In Enrique Diez Canedo and Fernando Fortún's seminal anthology *La poesía francesa moderna*, which Vallejo knew well, he would have come across the poem 'Impresiones de regreso' (originally 'Impressions de retour') by Émile Despax, which describes a return home whose uncertainties and disappointments are evoked in religious terms strikingly similar to those used in *Trilce* XIX:

> Tan indefenso el hombre, tan cobarde se siente,
> que recobra el pueril corazón maleable.
> Teme a los pensamientos malos de tal manera,
> que parece que un ángel cruza por la pradera.
> ¡Bruma del prado! ¡Lienzos blanquísimos que un día
> el altar adornaron para el mes de *María*!
> pero *el ángel* de pies de plata no ha venido.
> Tan sólo, en *el establo*, de una esquila el sonido.
> ¡Belén! ¡Belén! Cómo éste soñaba un cielo, mudo,
> sobre el *buey*, sobre *el asno*, sobre el niño desnudo.[13]

The parallels (specifically, the prefacing of a disenchanted Nativity scene with a description of man as 'indefenso' and 'cobarde') appear too close to be coincidental, though again Vallejo has methodically coarsened and colloquialized his impeccably arranged and articulated Gallic model.

As Julio Ortega points out, *Trilce* XIX is not simply a piece of secular proselytizing arbitrarily wedged into a poetic mould. As he puts it:

Más que luchando por forjar un significado predeterminado, que supondría un filosofismo aleccionador, el poeta parece embarcado en una secuencia de ejemplos o demostraciones, como si su método de articulación pasase por la desarticulación previa del sentido global en la antítesis y el paralelismo asimétrico de las figuraciones sucesivas.[14]

In fact, the poem is not entirely free of what might broadly be termed 'didactic' elements, but there is nevertheless running through it a dialectical tension between advocacy and enquiry, confident assertion and anguished uncertainty, and that tension remains deliberately and indeed necessarily unresolved at the close. Its ultimate source consists in the co-implicated questions of whether some form of radically secularized hope can ever replace the series of religious myths with which man has oriented and consoled but also deceived himself throughout history and, even if it can, of what form that hope might take and what possibilities it might offer in a world emptied

---

[13] *La poesía francesa moderna*, ed. by Enrique Diez Canedo and Fernando Fortún (Madrid: Renacimiento, 1913), pp. 344–45 (emphasis added).

[14] *Trilce*, ed. by Ortega, p. 115.

of every transcendental illusion and sense-making metanarrative. The poem oscillates between surges of optimism at the thought that the Christian era might finally be coming to an end and fear about what might emerge in its wake, a fear punctuated by intermittent outbursts of defiance. That oscillation begins in the opening couplet, in which Hélpide, imagined as offering a possible wake-up call from two millennia of metaphysical slumber, is presented in markedly, perhaps deflatingly materialist terms, and via a sort of ungainly, two-line hyperbaton-cum-anacoluthon which looks like a parody of the exalted, classical invocation of the muse. That opening address is extremely difficult to paraphrase, but if we assume for a moment that Vallejo is mocking or at least toying with classical models, and we accord the verb *trastear* one of the meanings which makes most grammatical sense ('Pisar las cuerdas de los intrumentos de trastes' or 'Discurrir con viveza y travesura sobre algún asunto', according to the *DRAE*), we quickly form a picture of a distinctly unpoetic figure gabbing merrily away about man's existential predicament or strumming casually on a guitar in front of a poet who has just fallen out of bed, thus clearing away the night's cobwebs.[15] Alternatively, if we take *trastear* to mean 'to shift around', we might imagine Hélpide as a maid turning up first thing in the morning to put an untidy house in order (*escampar* can be used both transitively and intransitively to mean 'to clear up', in the latter case in relation to the weather). Yet *trastear* can also mean 'To complicate, mix up' (the *DRAE* lists *enredar* as an equivalent). This might initially appear nonsensical, given that it follows 'escampas', but the resulting paradox might convey the sense that the setting out of man's stall for the dawning of a momentous new day is likely to be a complex and hazardous process. All three possibilities, then, are apposite in the overall context of the poem: some form of root-and-branch existential clear-up operation is taking or needs to take place, and hope of some sort will be required in order to effect it. Given that Vallejo has couched his opening salvo in such densely ambiguous terms, we should refrain from choosing definitively between them. Certainly, any Hellenism here is hedged around with and complicated by a mischievous sense of irony that we never find in González Prada's rhapsodic paeans to antiquity, and Vallejo's poem is both richer and more troubling as a consequence.[16] The

---

[15] To gain an idea of just how intractable these lines are, consider Clayton Eshleman's embattled rendering: 'To rummage, sweet Hélpide, you clear, | how we remain from so remaining ourselves'. See César Vallejo, *The Complete Poetry* (Berkeley: University of California Press, 2007), p. 203.

[16] In his 'Neologismos en la poesía de César Vallejo' Giovanni Meo Zilio has even suggested that Vallejo added an 'H' to what, after the original Greek, ought to be 'Élpide', to suggest *Helpis*, a genus of jumping spider. See *Lavori della Sezione del Gruppo Ispanistico I*, ed. by Oreste Macrí (Florence: Casa Editrice D'Anna, 1967), pp. 11–98 (p. 37). This would certainly add a further note of bathos, and spiders carry connotations of awkwardness and helplessness in other poems (not least 'La araña' from *Los heraldos negros*), though it is difficult to see what specific significance the allusion might have here. Might it be instead that Vallejo was thinking of the English word

tonal slipperiness is reflected in the hiccoughing dactylic/trochaic rhythm of line 2, further accentuated by the docking of a syllable from what we expect to be a second hendecasyllable, achieved by the bludgeoningly ungrammatical use of 'tan', where 'tanto' would have made more sense and given the 'right' count, and the tongue-twisting polyptoton of 'quedamos'/'quedarnos'. I shall say more about the significance of Vallejo's aesthetic effrontery in these opening lines below, but for the moment we might simply note that the depiction of hope is far from unequivocally triumphal, and that the seeds of the uncertainty which emerges unmistakably at the end of the poem are effectively sown here.

The last three lines of the second stanza provide one of the 'ejemplos' or 'demostraciones' described by Ortega—that of the stable in Bethlehem given a scatological overhaul—but the third stanza ushers in a change of tack and tone in the form of an impassioned and extended exhortation which culminates in the subsequent couplet, where a triumphalist note does, briefly, intrude. The gist of the stanza—again, the syntax is somewhat hazy—seems to be that a total, top-to-bottom reconception of the world and the way we understand and inhabit it, from 'lo más nada' all the way up to 'la ilusión monarca', is necessary if man is to be roused from his ontotheological torpor. No critic has remarked on the order in which the various elements listed in lines 8–11 are presented, but they appear to be arranged chiastically, moving down from the 'alma' to 'el sin luz amor, el sin cielo' (presumably sexual love, devoid of transcendental, spiritual significance), then to 'lo más piedra, lo más nada' (inanimate matter and the underlying void), before finally reascending to 'la ilusión monarca'. As we shall see presently, this sweeping movement up and down the chain of being seems to have been carefully plotted. The following couplet, meanwhile, a combative résumé of the previous stanza, is a call to arms, a proto-Sartrean exhortation to jettison reassuring 'essences' and embrace existential contingency, a move which will entail relinquishing definitively all the false securities of the past.

It is at this seemingly exultant juncture that a significant element of doubt enters. What if such a radical break is simply not possible, and man is condemned for ever to replace one set of 'mitos' with another? Is Vallejo's radically secularized 'Hélpide' in the last instance any less of an 'ilusión monarca' than the Gospel narrative? Alternatively, can any justifiable form of hope remain in a world without an overarching order, meaning, or purpose, and is Hélpide's message in reality one of despair; she is, after all, said to arrive 'masticando hielos'?[17] Might there have been more instinctive bravado than genuine con-

'help' when he altered the spelling? That would certainly work both semantically and tonally in the context.

[17] For some brief but incisive comments on these questions see John Gray, *The Silence of Animals: On Progress and Other Modern Myths* (London: Allen Lane, 2013), pp. 77 ff.

viction in the preceding declamations? The poet initially rebuffs this latter possibility with a gesture of pure defiance—'mastiquemos brasas'—but this does not succeed in dispelling his deeper misgivings. Lines 17–18 now revisit and summarize in more sober and stark terms the consequences of the fundamental dismantling celebrated in stanza 3. In a universe in which there is no longer any qualitative difference between 'alma' and 'sin luz amor', between 'lo más nada' and 'la ilusión monarca', in which all hierarchies have collapsed and there is no other-worldly 'beyond' or 'essence' to which to aspire, how can man find his bearings, and on what grounds would he do so? The poem cannot answer this consequent and crucial question, and thus ends on a note of muted, troubled uncertainty, putting the epistemological ball firmly in man's court and then falling silent. Various critics have commented on the presence and significance of the cock in the final line. Jean Franco asserts that 'The cock which had, with its crowing, signalled Peter's denial of Christ is now unsure of itself; the animal order no longer confirms the supernatural order but speaks only of uncertainty', and rather oddly infers from this that 'The poem ends on a comic note'.[18] André Coyné, meanwhile, claims that as a consequence of the desacralization of the Gospel scene the cock is reduced to 'su función de veleta, de aquello que mira ahora hacia un punto, más tarde hacia otro etc.', a less problematically specific and by no means unreasonable reading, for which he is nevertheless ridiculed by Abril.[19] Ortega is surely right in arguing that the cock is 'no necesariamente el que le cantó a Pedro sino el que está citado en la segunda estrofa de este poema "inocente"',[20] to which we might add that the whole poem is a sort of extended metaphorical aubade in which the cock plays its customary role of heralding a new dawn, but in this case a radically new one, robbed of all the quotidian certainties of those which have preceded it.

Almost every element considered in the foregoing analysis has an analogue, often a specific analogue, in the work of González Prada. As should be evident from the examples of his Hellenism cited above, González Prada was an implacable, lifelong enemy of religion in general and Christianity in particular, especially in its institutional guises, and his speeches and essays overflow with exhortations to his listeners/readers to reject the obscurantism and bigotry bred by religious thought and embrace a purely secular reason, specifically scientific reason (he was an avid reader of Feuerbach, Darwin, Spencer, Renan,

---

[18] Franco, *César Vallejo*, p. 86.
[19] André Coyné, *César Vallejo* (Buenos Aires: Editorial Nueva Visión, 1968), p. 228; Abril, *Exégesis trílcica*, p. 52. Abril's own reading is both far less intelligible and far more questionable: 'El verso con el que remata el poema, de manera coherente con el resto de la historia, en una especie de simbiosis (la conciencia de Pedro=la inocencia animal), aporta la negación de la negación' (*Exégesis trílcica*, p. 44).
[20] *Trilce*, ed. by Ortega, p. 115.

Haeckel, etc.), in which he saw humanity's only chance of enlightenment. The following passage, from a speech at the Teatro Olimpo (1888), is typical:

Algo muere, pero también algo nace: muere la mentira con las lucubraciones metafísicas y teológicas, nace la verdad con la Ciencia positiva. Una vieja Atlántida se hunde poco a poco bajo las aguas del Océano; pero un nuevo y hermoso continente surge del mar, ostentando su flora sin espinos y su fauna sin tigres.[21]

He predicated his hope for the future on the idea that religion was a historical or evolutionary accident, a temporary if regrettable juvenile interlude from which humanity was destined to emerge:

Si [la religiosidad] fuera inherente al hombre, su desaparición causaría efectos mórbidos; pero sucede lo contrario: cuando más brilla en el cerebro la inteligencia, más se nubla en el corazón el sentimiento religioso. La religiosidad no pasa de accidente en la marcha de la Humanidad, corresponde a un período intermediario de la evolución mental, oscilando entre la absoluta ignorancia y la plena ilustración [. . .] Querer, pues, que la inteligencia no salga de la religiosidad vale tanto como pretender que un organismo se detenga en la niñez o en la adolescencia.[22]

That hope is clearly reflected in *Trilce* XIX, and González Prada often expresses it with the sort of ardour we find in stanzas 3 and 4. Indeed, line 12 looks very much like a direct borrowing from his work. It is a line that might appear to offer meat and drink to theorists of a postcolonial persuasion, who would doubtless see it as an example of the ventriloquized subaltern subject haplessly parroting the discourse of his colonial masters—it was Cortés who enjoined his men to burn their boats so that they could not abandon their imperial mission—but its likely origin suggests otherwise. In his essay on Renan, González Prada upbraids the French thinker for clinging on to certain irrational beliefs (in particular the view that man did not evolve like the other animals) which his championing of science should have led him to abandon, in the following terms: 'Renán costeó el continente científico a manera de un Américo Vespucci: *pero no penetró en él como un Hernán Cortés* o un Pizarro.'[23] In other words, Renan refused to burn all his metaphysical boats and thus remained partially mired in the world of myth and superstition. Vallejo, surely paraphrasing González Prada, urges us to go the whole hog. Elsewhere, González Prada says that man's obsession with myth-making and 'siguiendo lo imposible' has led him to turn his back on 'la constancia y la firmeza' of nature, 'imarcesible flor de lo Infinito'. Again, the terms he uses manifestly prefigure those of *Trilce* XIX: '*Cifrando en viejos mitos la esperanza,* | *Te olvida*

---

[21] 'Discurso en el Teatro Olimpo', in *Páginas libres*, pp. 63–73 (p. 72). For the clearest if least subtle statement of his views see the unpublished early sonnets 'Los dioses', 'La ciencia', and 'La religión', in *Cantos del otro siglo*, in *Obras*, VII, 205–464 (pp. 211–12, 214–15). These poems were written during González Prada's militantly positivist phase.
[22] González Prada, 'Instrucción católica', p. 145.
[23] González Prada, 'Renán', p. 200 (emphasis added).

el hombre y al error se lanza.'[24] Yet despite his professed confidence in science and reason, González Prada periodically pauses to wonder whether a godless universe might not be one necessarily devoid of a fundamental rationale, meaning, and hope, for all that we might understand its purely mechanical workings. Thus the significantly entitled 'La esperanza' opens exultantly with the lines: 'La Ciencia triunfa, La Razón domina | Y el reino estéril de la Fe sucumbe.'[25] Yet the poet's thoughts soon turn to the chill enigmas of 'la fosa' and 'el polvo'—death without prospect of return or redemption—and by the final stanza he is in despair, describing man's fate in a manner which seems to foreshadow lines 17–18 of Vallejo's poem:

> *No más delirios de escalar las nubes,*
> *No más ensueños de futura vida:*
> *Al borde oscuro de la fosa*
> *Detenga el vuelo la esperanza.*[26]

Yet dejection is not González Prada's only response to the emptiness and purposelessness of the cosmos, and streams of darkling, Schopenhauerian musings are often illumined by dramatic shafts of Nieztschean yea-saying, in which he vows to embrace and affirm the universe in all its apparent absurdity. We find precisely the same pattern in Vallejo's poem, couched in language almost identical to that employed at comparable moments by González Prada. Franco says of the quasi-Petrarchan antithesis in lines 15–16: 'The instability of language is underscored by the purely natural opposition of "chewing ice" and "chewing coals", since neither substance belongs to the supernatural order.'[27] In fact, language and the supernatural order have nothing to do with it, as Vallejo is merely echoing here a passage from González Prada's 'La hora negra'. That poem begins by painting a terrifying picture of a stonily indifferent universe ruled only by 'dolor'—again, Schopenhauer's is the informing philosophy, via the poetry of Jean Lahor, from which González Prada takes his epigraph—in which men's lives are no more than ephemeral 'desdeñables episodios en el drama de los mundos'.[28] However, the murk begins to lift when the poet sees spring return, and with it exuberant new life, evoked in enticingly erotic terms. Tempted by 'el placer y la dulzura' which 'la copa inagotable de la vida' proffers, he asks himself:

---

[24] See *Minúsculas* (1901), in *Obras*, v, 177–224 (p. 191, emphasis added).
[25] González Prada, *Exóticas*, p. 328.
[26] Ibid. (emphasis added). This poem may also be a source for *Trilce* XXXI ('Esperanza plañe entre algodones'), which, thematically at least, is very close to XIX and also reads very much like a more experimental rehashing of one of the series of poems in *Los heraldos negros* inspired by Vallejo's readings of González Prada.
[27] Franco, *César Vallejo*, p. 86.
[28] González Prada, *Exóticas*, p. 333.

> ¿Porqué de las manos alejar el néctar?
> ¿Porqué de luto vestir el alma
> En lúgubres festines de eléboro y acíbar?

Finding no higher reason to spurn life's sensuous pleasures, he elects to embrace them, and in joyously defiant terms:

> Antes de ser un *glacial, emblanquecido polvo*,
> Seamos *fuego de amor*, seamos *llama*:
> Vivamos la vida, gocemos el goce.
> Condensemos —pobres seres de un instante—
> Lo Infinito en un abrazo,
> La Eternidad en un beso.[29]

These lines consciously pick up and effectively invert a similar but far gloomier reference earlier in the poem: 'Nos dormimos con las llamas en las venas, | Despertamos con los hielos en la frente.'[30] In classically Epicurean mode, González Prada is advocating a 'hot' response to a frigid cosmos, and this is precisely what Vallejo is doing in *Trilce* XIX, though the latter's clipped, graphic formulation is more memorable than that of his excessively rhetorical model.

González Prada's thought also casts significant light on the hesitant closing line of the poem, and should put us on our guard against interpreting it too negatively, despite Vallejo's choice of the more fragile, lower-case 'hombre' as opposed to González Prada's confidently capitalized 'Humanidad' (and, of course, his own Hélpide). For González Prada doubt and uncertainty were defining traits of our humanity and, far from being defects, were near-heroic intellectual and moral virtues, the wellsprings of all authentic and fruitful (i.e. scientific) thinking, and vital weapons in the battle with religious dogmatism, which 'resuelve *a priori* los problemas físicos y morales'.[31] Crucially, he also viewed them as the sources of inspiration for the greatest poetry. Passages such as the following abound in his prose writings: '*Hay más poesía en la duda varonil del sabio que en las afirmaciones pueriles del creyente: derribadas las barreras de las religiones caducas, el hombre tiene a su disposición lo Desconocido* para colmarlo de hipótesis racionales';[32] and:

> *La duda* y *la incertidumbre* desenvuelven a nuestra imaginación un espacio sin límites. *Al dudar*, afirmamos nuestra personalidad, crecemos, *nos sentimos más hombres* [. . .] De los espíritus sumisos, aunque escépticos, surge una poesía melancólica, serena y

---

[29] Ibid., p. 334 (emphasis added).

[30] Ibid., p. 333. We find precisely the same terms of opposition in 'Mi verdad' from the same collection (*Exóticas*, pp. 324–25): 'Como el hierro candente, nos abrasa el hierro helado' (p. 325). This poem also begins in the icy 'noches hiperbóreas de la mente' and ends with the celebration of a 'forma tangible', in this case that of the 'ardientes, vibradoras carnes' of a woman.

[31] González Prada, 'La instrucción católica', p. 143.

[32] 'Los fragmentos de Luzbel', in *Páginas libres*, pp. 235–53 (p. 253, emphasis added).

estoica; de los negadores y rebeldes, una inspiración acre, desesperada y batalladora. *Los trozos más celebres de las antologías, los versos que más brillan en el tesoro poético de la Humanidad, se hallan impregnados de negación y duda*, no de evaporaciones míticas ni delicuescencias dogmáticas.[33]

His poetry tells the same story. In 'Mi verdad', which opens with a long, unsparing gaze into the abyss, he berates human beings, with their self-deluding 'filosofías' and 'religiones', as 'ilusos incurables' who throughout history have done no more than replace 'mentiras viejas' with 'errores nuevos', championing instead '[la] duda viril y austera', which he describes as the 'manjar de fuertes y de libres'. Even in 'La esperanza', one of his bleakest utterances, we hear the 'grito heróico de la duda' ringing out in the void.[34] In the prose poem 'Duda', meanwhile, the poet is seduced into boarding a ship by a 'velada mujer misteriosa', who, when questioned, says that she is the embodiment of 'divina hermosura', 'la Helena de París, la Venus de Milo'. When he asks her name, she replies: 'Me llamo la Duda, la fiel compañera del sabio, la vista del ciego, la fuerza del débil. La Fe me proscribe, la Ciencia me aclama.'[35] Enraptured, the poet exclaims '¡Partamos, partamos! ¡Gloriosa la vida vivida contigo! ¡Gloriosa la muerte venida por ti!' Doubt, then, while it can obviously never solve man's existential dilemmas, and must necessarily leave him 'recorriendo siempre | los indecisos mares de la incertidumbre' ('Mi verdad', p. 325), constitutes the most scrupulous and courageous way of confronting them. Typically, Vallejo is much less explicit about this. The unresolved dissonance with which *Trilce* XIX concludes places the accent on the uncertainty itself, rather than its heroic quality, and the poem is all the better for it.

Yet it is not only in the 'content' of Vallejo's poem that González Prada's influence can be felt. The latter also had much to say about poetic form and language, experimented imaginatively with both (but particularly with the former) in his own verse, and, crucially, made a number of key recommendations to the young poets of the day with regard to how they should go about expressing themselves authentically both as men of their age and as Spanish Americans. Vallejo seems to be espousing and responding to just about all of his precepts and promptings in *Trilce* XIX. González Prada was particularly concerned that the new generation should avoid slavishly imitating age-old poetic models, since:

Ningún autor con lenguaje avejentado, por más pensamientos juveniles que emplee, logrará nunca el favor del público, porque las ideas del siglo injeridas en estilo vetusto

---

[33] 'La poesía', in *Nuevas páginas libres*, in *Obras*, I, 289–493 (pp. 333–44 (p. 338, emphasis added)).
[34] González Prada, *Exóticas*, pp. 325, 328.
[35] Ibid., p. 348.

recuerdan las esencias balsámicas inyectadas en las arterias de un muerto: preservan de la fermentación cadavérica; pero no comunican lozanía, calor de vida.[36]

What was true of antique forms and modes of expression in general applied *a fortiori* to those inherited from Spain. With certain honourable exceptions (especially Quevedo—also a favourite of Vallejo), González Prada saw Spanish poetry as hopelessly anachronistic and parochial, a grotesque and lifeless aesthetic offshoot of Spain's ultramontane Catholic tradition.[37] In both his prose and his poetry, he deplored starchy academicism, airless neoclassicism, and the adoption of form and metre simply for their own sake as damagingly retrograde. A spirited 'Ritmo sin rima' from *Minúsculas* is effectively a verse manifesto for his aesthetic. It opens with a volley of questions: '¿Son inviolables doncellas los léxicos? | ¿Son las palabras sagrados cadáveres? | ¿Momias de reyes, en pétreos sarcófagos?' These he answers with a declaration of aesthetic war on the ossified forms and diction of the past and sterile scholarly prescriptiveness, and with a call for poetry to speak the language of the day:

> ¡Guerra al vetusto lenguaje del clásico!
> ¡Fuera el morboso purismo académico!
> Libre y osado remonte el espíritu.
>
> Vista ropaje del siglo la idea:
> Deje el raído jubón de Cervantes,
> Rasgue la vieja sotana de Lope.

The poem closes with a plea to the American poet to adopt a new emblem: 'Tímido esclavo del Verbo ancestral, | No ames el cóndor ni el águila: ten | De ave-pegaso un dormido avestruz.'[38] In a pointed, perhaps comically bathetic gesture of disrespect, he rejects the traditional symbolic birds of both indigenous and colonial imperialism, as well the winged horse of Greek myth, and advocates instead the lowly, flightless rhea as a poetic standard. And Vallejo for one seems to have adopted it, since he entitled one of the poems in *Los heraldos negros* 'Avestruz'—an early indication of the esteem in which he held González Prada's views.[39] In 'La poesía', meanwhile, González Prada says more about how poetry might break free of its ancestral shackles by allowing

[36] González Prada, 'Conferencia en el Ateneo', p. 50.
[37] In 'La poesía' he refers disparagingly to Spain's 'espíritu regional y estrecho', which results from 'el odio al extranjero y el amor a las tradiciones religiosas', adding that 'En el verso castellano se oye el clamor de una secta o un partido, mas no se siente latir el corazón de la Humanidad' (p. 336). He dismisses Spanish poets and their American imitators as death-dealing 'anacronismos vivientes', devoid of a vitality which he again describes in Hellenic terms : 'En lugar de trascender a néctar y ambrosía, huelen a incienso o pólvora, cuando no a humedad de cripta ni a emanación de cuartel' (p. 336).
[38] González Prada, *Minúsculas*, p. 211
[39] *Los heraldos negros*, p. 73. The poem was originally published in *Mundo Limeño*, 20 (February 1918), shortly after Vallejo had moved to the capital and just before he interviewed González Prada. In her *Poetry in Pieces: César Vallejo and Lyric Modernity* (Berkeley: University of California

subject matter freely to shape form and versification, rather than arbitrarily imposing the latter on the former:

Al descubrirse las relaciones íntimas de las cosas, brotan las figuras retóricas y, por consiguiente, se ensancha el horizonte poético. La versificación, desdeñando las onomatopeyas y todas las demás puerilidades seniles, armoniza el ritmo de la palabra con el ritmo silencioso de la idea. El lenguaje, lejos de esclavizarse a la rima o petrificarse en el arcaísmo, vuela libre y modernizado, no admitiendo la imposición de las academias oficiales ni reconociendo más autoridad que el uso.[40]

He attempted to implement all of these principles in his own verse, especially in the second section of *Exóticas*, where we find him experimenting freely with rhythm and with stanza and line length, and dispensing completely with rhyme. Later poems from *Los heraldos negros*, such as 'La araña', 'El palco estrecho', 'Rosa blanca', and 'Espergesia', suggest that his example was rubbing off on Vallejo as early as 1918, though the first two of these are still *silvas*, albeit highly inventive ones. Indeed, although Vallejo's poetry had undergone a lexical and expressive sea-change by the time he composed *Trilce* XIX, even this poem contains significant metrical regularities and remains haunted by the ghost of *silva* form and the faint echoes of rhyme.[41]

Yet perhaps the most important precedent for some of the more radical innovations in *Trilce* XIX, and indeed the collection as a whole, is González Prada's aforementioned speech to the Athenaeum, in which he sets out at greatest length his template for an authentically American poetics. He begins by drawing attention to the growing historical cultural, racial, and geopolitical divide which separates America from Spain, and warns of the arrested intellectual development which will result from continued dependence on the motherland:

La dependencia intelectual de España significaría para nosotros la indefinida prolongación de la niñez. Del español nos separan ya las influencias del clima, los cruzamientos

---

Press, 2011), Michelle Clayton devotes several curious pages to what she terms 'ostriches' in Vallejo's poetry (pp. 89–85) and examines 'Avestruz' in some detail, though without attempting to identify any source (pp. 90–91). There may be a distant echo of González Prada's enjoinder in the parenthetical line '(¿Cóndores? ¡Me friegan los cóndores!)' from the much later 'Telúrica y magnética' (1931?), an attempt to write a specifically Peruvian poem which avoids all the clichés of *peruanidad*. See *Poemas humanos/España, aparta de mí este cáliz*, ed. by Francisco Martín García (Madrid: Castalia, 1987), p. 92.

[40] González Prada, 'La poesía', p. 343.

[41] Lines 1, 3, 6–8, and 14–15 are regular hendecasyllables, while line 2 is a consciously truncated one (see above), and Vallejo's liberal use of *sinafía* or interlinear elision (a device he also employs in 'Romería' (*Los heraldos negros*, p. 79) and 'El palco estrecho') across lines 3–6 means that lines 4–5 can be counted as hendecasyllables. Similarly, lines 17–18 are heptasyllables and pervasive *sinafía* makes lines 9–11 into near heptaysllables. The rhymes in stanza 2 (especially lines 5–6) seem deliberately childish, and the delayed assonantal rhyming of 'alma', 'nada', and monarca', 'cielo' and 'hielo' (and perhaps even the minimal resonance of 'maría ecuménica' in 'última esencia') are surely significant, as is the juxtaposition of the two disyllabic infinitives in lines 17–18.

etnográficos, el íntimo roce con los europeos, la educación afrancesada y 64 años de tempestuosa vida republicana [...] Vamos perdiendo ya el desapego a la vida, desapego tan marcado en los antiguos españoles, y nos contagiamos con la tristeza gemebunda que distingue al indígena peruano.[42]

That final, similarly cool reference to Peru's Indigenous heritage indicates that González Prada's poetics, distancing itself equally from the two 'poles' of Peruvian national identity, is essentially one of *mestizaje*, and perhaps explains why he should have expressed a preference for the rhea, a native bird with no atavistic cultural or racial connotations, over both the eagle and the condor.[43] All of the socio-cultural differences pinpointed by González Prada manifest themselves in the Spanish spoken in the Americas:

No hablamos hoy como hablaban los conquistadores: las lenguas americanas nos proveen de neologismos que usamos con derecho, por no tener equivalentes en castellano, por expresar ideas exclusivamente nuestras, por nombrar cosas íntimamente relacionadas con nuestra vida.[44]

He welcomes 'el neologismo, el extranjerismo o el provincialismo' as elements 'que rejuvenecen y enriquecen el idioma' and argues that literary language ought to reflect everyday speech ('El escritor debe hablar como todos hablamos, no como un Apolo que pronuncia oráculos anfibológicos') since 'Los idiomas se vigorizan y retemplan en la fuente popular, más que en las reglas muertas de los gramáticos y en las exhumaciones prehistóricas de los eruditos'.[45] Again, he endeavours to put theory into practice in his own verse, where we find him creatively tinkering with popular forms (especially in *Minúsuclas*), adopting foreign ones (the Vilanelle, Triolet, Pantoum, Spenserian stanza, etc.), consistently eschewing stilted and overblown rhetoric, and conducting modest experiments in neologism, experiments which Vallejo was already imitating (and in some instances reproducing verbatim) in the poems of *Los heraldos negros*.[46]

[42] González Prada, 'Conferencia en el Ateneo', p. 53.

[43] González Prada always championed the cause of Peru's Indians, but in his later thought did so on socio-economic and historical rather than purely ethnic grounds, having come to find all forms of supposedly 'biological' thinking about race both intellectually suspect and morally repugnant. He was consequently convinced that the 'Indian problem' could not be solved by an attempted return to some pre-Hispanic 'utopía arcaica' (to borrow Vargas Llosa's phrase), and that social harmony and justice in Peru could only be achieved via the integration of its different ethnic groups. Thus, after a youthful flirtation with *Indigenismo* (in the form of the saccharine *Baladas peruanas*, published posthumously in 1935), he came to see the more totemic forms of *Indigenista* art as both distorted and anachronistic. See 'Nuestros indios', in *Obras*, III, 185–210 (especially p. 209). In his 'Discurso en el Politeama' (1888) (*Páginas libres*, pp. 86–92), meanwhile, he notes that even Peru's coastal *mestizos* are the products of a double servitude, being descendants of both the 'súbditos de Felipe II' and the 'súbditos de Huayna-Capac' (p. 88).

[44] González Prada, 'Conferencia en el Ateneo', p. 53.

[45] Ibid., p. 51.

[46] For example, the line 'en la multicencia de un dulce noser', from 'Para el alma imposible de

González Prada's rejection of formal Iberian Spanish extends to pronunciation and even spelling: 'Hasta en la pronunciación, ¡cuánto hemos cambiado! [...] Señores, el que habla en este momento ¿qué sería en alguna academia de Madrid? Casi un bárbaro, que pronuncia la *ll* como la *y*, confunde la *b* con la *v* y no distingue la *s* de la *z* ni de la *c* en sus sonidos suaves.'[47] An enduring sense of linguistic propriety seems to have kept such 'barbarism' in check in his own poetry, but no such scruples inhibited Vallejo, as the deliberate misspelling of 'has' in line 8 of *Trilce* XIX, often erroneously 'corrected' by editors and commentators, as well, perhaps, as the 'H' (to be comically aspirated, perhaps, like Cortázar's Holiveira?) added to 'Helpide's' name, along with countless comparable examples, especially of an often exaggerated betacism, in other *Trilce* poems makes clear.[48] It is surely noteworthy, then, that in the interview with González Prada we find Vallejo quizzing him about the place of 'audacias de expresión' and even 'incorrecciones gramaticales' in poetry, as if seeking his mentor's approval before trying them out. González Prada assures him that 'los defectos de la técnica' and 'incongruencias en la manera' are of no import, that solecisms 'pasan por alto' and 'las audacias precisamente me gustan'. The key thing, he stresses, is to 'ir contra la traba, contra lo académico'.[49] Vallejo never looked back, and the licence to write aggressively against the grain would eventually result in the poems of *Trilce*.

In the light of the above, it seems clear that just about every formal and expressive element of *Trilce* XIX, the stanzaic and metrical irregularities, the almost jaunty irreverence with respect to the classical tradition, the eye-catching neologisms, the pervasive colloquialism and orality and concomitant misspellings, is in part or in whole attributable to the influence of González Prada, and that all form part of a nascent, Americanist poetics, a poetics which, it turns out, may also underpin Vallejo's choice and treatment of his subject matter. This may seem like an odd claim, but González Prada, anticipating the arguments of a Carpentier or a Borges by more than half a century, insisted that for American expression to be genuine it must break free of the narrow, cliché-ridden confines of *costumbrismo* and eschew the facile pictorialism of local colour:

mi amada' (*Los heraldos negros*, p. 124), is pieced together from two poems by González Prada. We find the compound noun 'noser' in a 'Triolet' from *Minúsculas* (p. 211), while in 'La nevada', from *Exóticas*, he refers to the 'triste blanquecencia' of the 'selénico paisaje' of a nocturnal snowfall (p. 318).

[47] González Prada, 'Conferencia en el Ateneo', pp. 53–54.

[48] Franco has 'haz' for 'has' (*César Vallejo*, p. 85); likewise Stephen Hart in *Religión, política y ciencia en la obra de César Vallejo* (London: Támesis, 1987), p. 90, Clayton Eshleman in *The Complete Poetry*, p. 202, and James Higgins in *César Vallejo: An Anthology of his Poetry* (Oxford: Pergamon, 1970), p. 105. The standard spelling even appears in Américo Ferrari's edition of the *Obra poética* (Paris: Colección Archivos, 1988), p. 191. Silva-Santisteban, whose text reproduces that of the original manuscript, has 'has' (*Poesía completa II*, p. 60), as does Ortega (*Trilce*, p. 111).

[49] Vallejo, 'Con González Prada', p. 554.

Los literatos del Indostán fueron indostánicos, los literatos de Grecia fueron griegos, los literatos de América y del siglo XIX seamos americanos y del siglo XIX. Y no tomemos por americanismo la enumeración de nuestra fauna y nuestra flora o la minuciosa pintura de nuestros fenómenos meteorológicos, en lenguaje saturado de provincialismos ociosos y rebuscados. La nacionalidad del escritor se funda, no tanto en la copia fotográfica del escenario (casi el mismo en todas partes), como en la sincera expresión del yo y en la exacta figuración del medio social.[50]

For González Prada, speaking universally as a man of one's age was as important as speaking locally as an American, and he would doubtless have endorsed Unamuno's dictum, often quoted by Carpentier, that 'Es de dentro y no fuera, donde hemos de hallar al hombre; en las entrañas de lo local y circunscrito, lo universal, y en las entrañas de los pasajero, lo enterno.'[51] When it came to poetry, he stressed time and again that to be truly modern, writers must consign to the past the phantoms of theology and metaphysics and the simultaneously genteel and airy versifying in which they were so often cloaked, and adopt a world-view which was, at its core, scientific and materialist. In his speech to the Ateneo, immediately after his tirade against literary parochialism, he urges:

Acabemos ya el viaje milenario por regiones de idealismo sin consistencia y regresemos al seno de la realidad, recordando que fuera de la Naturaleza no hay más que simbolismos ilusorios, fantasías mitológicas, desvanecimientos metafísicos. A fuerza de ascender a cumbres enrarecidas, nos estamos volviendo vaporosos, aeriformes: ¡solidifiquémonos! Más vale ser hierro que nube.[52]

At the close of his speech at the Teatro Olimpo he is more specific:

Empiece ya en nuestra literatura el reinado de la Ciencia. Los hombres no quieren deleitarse hoy con música de estrofas insulsas y bien pulidas ni con períodos altisonantes y vacíos: todos, desde el niño hasta el viejo, tenemos sed de verdades.[53]

Modern science, 'robustecida por la sangre del siglo', is, he claims—and here we come full circle—propelled by a quest for truth which is Hellenic in origin: 'sabe a miel de panales griegos'. It is this questing spirit which offers hope

[50] González Prada, 'Conferencia en el Ateneo', p. 54.
[51] See 'Arte y cosmopolitanismo', in *Contra esto y aquello*, 2nd edn (Madrid: Renacimiento, 1928), pp. 203–13 (p. 206). González Prada says much the same thing in 'La poesía'. Denouncing in 'el exagerado amor a la patria' a 'fanatismo laico, tan absurdo y estrecho como el fanatismo religioso', he says, 'El hombre encerrado en el círculo de una patria vive moralmente solo [. . .] Quien habla de sí mismo, de su familia o de su nación, merece un auditorio reducido; pero quien habla en nombre de la Humanidad tiene derecho a ser escuchado por todos los hombres' (p. 339). He cites Homer, Shakespeare, Goethe, and Lamartine as examples, and dismisses the bellicose 'canciones nacionales' and 'odas patrióticas' which peppered the first half of the nineteenth century in Spanish America as so many empty 'ejercicios de retórica' (p. 341).
[52] González Prada, 'Conferencia en el Ateneo', pp. 54–55.
[53] González Prada, 'Discurso en el Teatro Olimpo', p. 72 (emphasis added).

of rebirth and renewal—'trasciende a juventud'—in a world emerging from 'milenios enteros de Teología y Metafísicas'.[54]

Trilce XIX, as well as a host of other poems in the collection, not only meets but triumphantly exceeds all González Prada's requirements, not least his demand that poetry come down from the clouds and 'solidificarse'. Eschewing the jingoistic tub-thumping and insular expressive nativism which characterized the work of contemporaries such as Santos Chocano, the self-proclaimed 'Cantor de América', and leaving definitively behind Vallejo's own early— though far less strident and mannered—forays into *Indigenismo* in the poems of 'Nostalgias imperiales' from *Los heraldos negros*, it nevertheless remains a consciously American poem, and it does so by dealing with a universal, broadly scientific theme in an idiom and a style which treat the poetic tradition with a liberating impertinence.[55]

Xavier Abril was, it seems, right to identify in *Trilce* XIX a more radical rewriting of a poem such as 'Los dados eternos', but was either unaware of or had no interest in exploring the full import and implications of his insight. That is what I have attempted to do here, and I shall conclude with a few brief remarks on how full understanding of the latter might help us situate the poem within Vallejo's work as a whole, and on the light which the many links with González Prada cast on his evolving *vanguardismo*. Juan Espejo Astrurrizaga's detailed if unverifiable chronology of the *Trilce* poems, the only one we possess, should put us on our guard against seeing in the collection an unfaltering aesthetic march towards the wilder shores of avant-gardism. Instead, it seems to show a Vallejo flitting back and forth unpredictably between the most rebarbative hermeticism and much more readily comprehensible forms of expression. Thus, at least according to Espejo, the nigh-on unfathomable Poem XXV (1919) and the barely less opaque Poem IV (1919) pre-date relatively straightforward pieces such as Poems XXVIII (1920), LXIII (1920), and LXI (late 1920 or early 1921).[56] He dates our poem as late as August–September 1920, but it is nevertheless both licit and illuminating to view it, at least in stylistic terms, as a transitional piece, a combination of the old and the new in which we can see the Vallejo of 'Los dados eternos' or 'Espergesia' sometimes boldly, sometimes more tentatively essaying new techniques or modes of articulation against a more traditional formal and linguistic backdrop. The first two lines, for instance, provide an excellent example of the unnerving capacity he developed to speak conversationally, even offhandedly, in an idiom whose meaning and tone the reader nevertheless struggles to grasp,

---

[54] 'Discurso en el Politeama', p. 89.

[55] Something similar might be said of other predominantly 'scientific' poems in *Trilce*, especially XXXVI but also V.

[56] See *César Vallejo: itinerario del hombre 1892–1923* (Lima: Editorial Juan Mejía Baca, 1965), pp. 112–14. These are by no means the only examples.

despite having the uncomfortable impression that both ought to be perfectly clear. Elsewhere, however, this refreshing if perplexing garrulous obliquity gives way to something more blunt and prosaic, as in much of lines 13-18. Grammatical, syntactic, and orthographic irregularities are still the exception rather than the rule, and they are not pressed to the extremes that we find in many other poems. Similarly, metrical deviations remain partially anchored by the still prevalent *silva* form. Yet, however problematic we may find them from an aesthetic point of view, it is precisely these expressive discrepancies, as well as the ubiquitous residue of a more conservative poetic language, that allow us to perceive both the intellectual and the expressive origins of the poem in the work of González Prada. If accepted, this claim might also serve as a partial corrective to those overarching literary-historical interpretations of Vallejo's œuvre determined to situate it within the broader (and primarily European) currents of modernism, and to make its author at least an honorary member of the international '1922 Club', along with Joyce, Eliot, Rilke, etc. Here chronology really does count, as does the simple fact that Vallejo could read neither English nor German and, prior to leaving for Paris in 1923, had insufficient French to broach most francophone poetry in the original language.[57] That many of the more extravagant linguistic innovations—the brutal solecisms and studied syntactic blundering, the archaisms, neologisms, and flagrant misspellings—modestly incorporated into *Trilce* XIX but lavishly deployed throughout much of the rest of the collection may be homespun rather than imported renders Vallejo's imaginative achievement if anything all the more remarkable.

CHRIST CHURCH, OXFORD   DOMINIC MORAN

[57] Clayton makes various comparisons between Vallejo's poetry and both Joyce's prose (particularly that of *Ulysses*) and Rilke's *Sonnets to Orpheus* (*Poetry in Pieces*, pp. 18–19, 87, 95–96, 118, 120), though (even if he could have read it) the former appeared in February 1922, when, according to Espejo Asturrizaga, all but two of the *Trilce* poems had been written (*Itinerario del hombre*, p. 114), and the latter was not published until 1923.

'DIE JUDEN SCHIESSEN!' TRANSLATIONS BY HERMANN ADLER AND WOLF BIERMANN OF YITZHAK KATZENELSON'S EPIC POEM OF THE WARSAW GHETTO

In 1996, in an article on 'the scandal of Jewish rage', Naomi Seidman compared the well-known French edition of Elie Wiesel's survivor testimony, *La Nuit*, with the Yiddish memoir from which it had emerged, suggesting that Wiesel had downplayed the expression of anger and desire for violent vengeance in the earlier text in favour of a haunted, internalized, death-ridden image of victimhood in the later version.[1] Seidman suggested that this was not simply a case of Wiesel's changing attitude to his own experience, but of deliberate distortion intended to make his text acceptable to a majority culture that felt uncomfortable about Jewish anger and defiance and preferred a Christ-like image of passive suffering that it had the cultural resources to deal with.

Rage is a 'scandal' that disrupts carefully constructed patterns of social harmony and the political interests that rely on them. It is offensive because it attacks the sensibilities of those whose self-image relies on a commitment to reconciliation, and it is unreasonable because it exposes the interests behind reasonableness itself. For all the decades of reconciliation work and the establishment of politically acceptable ways of talking about the Holocaust, there is a residue of violent but unfocused emotion that is excluded from the patterns of polite public memory work. This is of vital interest for exploring how translations of texts arising from the Holocaust mediate the language of rage and vengeance between cultural contexts in which it has a very different status and potential effect.

This article will consider two of the German translations of a Yiddish text from the Warsaw Ghetto Uprising, both of which confront the issue of a 'scandalous' rage and desire for violent vengeance that refuse to take their place in the scheme of reconciliation, dignified mourning, and working through of the past. I propose that taking translation seriously as an activity inevitably involving creation as well as communication and mediation can move us beyond the sometimes sterile debate about whether it is possible for victims' experiences to be 'understood' in a new language or cultural context; instead, we can ask questions about the position from which the victim is able to speak in translation, as well as about the function of the text in a new cultural and linguistic context.

Arno Lustiger has called Yitzhak Katzenelson's Yiddish poem *Dos lid*

[1] Naomi Seidman, 'Elie Wiesel and the Scandal of Jewish Rage', *Jewish Social Studies*, 3 (1996), 1–19.

funm oysgehargetn yidishn folk (*The Song of the Exterminated Jewish People*) 'das wichtigste und ergreifendste poetische Werk des Holocaust'.[2] In Israel, Katzenelson enjoys the status of a significant poetic spokesman for the Ghetto fighters, and his work has played a defining role in creating and preserving the image of the Jewish combatant and resistance fighter.[3] Katzenelson wrote the text in the internment camp at Vittel between October 1943 and January 1944 after escaping the destruction of the Warsaw Ghetto. As a well-known writer, he had been charged by his fellow Ghetto fighters with the task of bringing information out of the Ghetto. He had been provided with a forged Honduran passport and was interned at Vittel, where foreign citizens were detained awaiting prisoner exchanges. Katzenelson hid the poem and other texts before he was finally transported to Drancy and then Auschwitz in April 1944. The poem was first published in Paris in 1945.[4]

Katzenelson's poem is an epic narrative of the German occupation of Warsaw, the construction of the Ghetto, the 'treachery' (as Katzenelson saw it) of the Judenrat under Adam Czerniaków, the deportation of the Jews, and finally the Uprising of April and May 1943 and the destruction of the Ghetto. The story is narrated in rhyming quatrains, in fifteen parts of fifteen stanzas each; as the text proceeds to its catastrophic conclusion, the lines lengthen, giving the impression of a strict compositional principle coming under extreme tension from the pressure of the events described. Katzenelson's language is a virtuoso display, mixing high and low registers, lament, narrative, and political invective, and rising to moments of rhythmic intensity when describing both the worst atrocities and the Ghetto fighters' response.

The narrative is many-layered. On one level, it is concerned with the possibility of making art on behalf of a people about to be exterminated, using a language that is dying with them. It is also a demonstration of Jewish resistance to National Socialism, made for an audience (God, Jews outside the Nazi sphere of influence) whose interest cannot be taken for granted, as well as a defiant statement of Jewish cultural identity at the moment of crisis. The text's

---

[2] Arno Lustiger, *Zum Kampf auf Leben und Tod! Das Buch vom Widerstand der Juden, 1933–1945* (Cologne: Kiepenheuer & Witsch, 1994), p. 88.

[3] On Katzenelson's biography see Tsiporah Katzenelson-Nakhumov, *Yitzhak Katzenelson: sayn leben un shafn* (Buenos Aires: Tsentral-farband fun Poylishe Yidn in Argentine, 1948).

[4] The publication history of Katzenelson's text is complex, especially given the existence of two manuscripts, one of which was buried in Vittel and the other smuggled out; both manuscripts are now held by the Ghetto Fighters' House, Tel Aviv. Quotations in this article are from the following edition, available online at the National Yiddish Book Center, Amherst, MA (http://www.yiddishbookcenter.org): Yitzhak Katzenelson, *dos lid funm oysgehargetn yidishn folk* (New York: Ikuf, 1963). References are given in parentheses as Katzenelson, by stanza (e.g. III. 6=part III, stanza 6) and page numbers. I have transliterated Katzenelson's text using the YIVO standard transliteration system; although this is in no sense a neutral system, being a compromise with the phonetic values of English, it does provide a useful contrast with the German-inflected transliterations provided by the translators.

linguistic identity is vital: Katzenelson wrote in both Hebrew and Yiddish, but chose Yiddish for this great, final statement, as the everyday language of Eastern European Jewry, and thus as a statement of identity. The attitude of the text towards the languages spoken by Jews is clear: Jewish figures who speak Polish, or who cannot speak Yiddish properly, are the informers, Ghetto policemen, and other traitors, who are not true Jews. Katzenelson calls them 'meshumodim un erev meshumodim' (converts and those on the eve of conversion), whose Star of David on their uniform caps looks to him like a swastika (Katzenelson III. 6, p. 28).

The opening of the poem makes a connection with the roots of Jewish poetry in the psalms, referring to David and his harp (as well as cheekily referencing the characteristic invocation of the Muses at the beginning of classical Greek epics such as Homer's *Odyssey*):

> 'zing! nem dayn harf in hant, hoyl, oysgehoylt un gring,
> oyf zayne shtrunes din warf dayne finger shver,
> vi hertser, vi tseveytikte, dos lid dos letste zing,
> zing fun di letste yidn oyf eyropes erd.'
>
> vi ken ikh zingen? vi ken ikh efenen mayn moyl
> az ikh bin geblibn eyner nor aleyn —
> mayn vayb un mayne eyfelekh di tsvey — a groyl!
> mikh groylt a groyl... me veynt! ikh her vayt a geveyn.
> (Katzenelson I. 1–2, p. 19)

Katzenelson turns the words of Psalm 149 around: instead of singing the Lord a new song, this is the last song, shouted at the heavens on behalf of his people to see if God is still there, and bringing to a catastrophic end the era of Jewish creativity that began with the psalms. The whole text is rich in interpretative possibilities,[5] but my interest here is in how the German translations respond to it. Where the original is about the possibilities of speech—and specifically art—in a situation where the Yiddish-language culture in which this speech was embedded and that had made it possible is on the point of extinction, the translations are about the meaning of this kind of speech in a context where the Yiddish-speaking world has been destroyed. The emphasis is on the 'how' of 'How can I sing?'.

The first part of the poem ends with the poem's speaker gathering his dead and dying people around him and choosing to represent them through his song in a final, communal act of defiance and self-identification. So any translation—not just one into German—needs to address the question of the meaning of this kind of speech *after* the catastrophe rather than during it, as

---

[5] See e.g. Susan Gubar, 'The Long and the Short of Holocaust Verse', *New Literary History*, 35 (2004), 443–68; Alvin H. Rosenfeld, 'The Jewish Writer at the End of Time', in *Identität und Gedächtnis in der deutschen Literatur nach 1945*, ed. by Dieter Lamping (Berlin: Schmidt, 2003), pp. 17–28.

well as the text's refusal to adopt a position of passive victimhood that is available for emotional identification. The translator is also faced with the issue of rendering a voice that speaks so clearly on behalf of a particular linguistic culture and refuses assimilation into what it identifies as non-Jewish languages.

The German translation brings with it additional problems, however. Since the poem's speaker is able to sing only when he overcomes his isolation and individualism and speaks with the voice of his people, a translation faces the problem of producing a text that speaks against the culture in whose very language it now speaks. Can one translate it into the language of the perpetrators without falsifying the subject position of the victim? Or without putting the text to use in supporting either identification with the victims or reconciliation between victims and perpetrators? These are both positions that Katzenelson would have rejected, since both occur at the cost of the victims. How does one deal with the specific similarities and differences between the languages in a text that insists on the implacable otherness of everything German? Is it possible to preserve that sense of otherness, or do the needs of German-language discourse about the Holocaust simply assimilate the subject position of the victim into a self-absorbed ethics of self-criticism? A translation might therefore entail abandoning the expression of rage and pain for its own sake, defusing it by inserting it into a meaningful narrative of mourning and 'working through' the past, where it can do constructive and positive work instead of being unreasonable and embarrassing.

The Translations

Katzenelson's poem has received little attention in English,[6] but in Germany, thanks to the commitment of the Evangelisches Bildungswerk, the historian Arno Lustiger, and the singer-songwriter Wolf Biermann, from the 1990s it achieved popular and political acknowledgement, including a performance by Biermann in the Bundestag on Holocaust Remembrance Day in 2005. Biermann's version of the poem, which is designed for performance, is worth discussing in its own right, but Katzenelson's text has in fact been translated into German on two other occasions, and Biermann's is situated in a network of translations that refer to each other as well as to the original text, and all of which make a case for the significance of the translation of this particular work into German.

The first translation was published by Hermann Adler in 1951, with a new edition in 1992 to mark the fiftieth anniversary of the Wannsee conference, following a reading organized by the Evangelisches Bildungswerk in Berlin

---

[6] See Yitzhak Katzenelson, *The Song of the Murdered Jewish People*, trans. by Noah Rosenbloom (Israel: Ghetto Fighters' House, 1980).

on 9 November 1990.[7] In response to this republication, Arno Lustiger made a romanized transcription of the Yiddish text, which formed the basis of Biermann's performing version.[8] Following this, and in response to a critical article by Hubert Winkels in *Die Zeit* in 1994,[9] the translator of Katzenelson's Vittel diary, Helmut Homfeld, published privately what he considered to be a more faithful translation.[10] The translators all describe themselves as motivated by factors arising from their biographies—the biographical material helps to justify making this text accessible to a German public—and both versions from the 1990s are presented as responses to earlier translations.

According to Hermann Adler's own account, he was commissioned to translate Katzenelson's work into German in 1949 by the Israeli Minister of Education (and future President) Zalman Shazar.[11] Adler, himself a survivor of the Warsaw Ghetto, was from an assimilated Jewish background in Nuremberg, so his cultural co-ordinates were German, and his concerns were with the possibility of salvaging a form of German Jewish culture after the Holocaust, as well as with questions of Christian–Jewish coexistence, none of which were of any interest for Katzenelson. Having known Katzenelson in Warsaw, and being himself the author of several volumes of German poetry arising from his experiences, it is likely that Adler was judged a useful mediator between victims and perpetrators. Certainly, Adler took this role seriously, positioning himself as mediator between Christians and Jews, Yiddish and German, and different culturally conditioned conceptions of aesthetic quality.

Biermann, whose Jewish Communist father had been murdered in Auschwitz, identifies his version of the text as a personal project to refute the view that Jews went passively to their deaths, 'die ganze Kälber-selber-Schuld-Arie', as he calls it, responding to Katzenelson's sarcastic dismissal of the same attitude: 'Aza a folk! vos hot gelosn zikh vi kelber oysshekhtn, aza a folk!' (Biermann, p. 23; Katzenelson xiv. 5, p. 72). He writes that the idea arose from discussions with Lustiger, who showed him the transliteration that he had made and who saw the publication as part of a long-term project documenting Jewish resistance to National Socialism. The edition presents Biermann as equal author of a text to put alongside Katzenelson's poem; this

---

[7] Jizchak Katzenelson, *Dos lid funm ojsgehargetn jidischn folk/Das Lied vom letzten Juden*, ed. by Manfred Richter, trans. by Hermann Adler (Berlin: Hentrich, 1992) (henceforth Adler 1992).

[8] Itzhak Katzenelson and Wolf Biermann, *Dos lied vunem ojsgehargetn jidischn volk/Großer Gesang vom ausgerotteten jüdischen Volk* (Cologne: Kiepenheuer & Witsch, 1994) (henceforth Biermann).

[9] Hubert Winkels, 'Rettung ins Wort', *Die Zeit*, 12 February 1994, pp. 11–12.

[10] Jizchak Katzenelson, *Das Lied vom ausgemordeten jüdischen Volk*, trans. by Helmut Homfeld (Rendsburg, Vierzonstr. 5: H. Homfeld, 1996); see also Jizchak Katzenelson, *Oh, Mein Volk! Mein Volk . . .: Aufzeichnungen aus dem Internierungslager Vittel*, ed. and trans. by Helmut Homfeld (Berlin: OMNIS, 1999).

[11] Hermann Adler, 'Zur Entstehung der Katzenelson-Nachdichtung', in *Gesänge aus der Stadt des Todes: Todeslagergedichte aus dem Wilnaer Ghetto 1941/42* (Berlin: Hentrich, 1994), p. 90.

applies whether Katzenelson's text is present in the edition or not. The hardback edition from 1994 referred to here presents Biermann's text alongside Lustiger's transliteration and a facsimile of one of Katzenelson's manuscripts, while a parallel edition in paperback simply provides Biermann's text, meaning that Katzenelson is given as the author of a text that does not appear in the book. Both editions provide Biermann's accompanying essays.

By contrast, Adler is presented as 'Nachdichter' for the poem, in other words in a dependent rather than equal relationship with Katzenelson, despite the freedom implied by the term. The first edition, which appeared in Zurich in 1951, did not feature the original text in parallel, but the 1992 edition comprises the original, a romanized transliteration by Claudia Bloß (making the text legible by a German-speaker), and Adler's translation. With three texts set side by side on the page, the poem is not easy to read as a narrative, and attention is thrown onto the relationship between them: the inclusion of the original text in Hebrew letters is a useful reminder of cultural difference and ensures that the German reader is aware that the transliteration is a compromise made for his or her sake.

Homfeld claims to speak on behalf of the author, with authority gained from his translation and editing of Katzenelson's Vittel diary: the aim of his 'wörtliche Übersetzung' is to convey 'wie denn nun Katzenelson wirklich formuliert und mithin gedacht hat'.[12] His translation is described as non-literary, aiming instead to grasp the essence of Katzenelson's thought, which is seen to be something separate from his style: 'Leider geht bei einer wörtlichen Übersetzung der "Klang" des Jiddischen weitgehend verloren. Auch das Versmaß und der Reim lassen sich kaum übertragen.' Thus the cultural specificity of the text, which is part of its meaning, is sacrificed in the name of a literal rendering of its content. One can see this as a useful task as a complement to the two other translations; however, since both texts now come with a romanized transcription of Katzenelson's Yiddish, meaning that the German-speaking reader is able to make comparisons between them, the word-for-word translation may be superfluous.

The translations by Adler and Biermann/Lustiger were both widely read and performed in public, and they have a particular linguistic interest. In their very different ways, these two translations work with aesthetic approaches that seek disruptive interventions in the contexts of their production: they intervene against a tendency to overlay Holocaust remembrance with a sonorous rhetoric of reconciliation or elegiac beauty of language, doing this through particular, and very different, linguistic strategies. They are stylized and rhetorical, working against sentimentality and identification with the victims,

---

[12] Homfeld, 'Einleitung' [n.p.]. Homfeld here cites correspondence with the publisher Hentrich; Homfeld eventually published the translation himself, however.

looking for ways of singing an impossible song rather than resorting to a consensual realism.

Adler's text presents a view of the German language as having been subject to destructive forces itself, and refuses any kind of beauty, even where the original offers it; it also insists on the fundamental difference between Yiddish and German, suggesting that reconciliation is possible only through acknowledgement of radical otherness. Biermann's text tries to shake up established ways of talking about violence and victimhood, confronting readers with a victim with whom identification is not possible: it is not polite or reasonable, and makes no offer of reconciliation to the German reader, instead exaggerating the original's violence and cynicism. Their strategies are supported by an implied relationship with the Yiddish original and with a particular understanding of the relationship of the language to German, reflecting the translators' political intentions.

Questions can certainly be raised about whether these strategies respect the cultural integrity of the original or whether it is assimilated to the needs of the new German context, which is a particularly sensitive issue in this case. Editions with a romanized transliteration of the Yiddish in parallel raise questions about the politics of transliteration, since there is no neutral transliteration system: they all have both to negotiate between the various different regional pronunciations of the language and to make particular compromises with the writing system of another language.

Producing a transliteration for a German-speaking readership can give the impression that Yiddish is little more than a dialect of German (or even a substandard 'Judenjargon'), understandable and accessible with little effort: the two translations under scrutiny here approach this political problem in very different ways.

The Relationship of German and Yiddish in the Paratexts

The translators' view of the relationship of Yiddish to German can give us an insight into their strategies, since they are both concerned very concretely with making German work as a medium for speech about the Warsaw Ghetto, as well as showing where it cannot work as a means of conveying the experiences of Yiddish-speaking victims. Hermann Adler's 1951 introduction to the text presents it as a force for reconciliation. A few statements seem to indicate that he, or those who commissioned the translation, is willing to speak on behalf of Katzenelson in the name of contemporary political realities:

Vielleicht wird in dieser deutschsprachigen Übersetzung aber doch das letzte Stammeln eines Sterbenden vernehmbar und sein letztes Warnen so, daß es der tote Dichter noch vermag, auch in der Sprache derer zu mahnen, die er nicht mehr hat vergeben können, und wo aus des Dichters letztem Stammeln Anklagen gellen, sind es nicht Anklagen eines Hassenden, sondern Anklagen eines Gefolterten, der nur deshalb so heftig hat anklagen können, weil er um Liebe und Barmherzigkeit wußte.

Als Warnung diene seine Dichtung, und seine Warnung wirke versöhnend.[13]

This reads as an attempt to defuse the anger of the text for a public sphere in which reconciliation and *Wiedergutmachung* are being discussed: it does not want to rock the boat. The phrase 'in der Sprache derer [. . .], die er nicht mehr hat vergeben können' is particularly unfortunate. Adler connects Katzenelson's vision of apocalyptic conflagration with the threat of nuclear war, allowing his German readers to position themselves as potential victims too:

Wüchse nämlich der Haß weiter, heute, da die Menschheit in ihrer Gesamtheit vor der Möglichkeit steht, ausgerottet zu werden, dann könnte geschehen, was der entsetzte Dichter prophetisch ausruft: Aufsteigen wird die Erdenflamme, um den Himmel zu verbrennen, und verbrennen wird des Himmels Flamme unsre Erd. (Adler 1951, p. 7)

Adler had worked for Jewish-Christian reconciliation in the immediate postwar years, and his own poetry was marked by attempts to reconcile images from the two traditions, and to make Jewish experiences of suffering understandable in Christian terms, while at the same time emphasizing the Jewishness of Jesus: this perhaps explains his strategy in the translation of introducing comparisons of the suffering of Jewish children in the Ghetto to the suffering of Christ.

However, there is more to this translation than Adler's attempt to make it 'salonfähig'. The word 'stammeln' is the key here, giving us an indication of Adler's view of the text, and consequently of his translation strategy. Other critics, such as Alvin Rosenfeld, have also taken this view, stating that the text 'manifests a helplessness of poetic means' and shows 'language in a state of breathless exhaustion'.[14] Discussing the work in terms of 'stammeln' rather than 'singing', which is the claim it makes for itself, downplays the articulacy and linguistic sophistication of the text, but gives us an indication of Adler's translation programme:

Die yiddische und die deutsche Sprache sind verwandt, und dennoch ist es, beispielsweise, für das yiddische Wort schmerzvollen Humors, verzweifelter Ironie, banger Zärtlichkeit, befreienden Spottes, anklagender Verwünschung, gottnaher Gottesleugnung, fordernder oder verzichtender Gläubigkeit nur scheinbar möglich, das entsprechende deutsche Wort zu finden; niemand kann den Ton des yiddischen Wortes in gleicher Weise deutsch erklingen lassen, am allerwenigsten durch wörtliche Übersetzung. In großer Erregung gesprochen, klingt die deutsche Sprache abgehackt, gleichsam staccato, die yiddische hingegen steigert sich zu einem atemlosen Legato. (Adler 1951, p. 7)

[13] Jizchak Katzenelson, *Das Lied vom letzten Juden*, trans. by Hermann Adler (Zurich: Oprecht, 1951), p. 7 (henceforth Adler 1951).
[14] Rosenfeld, 'The Jewish Writer at the End of Time', p. 20.

What is important here is not whether this assessment of the difference between the languages makes sense, but the way in which Adler constructs that difference in order to stress the distance between them. He clearly does not wish his translation to echo German religious language, or poetry, or political rhetoric, and denies it the resources that Katzenelson drew on in his poem. His comments are also designed to establish the status of Yiddish as a language independent of German, rather than as a substandard or dialect variant, and to justify his own translation practice by stating that a direct translation of words with shared roots or similar grammatical structures will somehow miss the essence of the text, which cannot be accessed through German.

It is not a strategy that tries to reproduce a similar effect in translation, but one that deliberately sets out to produce a different effect, one that is more appropriate to the context. Confronting the reader with harsh, staccato German works against any desire to overlay the experience with false elegiac beauty. It is an intervention against certain stylistic tendencies in the literature of the 1950s and against a tendency to seek reconciliation in aesthetic harmony. It is not a 'smooth' translation that ingratiates itself with the reader. The broken syntax means that it is at times hard to follow the narrative (often frustratingly so): the reader is forced to focus on interpretation rather than story, and is denied easy identification with the victims. Whatever the problems with the translation, there is intrinsic interest in a text that makes an offer of reconciliation while pursuing strategies that make it difficult.

Biermann and Arno Lustiger try hard to disguise their disapproval of Adler's work, but it is clear that an improved translation is part of what motivated them to create their own version. Biermann writes thus about Adler's version, damning with faint praise:

> Zur deutschen Übersetzung, die es schon gab, will ich und darf ich kein Wort sagen. In der sogenannten Kunst gibt es wohl Haß und Liebe, es gibt Kunsturteile und Geschmacksurteile, es gibt wechselnde Moden, denen keiner ganz entgeht — aber es gibt keine nettgemeinten Artigkeiten. Es war ohne allen Zweifel ein großer Verdienst von Hermann Adler in Basel, daß er Katzenelsons Poem ins Deutsche brachte. Trotzdem wird Arno Lustiger gewußt haben, warum er mich in dieses Werk von Katzenelson reinzog, und das mag genügen. (Biermann, p. 209)

On his reasons for producing the new version, Lustiger writes:

> Ich kannte sehr wohl eine ältere deutsche Übersetzung, sie stammt von Hermann Adler und erschien kurz nach dem Krieg. Weil ich aber das jiddische Original kenne, war ich nicht glücklich mit dieser deutschen Version. Ich wollte also deutsche Verse, die der poetischen Kraft des jiddischen Originals entsprechen. Und so bat ich meinen Freund Wolf Biermann, sich an Katzenelsons Versen zu versuchen. Er tat mir den Gefallen. Aber dann ließ ihn dieses Werk nicht mehr los. So verführte ich — ohne es darauf anzulegen — den Dichter und Sänger, das gesamte Poem von Jitzchak Katzenelson in

ein Deutsch zu bringen, das stark und lebendig genug ist, um junge Menschen in diesem Land zu erreichen und womöglich zu erschüttern.[15]

It is notable here that Lustiger sees no difficulty in finding an appropriate German style for this text: there is no agonizing here about the issue of *Opfer- und Tätersprache*, and no perceived need to stress the separateness of the languages.

Biermann continues in this vein:

Ich habe die herzzerreißenden jiddischen Verse nun in meine kopfzerbrechliche deutsche Sprache gebracht. Der Umstand, daß dieses Gedicht der Opfer in die Sprache der Täter transportiert werden muß, bekümmert mich dabei gar nicht. Mein Deutsch ist das von Hölderlin und Büchner und Heine und Rosa Luxemburg, es ist meine Muttersprache von Emma Biermann, es ist unsere Vatersprache von Bertolt Brecht und kein Schweinefraß, zusammengemanscht aus Abfällen von Bismarck, Hitler, Honecker, Blödel-Otto, Leni Riefenstahl, Mielke und Stolpe. (Biermann, p. 9)

This is a refreshingly practical dismissal of a philosophical tradition that questions the possibility of talking about the Holocaust in German, and that critiques the appropriation of the subject position of the victim in the language of the perpetrators: here, there is a strong, expressive tradition of literary-political German to set against a tradition of linguistic corruption. This is a writer making space for himself to work and locating a set of literary resources for the job in hand: language is not in itself a barrier to understanding.

The translation difficulties that Biermann discusses are less comprehensive than those identified by Adler. Biermann suggests that problems arise from the similarity of the lexical roots, mentioning a few cases of 'false friends' (Biermann, pp. 197–212). Whereas Adler had stressed separateness, an entirely different mode of expression and world-view—perhaps in order to play up the necessity of the task of reconciliation by forcing his German reader to acknowledge the legitimacy of the otherness of the text—Biermann suggests that closeness can lead to problems of understanding, which can be overcome with a little awareness and effort. The politics of the relationship between German and Yiddish have been transformed.

In his initial 1951 publication Adler had not included the Yiddish text, meaning that it is hidden and inaccessible to the German reader. This is of a piece with Adler's emphasis on difference: the translation is not presented as a dialogue with the original text, and the German reader is not encouraged to think that the original is accessible. By contrast, Lustiger has produced a transliteration that represents a compromise between a particular high-status Yiddish pronunciation ('Litvish Yiddish') and the phonetic values of

---

[15] Arno Lustiger, 'Anmerkungen zu Katzenelsons Werk und zur phonetischen Transkription', in Biermann, pp. 229–32 (p. 229).

the German writing system. Transliteration is always a political issue, and this reading version makes an offer to the German reader in line with Biermann's comments, namely that understanding is possible with a little sympathetic effort: 'das von mir angewandte Transkriptionssystem [wird] dem deutschen Leser ermöglichen, den jiddischen Text phonetisch korrekt zu lesen und ihn einigermaßen zu verstehen'.[16]

To illustrate how far this departs from Katzenelson's own conception of the linguistic situation, instances can be adduced from the text in which attention is drawn to linguistic difference. The original poem makes a stark distinction between Polish- and Yiddish-speakers that, while certainly a simplification of the multilingual reality of the Ghetto, reflects a rejection of compromise and assimilation. Polish is associated with situations of communication with the occupying authorities, and is the language of the Judenrat and of Jewish traitors. The German language is barely mentioned throughout, preparing for the moment towards the end when the Uprising breaks out, and Katzenelson puts the words 'die Juden schießen' in the mouths of individual Germans before they are killed: the words are transliterated into the text's Hebrew script, but clearly retain their character as German: יודען (yuden) instead of ייִדן (yidn). The German words are repeated throughout the staging of the final battle, finally coming to characterize the shocked and fearful response of the whole nation to the Uprising: 's'iz a ruf gevezn fun a merder-folk, fun akhtsik milion' (Katzenelson XIV. 1, p. 71).

This is the opposite process to the sympathetic opening suggested by Lustiger's German transliteration, suggesting that the assimilation of the desperate words of a dying German into the Hebrew characters is in itself an act of vengeance. For once, the victims are able to make meaning on their own terms. This is the key moment in the text, when the victims become visible on their own terms to the world beyond. It reverses the power imbalance represented by the rendering of Yiddish through the German writing system and displays German words defined and captured in the structures of meaning created by the Jewish resisters. It is also a response to a moment earlier in the text where the speaker recalls being subject to the gaze of a German that defines the relationship between victim and perpetrator. For Katzenelson, it is the gaze of the perpetrator that defines the victim and is the origin of violence:

du host gezen vi der oysvurf hot gekukt [. . .]
Khane, er hat dokh undz, undz alemen derharget dokh in yenem groylikhen moment
i mikh, i dikh, di kinder undzere dos gantse folk dos yidishe in goyishn in land
er hot farmostn mit a blik a shtolenem zikh un hot adurkhgefirt un hot farlendt!
(Katzenelson X. 4–5, p. 56)

The translations have to deal with the issue of the victimizing German gaze

[16] Ibid., p. 232.

while rendering the victim's perspective in the same language. Both address—
or perhaps avoid—this issue by shifting the perspective to the character of
the perpetrator, interpreted in contrasting ways. Adler stresses sadism, hate,
and 'Verrohung', and, by inserting references to Caesar and to Christ's last
words, interprets the gaze in terms of the killing of Christ, shifting away from
Katzenelson's speaker's voice (I discuss Adler's religious programme below):

> Wie loderte sein Haß, wie war sein Blick verroht [. . .]
> Uns alle hat sein Schuß getroffen. Keiner, Chane, lebt seit jener Nacht.
> Tot liegen wir. Tot sind die Kinder. Jeder Jude starb mit uns: im Christenland.
> Des Mörders Augen glänzten blau. Er kam, sah, tötete — Vollbracht! Es ist vollbracht!
> (Adler 1992, pp. 107–08)

Biermann emphasizes the gaze, strengthens the language of anti-Semitism,
and shifts the perspective to the voice of the perpetrator, ironizing characteristic post-war defence strategies:

> Hast gesehn, wie dieser Abschaum glotzt und stutzt? [. . .]
> Ich sage dir: Der hat uns, Chanele, im Grunde alle umgebracht
> Ermordet hat er uns und grad in diesem schrecklichen Moment
> Mich hat er umgelegt mit diesem Schuß, dich, unsere Kinderchen
> Das ganze Volk der Juden hier in diesem Land der Judenhasserei
> Er hat uns abgeschätzt mit einem Blick stahlhart, hat funktioniert
> Und hat wahrscheinlich nichts als seine Pflicht getan, ganz konsequent
> (Biermann, p. 109)

Where Katzenelson's text is about self-assertion against the victimizing gaze,
the translations need to work from within the perpetrator culture and to
divide the gaze against itself.

For Katzenelson, the Ghetto fighters' struggle is a clash of the Jewish with
the non-Jewish world, absolute separateness is emphasized, and the Germans
are simply the worst manifestation of a general hostility to the Jews. The text
concludes with a rejection of any future idea of reconciliation: no Jew will in
future sacrifice anything to improve the world for others. This is the problem
that post-war German translators have to deal with: if the sacrifice enacted in
this text now serves the cause of reconciliation, or if its readers are given the
opportunity to identify with the victims rather than seeing themselves in the
position of the 'merder-folk', then its message has been falsified. In the light
of this discussion, therefore, I will look at two aspects of the translations: the
treatment of the religious language, and the staging of the acts of violence
described in the text.

Religious Language

Both translations adopt particular positions on the text's religious language.
Where Adler introduces Christian imagery and suggests a potential for recon-

ciliation that Katzenelson would have rejected, Biermann seems to confuse Katzenelson's bitterness and 'revolt against God' with an outright rejection of religion. To illustrate this, I will look at a passage in which Katzenelson nostalgically describes the life of Jewish Warsaw before the occupation:

varshe! di alt-yidishe, di fule vi a shul yom-kiper, vi a mark oyf a yarid,
yidn varshever, yidn handlndike oyfn mark, yidn davnendike in di shul
azoy umetik un azoy freylikh — o, parnosse-zukhndiker un gotzukhndiker yid!
varshe di farmoyerte arum, di opgeshlossene — iz geven mit dir ersht ful!
[...]
di ershte umtsubrengen sen' gevezn kinder, yessoymimlekh farlosene, es heyst
dos beste oyf der velt, dos sheynste vos di erd, di finstere farmogt!
o, fun die elntste yessoymimlekh in kinderheymen volt gevoksn undz a treyst,
fun di umetikste, shtume penimlekh, di khoyshekhdike, volt getogt undz, volt getogt!
(Katzenelson VI. 2 and VI. 4, pp. 39–40)

Adler has this:

Mein Warschau, Judenstadt, voll warst du wie die Häuser Gottes am Versöhnungsfest,
Voll wie ein Markt. Wo seid ihr, Juden Warschaus, Händler, Betende im Gotteshaus,
Getroffene und dennoch Hoffende? Brotsuchende. Gottsuchende. Der Rest
Vom Rest entschwand. O Stadt, umlauerte, verschlossene — du speist dein Leben aus!
[...]
Am Anfang fielen die Verwaisten, längst Verlassenen. Sie lebten freudenlos.
Sie starben sehnsuchtsvoll. Gott weiß: sie waren edle Sprossen einer edlen Saat.
Als Schwacher mit den Schwachen litt, vor Gott, der künftige Erlöser. Seelengroß,
Erniedrigt nur. Wer hofft noch auf Erlösungstaten? Nur die Untat gilt als Tat.
(Adler 1992, p. 67)

Here, the phrases 'Getroffene und dennoch Hoffende' and 'der künftige Erlöser' introduce ideas of suffering and redemption not in the original, which simply describes a mixture of emotions: a description of the religious and political variety of the Jewish population of Warsaw becomes an image of a people seeking redemption. This is taken up in the next stanza cited here, which inserts a reference to Christ suffering alongside the poor and weak.

It is tempting to see in this a falsification of Katzenelson's text for the purpose of making it accessible to a Christian readership, but there is more to it than this. Part of Adler's literary project was to re-emphasize the significance of the Jewishness of Jesus, to persuade the German churches to make this awareness part of their theological apparatus and to use it in a self-critical awareness of their role during the Nazi period.[17] Adler's version offers his Christian readers a route to understanding, while simultaneously making clear the gulf between their world and that of the text and refusing

---

[17] See e.g. Friedrich Heer, *Gottes erste Liebe: Die Juden im Spannungsfeld der Geschichte* (Frankfurt a.M.: Ullstein, 1986).

them linguistic resources to deal with the events described in a familiar or comforting way. The final lines of part VI will illustrate this:

> zey zen' geven di ershte, di genumene tsum toyt, di ershte oyf der fur,
> men het gevorfn in di vegener di groyse zey, vi hoyfns mist, vi mist —
> un avekgefirt zey, oysgeharget zey, farnikht zey, s'iz keyn shpur
> fun zey, fun mayne beste nit geblibn mer! okh vey iz mir un vind iz mir, un vist!
> (Katzenelson VI. 15, p. 42)

> Am Anfang fielen die Verwaisten. Flammen warteten auf sie. Hoch stieg der Rauch.
> Die Mörder warfen sie auf Wagen. Unrat wird so fortgefahren. Gassenkot.
> Dann rief der Mord: Zum Freudenfeste! Und? Verwaiste waren Opfer. Nicht ein Hauch
> Von ihnen blieb. Mit jedem starb ein Nazarener. Wehe uns, wer herrscht? Der Tod.
> (Adler 1992, p. 73)

While one might baulk at the bathos in the personification of Death and the *Totentanz* reference here, Adler's refusal to imitate the very powerful rhythmic lament in Katzenelson's text is telling. The translation refuses the German reader permission to lament the dead with the author, or even to join in the expression of emotion in the same way; the lament is a public, communal expression of emotion from which the perpetrators are excluded. Instead, they are confronted with a reversal of the Christ-killer calumny against the Jews, for here it is the goyim who have killed Christ in these children. The relationship of the translation to the original suggests that it is the perpetrators' business alone to be concerned with this; for Katzenelson and the people his text speaks to, it is irrelevant. Biermann's version, by contrast, joins his voice to Katzenelson's, stressing the closeness of the word roots, which even permit imitation of the alliteration: 'Weh ist mir, wund bin ich und verwüstet bis ins Mark' (Biermann, p. 83).

Biermann takes a very different attitude towards the text's religious language, introducing elements of critique where Katzenelson simply celebrates Jewish cultural diversity:

> Ach Warschau, Stadt der Juden, ein Gewimmel war das einstmals, Jom Kippur
> Ein endloses Versöhnungsfest mit Beten, Streiten, Handeln in der Synagog
> So traurigfroh war alles, einer suchte Geld, ein andrer Jude suchte nur
> Nur Gott und suchte Wahrheit, wenn er sich was in die Tasche log.
> [...]
> Zuerst warn Kinder dran mit Sterben. Waisenkinderchen, verlaßne Brut
> Sie warn das Liebste, Schönste, was die finstre Erde je gebar. Aus ihrem Angesicht
> Aus diesen Waisenkinderchen hätte uns erwachsen können Lebensmut
> Aus diesen traurigdüsteren Gesichtchen hätte uns gestrahlt ein Morgenlicht.
> (Biermann p. 79)

Note here that Biermann has brought together the worlds of market and synagogue, which are separate in the original, and has introduced a new note of irony. Biermann's version could be seen as working in the service of a liberal-enlightened polemic against National Socialism, which might entail a critical stance towards religion in general, whereas Katzenelson stresses the unity of a specifically Eastern European Jewish culture that encompasses variety and contradiction, and has little to learn from a liberal critique.

The Staging of Violence

Biermann's text is the version that deals most specifically with the issue of the desire for violent retribution and the inappropriate expression of that desire in the context in which the translation intervenes. Biermann works with a technique of aesthetic excess in rendering the descriptions of violence in the text, showing that the depiction of suffering and retribution has a different kind of significance in the new translation context. Biermann locates in Katzenelson's text the idea of the staging of the revolt for the benefit of external observers, emphasizes it, and puts it to a new use.

The text opens with the poet's demand to himself to sing the last song on behalf of his people in a challenge to God to show himself. On one level, the poem is structured as a drama staged for external observers—specifically God and the Jewish community abroad who may gain access to the smuggled text—and within the text itself, the German occupiers and their helpers. Towards the end, Katzenelson closes the circle, stating that at least their actions have been visible, whether or not anyone was there to see them:

> der geto brent, er brent oyf zayne moyern un zayne letste yidn, s'fayer hesht un hesht,
> der himl iz geven baloykhtn un oyb s'iz do dort ver, hot tsugekukt zikh un gezen
>   di end.
> (Katzenelson XIV. 15, p. 74)

Biermann's version of this stanza expands the theatrical metaphor, emphasizing the idea of purposeful staging and expressing the certainty that somebody is watching, which Katzenelson's original does not:

> Die Mauern brennen restlos aus, mit ihnen auch der kleine Judenrest
> Das Feuer wütet und beleuchtet schön die Szenerie. Der höh're Zweck
> Ist klar: Das Ghetto brennt so hell, damit er, der da in der Loge glotzt
> Den letzten Akt von oben sehen kann. Das war das End vom Lied.
> (Biermann, p. 155)

This moment is a key to understanding Biermann's strategy: this text is for an existing German audience, and the display of violence and resistance has a present function beyond simple commemoration.

The change in emphasis has to do with the new audience and their expectations: where Katzenelson wrote for a potential Yiddish-speaking audience that was rapidly being exterminated, Biermann is writing for the descendants of the perpetrators. He is not writing in a situation in which knowledge about the Holocaust needs to be gradually established, but is trying to shake up ritualistic forms of remembrance: 'der kleine Judenrest' is a linguistic provocation of a kind uncharacteristic of Katzenelson's style, a brutally impersonal compound that throws a stark light onto the observer's indifference to mass murder. Biermann also confronts German audiences with a victim who refuses to be a victim, who cannot be identified with, and whose text does not conform to the expectations of the Holocaust testimony.

Biermann's language is a performance of violent spectacle. It is not directed against the coherence of German syntax, as Adler's is, but instead takes a scandalous pleasure in its own virtuosity, even when describing the most appalling events. This example is taken from the most upsetting sequence in the text, in which a rabbi and a shammes are hounded by a group of soldiers before the synagogue is burnt down. One of the soldiers theatrically humiliates the pair in various ways, in a grotesque parody of 'teaching them a lesson'. In this stanza, which has a subtext of sexual violence, he has tried to force the shammes to spit into the rabbi's mouth:

'kuk, kuk zikh ayn un lern oys zikh, shmutsiker du yid, kuk vi azoy men shpayt —
un s'hot der daytsh in ofenem in moyl in rov arayngekhraket: 'shling's arop!'
der rov er hot's aropgeshlungen un s'vendt der daytsh tsum shames zikh un tayt,
tayt oyfn rov: 'du zest, er folgt!' der shames hot gekhapt zikh farn kop.
(Katzenelson VIII. 11, p. 49)

'Nun schau, du Saujud, dreckiger, schau zu und lern mal, wie man richtig spuckt!'
Der Deutsche rotzt dem Rabbi in den Rachen und schreit: 'Schluck! Und mogel nicht'
Der Rabbi würgt die Rotze runter, und der Deutsche sagt zum Schammes: 'Guck
Wie prima der gehorchen kann!' Der Schammes aber schlägt die Hände vors Gesicht
(Biermann, p. 95)

Where the shammes refuses to watch, we are forced to—but what are we watching? Ultimately, we are watching a linguistic performance demonstrating the theatricality of violence and pleasure in its performance. Katzenelson's language is also striking here, but he uses the syntactical resources of Yiddish to focus on the victim, the movement of the language mirroring the movement of the act of violence: 'un s'hot der daytsh in ofenem in moyl in rov arayngekhraket.' Biermann's alliteration emphasizes the action rather than the victim, making us take the place of the aggressor, or at least not permitting us to identify with the victim. By contrast, Adler's version plays down this moment: 'Dem Rabbi speit der Söldner in den Mund' (Adler 1992, p. 91).

The text's strategy of excess—drawing attention to the language in a way beyond what would be needed to describe the situation—prepares the way for the outburst of violence at the text's close. Katzenelson describes with satisfaction the deaths of ambushed Germans, giving the killing meaning in terms of rescuing the honour of his people even during its destruction:

> der lezter yid — koym leygt avek er a rotseyakh ratevet zayn folk!
> man ken a folk an oysgehargetn shoyn rateven.
> (Katzenelson XIII. 12, p. 70)

The meaning of the description of these killings in German is different, and the translators are faced with the choice of how to present Katzenelson's contempt and satisfaction to their readership:

> zey hobn nit gevust, zikh nit gerikht — '*die Juden schießen!*' ikh hob gehert dem oysvurf's ekldike shtim
> eyder nokh die umreyne neshome s'iz aroys, s'iz nit geven keyn oysruf, nor beys vunder — s'taytsh?!
> a shtoynen vist un oysterlish un umgerikht azoy: '*die Juden schießen!*' o, nisht aleyn fun im,
> s'iz a ruf gevezn fun a merder-folk, fun akhtsik milion: zey oykh! di yidn makhn's oykh vi mir, vi yeder daytsh.
> (Katzenelson XIV. 1, p. 71)

Adler tones down the contempt, removing words like 'ekldik' and 'umreyn', weakening the word 'oysvurf', introducing verbs such as 'heulte' and 'büßt' that might evoke pity, and he omits the sardonic pleasure in the dying man's expression of surprise ('s'taytsh?!'):

> Das hat der Deutsche nicht gewußt.
>   Wahrhaft — Juden schießen! Wann im Ghetto heulte so ein Jude, wie
> Der Deutsche heulte, ehe seine Seele wich?
>   Vielleicht kein Auswurf? böses Wunder nur? ein Narr, der büßt?
> Der Schrecken gellte durch die Judenstadt:
>   Die Juden schießen! Und es war kein Einzelner, der sterbend schrie.
> Aufschrie das Mördervolk. Millionen brüllten: Seht —
>   Die Juden! Juden schießen so, wie jeder Deutsche schießt!
> (Adler 1992, p. 146)

Where Adler introduces the possibility that the dying man may be repenting, Biermann intensifies Katzenelson's tone. The stronger word 'röcheln' connects the individual with the eighty million murderers in the place of 'ruf'; his soul is 'schwarz' as well as 'unrein'; 'Mörderfressen' intensifies the speaker's grotesque pleasure. Biermann makes an even more direct connection between the bullet and the 'Staunen' that it produces:

> Das hat den Deutschen überrumpelt, schwer verwirrt
> 'Die Juden schießen ja!' — er röchelte dies deutsche Wort
> Als unrein seine schwarze Seele aus dem Körper wich
> Böses Erwachen, reichlich spät im letzten Sterbehauch

> Und mit der Kugel hat ein Staunen da den Deutschen kalt erwischt
> 'Die Juden schießen ja! Verbrecher! Mörder! Mord!'
> Achtzig Millionen Mörderfressen röchelten im Schreck:
> 'Die also auch! Wie wir, so machen es die Juden auch!'
> (Biermann, p. 147)

All the acts of violence in the text are staged for someone else's observation, to demonstrate something about power, and all are connected with feelings of enjoyment on the part of one of the parties. By confronting his audience with the spectacle of a victim who revels in the painful death of an individual who could potentially be a family member of anyone in his audience—and this is not the only occasion in the last few pages of the text—and by drawing attention to the aesthetic pleasure of the German linguistic performance, Biermann's text brings to light something forbidden, namely the pleasure involved in inflicting violence and our implication in that pleasure as observers. He makes it very difficult for the German reader to know what position to take up.

Katzenelson does not conform to the image of the reasonable victim, whose pain and anger are expressed only in the expected ritual contexts, whose media presence supports processes of public commemoration, and who provides messages against violence and intolerance. Katzenelson's text, when read in the new context opened up by Biermann's translation, seems to bring to speech hidden desires and fears, which are unconstructive and unreasonable, but unreasonable only because they are in excess of the 'reasonable' consensus of narratives of mourning, remembrance, and reconciliation that give everything a direction and a meaningful narrative function.

Read in terms of theories of mourning, or of theories that contrast the compulsive repetition of traumatic events with a more constructive, enlightened 'working through' of trauma, the performance offered by Katzenelson's text, particularly in Biermann's translation, might feel like a setback, a *Rückfall* into traumatized, compulsive 'acting out' of the experience of violence. But this underestimates the element of aesthetic calculation in the translation strategies adopted to make this text available to an audience for which it was never intended. While Adler's version makes an offer of reconciliation—while showing how much work there is still to do and laying the burden of responsibility clearly onto the German reader of the text—Biermann intervenes against ritualized cultural narratives of remembrance, staging a confrontation with the rage, pain, and violence that have had to be repressed, and reminding us that the price of reconciliation is always paid by the victims.

UNIVERSITY OF EDINBURGH   PETER DAVIES

WRITERS' LINGUISTIC OBSERVATIONS AND CREATING MYTHS ABOUT LANGUAGES: CZESŁAW MIŁOSZ AND JOSEPH BRODSKY IN SEARCH OF THE 'SLAVONIC GENIUS OF LANGUAGE'

Introduction

The long tradition of making evaluative judgements about the Slavonic languages on the part of both native speakers and outside observers has led to the creation of a corpus of colourful descriptions and produced a variety of linguistic myths. From the position of 'pure' linguistic science language myths are usually considered to be prejudices, and some of them are often qualified as being akin to racism and sexism.[1] However, in the wider context of the humanities the entire range of statements of this sort, regardless of whether they give preference to one language over another, forms a significant element of the cultural history of a particular nation and hence requires not only a classification of all their possible structures and metaphoric figures, but also a thorough exploration of the cultural links and ideological roots from which they grow. Thus we have two major overlapping groups of discourses—one that is located within the framework of descriptive linguistics, and one that originates elsewhere but which incorporates the linguistic argument. Discourses of the second group are common in philology, like linguistic purism, as well as in various kinds of language-related speculations based on national stereotypes found in literature, journalism, individual reflections, oral folklore, and jokes.

This not only brings about a new interdisciplinary subject of research, but also demands appropriate methods for dealing with such multifaceted topics as judgements on languages. On the one side we have schools of linguistics, on the other side there is literary and language critique and a whole domain of discourses which incorporates individual and collective wisdom about language(s), with all possible projections onto the mental and cultural peculiarities of a particular nation. Looked at more generally, the epistemology of linguistic science comes into contact with what can be called the 'imageology'[2] of naive linguistics, creating a large area of overlap where de-

---

Note. All translations of quotations from sources in languages other than English, as well as instances of emphasis by the use of italics, are mine except where I have indicated that italics are used in the original version.

[1] Laury Bauer and Peter Trudgill, 'Introduction', in *Language Myths*, ed. by Laury Bauer and Peter Trudgill (London and New York: Penguin, 1998), pp. xv–xviii (p. xvii). The purpose of this book is to expose some of these stereotypes. See the chapters 'French is a Logical Language' (pp. 23–31), or 'Italian is Beautiful, German is Ugly' (pp. 85–93).

[2] Linguistic imageology is, in our opinion, a useful term for the field of research which would cover myths and conceptual metaphors of languages as they are understood in Richard Watts,

scriptions of the former interact with judgements of the latter. Consequently, the main purpose of research in this field would consist in seeking answers to the following questions. From and to what features of 'national world-view'[3] are linguistic links drawn? Which features of a language and which linguistic categories are selected for these links and for language-related judgements in general? What are the ideological or political roots of these links? What techniques are used in establishing these links?

Judgements on language matters made by recognized writers comprise a particularly interesting subject because the 'judges' themselves are not only sensitive and influential users of their language, but, owing to the nature of their work, have the skills and authority to speculate on these matters in ways that often go far beyond the common stereotypes. Moreover, either they openly declare the ideological motivations that lie behind their statements, or these motivations can be decoded from their aesthetic or ideological creed. Their reflections can be particularly acute if they live and work in two (or more) language environments, as was the case with Czesław Miłosz and Joseph Brodsky, two Nobel Prize winners who both spent a significant period of their creative lives as émigrés. The linguistic competence of both poets can hardly be doubted. Miłosz extensively translated from Spanish, and from and into French and English; he knew Latin and in his sixties learnt Greek and Hebrew.[4] Like Miłosz, Brodsky had extensive experience in translating poetry into Russian, mostly from English, but also from Polish, Czech, and other Slavonic languages. English, along with his native Russian, also became the main object of his linguistic observations, which are lavishly scattered throughout his prose. The two men respected each other highly as poets, and despite the age difference remained good friends from the time of their

Language Myths and the History of English (Oxford and New York: Oxford University Press, 2011); see the introductory chapter 'Metaphors, Myths, Ideologies and Archives', pp. 3–23. The main purpose of the studies on linguistic imageology, however, would not be checking their credibility, but rather understanding their roots and building a typology of the models they are created by. The boundaries of Slavonic linguistic imageology as a research field at the intersection of linguistics and cultural studies were briefly outlined in my paper 'Slavianskaia lingvisticheskaia imagologiia segodnia: "obrazy iazyka" i sposoby ikh sopriazheniia s mental'nost'iu i kul'turoi' at the Thirteenth International Congress of Slavists in Ljubljana, 2003; full text in Russian available at <http://dspace.gla.ac.uk/bitstream/1905/42/1/KhairovEd.pdf> [accessed 31 August 2013].

[3] I am aware of the fact that this notion as well as the notion of 'ethnic mentality' is not sufficiently well defined and too tainted by numerous speculations. For more about these concerns see Shamil Khairov, 'Kniga Nadezhdy Zharintsevoi "The Russians and their Language" (1916) i sovremennye kul'turologicheskie interpretatsii russkogo iazyka', in *Ot lingvistiki k mifu: lingvisticheskaia kul'turologiia v poiskakh 'etnicheskoi mental'nosti'*, compiled by Anna Pavlova (St Petersburg: Anthology, 2013), pp. 289–315.

[4] Miłosz gives a brief account of his experience as a translator in the introduction to a collection of his translations from a number of languages in his essay 'Gorliwość tłumacza', in Czesław Miłosz, *Ogród nauk* (Paris: Instytut literacki, 1979), pp. 171–74. The role of the different languages that Miłosz encountered in his lifetime is discussed in Elena Brazgovskaia, *Cheslav Milosh: iazyk kak personazh* (Moscow: Letnii sad, 2012), pp. 108–24.

first personal contact, which was established by Miłosz's consolatory letter to Brodsky upon the arrival of the latter in the United States. As they conformed to a similar scheme—'two Slavonic writers in exile'—their linguistic experience and opinions provide us with valuable material which allows us to examine to what extent their linguistic views overlap, when they follow and when they deviate from common stereotypes, what individual descriptions of languages they come up with, and how their philosophical creed and origin might influence their judgements.

At this point it is important to make a disclaimer: this article is not about two creative biographies,[5] but is written from a different perspective. It is about the nature of language-related statements made by writers, especially by those who work in exile and with their linguistic observations contribute to language myth-making. In this article we deal only with the poets' explicit language-related statements. Linguistic metaphors and language as a motif in their poetry are not discussed here.[6]

The list of linguistic features traditionally used in mapping the metaphysics of a particular Slavonic language or in specifying the 'Slavonic linguistic perception' of the world in general ranges from detecting traces of 'national character' in semantic structure or value of a single word (the 'key-words' approach)[7] to highlighting selected typological peculiarities of a particular language system. Within the domain of grammar the following 'specific' Slavonic features are most often identified:

- free word order as a reflection of the 'flexibility of mental processes';
- the role of inflection in thought;
- a highly developed system of word formation, with special reference to expressive models of suffixation such as diminutives and augmentatives;
- the influence of grammatical gender on the perception of the outside world;
- impersonal verbs and sentences in relation to personal will and choice;
- Peculiarities of the tense and aspect system of the Slavonic verb.[8]

As will be shown, the language-related statements of Czesław Miłosz and

[5] Regarding a comparative view of the biographies of the two poets, the most remarkable work is a book by Irena Grudzinska Gross, *Czesław Miłosz and Joseph Brodsky: Fellowship of Poets* (New Haven and London: Yale University Press, 2010). The author knew both poets personally and devotes a considerable part of her book to their language attitudes. See also Bożena Karwowska, *Miłosz i Brodski: recepcja krytyczna twórczości w krajach anglojęzycznych* (Warsaw: IBL, 2000).

[6] For a treatment of the language theme in Miłosz's creative work, thought, and life from a broader perspective see Brazgovskaia, *Cheslav Milosh*.

[7] Probably the most frequently quoted source in this respect is Anna Wierzbicka, *Understanding Cultures through their Key Words: English, Russian, Polish, German, and Japanese* (Oxford and New York: Oxford University Press, 1997).

[8] See e.g. Boris Gasparov, 'Lingvistika natsional'nogo samosoznaniia', *Logos*, 14 (1999), pp. 48–67.

Joseph Brodsky reflect and refine some existing language myths, but also contain many apt descriptions and metaphors that complement these common stereotypes. Examination of these statements reveals two distinct themes: one that depicts the character of Slavonic languages, either seen individually or in contrast with other European languages, predominantly English; and the other that contrasts Polish and Russian, revealing the mechanisms of cross-evaluation when the structural differences between two languages are neutralized by their common origin and the similarity of their grammatical structure.

The 'Slavonic Genius' of Language: Polish and Russian vs. English

MIŁOSZ

The most articulate expression of Czesław Miłosz's language attitudes can be found in his collection of essays *Ogród nauk* (*Garden of Sciences*), and particularly in one essay from this collection entitled 'Język, narody' ('The Language, the Nations').⁹ This essay was written as a critical response to a series of publications in the London-based newspaper *Wiadomości* in 1972–73 by the Polish émigré translator and essayist Jan Darowski. In this essay Miłosz uses the concept of the *genius of language*, invented by the leaders of the French Enlightenment and widely applied ever since in language-related contexts. Miłosz paraphrases Darowski's views as follows:

All one needs is to have an ear in order to express one's opinion on the Slavs: the Slavonic languages—with their groups of hushing consonants, with their multi-syllable words—are clumsy and inconvenient. And they are absolutely useless in the domain of intellectual activity [...]. One can discern in these languages the Slavonic laziness, the individual's incapacity for independent thought, an inclination to fall into line with major movements—hence those slavophilisms, Messianisms, panslavisms etc. [...] Polish makes human contact with life unserious (chrząszcz brzmi w trzcinie) as if putting the fool's cap of its ć, ś, sz, and cz on words which sound solemn in other languages. 'Amour, love, or Liebe as *miłość*! Mors, death, Todt as *śmierć*! Bonheur, happiness as *ščęśče* [sic]!' [...] Every discussion [in it] quickly and irrepressibly turns into a sort of irritating quarrel, into oppressing the other's personality, into depriving the other of the right to speak. Our language does not let the speakers enjoy the easy communication with another sovereign person present in the language of the Anglo-Saxons, which is relaxed and economical, and which spares the nerves of its listeners.¹⁰

However, qualifying Darowski's articles as a typical Slavonic manifestation of self-deprecation, Miłosz warns readers against stigmatizing his opponent as a vulgar language determinist. In his essay he descends from the abstract to

---
⁹ Czesław Miłosz, 'Język, narody', in Miłosz, *Ogród nauk*, pp. 121–37 (Miłosz's emphasis).

¹⁰ Ibid., pp. 121–22. 'W Szczebrzeszynie chrząszcz brzmi w trzcinie' is the initial line of a humorous poem by Jan Brzechwa; its deliberate concentration of hissing consonants is often used as a tongue-twister.

the literary and historical grounds: he treats such linguistic speculations as an attempt at 'liberation', a search for the reasons why Poland had found herself on the margins of European civilization, and points to language as a response to the challenges of history. The Polish language is treated here by Miłosz in an ambiguous manner: on the one hand it is only a tool, the efficiency of which can be questioned in evaluative terms, while on the other it is an active subject endowed with a certain inner power and independence (an image of language widely accepted outside descriptive linguistics). Noting Darowski's accusation that Polish hampers the development of an adequate network of abstract concepts and thus puts obstacles in the way of social communication and technical progress, Miłosz does not directly refute this opinion.[11] Moreover, a few months later he makes a similar statement himself, albeit balancing it with the positive quality that Polish has of being *sensual*. Apparently adhering to the old notion that languages can be classified according to whether they are sensual (poetical) or logical, he claims that 'the Polish language is very bad at sustaining lofty flights of philosophy. Polish just *isn't concise enough*; it's *sensual. All abstractions sound heavy and artificial* in Polish.'[12]

In 'The Language, the Nations' Miłosz sets out his own view of the metaphysics of his native Polish as contrasted with that of English and, in some respects, French. Miłosz is convinced that English cannot serve as an ideal language for the Slavs. He champions the notion of the inner ability of a language to respond to the demands of civilization and refuses to admit that languages simply adjust and reflect the development of the latter. Miłosz points to the fields where English is left behind by its main donor, French, and lists the semantic fields that divide the metaphysics of these two languages from each other, namely, being (l'être), becoming (le devenir), and duration (la durée). He attributes to English such features as *compactness*, *solidity*, and *sobriety*, which he thinks are due to its Anglo-Saxon component. Although compactness is measurable and can refer either to the number of words needed to express an idea or to the average length of a word or sentence, the other two features are clearly relative. Some forms of compactness can become negative: the abundance of monosyllabic words, these 'verbs-for-everything' (*do*, *bring*, *make*, *speed*, *catch*, etc.), which, while being valuable in a technical civilization as useful tools for naming non-traditional phenomena, can, according to Miłosz, '*eat away at the very substance of the language*'.[13]

Another linguistic category used by Miłosz as a cultural argument is grammatical gender. He argues that English, being deprived of grammatical gender, is *isolated from nature, cold,* and '*bears the stamp of human loneliness*'.[14] It

[11] Ibid., p. 123.
[12] Ewa Czarnecka and Alexander Fiut, *Conversations with Czeslaw Milosz* (San Diego: Harcourt Brace Jovanovich, 1987), p. 254.   [13] Miłosz, 'Język, narody', p. 124.
[14] Ibid.

would be difficult to find a more striking example of making a grammatical feature emanate extra-linguistic values. In the spirit of tradition, grammatical gender is used by Miłosz to highlight certain generic metaphysical qualities of the Slavonic languages, the most remarkable of which, according to him, is the strong individualizing of plants, animals, and inanimate objects. The link between grammatical and natural gender opens up the possibility of various sorts of personification and allegedly imposes a more vivid, animated, and 'ensouled' perception of the world. He notes that French also carries the mark of alienation from nature, but at least it keeps the feminine and the masculine genders, while English, which uses neuter to refer to everything except people, only stimulates such alienation.

Since grammatical gender is equally embedded in all Slavonic languages, it is easy to extend the Polish–English opposition and include all Slavonic languages, which, as will be shown later, makes the further detection of metaphysical differences between closely related languages such as Russian and Polish very difficult, especially if one wants to base them on palpable linguistic grounds. The natural and cultural connotations of grammatical gender have been a subject of observations in translation studies and studies in folklore for decades, and Miłosz's bold descriptions only draw the essence of their metaphysical potential.

BRODSKY

Depending on his needs, Brodsky could either associate a language with a given political system or, on the contrary, detach the former from the latter:

This country [Russia], with its *magnificently inflected language capable of expressing the subtlest nuances of the human psyche*, with an incredible ethical sensitivity (a good result of its otherwise tragic history), had all the makings of a cultural, spiritual paradise, a real vessel of civilization. Instead, it became a drab hell, with a shabby materialist dogma and pathetic consumerist gropings.[15]

Here immanent features of Russian are opposed to something of a completely different nature—the Soviet environment—and in his autobiographical essay Brodsky endows the English language with values of the political system he sympathizes with. Regarding the question why he wrote this essay in English and not in his native Russian, the reason he states was to liberate his late parents from 'their captivity', 'to grant them a margin of freedom' represented by English. Despite the reassurance that 'one shouldn't equate the state with language', he associates Russian in this context with all the Soviet bureaucratic harassments his parents encountered during their unsuccessful applications to visit him in the United States. Brodsky wants to please his dead parents

[15] Joseph Brodsky, 'Less than One', in Joseph Brodsky, *'Less than One': Selected Essays* (Harmondsworth: Penguin, 1987), pp. 3–33 (p. 26).

by 'transferring' them to the language realm preferred by him (though not necessarily by them), suggesting that 'English offers a better semblance of afterlife.'[16] Here Brodsky follows an old formula expressed long before him: 'As England is the Land of Liberty, so is her language the Voice of Freedom.'[17]

A significant difference between the two poets on these matters is that while Miłosz highlights both strong and weak sides of English, taking a somewhat technical approach, Brodsky's gravitation towards English, as David Bethea points out, is both 'ethical' and 'aesthetic'. Bethea shows that Brodsky's 'idiosyncratic (and belatedly romantic) view of language and national character' is, in fact, a significant element of his exile creation strategy, in which, as Bethea notes, English plays the role of 'the necessary antidote to the false letter of the Soviet'.[18] It can be added that Brodsky does not stick only to this modern political opposition of the Soviet and the West, but also takes a broader view, commenting on the primeval metaphysical opposition between these two languages as representatives of two types of culture.

BRODSKY ON THE EASTERNNESS OF RUSSIAN

The 'Easternness' of Russian culture, if not of the Russian language as such, has been noted by writers and philosophers for a long time. In 1925 it attracted the attention of the young Nikolai Trubetskoi, then a leading Eurasianist, but later one of the most prominent linguists of the last century. Having emphasized the significance of the 'Mongolian certificate' for Russian culture, Trubetskoi failed, however, to provide convincing linguistic arguments in support of his Eurasianist theory.[19] Brodsky offers his own perception of Russian as a language of an Eastern nature. He indeed finds the Russian mind 'continental', and even 'claustrophobic', but where the Russian language is concerned, its Easternness, in Brodsky's view, is revealed in its predilection for rhetorical bombastic decorations, which places it among the languages of the East, in contrast to the 'concise', 'rational', 'truth-telling' English.[20] Brodsky must have known perfectly well that the statement concerning the 'truth-telling'

[16] Joseph Brodsky, 'In a Room and a Half', in Brodsky, *Less than One*, pp. 447–501 (pp. 460–61).
[17] George W. Lemon, *English Etymology; or, A Derivative Dictionary of the English Language* (London: G. Robinson, 1783); here quoted from Tony Crowley, *Language in History: Theories and Texts* (London and New York: Routledge, 1996), p. 71.
[18] David M. Bethea, *Joseph Brodsky and the Creation of Exile* (Princeton: Princeton University Press, 1994), p. 121.
[19] Nikolai Trubetskoi, 'O turanskom elemente v Russkoi kul'ture' (1925), repr. in *Etnograficheskoe obozrenie*, 1 (1992), 92–106. On Trubetskoi's early writings in a wider Eurasianist framework see Patrick Sériot's critical study: Patrik Serio, *Struktura i tselostnost': ob intellektual'nykh istokakh strukturalizma v Tsentral'noi i Vostochnoi Evrope. 1920-30-e gg.* (Moscow: Iazyki slavianskoi kul'tury, 2001), pp. 67–86.
[20] Interview with David Bethea, in Iosif Brodskii, *Bol'shaia kniga interv'iu, sostavlenie i fotografii Valentiny Polukhinoi* (Moscow: Zakharov, 2000), pp. 505–52 (p. 541). In all further references to this volume the abbreviation *BKI* is used.

quality of English could easily be challenged: it would have sufficed to refer to Orwell, one of his beloved English authors, who wrote extensively about the corruption of language. Nevertheless, Brodsky claims that English has a core of anti-rhetoric. Furthermore, he associates English with an aspiration for global order ('стремление к мировому порядку'). He sees Russian as representing the *reflexive* and English the *rational* type of culture,[21] and sometimes relates this opposition to the opposition of *analytical* and *synthetic* which he likes to use in his language critique:

[. . .] The English, for example, are exceedingly rational. At least, externally. That is, they often are likely to lose track of nuances, all those so-called 'loose ends.' [. . .] Just suppose that you cut through an apple and remove the skin. Now you know what is inside the apple but by the same token you lose sight of both its bulges, both its cheeks. Russian culture is interested precisely in the apple itself, taking delight in its color, the smoothness of its skin, and so forth. [. . .] Speaking crudely, these are different ways of relating to the world—*rational* and *synthetic*.[22]

Evaluating Polish and Russian

MIŁOSZ ON THE ENERGY, HEALTH, AND EUPHONICS OF POLISH

The whole gamut of language-related discourses—from single reflections to language myth-making—is full of evaluative ingredients, which traditionally take the form of metaphors of a biological, botanical, industrial, or medical character. And the further the discourse is from descriptive linguistics, the more active a role language is assigned in it. Miłosz tends to adopt a traditional approach when applying the concepts of health and vitality to the state of the Polish language. The *illness* of contemporary Polish, in Miłosz's opinion, lies in its *talkativeness* ('gadulstwo'), the quality that typologically can be matched with the 'rhetorical core' of Russian noted by Brodsky. Miłosz believes that Polish is *losing its energy* through the massive borrowing of new words. In answer to the hypothetical argument that a process of constant change is a normal phenomenon for a language, Miłosz expresses his doubts as to whether these changes are always for the better. It is worth noting that when Miłosz speculates on the subject of the energy, strength, and health of the Polish language, he in fact means Polish literature. The state of a language for him is a visible external symptom of the inner state of a literary organism. Thus he treats language as a mirror of literature, while Brodsky turns this relationship upside down (as will be shown below). Miłosz warns Polish poets and writers against unfounded wordplay, an infatuation with irony, a worship of foreign words, and empty talkativeness in general. Miłosz finds

[21] Interview with Annie Epelboen, *BKI*, pp. 130–53 (pp. 138, 142–43, 153).
[22] Marianna Volkova and Solomon Volkov, *Iosif Brodskii v N'iu Iorke: fotoportrety i besedy s poetom* (New York: Slovo, 1990); quoted from Bethea, *Joseph Brodsky and the Creation of Exile*, p. 227.

Polish *not established* ('ustawiony') firmly enough, which makes it weak and non-resistant to influence from outside. He points to the early 1900s, the time of Polish modernism, as one of the weakest periods in the history of Polish literature and, thus, the Polish language. He qualifies Polish as *rich, warm,* but at the same time *capricious,* which is another source of its difficulties. Miłosz appeals to writers not to take a passive role in their interaction with the language. Even a talented writer can be a loser in this interaction, if he lets himself be driven by the natural forces ('żywioł') of his tongue.[23]

While Brodsky refers to the inarticulate buzz of language ('гул языка') which poets tune in to, Miłosz touches on concrete matters of the euphony of Polish. In a passage concerning the weak representation of the rural element in twentieth-century Polish Miłosz suspects that the blame lies with the immanent disadvantages of the rural dialects, such as their *rustling character* ('szelestliwość') and the weakness of their rhythmical structure. This is the reason why, in his opinion, no great Polish poets came from the countryside.[24] Sometimes Miłosz cannot restrain himself from making an ironical comment on the euphonics of a particular Polish word, as if hearing it with a stranger's ear. For example, he qualifies the word *rzeczywistość* as 'ochydne w dźwięku słowo' (a word that sounds disgusting).[25] Intentionally or otherwise, Miłosz does not dismiss the idea of judging languages on euphonic grounds. It should be mentioned here that comments on euphony in the Slavonic languages consist of a variety of long-standing myths, and scholarly arguments on this topic usually refer to their relative nature and lack of credibility.[26] But the construction of these myths—i.e. what features and what reasons make a language, its idiom, or a particular word euphonic—still awaits a proper classification.

BRODSKY ON THE NET OF RUSSIAN SYNTAX AND THE 'TRAGIC CORE' OF RUSSIAN

In contrast with Miłosz, who warns writers not to be driven by the natural forces of their language, Brodsky believes that true poets and writers inevi-

---

[23] Miłosz, 'Język, narody', pp. 128–29. Miłosz repeats his statement about Polish *having no established voice* elsewhere: Czesław Miłosz, 'Mickiewicz', in Miłosz, *Ogród nauk*, pp. 138–42 (p. 139). [24] Miłosz, 'Język, narody', p. 130.
[25] Czesław Miłosz, 'Rzeczywistość', in Miłosz, *Ogród nauk*, pp. 30–38 (p. 30).
[26] As in a comment made by Ivan Lekov: 'The statements on euphony cannot be scientifically credible. According to certain amateurish opinions euphony derives from an abundance of palatal sounds (as in Polish), while according to other opinions it originates in energetic and hard sounds (Bulgarian), or in clear vocalism (Serbian and Croatian). To the Southern Slavs the consonant clusters of Northern Slavonic languages do not sound euphonic, and to the Northern Slavs, for instance, the Bulgarian "dark" vowel ъ is peculiar and difficult to pronounce and so is usually replaced by other/similar vowels—*e, o, a.* Hence, the impression that euphony or its absence is relative and arbitrary' (Ivan Lekov, 'Sistema ot osnovni zakonomernosti v kharakterologiiata na slavianskite ezitsi', in *Zakonomernosti na razvitieto na slav'anskite ezitsi,* ed. by Ivan Lekov (Sofia: BAN, 1977), pp. 7–36 (p. 31)).

tably do exactly that, as was the case with Dostoevskii or Platonov. And in his contemplations of the ways in which languages put crucial pressure on their writers, or, in a wider context, their speakers, he deviates from qualities traditionally assigned to the Slavonic languages as reflectors of their metaphysical peculiarities. His 'Catastrophes in the Air' is not just a literary essay; there is no problem about assigning it to the category of works about the philosophy of language. In this essay Brodsky attributes to language even more power than is the case in neo-Humboldtian discourses on linguistic relativism. Like Miłosz, Brodsky is far from being apologetic about his native tongue, but the ethical scale of his statements is set much higher. In the paragraphs relating to Platonov Brodsky discovers in Russian such features as destructive revolutionary *eschatology*, relentless *absurdity*, a *tragic core*, bringing about *social evil* and *dead-end psychology*. The following statement from this essay perfectly illustrates Brodsky's extreme evaluations:

Platonov speaks of a nation which in a sense has become the *victim of its own language*; or, to put it more accurately, he tells a story about this very language, which turns out to be capable *of generating a fictitious world*, and then falls into *grammatical dependence* on it.[27]

This image of Russian reaches its peak in the claim that in Platonov's case, Russian '*language is a millenarian device*, history isn't'.[28] What makes it interesting to a scholar of language myths is that a similar kind of inverted logic can be found in numerous speculative texts originating in the marginal zones of linguistics and cultural studies that have emerged in Russia in the last two decades under the name 'linguistic culturology'. According to one of them, for instance, the reason why the formal rules of duelling took so long to be adopted in eighteenth-century Russia lies in the structural difference between the Russian and French languages. The 'flexible' Russian grammar allegedly tended to encourage a spontaneous fight, but with the gradual acquisition of foreign languages by the Russian nobles the 'regular' grammar of French and English persuaded them to accept the formal and meticulously structured rituals of duelling. So the more the Russian upper classes became fluent in French, the more they liberated themselves from the 'chaotic' metaphysical influence of their native tongue, which in this particular case was 'responsible' for the emotional and immediate method of resolving conflicts.[29]

Brodsky's statements are not so straightforward, though; he is trying to find the embedded ethical proclivities of his native tongue. In Tsvetaeva's writing Brodsky finds in Russian the best match to the spirit of Calvinism:

---

[27] Joseph Brodsky, 'Catastrophes in the Air', in Brodsky, *Less than One*, pp. 268–303 (p. 290).
[28] Ibid., p. 288. See also his notes on eschatology in Russian on pp. 283, 286–87.
[29] Alla Mel'nikova, *Iazyk i natsional'nyi kharakter: vzaimosviaz' struktury iazyka i mental'nosti* (St Petersburg: Rech', 2003), pp. 299, 303, 309.

One of the possible definitions of her [Tsvetaeva's] creative production is *the Russian subordinate clause put at the service of Calvinism*. Another variation is: *Calvinism in the embrace of this subordinate clause*. In any case, no one has demonstrated the congeniality of the said *Weltanschauung* and this grammar in a more obvious way than Tsvetaeva has. Naturally, the severity of the interrelation between an individual and himself possesses certain aesthetics; but it seems there is no more absorbing, more capacious, and more natural form for self-analysis than the one that is built into the multistage syntax of the Russian complex sentence. Enveloped in this form, Calvinism 'takes' the individual much further than he would happen to get had he used Calvin's native German.[30]

Remarkably, Brodsky is wrong in identifying German as Calvin's native language (it was French), but in creating myths on languages it is the very fact of the metaphysical opposition as such that often makes up the main point. The word 'Calvinism' constantly appears in Brodsky's essays and interviews when these two subjects, Marina Tsvetaeva and Russian syntax, are linked. In Brodsky's context Calvinism is a severe moral self-treatment, but here Brodsky contradicts his own statements in which he makes Russian grammar partly responsible 'for the *moral ambivalence* and the diminished willpower' endemic to his generation.[31]

Although Brodsky joins the chorus of statements about the warm-heartedness and the spiritual nature of Russian, he finds the latter reflected neither in its gender-imposed personification nor in the extensive use of expressive suffixation, but, above all, in its syntactic flexibility and lack of constraints. The free word order can not only bring 'moral ambivalence', but also refines the perceptive abilities:

[. . .] The noun [in Russian] could easily be found sitting at the very end of the sentence. [. . .] All this provides any given verbalization of the *stereoscopic quality of the perception* itself, and (sometimes) sharpens and develops the latter.[32]

Like Miłosz, Brodsky in his language critique also touches upon the length of Russian words, as if polysyllabic units are able to emanate euphonic magic. His main focus, however, remains on the syntax: he thinks that the lack of set limits in the Russian complex sentence can deceive a writer and lure him to unknown and unpredictable products, quite in compliance with the stereotype of the irrationality and flexibility of the 'Russian national character':

As intricacies go, Russian, where nouns frequently find themselves sitting smugly at the very end of sentences, whose main power lies not in the statement but in its subordinate clause, is extremely accommodating. This is not your analytical language of 'either/or'—this is the language of 'although'. Like a banknote into change, every stated

[30] Joseph Brodsky, 'Footnote to a Poem', in Brodsky, *Less than One*, pp. 195–267 (pp. 232–33).
[31] Brodsky, 'Less than One', p. 9.
[32] Joseph Brodsky, 'The Child of Civilization', in Brodsky, *Less than One*, pp. 123–44 (p. 124).

idea instantly mushrooms in this language into its opposite, and there is nothing its syntax loves more than doubt and self-deprecation. Its *polysyllabic nature* (the average length of a Russian word is three to four syllables) reveals the elemental, primeval force of the phenomena covered by a word a lot better than any rationalization possibly could, and a writer sometimes, instead of developing his thoughts, stumbles and simply revels in the word's euphonic contents, thereby *sidetracking his issue in an unforeseen direction*. And in Dostoevsky's writing we witness an extraordinary friction, nearly sadistic in its intensity, between the metaphysics of the subject matter and that of the language. [. . .]. His treatment of the human psyche was by far too inquisitive for the Russian Orthodox he claimed to be, and it is *syntax* rather than the creed that is *responsible for the quality of that treatment*.[33]

Ignoring the presupposition held in linguistics that inflection, owing to the rules of grammatical agreement and government between the elements of a sentence, represents grammatical regularity and order, Brodsky renders Russian grammar as 'irregular'.[34] And the Russian complex sentence is linked by him with a Russian type of mind that can easily fall into an abyss of subordinating statements, albeit that the same syntactic substructure is also able to explore the human psyche in all its depths:

Its subordinate clauses often carried him farther than his original intentions or insights would have allowed him to travel. [. . .] A born metaphysician, he [Dostoevskii] instinctively realized that *for the human psyche, there was no tool more far-reaching than a highly inflected mother tongue, with its convoluted syntax*.[35]

Brodsky does not explain how Russian syntax and Russian grammar in general can demonstrate such different, if not opposite, qualities—the Calvinist moral challenge, the sidetracking of a writer's thoughts in unforeseen directions, and the moral ambivalence in Tsvetaeva's and Dostoevskii's writings and his own reflections respectively.

It should be noted here that Miłosz mentions the deceptive flexibility of Polish syntax too, although in a narrower context, when he looks for the reasons why Polish was losing its density and strength in the 1900s:

They [Polish writers] knew everything; they read everything, including Nietzsche, Baudelaire, and the French symbolists, but everything they wrote turned into a mush. In that attempt to accept the new intellectual content Polish lost out, because, *lured by the efficiency of syntax*, they fancied that everything was permitted.[36]

The comparison of Miłosz's and Brodsky's language critique makes it clear that the latter constantly moves from observations of a more technical or perceptional kind to conclusions on an ethical level, from literary matters

[33] Joseph Brodsky, 'The Power of the Elements', in Brodsky, *Less than One*, pp. 157–63 (pp. 160–61).
[34] Ibid., p. 160.
[35] Brodsky, 'Catastrophes in the Air', p. 278.
[36] Miłosz, 'Język, narody', p. 129.

to the peculiarities of the Russian psyche. Brodsky's range of conclusions is more grandiose. He wants to be paradoxical in his metaphysical revelations: the 'intricacies' of Russian grammar provide, according to him, an excellent *playground for evil to disguise itself*, while English, with its 'truth-telling proclivity', is unsuitable for this purpose.[37]

THINKING IN A LANGUAGE

Another significant point of comparison is to examine how the two writers project the interrelationship of language and thought onto their own mental processes and whether they attribute any values to the languages involved.

Since Miłosz does not write his original literary work in English, he claims that he conducts all his creative activity within the domain of his native Polish:

> In the first place my continuing to write in Polish indicates a continuing involvement in the whole Polish mess. In the second place, it's the product of my sense of guilt. In a way, to write in Polish is, of course, to converse with the dead. [...] For me there's no other way out except to write in Polish. I have said somewhere that there are writers who think more in ideas or images, whereas I think in language itself, so I simply had no other choice.[38]

After settling in the United States, Miłosz started to promote contemporary Polish poetry by translating it into English, and with time he also gradually switched to translating his own poems; thus he adopted the practice of re-creating his works in English, but he does not speculate much on the linguistic side of this process.

As for Brodsky, he positions himself as a Russian poet, but an anglophone writer. That is why his reaction to statements that a writer must be a monoglot is so blunt: he qualifies this notion as 'a provincial nonsense'.[39] He emphasizes that he thinks neither in Russian nor in English: 'People don't think in languages. When thoughts come I formulate them in Russian or in English. People do not think in languages.'[40] Brodsky applies different 'language–thought' schemes depending on the time, the situation, and the public scale of his words. Before his departure from the USSR he was expressing his worries about language, as Liudmila Shtern recollects:

> One day he was saying that he would get suffocated and become silent as a poet, and another day—that he was afraid of being left without the nutrient medium of the Russian language and being made silent: 'You know, here you listen to the language in a tram, in a bath house or at the beer stalls. But there [abroad] you'll have only the

[37] Brodsky, 'Less than One', p. 31; 'Catastrophes in the Air', p. 283. See also Brodsky's interview with David Bethea: *BKI*, p. 541.
[38] Czarnecka and Fiut, *Conversations with Czesław Miłosz*, p. 264.
[39] Interview with John Glad, *BKI*, pp. 109–21 (p. 117).
[40] Interview with Lisa Henderson, *BKI*, pp. 327–35 (p. 330).

language that you brought with you, because a poet cannot live without a language environment.'[41]

In his letter from America to the same correspondent, who was about to emigrate from the USSR and was worrying about her knowledge of English, he encourages her with the words that 'there are no foreign languages as such—there is only a different set of synonyms'.[42] But his later statements about the language of his intellectual existence were, without doubt, determined by his new status and location. He made all possible efforts towards a transition to English not only as the language of everyday existence but also as the language of his writings, something that can also be interpreted as his escape from being 'locked' in one culture.[43] He admits that if he were to return to Russia, he 'would be exceedingly bothered by the inability to use an additional language'.[44] Considering Brodsky's inclination towards English and Western culture as a form of his self-representation strategy, Karwowska points out that despite all this, Russian remained for him a kind of 'motherland in exile',[45] using another broad metaphor from the line *language as locus of existence*.

Miłosz, by contrast, is happy not to have moved away from his native tongue:

I cannot stand writing in a foreign language; I am incapable of it. [. . .]. How glad I am now that I clung to my native language (for the simple reason that I was a Polish poet and could not have been otherwise); that I did not emulate those émigrés in France and the United States who shed one skin and language for another. I would not deny that my Polish served my pride by erecting a protective barrier between myself and a civilization in the throes of puerility [*qui sombre dans l'idiotie*].[46]

Inter-Slavonic Reflections: Brodsky and Polish; Miłosz and Russian

Examining inter-Slavonic linguistic perception of languages is a difficult task, because in this domain statements based on a structural contrast between languages or on language data in general are rarely applicable. Arguments of this type are more heavily loaded with stereotypes and prejudices of all

[41] Liudmila Shtern, *Brodskii: Osia, Iosif, Joseph* (Moscow: Nezavisimaia gazeta, 2001), p. 124.
[42] Ibid., p.134.
[43] Grudzinska Gross devotes a separate chapter to comparison of both poets' positions concerning English and their principles regarding English translations of their own poetry (*Czesław Miłosz and Joseph Brodsky*, pp. 221–58). She points out Brodsky's constant desire to escape from 'one-languageness' (p. 223).
[44] Volkova and Volkov, *Iosif Brodskii v N'iu Iorke*; quoted from Bethea, *Joseph Brodsky and the Creation of Exile*, p. 228.
[45] Karwowska, *Miłosz i Brodski*, p. 109.
[46] Czesław Miłosz, *Ziemia Ulro*, trans. by Louis Iribarne as *The Land of Ulro* (Manchester: Carcanet, 1985), p. 78

sorts, from cultural rivalry to religious zeal or the remembrance of a turbulent history of coexistence.

BRODSKY AND POLISH

There is a strong discrepancy in the amount of attention that Miłosz and Brodsky devote to each other's languages, which can be simply explained by the asymmetrical interrelations of their respective countries of origin. Brodsky's perception of Polish does not occupy a significant place in his linguistic speculations. He belonged to the younger post-war generation, and, as for many in the Soviet Union, Polish became for him a sort of a cultural window onto Europe. As seen from behind the inner, Soviet, 'iron curtain', Polish was for liberal minds the language of a nation upon whom Communism was imposed, but who, despite this burden, managed to remain European and relatively modern. It is a well-known fact that even under Communist rule Poland was much more liberal than the USSR both in terms of censorship and regarding the selection of foreign authors for translation. At the beginning of his literary career Brodsky learnt Polish in order to be able to translate from it. He was given the task of translating a number of Polish poets, and participated in events devoted to the promotion of Polish literature.[47] Brodsky had no inherited 'imperial' bias regarding Poland and hence against the Polish language. On the contrary, he extends his sympathy for Poland as a country to the Polish language. His early perception of everything Polish was very positive and even Romantic. His personal encounters added to his enthusiasm for Polish. This corresponds to the generally positive, Romantic perception of Poland in post-Stalinist Russia, especially among pro-Western intellectuals.[48] As a poet sensitive to linguistic matters, Brodsky cannot avoid the temptation of making remarks about Polish. While he never openly reflects on the semantic models of Russian words, he occasionally examines the structure of a Polish word, being fascinated by the way in which it reveals the Poles' aspiration for independence:

I remember how strong an impression the Polish words *podległość* ('dependence') and *niepodległość* ('independence') made on me at that time: not the etymological analysis as such but the simple feeling of these words.[49]

In these words Brodsky is recognizing a live model, an explicit sexual meta-

[47] Brodsky mentions one of these events in his letter to the editor of *Vechernii Leningrad* as a response to the libel against him. See Iakov Gordin, *Pereklichka vo mrake: Iosif Brodskii i ego sobesedniki* (St Petersburg: Izdatel'stvo Pushkinskogo Fonda, 2000), p. 168. Brodsky later confirmed his passion for Polish poetry in a number of interviews with Polish media.
[48] The Polish historian Andrzej Walicki, for example, mentions a number of instances of Polonophile attitudes encountered during his visits to the USSR. See Walicki, *Spotkania z Miłoszem* (London: Aneks, 1985), pp. 108–09.
[49] Interview with Jerzy Illg, *BKI*, pp. 315–28 (p. 326).

phor: *nie-pod-leg-ł-ość* (not-lying-under), a refusal to lie down under anybody, and he perceives this as a feature of the Polish mentality, thereby paying an indirect compliment to the related culture. After leaving Russia, Brodsky's positive sentiments refer almost exclusively to Polish poetry, which he ranks very highly. Brodsky encouraged his students to learn Polish, in order 'to be able to read the best poetry in the world',[50] which itself is an example of an evaluative formula: *a language is valuable because a valuable literature is written in it*.

MIŁOSZ AND RUSSIAN

Miłosz's knowledge of Russian is much deeper and his attitude towards Russia and Russian culture is much more complicated and rooted in the history of Polish–Russian affairs. Brodsky visited Poland only twice, both times coming from the West, whereas Miłosz grew up in the Polish community in Vilnius (Polish Wilno) within the borders of the Russian Empire, which Lithuania was then part of, but never visited Russia after Poland acquired its independence. The home language of his family and his language of education was Polish, but the official state language in pre-1917 Lithuania was Russian. He made a trip to Siberia with his family in his early childhood, and some time later, after the outbreak of the First World War, spent another four years deep in Russia in connection with his father's work as a communications engineer. This is how he describes his linguistic state of mind at that time: 'I was *under the sway of the Russian language* until the spring of 1918. *I was bilingual*.'[51]

Living in a country situated between two major European powers—Prussia (later Germany) and Russia (later the Soviet Union), the Poles had for centuries identified their position as being located between two evils. Quite naturally, Miłosz was always aware of Russia's sinister presence and her permanent shadow over Polish destiny. This, however, did not mean a sweeping rejection of everything Russian. His solid knowledge of Russian classical literature and socio-philosophical thought gave him a deeper insight into both Russian and Polish nationalisms. His *Native Realm*, in which he puts his personal biography in a wider European context, contains enough material for a separate article on how Poles perceive Russia, and the language component is an important part of Miłosz's view of Russia.

From our perspective, the main task in understanding his image of Rus-

[50] Grudzinska Gross, *Czesław Miłosz and Joseph Brodsky*, p. 91. As the author notes, 'his Polish translations were more numerous than from any other language (English later won over)'. Gross also gives a detailed record of the Polish poets translated by Brodsky into Russian and English (pp. 182–83). Karwowska notes that Brodsky's assessment of the poetry of Slavs he translated in the USSR could depend on who the interview was given to: see Karwowska, *Miłosz i Brodski*, p. 96.

[51] Czarnecka and Fiut, *Conversations with Czesław Miłosz*, p. 17.

sian would be the separation of the national Polish element from the generic Slavonic heritage which Poles share with Russians and other Slavs. An additional complication here is the strongly asymmetric influence coming from the Russian side. Miłosz was fully aware of the problem of the undesirable penetration of Russianness into Polish national consciousness. The above-mentioned complexity is well illustrated by the following statement:

> One should not underestimate the defensive gesture of collective Polishness [zbiorowości polskiej] and of the national taboo. For a foreigner this kind of Polish 'nationalism' is incomprehensible, but we know how much of a Russian is sitting in each of us, and this is not the same thing as enmity of the Mexicans towards 'gringos', the Yankees, because we are threatened by Russification from inside, at least, *through the language*.[52]

Being aware of all cultural differences, including those shaped by Orthodox Christianity and Polish Catholicism, Miłosz does not perceive everything Russian in only one colour, and the Russian language appears in his statements as both sinister and attractive:

> Poles, it would seem, are able to get an intuition of 'Russianness' mainly through the language, which attracts them because *it liberates their Slavic half*; in the language is all there is to know about Russia. The very thing that attracts them is at the same time menacing.[53]

Miłosz characterizes the Russian language in various modes: it is a language strong and powerful in 'tone', it is a language of humour and laughter, but it is also a language of unwanted values, a language to be held at a distance and to be prevented from intruding into the Polish national psyche. Written in the last years of Stalin's rule, his book *The Captive Mind*, which made Miłosz's name as a prose writer, is set in the anti-Communist, pro-Western post-war political context. But the old 'inherited' perception of Russia and the stereotype of the Russian language held by the Poles are clearly evident in it. The threat of sovietization via the spread of the Russian language here overlaps with older fears of Russification.[54] And yet Miłosz never rejects the attractive, '*brutal-sweet*', and enigmatic component of the Russian language. Six years later, in 1959, he describes the presence of the Russian language in the everyday life of a Polish family in pre-war times as follows:

> To me, Germans, except for the cruel myth of the Knights of the Cross, meant nothing; I did not know their language. [. . .] Russia, however, was relatively, but only relatively, concrete, as a chaos and an infinity remembered from childhood and, above all *as a language*. At the dinner table in our shabby, miserable (as I know now) home,

---

[52] Letter to Andrzej Walicki of 19 November 1960, in Walicki, *Spotkania z Miłoszem*, p. 97.

[53] Czesław Miłosz, *Rodzinna Europa*, trans. by Catherine S. Leach as *Native Realm: A Search for Self-Definition* (London and Manchester: Sidgwick and Jackson, 1981), p. 138.

[54] Czesław Miłosz, *Zniewolony umysł*, trans. by Jane Zielonko as *The Captive Mind* (London: Secker and Warburg, 1953), p. 19.

Russian had been *the language to make jokes in*, whose *brutal-sweet nuances* were untranslatable.[55]

Native Realm has a subtitle 'Search for Self-Definition', and in it Russia plays the role of a mirror to reflect the significant and the sensitive points of the author's Polishness. The Russian national character is shown here from the Polish point of view partly by comparing two cultures, in which the language component is fully fused. As for the perception of Russian within this fusion, Miłosz recalls a remarkable exercise he used to perform in his younger years, which gave him 'a good deal to think about':

One had to take a deep breath and pronounce [in Russian] first in a deep *bass* voice: 'Wyryta zastupom yama glubokaya' ['A deep pit dug out with a spade'], then to chatter quickly in a *tenor*: 'Wykopana szpadłem jama głęboka' [*the same in Polish*]. The arrangements of accents and vowels in the first phrase connotes *gloom, darkness, and power*; in the second, *lightness, clarity, and weakness*. In other words, it was both an exercise in self-ridicule and a warning.[56]

This impression that Russian has a darker, denser, more tragic, and even fearful 'voice' is intuitive and impossible to prove, but it is also traditional, almost a commonplace. It was not an individual impression unique to Miłosz, and it cannot be based purely on a euphonic notion, detached from the relative size and the history of relations between the two countries. Similar descriptions of Russian had been formulated a hundred years before Miłosz. Here he follows his famous predecessor Adam Mickiewicz, who in one of his Paris lectures contemplates the 'tone' of Russian, coloured with fear, a heritage from Genghis Khan, and the tone of Polish:

The Polish language that flourished in the gentle warmth of Christianity had a different sound. In the tone of Poles there was something similar to the tone of the French monarchy of the Middle Ages, to the *tone of the time of chivalry*. But [. . .] Europe went in a different direction. The Christian tone of Poles started to weaken too; Poles retained it, but they already *did not have the strength to raise it to the force of the Russian tone*. Now the Russian soldiers still laugh at the Polish officers as if they beg their soldiers to open fire, as if they bow before the line.[57]

The alleged ability of Russian to 'add force to a phrase' is also mentioned

---

[55] Miłosz, *Native Realm*, pp. 137–38.
[56] Ibid., p. 138. 'Вырыта заступом яма глубокая' is the first line of a poem by Russian folk-style poet Ivan Nikitin (1824–1861).
[57] Adam Mickiewicz, 'Literatura Słowiańska, Wykłady w Collège de France, Kurs Drugi, Rok 1841–1842, Wykład XXXIII', *Dzieła*, 10 (Kraków: Czytelnik, 1949), 395–405 (p. 398). In this lecture Mickiewicz also mentions the French tone, which Poland understood and was inspired by. The French tone of Napoleon is perceived in a rather abstract and symbolic manner, while the Russian tone in his contemplations is endowed with physical vocal features, as follows: 'There have been many attempts to imitate imperious gestures of the tsars; the Russian generals and officers tried to simulate the hoarse voice of the Romanovs, which indeed contained something fearful' (ibid., p. 399).

by Miłosz in *The Land of Ulro*, where he lists Russian along with Latin and French among the languages that made an impact on his 'internal rhythm'.[58] Miłosz calls for resistance to the influence of Russia and the Russian language, but at the same time admits having 'almost exaggerated sympathy for Russians taken individually'. He complains about the lack of a proper tool to describe how and why these contradictory attitudes can 'hang together'.[59] To Miłosz the difference between the two national psyches lies in the broader Polish view of the world against that of the Russian, but also in the presence of the eschatological element in the latter:

> The Poles are closely related to the Russians and menaced enough from within by the weakness of their own individualist ethic to be fearful. But their history, which made them what they are, was on the whole deprived of eschatology.[60]

The Polish metaphysical standing is more material, more balanced, less extreme:

> To me, the 'depth' of Russian literature was always suspect. What good is depth if bought at too high a price? Out of two evils, would we not prefer 'shallowness' provided we had decently built homes, well-fed and industrious people?[61]

Brodsky, as was noted above, refers to eschatology too, but in direct connection with the Russian language as such: he champions the idea that eschatology is one of its inherent features.

In discourses of this kind, images of national characters inevitably overshadow images of languages, with distinct linguistic elements virtually disappearing from view. Where inter-Slavonic perception of languages is concerned, the grammatical structure of the languages involved provides observers with almost no grounds for comparison, in contrast with the Slavonic–Western oppositions. Almost all evaluations and attitudes here have an 'ideological' character, and, being projected from outside, they refer to a particular language in general as a representative (or mirror) of its speakers.

The use and appreciation of Russian was taboo among both pro-Western liberals and nationalists in Communist Poland, and being aware that such an attitude towards Russian as an unwanted lingua franca had not disappeared with the fall of Communism, Brodsky, on the occasion of receiving an honorary doctorate from Katowice University in 1993, gave his speech in English rather than Russian.[62] And this 'asymmetrical' position of Russian is vividly illustrated by Walicki from the opposite perspective by the following anecdote:

[58] Miłosz, *The Land of Ulro*, p. 47.
[59] Miłosz, *Native Realm*, p. 146.
[60] Ibid., p. 144.
[61] Ibid., p. 145.
[62] According to Grudzinska Gross, 'fearing, that he might offend Polish national sensibility' (*Czesław Miłosz and Joseph Brodsky*, p. 189).

Spring 1976, the house of Mr and Mrs Miłosz in Berkeley. [. . .] At a certain moment, just before the meal was served, Miłosz got into a merry mood and started singing in Russian (in the house of his parents, as we know from his essay on Russia, Russian was the language of humour). Mrs Miłosz immediately summoned him to order, reminding us that 'in her house this language was not used'.[63]

Despite his excellent knowledge of Russian and his academic duties, which included lecturing on Russian literature, and Dostoevskii in particular, Miłosz almost never translated from Russian, for which he gives a reason that is not surprising in the light of this topic: that Russian with its '*great power of attraction*' might pose a 'threat' to his way of thinking and writing in Polish.[64]

Conclusion

Questioning the verity of evaluative language-related statements by referring them to the language system taken 'in itself and for itself' is not the main purpose of this exercise; these statements and their core content can be understood only against a wider cultural and historical background. In fact, the very idea that languages or their elements can be valued according to criteria divorced from cultural and political history is open to serious question.[65] Particular episodes from the cultural history of nations bring to life different oppositions. As far as Slavs are concerned, the promotion of the unique nature of their language(s) as a reflection of their 'national soul', in an effort to equate them with the more established European languages, always appeared on the agenda in times of their cultural and political revival and self-identification.[66] Vladimir Macura, for example, points out that in the context of the Czech National Revival a Slavonic language can be qualified both as illogical and as 'the most logical', because the political meaning of the attribution refers to a 'quality' that has to make the language in question different from other languages (in that particular case, German).[67]

The fact that in recent decades there has been a flourishing of speculative

[63] Walicki, *Spotkania z Miłoszem*, p. 98.
[64] Miłosz, 'Gorliwość tłumacza', p. 171.
[65] Even the common perception that the vast distances and harsh climate of Russia are reflected in the dramatic core of Russian, so deeply rooted in stereotypes of Russianness and the Russian language, is hardly proved by the linguistic facts and can be challenged by a socio-historical approach. See, for instance, how Leonid Batkin challenges Dmitri Likhachev's opinion about 'embedded' Russian concepts *udal'*, *prostor*, and *volia* taken in isolation from social and historical reality: Leonid Batkin, 'Po povodu "Zametok o russkom" D. S. Likhacheva', in id., *Pristrastiia: izbrannye esse i stat'i o kul'ture* (Moscow: Oktiabr', 1994), pp. 245–64 (pp. 253–56).
[66] Many speculations of this type can be found in periods of national revival. See e.g. Vladimir Macura, *Znamení zrodu: české obrození jako kulturní typ* (Prague, 1983). The chapter entitled 'Lingvocentrismus' (pp. 47–68) concentrates on the evaluation of different language strata in order to back up national cultural values. For most Southern and Western Slavs this is the middle of the nineteenth century.
[67] Macura, *Znamení zrodu*, pp. 38–39.

language-related judgements, particularly those published in Russia in a genre of so-called 'linguistic culturology', may be interpreted, on the one hand, as an effort to re-establish an 'original' national identity, thus helping to eliminate the demons of the Communist past, and, on the other hand, as a search for a vaccine against omnipotent globalization.[68] These texts are preceded by a long tradition of imaging languages along with depicting national psyches. Thus, not only does the typology of language-related statements require a proper gradation, but also the relationships between the discourses to which they belong need to be identified and classified whenever this phenomenon is described.

Comparing the linguistic observations of Czesław Miłosz and Joseph Brodsky, it is evident that the same languages may be endowed with different, sometimes contradictory, qualities depending on the observer's origin and location and, of course, the type of oppositions in which they are engaged. The Slavonic–English oppositions heavily exploit the structural differences between languages, linking them to differences in cultures and 'mentalities'. As for inter-Slavonic contexts, the structural references lose their illustrative value because they are not distinct enough to support ideological interpretations. The difference between the attitudes of Brodsky and Miłosz towards each other's language can be understood as a projection of the asymmetrical nature of Russian–Polish relations. The differences between how they contrast their native languages with English can only be understood if we bear in mind their individual exile strategies and their personal attitude to locus and history—more specifically, Miłosz's affinity to his roots and his acceptance of history on the one hand, and Brodsky's cosmopolitanism and his rejection of history on the other. That is why Miłosz's statements on languages are more earthbound and more prescriptive, and Brodsky's, on the contrary, more abstract and ethical. Brodsky's 'trademark' is putting the metaphysics of a language, whether Russian or English, ahead of history and literature.[69] It does not take long to notice that Miłosz's linguistic observations are pointed in two directions. In the first case he is in fact targeting Polish literature: in his language critique one can detect a certain pity, even reproach for the

[68] In the Slavonic world the quest to find connections between the meaning of specific national words and 'semantic' patterns of the perception of the world or moral values seems to be triggered by the works of Anna Wierzbicka. As far as Russian is concerned, the books of Vladimir Kolesov (see e.g. 'Zhizn' proiskhodit ot slova...' (St Petersburg: Zlatoust, 1999)) have become another popular example of this sort of literature. The ideas of Wilhelm von Humboldt and their reinterpretations have been brought back onto the agenda, often simplified and used for wide-ranging connections between language and all sorts of national habits or values. See the critical overview of neo-Humboldtianism in modern Russian Studies in A. V. Pavlova, 'Svedeniia o kul'ture i "etnicheskom mentalitete" po dannym iazyka', in Ot lingvistiki k mifu, pp. 160–240.

[69] For more on Brodsky's language myth-creation see Shamil Khairov, '"Esli Bog dlia menia i sushchestvuet, to eto imenno iazyk . . .": iazykovaia refleksiia i lingvisticheskoe mifotvorchestvo Iosifa Brodskogo', Novoe literaturnoe obozrenie, 67 (2004), 198–223.

underachievement of Polish literature at certain periods. His evaluation of Polish here has a more technical character. The second direction concerns the linguistic core of Polish identity, the conflict between the essence of 'Polishness', and the influence of 'Russianness' through the Russian language, which can to a certain extent be connected with the border zone of his birthplace. The references to linguistic elements in the first case are quite clear, but in the second, where languages are perceived as repositories of the national psyche, they inevitably become unarticulated, vague, and obscure.

The asymmetry in the attitudes of both poets to each other's language lies in the fact that Russian is not only a significant part of Miłosz's personal biography but is also ever-present in any consideration of the Slavonic beginnings of Poland's European destiny. Brodsky's attitude towards Polish can be described in linguistic terms as 'synchronic' and personal, whereas Miłosz's sentiments about Russian are clearly 'diachronic' and 'collective', since he often speaks on behalf of his compatriots. There is no evidence of Brodsky being involved in deeper metaphysical reasoning about Polish or any Slavonic language other than Russian.[70] The only metaphysical opposition he is interested in is that of Russian and English, which he characterizes in terms of an opposition between 'reflexive' and 'rational' cultures. Miłosz's concerns about his native Polish are those of a man responsible for a valuable inherited tool, while Brodsky expresses his absolute belief in the survival abilities of Russian and in its suprahistorical power.[71] Miłosz is a man of tradition: he is quite comfortable with the traditional list of metaphors applied to the image of a language: illness, strength, durability, its ability to respond to the challenges of the times. He does not look for answers outside history, while Brodsky, by contrast, is not interested in seeing things in a 'linear' sequence. Brodsky deliberately emphasizes his own theoretical constructions in his personal profile of a poet who is both a 'tool' of a spiritually endowed Russian but at the same time a thinker who belongs to the world of reason, i.e. to the cultural context of the West.

Both authors prove that the tradition of language myth-making and the search for the metaphysics of a language were still alive and thriving at the end of the twentieth century. The main problem of examining the subject re-

---

[70] In Brodsky's early language attitudes one can detect a popular thesis that not only does every stratum of a language reflect the national psychology but any change can damage the balance between the two. It is known that when he was still in Leningrad the young Brodsky was once about to send a letter to the editor of a daily newspaper in defence of Russian orthography against a proposed reform. In this letter he argued that despite a close genealogical relationship each Slavonic language conveys a different psychology, and thus any modification by analogy with a neighbouring language can be harmful to Russian: see Gordin, *Pereklichka vo mrake*, p. 141.

[71] See e.g. his statements in the interviews with Arina Ginsburg, Jadwiga Szymak-Reifer, and David Montenegro: *BKI*, pp. 371, 629, 272. See also Solomon Volkov, *Dialogi s Iosifom Brodskim* (Moscow: Nezavisimaia gazeta, 1998), p. 180.

mains in the nature of the domains involved: although the language references remain relatively (although only relatively) discrete and can at least be related to the customary descriptions used in linguistics, the second domain refers to diffused notions of national psyche, national spirit, and the perception of the world. Miłosz once warned one of his correspondents: 'We have to move away, and we can't do anything about this, from notions of "the spirit of the nation" as too much compromised, but at some point, when we have more refined tools, we'll return to them.'[72] It would be hard to disagree with this statement, but it seems as if there is still a long way to go before this refinement is obtained.

UNIVERSITY OF GLASGOW   SHAMIL KHAIROV

[72] Miłosz's letter to Andrzej Walicki of 19 November 1960, in Andrzej Walicki, *Spotkania z Miłoszem*, p. 167.

FREEDOM AND CAPTIVITY IN THE WORKS OF VLADIMIR SOROKIN AND VLADIMIR TUCHKOV

> Give beer to those who are perishing, wine to those who are in anguish; let them drink and forget their poverty and remember their misery no more.
> (BOOK OF PROVERBS)[1]

> To rule, you must see one purpose only: power. You must love one person only: yourself. Even your God must be your exclusive God, who justifies your every crime and covers it by his holy name.
> (STEFAN HEYM)[2]

Maksim Gor'kii's allegorical story 'About the siskin who lied, and the woodpecker, a lover of truth' ('O chizhe, kotoryi lgal, i o diatle — liubitele istiny') presents a debate between an 'idealist' siskin and a 'realist' woodpecker.[3] It takes place in a wood, which had hitherto been characterized by boredom and poor and uninspiring singing on the part of the birds. One day the grove's entire bird population is enraptured by the daring and beautiful song of a siskin, sitting high up in a tree. What ensues is an inspiring speech from the siskin, challenging the birds to leave the grove and move to another country, into a world of unheard-of achievement and gratification, into a new kind of great and happy life. The birds' enthusiastic response, however, is in turn interrupted by the woodpecker, who portrays the siskin as a deceiver who wrongly promises a better life without ever having been to that imaginary country. The woodpecker points out all the possible problems and contingencies which the birds might have to face in their quest for freedom. In the end, the birds reveal themselves to be too entrapped mentally to cope with the challenge of facing an unknown but potentially better life.

The post-Soviet fiction of Vladimir Tuchkov and Vladimir Sorokin is, among other things, concerned precisely with the situation described in Gor'kii's story. Some of their works depict individuals, or indeed a people, who, although in theory free, both by law (through the collapse of the Soviet system) and by nature (as humans), are not in fact free mentally. On the contrary, they are all too ready to sell themselves into serfdom in exchange for bread and a daily diet of abuse. It would seem from the texts to be analysed below that freedom and survival may be mutually exclusive, that survival is

---

[1] Proverbs 31. 6–7 (New International Version).
[2] Stefan Heym, *The King David Report: A Novel* (London: Quartet, 1977), p. 67 (Prince Jonathan to Princess Michal).
[3] Maksim Gor'kii, *Sobranie sochinenii*, 18 vols (Moscow: Gosudarstvennoe izdatel'stvo khudozhestvennoi literatury, 1960), I, 69–74.

available only at the cost of freedom, and vice versa. They exemplify the often all too real tension between Francis Bacon's admonishment: 'Why should a man be in love with his fetters, though of gold? Art thou drowned in security? Then I say thou art perfectly dead. For though thou movest, yet thy soul is buried within thee'[4] and Vladimir Lenin's insistence that freedom means first and foremost the 'freedom to provide for the most basic needs of the masses, above all freedom from hunger. "Everyone to have bread; everyone to have sound footwear and whole clothing; everyone to have warm dwellings"',[5] an opinion that might be considered reminiscent of the views of the Grand Inquisitor in Dostoevskii's novel *The Brothers Karamazov* (*Brat'ia Karamazovy*), to which we will return in due course.

The theme of freedom in the works of Sorokin and Tuchkov lends itself to analysis using the concepts of 'moral masochism', 'self-incurred immaturity', and an 'archaic relationship with the state', ideas which we shall outline before examining specific texts by the two writers. Let us begin with the concept of 'moral masochism', which has been defined by Daniel Rancour-Laferriere as 'a relatively mild disturbance in which the otherwise healthy individual searches for opportunities to suffer, to be humiliated, or to be defeated'[6] and is different from erotogenic or severe self-destructive behaviour. Although the Russian notions of *smirenie* ('humility') and *kenosis* ('self-emptying') originate in religious tradition, they can, from a psychoanalytical point of view, be approached as a manifestation of 'moral masochism', together with the Russian peasantry's tradition of fatalistic submission to *sud'ba* ('fate', 'destiny') and *rok* ('fate').[7]

The second concept that will be helpful in understanding the works of Tuchkov and Sorokin is that of 'self-incurred immaturity' ('selbstverschuldete Unmündigkeit'), a term used by Immanuel Kant in his 1784 essay *An Answer to the Question 'What is Enlightenment?'* to describe moral immaturity in contrast to age-related immaturity or legal dependence. Its opposite, moral maturity, must be earned and acquired through conscious effort of both intellect and character, namely 'enlightenment'. Kant proposed that '[e]*nlightenment is man's emergence from his self-incurred immaturity. Immaturity* is the inability to use one's own understanding without the guidance of another. This immaturity is *self-incurred* if its cause is not lack of understanding, but lack of resolution and courage to use it without the guidance of another. The motto

---

[4] *The Works of Francis Bacon*, ed. by James Spedding and others, 15 vols (Boston: Houghton and Mifflin, [n.d.]), XII, 395 <http://ia300227.us.archive.org/0/items/worksofbacon12bacoiala/worksofbacon12bacoiala.pdf> [accessed 18 March 2009].

[5] Andrzei Walicki, *Marxism and the Leap to the Kingdom of Freedom: The Rise and Fall of the Communist Utopia* (Stanford, CA: Stanford University Press, 1995), p. 279.

[6] Daniel Rancour-Laferriere, *The Slave Soul of Russia: Moral Masochism and the Cult of Suffering* (New York and London: New York University Press, 1995), p. 93.

[7] Ibid., pp. 66–77, 93–94.

of enlightenment is therefore: *Sapere aude!* Have courage to use your *own* understanding!'[8]

The third concept to be introduced here is that of an 'archaic relationship with the state',[9] which is a formulation used by the writer Vladimir Sorokin himself and describes a relationship between the people and the state and government characterized by a typologically patriarchal or quasi-religious system of unquestioning submission to authority and the latter's deification. Examples of an archaic concept of the state would be ancient Egypt, where the pharaohs were worshipped as gods. Influenced by the Judaeo-Christian tradition of seeking justice and righteousness, Russian thinkers and writers have traditionally attempted to overcome this archaic relationship with the state through critical engagement with their society, either by creating utopian visions of an alternative society or by representing social ills. Since the eighteenth century, the best-known Russian writers and poets, from Aleksandr Pushkin, Nikolai Gogol', Mikhail Lermontov, Lev Tolstoi, and Ivan Turgenev to Fedor Dostoevskii, Anton Chekhov, Evgenii Zamiatin, Daniil Kharms, Maksim Gor'kii, Anna Akhmatova, Iosif Brodskii, and Aleksandr Solzhenitsyn, have all suggested in their works an aspiration to individual moral and spiritual responsibility, and to their nation's collective social well-being. This has often included criticism of the government for its contempt for fellow men as well as discussions of the notion of freedom,[10] and has led to disagreements with the authorities, causing some writers to be condemned to exile, prison, and even death. Pushkin, for example, criticized Peter the Great in 1822 for his pursuit of power: 'Peter I had no fear of the freedom of the people and the unavoidable consequences of enlightenment, since he trusted in his own might and despised humanity, perhaps even more so than Napoleon.'[11] Dostoevskii discussed the notion of freedom in a number of his works, and in particular in the story 'The Grand Inquisitor' ('Velikii inkvizitor') in his novel *The Brothers Karamazov*, to which our discussion of Sorokin and Tuchkov will return below.[12] It will be suggested that even though the works by Sorokin and

---

[8] [Immanuel] Kant, *Political Writings*, ed. by H. S. Reiss, trans. by H. B. Nisbet (Cambridge: Cambridge University Press, 1991), p. 54 (emphases original).

[9] Brigitte Neumann, 'Der Tag des Opritschniks: Russland, Putin, der Autor Vladimir Sorokin und dessen neuer Roman', Bayerischer Rundfunk Munich, BR2 Kulturwelt radio broadcast on 21 January 2008, interview manuscript (para. 4 of 9). This and all subsequent translations from the Russian and German are my own unless otherwise indicated.

[10] See e.g. Richard Peace, 'Russian Concepts of Freedom', *Journal of Russian Studies*, 35 (1978), 3–15.

[11] A. S. Pushkin, 'Zametki po russkoi istorii XVIII veka', in *Polnoe sobranie sochinenii*, ed. by Maksim Gor'kii and others, 16 vols (Leningrad: Akademiia nauk SSSR, 1937–59), XI, 14–19 (p. 14).

[12] Dostoevskii's semi-autobiographical work *The House of the Dead* (*Zapiski iz mertvogo doma*) (1862) is also an obvious point of reference relative to the themes of imprisonment and freedom, but will not be considered in this article.

Tuchkov considered in this article do so differently, they nevertheless follow the Russian literary tradition of engaging with the relationship between power and freedom in their society.

The texts to be analysed are taken from politically and socially different periods of the first two post-Soviet decades. The immediate post-perestroika and post-Soviet era began with radical economic reforms, an all-permeating instability, and the emergence of Russian capitalism under President Boris El′tsin. Concomitant phenomena were a new degree of political and economic freedom, political chaos, and the rush to make money, out of which emerged the so-called oligarchs. The remainder of the 1990s witnessed a further erosion of the Kremlin's power over society, the regions, and other influential institutions, thrown into relief by a weakening and alcoholic president and all manner of political disputes. The new millennium's first decade under President Vladimir Putin turned out to be a time of economic restoration and bureaucratic centralization, increasing the Kremlin's power to the possible detriment of civil society and other state or constitutional authorities, such as Russia's parliament, the Duma. This third period was accompanied by the enormous personal popularity of President (and subsequently Prime Minister) Putin and significant economic improvement, as well as action by the Kremlin to neutralize the influence of the oligarchs. Viewed against this historical background, the stories by Tuchkov and Sorokin to be examined below can be seen to contain elements of social criticism by means of satire, irony, and parody, which link them with Soviet writers such as Zamiatin with his dystopian novel *We* (*My*), Mikhail Bulgakov with his work *The Master and Margarita* (*Master i Margarita*), and Aleksandr Zinov′ev and his satire *Yawning Heights* (*Ziiaiushchie vysoty*). It should be added that a number of features in some of the texts analysed below concern Russia's historical past and fictional, dystopian future. They could also be said, to some extent, to be features of the non-fictional world of post-Soviet Russian politics and society, in which citizens experience an arbitrary use of state power and in which the church appears to have become an instrument of the state in the service of an illiberal étatism.[13]

Vladimir Tuchkov's collections of stories entitled *Those Singing in the Internet* (*Poiushchie v Internete*, 2002)[14] and *Death Comes through the Internet*

---

[13] For scholarship on the relationship between the post-Soviet Russian government and the Russian Orthodox Church see e.g. John Anderson, 'Putin and the Russian Orthodox Church: Asymmetric Symphonia?', *Journal of International Affairs*, 61.1 (Fall/Winter 2007), 185–201; Joachim Willems, 'Die Russische Orthodoxe Kirche: Stütze der Macht und Spiegel der Gesellschaft', *Osteuropa*, 62 (June–August 2012), 179–89.

[14] Vladimir Tuchkov, *Poiushchie v Internete: skazki dlia vzroslykh. Odinnatsat′ zhizneopisanii novykh russkikh bankirov, terzaemykh rokovymi strastiami* (Moscow: Zakharov, 2002), also available at <http://magazines.russ.ru/druzhba/2001/9/tuch.html> [accessed 3 October 2007] (section 7 of 15).

(*Smert' prikhodit po Internetu*, 1998)[15] contain two of the stories on which we will focus: 'The Island of Freedom and Happiness' ('Ostrov svobody i schast'ia') and 'The Lord of the Steppe' ('Stepnoi barin'). Works by Vladimir Sorokin to be examined include sections of *Blue Lard* (*Goluboe salo*, 1999)[16] and *Day of the Oprichnik* (*Den' oprichnika*, 2006).[17] It will be argued that while Sorokin and Tuchkov differ in their treatment of the prison camp theme, and while this is not the only aspect of their work to be worthy of study, the two writers share a deep interest in examining the themes of freedom and of mental and moral entrapment. 'Moral entrapment' is understood here as a limitation on freedom which is rationalized and justified by both the oppressor and the oppressed through the espousal of ostensibly admirable ethical and religious values, such as *smirenie* on the part of the oppressed and the need to take responsibility for the welfare of the majority as a rationale on the part of the oppressors. This theme was of particular interest to Dostoevskii, as is evident from 'The Grand Inquisitor', *Crime and Punishment* (*Prestuplenie i nakazanie*), and *The Devils* (*Besy*).

Both Tuchkov and Sorokin take a subversive view of what Sorokin refers to as the 'great myth of Russian literature'.[18] This term encapsulates Sorokin's criticism of the pivotal significance which Russian culture traditionally ascribed to its literature as the source of supreme moral authority. This authority was, for example, embodied in the nineteenth-century novel, on the one hand, with its enormous social resonance, and in socialist realism, which was designed to be appropriate for serving the Communist Party's ideological purposes, on the other.[19] Sorokin and Tuchkov both use the grotesque as their principal literary device, mimicking and simultaneously distorting established literary styles and plots so as to challenge the reader's aesthetic expectations. Whereas Tuchkov's emphasis in his stories is on the darkly humoristic portrayal of psychopathological characters and the psychological malleability of people, Sorokin's works considered here appear to be more concerned with physical violence and the slave mentality, the absence of political culture among the Russian people, and the sacralization of the state.

Both writers draw heavily on the topoi, forms, and genres of nineteenth-century Russian literature, as well as of Soviet literature and official Soviet

[15] Vladimir Tuchkov, *Smert' prikhodit po Internetu: opisanie odinnadtsati beznakazannykh prestuplenii, kotorye byli taino soversheny v domakh novykh russkikh bankirov* (Moscow: NLO, 2001), also published in *Novyi mir*, 1998, no. 5, 68–76, and available at <http://magazines.russ.ru/novyi_mi/1998/5/tuch.html> [accessed 3 October 2007] (section 3 of 10).

[16] Vladimir Sorokin, *Goluboe salo*, 6th edn (Moscow: Ad Marginem, 2002).

[17] Vladimir Sorokin, *Den' oprichnika* (Moscow: Zakharov, 2006); Vladimir Sorokin, *Day of the Oprichnik*, trans. by Jamey Gambrell (New York: Farrar, Straus and Giroux, 2011).

[18] Cited in Sally Laird, *Voices of Russian Literature: Interviews with Ten Contemporary Writers* (Oxford: Oxford University Press, 1999), p. 159.

[19] Cf. Maksim Marusenkov, *Absurdopediia russkoi zhizni Vladimira Sorokina: zaum, grotesk i absurd* (St Petersburg: Aleteiia, 2012), pp. 15–18.

discourse. More specifically, both rely on the language and ideas of Tolstoi and Dostoevskii, and also of other writers such as Zamiatin, as primary sources of inspiration. Tuchkov uses Tolstoi's didactic peasant stories and fables as a template for his short stories, and Sorokin also copies Tolstoi's style, to extravagantly grotesque effect. Both authors' use of nineteenth-century lyrical language and idyllic description of the countryside, reminiscent of Tolstoi, Ivan Turgenev, Chekhov, and Ivan Bunin, and Sorokin's imitation of socialist realist literature seem to suggest at first the presence of a meaningful plot. Against expectation, however, the narratives turn into cascades of graphic and barbaric violence, sadism, masochism, and cannibalism, accompanied by a carnivalesque portrayal of lower body parts and their products, such as faeces. The Russian literary scholar Mikhail Golubkov has referred to this as embodying a 'merciless clash of two discourses, two languages, two incompatible cultural layers'.[20] These two 'incompatible cultural layers' refer to nineteenth-century literary and moral discourse, and the language and plotlines employed by Sorokin, which figuratively seek to 'destroy' this discourse.

This incompatibility may be analysed in terms of the grotesque, irony, and the comic. Philip Thomson argued that the grotesque can 'serve to bring the horrifying and disgusting aspects of human existence to the surface, there to be rendered less harmful by the introduction of a comic perspective'.[21] Furthermore, the grotesque operates on the principle of incompatibility and disharmony[22] between the reader's world-view and expectations, and the failure of his world-view and categories of understanding to deal with the represented world.[23] The grotesque questions mankind's very ability to understand the world. The world of the grotesque is uncanny and evades understanding. Moreover, it is critically directed at society, since it relies for its effects on the world-view, expectations, habits, and values which dominate it. Carl Pietzcker wrote that the grotesque, through its examination of the individual's ability to understand the world, occurs where people's value systems have been shattered, but have not yet been replaced by new ones.[24] Wolfgang Kayser regarded the grotesque as expressing an ambivalent experience of the absurdities of existence, and as an 'attempt to invoke and subdue the demonic aspects of the world'.[25] The monstrous, grotesque nature of certain works by

[20] '[Б]езжалостн[ое] столкновен[ие] двух дискурсов, двух языков, двух несовместимых культурных пластов' (Mikhail Golubkov, 'Russkii postmodernizm: nachala i kontsy', *Literaturnaia ucheba*, 6 (2003), 71–92 (p. 80)).
[21] Philip Thomson, *The Grotesque* (London: Methuen, 1972), p. 59.
[22] Ibid., pp. 18, 20–28, 58–59.
[23] Carl Pietzcker, 'Das Groteske', *DVjs*, 45 (1971), 197–211.
[24] Ibid., p. 211.
[25] Wolfgang Kayser, *The Grotesque in Art and Literature*, trans. by Ulrich Weisstein (Bloomington: Indiana University Press, 1957), p. 188.

Tuchkov and Sorokin foregrounds the absence of a moral and semantic grid, thereby describing the existence of post-Soviet men and women.

The clash of readers' expectations of narrative coherence with the actual development of plotlines—a clash which arguably dominates much of Sorokin's and Tuchkov's fiction in general—introduces an ironic dimension: Douglas Muecke argues that a text can be marked as ironic through 'some form of perceptible contradiction, disparity, incongruity or anomaly'.[26] The fact that a related feature of Sorokin's and Tuchkov's narratives, namely hyperbole, may have an ironic implication[27] may shed further light on their narratives, suggesting that the plotlines which Tuchkov's and Sorokin's readers encounter are not necessarily endowed with the approval of the implied author.

Before turning to discussion of the specific literary texts, one further aspect of the discussion's theoretical framework must be introduced. The concept of the carnivalesque will be used to position the texts in relation to the Russian literary tradition. Despite surface indications to the contrary, these texts may in fact be read as a continuation of traditional literary concerns with questions of morality. The texts by Sorokin and Tuchkov may be viewed constructively in terms of 'carnivalized' literature as constituting 'official literature's dialectical antithesis and parodic double',[28] and Sorokin's texts in particular are characterized by heterogeneity and ontological instability, stylistic heteroglossia and apparent incoherence of structure. Our textual analyses will show that Brian McHale's view of postmodernist fiction as a satirical, parodic, and antithetical counterpart to official literature applies to Sorokin's and Tuchkov's works. At the same time, what looks like a carnivalesque attack on the literary canon ultimately confirms its superiority. David Shepherd, for example, writes that carnivalistic transgression of hierarchy 'actually confirms and bolsters the security of the more enduring authority which it purports to challenge'.[29] As Shepherd goes on to point out, however, such carnivalistic subversion has a liberating effect since it offers a 'glimpse of a better alternative; hence the not uncommon description of Bakhtin as a utopian'.[30] Analysis of Tuchkov's and Sorokin's texts will illustrate that although these narratives treat the Soviet past and post-Soviet present satirically, they demonstrate that post-Soviet fiction is able to be both humorously critical and ultimately affirmative of Russia's literary tradition.

Scholarly interest in Tuchkov's short fiction has focused on an aspect that his poetics share with that of Sorokin, namely the creation of a

[26] Douglas C. Muecke, 'Irony Markers', *Poetics*, 7 (1978), 363–75 (p. 365).
[27] Cf. Linda Hutcheon, *Irony's Edge: The Theory and Politics of Irony* (London and New York: Routledge, 1994), pp. 156–59.
[28] Brian McHale, *Postmodernist Fiction* (Routledge: London and New York, 1987), p. 172.
[29] David Shepherd, *Beyond Metafiction: Self-Consciousness in Soviet Literature* (Oxford: Clarendon Press, 1992), pp. 119–20.
[30] Ibid., p. 120.

quasi-mythological space where pre-modern, Soviet, and post-Soviet times converge.[31] This can be seen in Tuchkov's anti-utopian story 'The Island of Freedom and Happiness',[32] which treats ironically the myth of 'New Russian' megalomania, that is the so-called New Russians' pursuit of self-gratification and power over others. The story also parodies the genre of utopia and addresses important philosophical issues relating to freedom, necessity, happiness, and evil. Evgenii, alias John, is a Russian multi-millionaire who wishes to build a Russian America, a place he calls Libertytown, somewhere in the middle of Russia. People excitedly volunteer to join the utopian project, and he creates a 'Free World' modelled on Californian laws, market economy, and democracy, perfectly copying Californian society, including the latter's demography. Unlike the situation in Russia proper, the new citizens of Libertytown are prosperous since they have money, houses, and careers; theirs is supposed to be an island of 'freedom and happiness in the huge surging ocean of Russian chaos!'.[33] Notwithstanding all this, selfish ambition, greed, strife, crime, and murder come into existence and multiply, prostitution flourishes, while political intrigue and unemployment begin to dominate. What has been said with reference to Aleksandr Zinov'ev's satirical novel *Yawning Heights* seems to be applicable to this story too: 'the utopian experiment put into practice is revealed as an arena not for the elevation and perfection of human nature, but for the continuous enactment of the worst elemental drives of greed, gluttony, status-seeking, in short, of narrow self-interest'.[34] Without collective experience of how to enjoy freedom responsibly and live simultaneously in peace, the enthusiasm of Libertytown's inhabitants for their new world soon turns into death and chaos and appears to provide posthumous proof of Catherine the Great's *Nakaz*, which stated that 'One should not suddenly and through general law create large numbers of free men.'[35] Social unrest gives rise to a national socialist party, and in the end a Fascist regime takes over and establishes a dictatorship, which among other things replaces dollars with the Reichsmark. The only way for John to restore his initial concept seems to be to ask the United Nations Security Council for military intervention (p. 86).

'The Island of Freedom and Happiness' not only mocks New Russians as

[31] Mark Lipovetsky, 'New Russians as Cultural Myth', *Russian Review*, 62 (2003), 54–71; Kapitolina Koksheneva, *Revoliutsiia nizkikh smyslov: o sovremennoi russkoi proze* (Moscow: Leto, 2001), pp. 109–13.

[32] Tuchkov, *Poiushchie v Internete*, pp. 73–86.

[33] 'Мы во что бы то ни стало станем маленьким островком свободы и счастья в огромном бушующем океане российского беспредела!' (p. 86).

[34] Edith W. Clowes, *Russian Experimental Fiction: Resisting Ideology after Utopia* (Princeton: Princeton University Press, 1993), p. 124.

[35] Section 250 of the *Nakaz*, cited in Uriel Procaccia, *Russian Culture, Property Rights and the Market Economy* (Cambridge: Cambridge University Press, 2007), p. 103.

they are often stereotypically perceived, as wealthy, self-absorbed and uncultured individuals with an unquenchable desire to display their riches instead of showing respect for others, but also makes comic use of German history as a backdrop to events: in the same way that the Weimar Republic began as a young democracy in the 1920s, but suffered from significant economic and social instability and discontent with the post-war settlement, and was replaced by a Fascist dictatorship in the early 1930s, the utopian 'Island of Freedom and Happiness' begins with euphoric post-Soviet enthusiasm for capitalism, democracy, America, and the West, but then goes through a powerful process of disillusionment.

The story can also be interpreted as criticizing the identification of material well-being with happiness. For many ex-Soviet people, as Vladimir Sorokin argues, 'even the last vestiges of a moral code have been destroyed [...] Many people seem to lack any criteria for evaluating reality at all.'[36] Moreover, Tuchkov's Evgenii builds his city not for the sake of liberating the people, but for his own glory. Even so, he cannot create Libertytown without them. The people, therefore, are a means to an end for him, not an end in themselves. Here Tuchkov touches on the fundamental issue confronting most human attempts to 'realize' utopia artificially: the sublime idea itself comes to take precedence over human beings, who regress from the level of moral and spiritual beings to that of freely utilizable objects or commodities.

Before moving on to our next text-based discussion, namely of Tuchkov's narrative 'The Lord of the Steppe' ('Stepnoi barin'),[37] it may be helpful to point to its intertextuality at the surface, the thematic, and the semantic levels. The story appears to contain a specific reference to the title of Turgenev's novella *Stepnoi korol' Lir* (*King Lear of the Steppe*, 1870) and to be generally linked with his *Zapiski okhotnika* (*A Hunter's Sketches*, 1852). Turgenev's novella, through its treatment of Shakespeare's *King Lear*, engages with the issue of power as well as historical issues and the dark sides of Russian society, such as serfdom. In addition, the novella reflects Turgenev's interest in types of Russian people and their passions and conflicts, set at the level of ordinary, everyday life.[38] Similarly, the earlier sketches in *Zapiski okhotnika* deal both with the theme of the Russian countryside, the forest and the steppe, and with that of serfdom.[39] A further parallel between Tuchkov's short fiction and

---

[36] Vladimir Sorokin, cited in Laird, p. 154.
[37] Tuchkov, *Smert' prikhodit po Internetu*, pp. 20–27.
[38] These themes in Turgenev are critically discussed in I. S. Turgenev, *Polnoe sobranie sochinenii i pisem v dvadtsati vos'mi tomakh*, ed. by M. P. Alekseev, *Sochineniia* (Moscow and Leningrad: Nauka, 1965), x, 415–23.
[39] See Victor Ripp, 'Ideology in Turgenev's *Notes of a Hunter*: The First Three Sketches', *Slavic Review*, 38 (1979), 75–88; and Thomas H. Hoisington, 'The Enigmatic Hunter of Turgenev's *Zapiski okhotnika*', *Russian Literature*, 42 (1997), 47–64 (pp. 47–48).

Turgenev's works is the fact that both frustrate contemporary readers' expectations that literary works should offer recognizable moral judgements.[40]

The narrative 'The Lord of the Steppe' tells the story of Dmitrii, a malicious but successful banker who purchases some land and sets about re-establishing the feudal system within its boundaries, with himself as *barin* ('lord') and people from the surrounding villages as serfs. In effect, by signing Dmitrii's 'employment' contract, these people voluntarily renounce their rights as free people and become his slaves. Their only remaining rights are that they are theoretically free to leave his employ on St George's Day, and, of course, far more importantly, that they receive wages. At the end of the first year, in spite of the systematic maltreatment and physical abuse which they have undergone, they agree to prolong their serfdom, confident that they will be able to opt out in several years' time with enough money to retire on in the outside world. In reality, however, the experience of living in this feudalistic microcosm manages to transform these people psychologically, as they become real serfs:

It took Dmitrii, who managed his business with a hard and merciless hand, about three years to instil a new self-consciousness, new morals, and a new sense of purpose in his serfs. They began to relate to their master no longer as to an ecccentric rich man, but as to their own father, a strict but just father, who continually looks after their happiness.[41]

In other words, the peasants develop a serf mentality, which makes their existence as serfs seem perfectly acceptable to them and which prevents them from seeing reality for what it is. In the serfs' imagination Dmitrii, the one who abuses them, has become a well-meaning father figure.

Above all, the story deals with the theme of freedom, with the tension between freedom and economic survival, and with the question of how much significance spiritual values such as freedom and human dignity have in the contemporary and, more specifically, the post-Soviet world. It also addresses the corresponding theme of moral masochism and the question of human psychological malleability, not as individuals, but as members of a collective.

In essence, Dmitrii's social project succeeds in making a number of free, albeit poor, individuals consciously and voluntarily renounce their liberty and human dignity in exchange for being mistreated on a daily basis and not even being fed very well. The story implicitly asks how far freedom and personal rights may be of use to individuals, or indeed to a whole people living

---

[40] Cf. Isaiah Berlin's Romanes Lecture of 1920, *Fathers and Sons* (Oxford: Clarendon Press, 1972), p. 18.

[41] 'Тода через три Дмитрий, ведя дело твердой и беспощадной рукой, сформировал в своих крепостных новое самосознание, новую мораль, новые ориентиры. К барину стали относиться уже не как к чудаковатому богачу, а как к отцу родному, строгому, но справедливому, беспрестанно пекущемуся об их благе' (p. 26).

in poverty and without any economic prospects, or to people who seem to lack any sense of purpose or vision for managing their own lives. In 'Stepnoi barin' the peasants derive their entire identity and purpose from subjection to someone else's 'dream', namely Dmitrii's sadism and his hunger for wealth and power.

'Stepnoi barin' operates to some extent as a reversal of Russian history by undoing the emancipation of the serfs, but perhaps more interestingly also inverts the account of the Israelites' Exodus from Egypt. The Israelites' complaint to Moses and God in the wilderness after their escape from Egypt was that they would prefer to be slaves, but supplied with garlic and meat, rather than suffer starvation in the desert. However, the Israelites had leaders who were committed to helping them to achieve their true identity and purpose, living as free men and proprietors of their own land. The editor of the biblical narrative makes it clear that the people needed to rid themselves of the slave mentality which they had acquired over the time of their servitude. This is why, in a possible sociological interpretation of the narrative, the people had to wander forty years in a desert which could have been crossed in a few weeks, so that the older generation could die and the young, who had never seen physical or mental slavery, could enter the Promised Land as truly free people.

By contrast, in 'Stepnoi barin' the Exodus story of a people moving from slavery to freedom is inverted, and Tuchkov's narrator calls Dmitrii's experiment 'anti-evolutionary' (p. 22). Although time and civilization move on, the people in the story are happy to revert to what at first glance appear to be long-forgotten forms of social organization.[42] The peasants feel relatively secure in their physical existence (something which they had apparently not felt in the world 'out there'), and indeed they are joined by a priest who 'was quite rightly disappointed by modern civilization'.[43] As it seems, the priest rediscovers his purpose by living with the suffering peasants and being cherished by them, rather than perceiving himself as being obsolete and without relevance in modern society. The same applies to the peasants. They have become an integral part of a society, however small, and have been given a sense of purpose and belonging. By and large, their life is predictable and bearable, and they receive attention (for in a twisted and masochistic way lashes can be a form of affection, too).[44] Apropos of Turgenev's 'Raspberry Spring' in *A Hunter's Sketches*, Victor Ripp writes that 'the peasants are part of a society that is not merely oppressive but also manages to insinuate its own rationality, a political

---

[42] Considering that the introduction of collective farms in the Soviet Union was popularly perceived to be a reimposition of serfdom, this kind of social organization may not have been as long-forgotten as suggested, after all.

[43] '[С]овершенно справедливо разочаровался в современной цивилизации' (p. 26).

[44] Cf. Rancour-Laferriere, pp. 154–55: love can be won through the acceptance of abuse.

system simultaneously so encompassing and persuasive that it is impossible to conceive of an alternative'.[45] In 'The Lord of the Steppe' Tuchkov appears to follow Turgenev in highlighting exactly this self-perpetuation of serfdom, be it political or psychological, even though, unlike Turgenev, Tuchkov does not conform to realist expectations, but alienates his fictional world from the real one by way of grotesque exaggeration. Christie Davies writes of such humour that it enables people to laugh 'at what appears to them to be a slightly strange version of themselves; almost as if they were to see themselves in a distorting mirror at a fair ground'.[46] The fictional world of 'Stepnoi barin' is incongruent with the reader's historical world, and so is surprising, or rather shocking, for the reader. At the same time, such an exaggeration of reality that foregrounds a combination of 'moral masochism' and its abuse by the powers that be allows critical emphasis to be placed on these features as persistent elements in Russian culture.

The questions of liberty and survival which arise in 'Stepnoi barin' are reminiscent of the discussion between the Cardinal Archbishop of Seville and Jesus in the chapter 'The Grand Inquisitor' in Dostoevskii's *Brothers Karamazov*.[47] In that story, the Cardinal defends himself and the elaborate system of religious and moral subordination and rule which the church has created over centuries in order to free mankind from what he regards as 'bad' freedom (represented by the archbishop as the freedom *to* sin and become involved in moral dilemmas which ordinary humans supposedly could not possibly bear). His arguments are in every way a misrepresentation of the purposes of Jesus. As evidenced by Jesus's actions in 'The Grand Inquisitor', which is in essence in line with his real counterpart in the Bible, he came to bring forgiveness and freedom *from* sin (he withstood the temptations in the desert) and healing and restoration to life (he resurrects the dead girl in the cathedral square), as well as unconditional love and acceptance of mankind (he kisses the Grand Inquisitor).

'The Grand Inquisitor' is founded on the premiss that the church had built a repressive system, which not only curtailed freedom but also kept people in collective immaturity and dependency, and claimed furthermore that such bondage was spiritually legitimate. Concerning the legend of the 'Grand Inquisitor', Dostoevskii wrote that:

---

[45] Ripp, p. 86.

[46] Christie Davies, *Jokes and their Relation to Society* (Berlin and New York: de Gruyter, 1998), p. 1.

[47] F. M. Dostoevskii, *Sobranie sochinenii*, ed. by L. P. Grossman and others, 10 vols (Moscow: Gosudarstvennoe izdatel'stvo khudozhestvennoi literatury, 1958), IX, 309–32. For a more extensive discussion of 'The Grand Inquisitor' and its treatment of the theme of freedom see Joseph Frank, *Dostoevsky: A Writer in his Time*, ed. by Mary Petrusewicz (Princeton: Princeton University Press, 2010), pp. 788–803, 872–78.

all of this for them is allegedly in the name of love of humanity: Christ's law, they claim, is burdensome and abstract, and too heavy for weak people to bear, and instead of the law of Freedom and Enlightenment, they offer them the law of chains and enslavement through bread.[48]

The real issue here is not the system as such, however, but the perversion of mind of those running and sustaining it, such as the Grand Inquisitor, who seriously believes that what he is doing is indeed on behalf of and for the benefit of the people. He is fully convinced of the goodness of the system, even if it results in such acts as the enthusiastic burning of fellow human beings as heretics, all 'ad majorem gloriam Dei',[49] to the greater glory of God.

In a way, 'The Grand Inquisitor' and 'Stepnoi barin' pose similar questions: What constitutes a socio-political system's moral legitimacy? What self-perception and consciousness of their own worth do people have? Is their (unfree) position imposed from above or in reality 'self-incurred immaturity'? How is freedom to be defined? Why do people voluntarily relinquish their freedom and dignity? Do they do so simply through necessity, the fear of responsibility and freedom, or could it be because of the drive to experience suffering? The disdain for both passivity and the fear of accepting responsibility for oneself which Kant expressed in *An Answer to the Question 'What is Enlightenment?'* may provide a possible answer: people's indolence and the convenient refusal to examine their social scripts; reactive or passive types of behaviour; and, presumably, lack of action in response to what reason tells them:

Laziness and cowardice are the reasons why such a large proportion of men, even when nature has long emancipated them from alien guidance (*naturaliter maiorennes* [those who have come of age by virtue of nature]), nevertheless gladly remain immature for life. For the same reasons, it is all too easy for others to set themselves up as their guardians. It is so convenient to be immature! [...] For enlightenment [from the yoke of immaturity], all that is needed is *freedom*. And the freedom in question is the most innocuous form of all—freedom to make *public use* of one's reason in all matters.[50]

Having examined the common thematic ground of 'The Grand Inquisitor' and 'Stepnoi barin', our discussion will now turn to the construction and presentation of semantic intention. Each of these narratives uses different narrative devices to interrogate the actions and reasoning of the protagonists, of the Grand Inquisitor as well as of Dmitrii and his serfs. The chapter about the Grand Inquisitor is an embedded story characterized as a *poema*, narrated by Ivan Karamazov to his younger brother; moreover, Ivan recommends to

---

[48] Dostoevskii in a commentary on 'The Grand Inquistor' sent to N. A. Liubimov, co-editor of the *Russian Messenger*, on 11 June 1879, quoted in Frank, *Dostoevsky*, p. 792.
[49] Dostoevskii, *Sobranie sochinenii*, IX, 312.
[50] Reiss, pp. 54–55 (emphases original).

Alesha that he should not take the narration too seriously.[51] In Tuchkov's story, however, the main device through which the implied authorial viewpoint becomes obvious is that of humour.

In 'Stepnoi barin' Tuchkov follows a humoristic strategy based on creating, then frustrating, certain expectations in the reader. By so doing, the author infuses a parodic and ironic effect into the narrative. Laughter is created furthermore by the contradiction between the rational and purposeful action which the reader would expect from the characters (such as not signing the serfdom contract) and the serfs' counter-productive and inappropriate action. Human inertia and indolence, the inability to react quickly enough to changing circumstances, which Henri Bergson identified as one of the main characteristics of humour,[52] is a clear element in Tuchkov's stories.

A few examples from 'Stepnoi barin' will suffice to illustrate Tuchkov's use of humour and irony and how they reveal the story's implied authorial viewpoint as being in opposition to the repugnant plot. The story's opening line ('Dmitrii was the product of great Russian literature')[53] might make the reader expect something 'great' of his character, since it speaks of his being a product of 'greatness' (p. 20). The omniscient narrator then proceeds to tell us that Dmitrii's favourite writers were Tolstoi and Dostoevskii, who, the narrator points out, are widely regarded as moralists. The rest of the paragraph makes it clear, however, that Dmitrii is not modelling himself on the positive example of 'great Russian literature' but takes it instead as something to react against: 'However, his character took shape not as the sum of the spiritual injunctions of which the nineteenth-century Russian novel is full, but rather as its opposition.'[54] The reader is surprised and disoriented by the fact that the study of the Russian classics has led to the celebration of greed and lust for power. The irony contained in the opening remarks is thus fully revealed.

A second example of Tuchkov's irony is as follows: 'To reinforce the educational impact, he occasionally came out into the courtyard to conduct trials, addressing the people in absolutely plain terms: "Well then, you little thieves, have you assembled for righteous judgement?"'[55] It is as obvious to the reader as it is to the narrator that there is nothing 'righteous' or 'educational' about Dmitrii's law court. In reality, the latter is nothing more than a pretext for

---

[51] 'Well, isn't this nothing but nonsense, Alesha, isn't it simply an incoherent poem of an incoherent student? [. . .] Why are you taking it so seriously?' ('Да ведь это же вздор, Алеша, ведь это только бестолковая поэма бестолкового студента [. . .] К чему ты в такой серьез берешь?' (Dostoevskii, *Sobranie sochinenii*, IX, 330)).

[52] Henri Bergson, *Laughter: An Essay on the Meaning of the Comic* (Rockville, MD: Arc Manor, 2008), pp. 10–14, 71, 87.

[53] 'Дмитрий был продуктом великой русской литературы.'

[54] 'Однако его характер сложился не как сумма духовных предписаний, которыми насыщен отечественный роман XIX века, а как противодействие им.'

[55] 'Иногда выходил судить во двор — для усиления педагогического эффекта, обращаясь к народу без всяких обиняков: "Ну что, ворюги, собрались на суд праведный?!"' (p. 23).

his abuse of power. The report about Dmitrii 'judging' his serfs is comic and ironic, since the context implies a negation of true justice and education.

Another instance in 'Stepnoi barin' of situational humour resulting from human inertia is offered by the following: the serfs ignore the opportunity to leave the estate on St George's Day. In effect heeding the advice from Proverbs cited in the epigraph to this article, Dmitrii had thrown a party for them the night before. Dmitrii reveals perfectly the psychological inertia which causes the peasants to adopt behaviour harmful to their own self-interest, which is clearly perceived as comic by the outside spectator, the reader. There is in the story a strong element of satire of the Russian people and of its 'slave soul':

> To all appearance, severe ordeals have tempered Russian men and women to such an extent that they are able to bear even truly inhumane adversities. This is how it has always been: under the Tatars, under Ivan the Terrible, under Peter the Great, under Stalin. Dmitrii fully confirmed this rule.[56]

Such instances of humour and irony are typical of the story as a whole, and justify the conclusion that the implied authorial viewpoint in 'Stepnoi barin' is one of disapproval for Dmitrii and his way of life.

Although Dmitrii's little feudal world can be seen as representing authoritarian or totalitarian societies where people are used as instruments for the attainment of some grand idea of order or ideological purpose, the specific references are to post-Soviet and Russian culture. To a certain extent, however, 'Stepnoi barin' can also be viewed as a broader satire on unmitigated capitalism, presented as depriving humans of their value and of the very freedom which it claims to promulgate. Again, the crucial question posed is as follows: what is of greater worth: being free but deprived of immediate prospects for the future, or having food, an occupation, a sense of usefulness, albeit at the price of slavery?

The story also embodies in the case of Dmitrii himself the individual's passions and pathological lust for power. 'Stepnoi barin' is just as much about Dmitrii, a cruel and mentally sick individual who suffers from an 'unusual state of mind' ('нестандартная психика', p. 23), to quote the narrator's characteristically ironic understatement. Dmitrii has devised his scheme in order to satisfy his own desire for possession, control, and violence. And his 'regime' is perpetuated by his son Grigorii, who, we are told, inherits his father's 'passion'.

Above all, 'Stepnoi barin' concerns the peasants who figure in the story, people who crave order, identity, purpose, stability, and some sort of satis-

---

[56] 'По — видимому, суровые испытания закаляют русского человека до такой степени, что он способен перенести еще и не такие невзгоды, поистине нечеловеческие. Так было всегда: при татарах, при Иване Грозном, при Петре Первом, при Сталине. Дмитрий вполне подтвердил это правило' (p. 25).

faction in life, however limited and fragile. Since they appear to be entirely fixated on the immediate, momentary, and physical aspects of existence, however, without any dreams or true vision for their future, they do not realize that what they are perpetuating is their own subordination to Dmitrii's desires: 'Where there is no vision, the people perish' (Proverbs 29. 18, Authorized Version). Tuchkov's characters appear to embody what the psychiatrist Viktor Frankl, a former Nazi camp prisoner, wrote about life in a concentration camp, likening it to a 'provisional existence':

> On entering camp a change took place in the minds of the men. [. . .] A man who could not see the end of his 'provisional existence' was not able to aim at an ultimate goal in life. [. . .] The prisoner who had lost faith in the future—his future—was doomed. With his loss of belief in the future, he also lost his spiritual hold: he let himself decline and became subject to mental and physical decay. [. . .] He simply gave up.[57]

Tuchkov foregrounds the process by which the people develop into serfs, namely by voluntarily agreeing to it and co-operating with it. This seems to reflect what the critic Rancour-Laferriere has observed in relation to Russian cultural history in general:

> Russia is customarily characterized as an 'authoritarian' or 'patriarchal' culture. This is no doubt true, but the very terms tend to attract blame toward those exercising 'authority' and draw analytic attention away from those who do the suffering and who might possibly be complicitous in the 'authoritarianism'.[58]

In the same vein, the historian Nicholas Vakar has argued that:

> [h]istorians who have written that the tyranny of the Czars conditioned the nation to accept the tyranny of the Communists have missed the fact that Russian habits of obedience have been the cause, not the result, of political authority.[59]

This acceptance of tyrannical rule appears to be motivated by what Sigmund Freud once defined as 'moral masochism', as contrasted with erotogenic and feminine masochism:

> The third form of masochism, moral masochism, is chiefly remarkable for having loosened its connection with what we recognize as sexuality [. . .] The suffering itself is what matters; whether it is decreed by someone who is loved or by someone who is indifferent is of no importance. It may even be caused by impersonal powers or circumstances; the true masochist always turns his cheek whenever he has a chance of receiving a blow.[60]

---

[57] Viktor E. Frankl, *Man's Search for Meaning*, trans. by Ilse Lasch (Boston: Beacon Press, 2006), pp. 70, 74.

[58] Rancour-Laferriere, p. 2.

[59] Nicholas Vakar, *The Taproot of Soviet Society* (New York: Harper, 1961), cited in Procaccia, p. 169.

[60] Sigmund Freud, 'The Economic Problem of Masochism', in *The Standard Edition of the*

It is in this context that Rancour-Laferriere speaks metaphorically of Russia's 'slave soul', a phrase to describe what is in his view a 'mentality that pervades Russia on all cultural levels'.[61]

A very instructive subject yet to be discussed is that of the serfdom contract which the people sign (p. 21). Tuchkov's use of anachronism and the juxtaposition of conceptually unrelated things, such as modern consumer technology with feudalism (Dmitrii prints two copies of the serfdom contract on a laser printer), serve to reinforce the story's comic and grotesque character. Intriguingly, the conclusion of a contract is by definition a rational act pursued to better an individual's situation, and the modern contract is a form of legally binding promise between ordinary individuals. It is a product of Renaissance, Reformation, and Enlightenment notions of human dignity and individual self-esteem and is based on a set of individual liberties and rights as prerequisites.[62] Uriel Procaccia writes that:

since Hegel also held that ownership of objects, including ownership of a person over [him]self, is essential to the definition of 'personhood' (*Persönlichkeit*), he reasoned that contracts were necessary for the mental construction of the self.[63]

In 'Stepnoi barin' the contract to surrender one's individual rights to another private individual would probably in many liberal democracies be regarded as void, since it does transgress commonly held moral bounds. More importantly, however, the notion of contract is turned here *ad absurdum*, into something self-defeating which contradicts normal logic and reasoning. A contract requires the individual's free consent, which can be exercised only if the person enjoys the necessary liberty to do so, as well as implicit and inalienable personal rights. Solzhenitsyn lamented that 'a helplessness bred by the absence of personal rights permeates the entire country'.[64] What is emphasized hyperbolically in this story is something which Lipovetsky identifies as 'the unity of Russian cultural dynamics despite all historical ruptures':[65] whereas technology and time move on and political systems replace each other, certain deeply rooted cultural features, specifically moral masochism, seem to continue their existence in today's post-Soviet Russian society.

Let us now turn briefly to Vladimir Sorokin's work *Day of the Oprichnik* (*Den' oprichnika*).[66] Making copious use of anachronism and antiquated lan-

Complete Psychological Works of Sigmund Freud, trans by J. Strachey, 24 vols (London: Hogarth Press, 1953–65), XIX: *1923–1925: 'The Ego and the Id' and Other Works* (1961), pp. 159–71 (p. 165).

[61] Rancour-Laferriere, p. 134.
[62] See Procaccia.
[63] Procaccia, pp. 78–79 (emphasis original).
[64] Solzhenitsyn, *Rebuilding Russia: Reflections and Tentative Proposals*, trans. by Alexis Klimoff (London: Harvill, 1991), p. 10.
[65] Lipovetsky, 'New Russians as Cultural Myth', p. 71.
[66] For recent scholarship on this short novel by Sorokin see e.g. Marusenkov, pp. 29–31, 63–65;

guage, the novel depicts Russia in the year 2027 as a reborn sixteenth-century Muscovite Rus', an ethnically Russian principality protected from the outside world by a 'Great Russian Wall', reminiscent of the Great Wall of China. Despite this reversion to an earlier state of Russian society, the technology is still that of the twenty-first century, as exemplified by modern cars and cutting-edge communication technology; information bubbles in the air depict the face of the absent interlocutor, mobile phones are a particular status symbol of the *oprichniki*,[67] and a walk through security corridors at an airport reveals on a glass screen all there is to know about you and your life. The state is ruled by the *gosudar'* ('sovereign'), aided in his task by a brotherhood of modern *oprichniki*, who directly serve their sovereign. They wear what are probably meant to be historical garments (red shirts, black kaftans, heavy gold earrings), prefer poleaxe-shaped beards, and drive red Mercedes cars. They are divided into two factions, a left and a right wing. They are organized in a way similar to that of a religious order, are ferociously Orthodox, and copy the most brutal techniques of torture and execution used earlier by Ivan IV's *oprichniki*. The state's historical view of itself is that it has finally achieved the long-awaited rebirth of 'Holy Rus'', an event which had been heralded sixteen years earlier by the laying of the foundation stone for the 'Great Russian Wall', which ended the series of *smuty* ('rebellions') reminiscent of the October Revolution of 1917 and perestroika of the late 1980s, eventually leading to an anti-liberal restoration. After the 'Red Rebellion' had passed, the 'White Rebellion' would have led to the break-up of the country, had not the ensuing 'Grey Rebellion' restored the power of the motherland.[68] The 'Great Russian Wall' or 'Western Wall' separates Russia from Europe, which is dependent on Russian gas exports. Western culture is officially despised even though it remains accessible, while Russia turns back to an idealized past peasant culture.

Sorokin's dystopia describes, by way of first-person narration, a day in the life of Andrei Danilovich Komiaga, who is a leading member of the corrupt right wing of the *oprichnina*. The story's narrative structure appears to be modelled on Aleksandr Solzhenitsyn's work *A Day in the Life of Ivan Denisovich*

Marina Aptekman, 'Forward to the Past, or Two Radical Views on the Russian Nationalist Future: Pyotr Krasnov's *Behind the Thistle* and Vladimir Sorokin's *Day of an Oprichnik*', *Slavic and East European Journal*, 53 (2009), 241–60; Dirk Uffelmann, 'The Compliance with and Imposition of Social and Linguistic Norms in Sorokin's *Norma* and *Den' oprichnika*', in *From Poets to Padonki: Linguistic Authority and Norm Negotiation in Modern Russian Culture*, ed. by Ingunn Lunde and Martin Paulsen, Slavica Bergensia, 9 (Bergen: University of Bergen, 2009), pp. 143–67; Kornelia Lienhart, *Neo-Opričnina: Aleksandr Dugins Utopie und Vladimir Sorokins Antiutopie* (Saarbrücken: VDM, 2011); Karlheinz Kasper, 'Terror der Opričnina oder Diktatur der Vampire? Sorokin und Pelevin warnen vor Russlands Zukunft', *Osteuropa*, 57 (October 2007), 103–25.

[67] *Oprichnik* is the historical term describing a member of Ivan IV's secret police.
[68] pp. 18, 38–39 in the Russian original; pp. 13–14, 30–31 in Jamey Gambrell's translation.

(*Odin den' Ivana Denisovicha*,[69] first published in 1962), which narrates an ordinary day in the life of the prison-camp inmate Ivan Denisovich. Sorokin's character Komiaga begins his day with prayer, and then proceeds to engage in pillage, rape, murder, and torture, which are followed by attending Mass, lunch, and the injection of some kind of drug. The afternoon is filled with extortion and a visit to a clairvoyant who burns Russian classics such as *The Idiot* and *Anna Karenina*, and who later receives the collected works of Anton Chekhov for the same purpose. At night, Komiaga's faction of the *oprichnina* assembles in the *bania* ('bathhouse') owned by its leader, where they feast, take drugs, exercise mutually ritualized cruelty, and engage in mass copulation.

A comparison of *Day of the Oprichnik* with Zamiatin's novel *We* may offer an instructive perspective on Sorokin's work. Both texts engage critically with utopian discourse, and share a number of specific parallels. Both are written in the form of diaries by leading functionaries who live in a fictional society cut off from the outside world by a great wall. In Zamiatin's *We* an established totalitarian society is portrayed from the point of view of a key engineer, D-503, who gradually comes to doubt the veracity of the 'truth' as promulgated by One State, which demands absolute compliance from all citizens. Through an apparently chance acquaintance with the rebel I-330, the hero is exposed to an outsider's perspective, which enables him to question his society's code, even if he is forced into line again at the end of the novel through the 'Great Operation'.

Sorokin's *Day of the Oprichnik*, on the contrary, is, according to Dirk Uffelmann, characterized by the narrator's 'attempt to internalize the righteousness of the norms he implements by murder, rape and arson'.[70] Uffelmann further writes that in this novel 'we learn a lot about a repressive system *in statu nascendi* from the perspective of an executor of the norm'.[71] The *oprichnik* eagerly aligns himself with his society's code, thereby helping to consolidate his society. While *Day of the Oprichnik* lacks any character development comparable to that of D-503 in *We*, the novel is still easily recognizable as an anti-utopia (with elements of science fiction), if not a parody on the utopian (and anti-utopian) genre itself, by way of its ironic implications and its satirical and grotesque character.

Key characteristics of *Day of the Oprichnik* are its explicit portrayal of violence and its revival of an archaic concept of the Russian state as an almost sacral and mythological entity which requires submission from its subjects. This can be seen in the typological, if ahistorical, conflation of the imagined

---

[69] Aleksandr Solzhenitsyn, *Odin den' Ivana Denisovicha: povest'*, in Solzhenitsyn, *Sochineniia* (Frankfurt a.M.: Possev, 1964), pp. 5–133.

[70] Uffelmann, p. 155.

[71] Ibid., p. 164.

political system of a future Russia and that of Ivan the Terrible. One of the continuities between the historical and the fictional future regimes is the arbitrary use of power by state servants, something which Dostoevskii's character Stepan Verkhovenskii had eloquently dubbed 'administrative ecstasy'.[72] This term denotes the sense of apotheosis which is experienced by a low-ranking public servant when eagerly making use of the opportunity to make petitioners feel their dependency upon him.

In *Day of the Oprichnik* violent acts of torture and execution, apparently corresponding to those of the historical *oprichnina*, are portrayed very graphically. In this respect Sorokin's novel seems to be concerned with the theme of manifold abuse and violence in Russian culture. In one scene the narrator is on an aeroplane to Siberia, and next to him sits a lady, the daughter of a former Duma clerk who had schemed with the chairman of the Duma to dismember Russia (he finds this out very quickly by running a security check on the woman on his mobile phone). He notices her watching a film during the flight entitled *The Great Russian Wall* (*Velikaia Russkaia Stena*), a propagandist account of the political sale of Russia in former times, possibly a reference to post-perestroika liberalization and geopolitical chaos.[73] The film is very violent, and he asks her how she, as a woman, can cope with seeing so much blood. To which she replies: 'Mister *oprichnik*, thanks to you Russian women have long been used to blood. To little blood and to great blood.'[74] By employing such wording, *Day of the Oprichnik* may be pointing towards Tat'iana Tolstaia's dictum concerning the 'Great Terror and Little Terror'. Tolstaia wished to distinguish between the 'Great Terror', the terror of the Stalin period and other periods in Russian history, such as that of Ivan the Terrible, and 'the Little Terror', by which she meant an ever-present everyday violence:

> In Russia, the 'little terror' has been around from time immemorial. It has lasted for centuries and continues to this very day. So many books have been written about the Little Terror! Virtually all the literature of the nineteenth century, which is so valued in the West, tells the story of the Little Terror, sometimes with indignation, sometimes as something taken for granted, and tries to understand its mechanisms [...]. What is Russian society and why is it the way it is? What can and must be done in order to free ourselves of this all-permeating terror, of total slavery, of fear of any and everyone?[75]

According to Mark Lipovetsky and Sven Spieker, Tolstaia thereby 'explains the phenomenon of the little terror by the contradiction in Russia between,

---

[72] '[А]дминистративный восторг' (Dostoevskii, *Sobranie sochinenii*, VII: *Besy: roman v trekh chastiakh*, p. 60).

[73] pp. 115–21 in the original; pp. 99–104 in the translation.

[74] 'Господин опричник, благодаря вам русские женщины давно привыкли к крови. К малой и к большой' (p. 118).

[75] Tatyana Tolstaya, 'The Great Terror and the Little Terror', in *Pushkin's Children: Writings on Russia and Russians*, trans. by Jamey Gambrell (Boston: Houghton and Mifflin, 2003), pp. 14–26 (p. 15).

is evidenced by the reference to a holy book and the founder of a 'better' society. Furthermore, a limited number of people are said to have incomparably greater value than the rest of society. Ivan wholeheartedly believes in the value of his mission, which to an outside observer appears redundant to the point of madness. He is proud to serve the state, and yet the superior collective entity which he glorifies actually deprives him of all value as an individual. His family name, Monakhov, which relates to the Russian word 'монах' ('monk'), is symbolic. Life as a monk in a religious order is traditionally associated with a very strict, reclusive, and self-sacrificial existence at the service of an order or monastic community, and ultimately of God. The state in 'The Swimming Competition' is itself deified and glorified as 'great'. Moreover, this is not just a socio-political form of organization, but some metaphysical and superhuman force,[85] as embodied in references to the night sky and the mysterious group of 513 people. This impression is further reinforced by references to places made of bronze or gold, traditionally used in the crafting and adornment of sacramental vessels, holy places such as temples and altars, and idols (cf. the golden calf in the Book of Exodus). The underlying concept of the state depicted here is an archaic one in which the state is endowed with a divine and patriarchal nature which enjoys unquestioned and absolute authority. The relationship of the people towards the state can correspondingly only be one of reverence and obedience.[86]

Ivan Monakhov is a perfect, if hyperbolic and grotesque, exemplar of what Andrei Siniavskii-Terts called:

the moral imperative of the Revolution, which justifies every manipulation with one's own conscience, transformed into simple conformism and subservience. And the 'new man' emerges as an ordinary recipient of orders, as an adjustable slave, as a mechanical executor of an alien decision.[87]

'The Swimming Competition' is a parody of socialist realist literary conventions pertaining to the hero as an utterly committed soldier or industrial worker. What Lipovetsky says of the writer Anatolii Kurchatkin might also be applied typologically to Sorokin: he 'revitalizes the Socialist Realist model of

---

[85] Cf. Marusenkov, pp. 84–85.

[86] In certain respects the world described in this story is reminiscent of the society portrayed in Zamiatin's *We*, where the state provides the absolute measure of authority, and where individuals are of no value vis-à-vis the collective entity. Individuals in *We* are mere 'ciphers', made to believe that they are building a bright future but in reality systematically enslaved and abused. The same state of mind, contempt for individual self-worth, and equanimity towards repression and even mass killing for the imagined good of the collective are also exhibited by Dostoevskii's characters Shigalev and Petr Verkhovenskii in *The Devils* and, of course, in the 'Grand Inquisitor' episode of *The Brothers Karamazov*. Like the works mentioned here, Sorokin's 'The Swimming Competition' also embodies a counterview by ironic implication, which is highlighted by means of exaggeration and the grotesque.

[87] Andrej Sinjawskij, *Der Traum vom neuen Menschen oder Die Sowjetzivilisation*, trans. by Swetlana Geier (Frankfurt a.M.: Fischer, 1989), p. 192.

an exemplary representative of the people (*narod*)—a Soviet worker/soldier/ party member who embodies ultimate *submission*, which the protagonist perceives as the highest privilege, though it leads to his self-destruction'.[88]

The only remedy that might help appears to be a change of identity, as advocated by Anton Chekhov in 1889. Chekhov had described himself as:

a young man, the son of a serf, a former shopkeeper, a chorister, a schoolboy, and a university student, brought up on reverence for rank, on kissing priests' hands, on veneration of other people's thoughts, thankful for every crust of bread, flogged many times [. . .] who lied to God and people, lied without need, simply out of the realization of being a nobody [. . .] this young man is squeezing drop by drop the slave out of himself, and wakes up one fine morning and feels that it is real human blood flowing in his veins, not a slave's.[89]

Chekhov's image was echoed by Evgenii Evtushenko a hundred years later when he said that 'today [this slavish blood] must not be squeezed out drop by drop but pumped out by the bucketful'.[90] The siskin in Gor'kii's allegory outlined in this article's introduction seems to have failed to motivate its fellow birds to engage in such a process.

These works by Sorokin and Tuchkov describe different societies with a shared emphasis on portraying an archaic culture. They contain 'an analysis of the inner mechanisms of a paradoxical cultural realm, which, apparently, is located *between* contemporary civilization and archaic ritualism'.[91] The 'archaic ritualism' referred to is the preoccupation with power as the 'sole value, the purpose of [the potentate's] world. It is totally self-sufficient, fully justifies itself, and for Tuchkov's New Russians serves as a religious absolute'.[92] This very attitude towards power is also well expressed in the second epigraph to this article, taken from Stefan Heym's novel *The King David Report*.

The archaic conception of power which Tuchkov projects onto the New Russians is directed in Sorokin towards the state and its servants: their consciousness is one of power which has been put at the disposal of a deified state. The state has assumed the role of a divinity, something which in Sorokin's words is:

closed, inaccessible, unpredictable, incalculable, and merciless. These were in effect the characteristics of power in Russia. And since they are divine, one can only submit and pray to this force. That is precisely what the authorities expect from the people.[93]

[88] Lipovetsky, 'New Russians as Cultural Myth', p. 59 (emphases original).
[89] Anton Chekhov to A. S. Suvorin, 7 January 1889, in A. P. Chekhov, *Sobranie sochinenii v dvenadsati tomakh* (Moscow: Khudozhestvennaia Literatura, 1963), XI, 317–18, cited in Leon Aron, *Russia's Revolution: Essays 1989–2006* (Washington: AEI Press, 2007), p. 153.
[90] Evgenii Evtushenko, 'Priterpelost'', *Literaturnaia gazeta*, 19 (11 May 1988), p. 13, cited in Rancour-Laferriere, p. 61.
[91] Lipovetsky, 'New Russians as Cultural Myth', p. 62 (emphasis original.)
[92] Ibid., p. 63.
[93] Vladimir Sorokin, in Neumann (para. 4 of 9).

The acceptance of the rulers' will as paramount has long been recognized as a leitmotif of Russian history, with the Tsar being traditionally regarded as 'the living icon of God'.[94]

Intriguingly, the archaic relationship of the Russian people with power in general and with the state in particular was publicly recognized and criticized by former Russian President Dmitrii Medvedev in his address to the Federal Assembly of the Russian Federation on 5 November 2008:

> The Constitution paves the way for Russia's renewal as a free nation and a society that holds law and the dignity of each individual as its highest values. The cult of the state and the illusory wisdom of the administrative apparatus have prevailed in Russia over many centuries. Individuals with their rights and freedoms, personal interests and problems, have been seen as at best a means and at worst an obstacle for strengthening the state's might. This view endured throughout many centuries. I would like to quote Pyotr Stolypin, who said, 'What we need to do first is create citizens, and once this has been achieved civic spirit will prevail of its own accord in Russia. First comes the citizen and then the civic spirit, but we have usually preached the other way round'.[95]

In conclusion, the works of Sorokin and Tuchkov analysed above reveal a clear concern with the theme of freedom. They relate to the immediate post-Soviet era with its all-permeating instability, and the emergence of Russian capitalism with all its significance for the ordinary people. More important, they treat what has been referred to as the 'Russian cultural dynamics' of 'moral masochism', 'self-incurred immaturity', 'slave soul', and an archaic relationship between the people and the state, which has arguably kept the Russian people in a state of legal and mental servitude for an unnecessarily long period. Both authors present an imaginary world in their fictions, a world which has certain specific features relating both to Russia's pre-revolutionary and immediate Soviet past, and to the post-Soviet Russian present. They describe the vulgarity, violence, and mental perversion which they perceive to be inherent in their culture. Both writers create ahistorical, hyperbolic spaces that implicitly foreground the abuse of power and ideology and cause the Soviet and the post-Soviet periods to intermingle with typologically ancient conceptions of power. By so doing, they foreground 'the unity of Russian cultural dynamics despite all historical ruptures between the prerevolutionary, Soviet, and post-Soviet periods'.[96] Although their works might be interpreted as doing an injustice to Russian culture, Russian literature, and the Russian people, this would not be a foregone conclusion, since the two authors present these themes carnivalistically and in grotesque, hyberbolic, ironic, and satiri-

---

[94] James Billington, *The Icon and the Axe* (London: Vintage, 1970), p. 35.

[95] Dmitry Medvedev, 'The Russian People Don't Need the State Watching their Every Step', *Jerusalem Post*, 12 November 2008, p. 15.

[96] Lipovetsky, 'New Russians as Cultural Myth', p. 71.

cal ways. Furthermore, the works analysed above deal with themes which were central also to the fiction of Dostoevskii and his religious quest, and also to Zamiatin, such as that of the relationship between the individual and power. The works considered not only relate themselves to the classics superficially by way of borrowing, or alluding to, titles from Turgenev's and Solzhenitsyn's works, for example, but also engage with their key concerns at a deeper level, in spite of all carnivalism at the level of plot, genre, and narrative structure. Although Tuchkov's and Sorokin's preoccupation with such issues proceeds from historical postulates different from those of the aforementioned classical writers, both writers deal with the same set of questions: freedom, evil, suffering, happiness, and necessity. It would appear furthermore—although this is more often implicit than explicit—that Sorokin and Tuchkov are both well grounded in the Judaeo-Christian and humanist tradition of an individual and social quest for moral truth, so characteristic of Russian literature of the past. It is suggested that this is not only the case with regard to their intertextual links with writers who belong to these traditions, but more significantly, that Sorokin and Tuchkov are also sympathetic to those traditions, despite surface appearances to the contrary.

HAMBURG   NICOLAS DREYER

REVIEWS

Stories and Minds: Cognitive Approaches to Literary Narrative. Ed. by LARS BERNAERTS, DIRK DE GEEST, LUC HERMAN, and BART VERVAECK. Lincoln and London: University of Nebraska Press. 2013. 236 pp. £20.99. ISBN 978-0-8032-4481-8.

The eight essays in this volume make a substantial contribution to cognitive narrative research, mapping out the potential of this domain and providing suggestive leads in several directions. In the process they defy the prejudicial view of cognitive narratology as unhealthily preoccupied with using theory of mind and mind-reading as a rather literal key to understanding fictional characters. One of the main ways in which these essays break out of that stereotype is by foregrounding the reader, a topical focus which itself embraces a number of distinct research questions.

Thus, Marisa Bortolussi and Peter Dixon draw attention to the crucial role of memory in the reading process, while Catherine Emmott, Anthony J. Sanford, and Marc Alexander discuss the complementary issue of the reader's attentional focus. By reading these two off against each other we encounter an implicit third question, brought to the fore in Elaine Auyoung's essay, namely the object of the reader's sense-making, and the extent to which inference in reading equates with our cognitive responses to partial cues in everyday experience. The representational focus of these essays provides a foil for the strongly enactivist perspective on the reader's imagination advanced by Marco Caracciolo; while Anežka Kuzičová addresses the absence, in the experiential emphasis of the preceding essays, of an adequate recognition that the textual encounter has a fundamentally communicative dimension—though the experiential (indeed, sensorimotor) core of the reading process remains a foundational assumption. It is left to Maria Mäkelä to question the primacy or adequacy of an experiential frame of reference in accounts of narrative interpretation, by emphasizing the communicative resistance to naturalization in literary narratives, at the level of the character-narrator but also, implicitly, the author. Roy Sommer's contribution re-establishes a crucial and welcome cultural specificity for the reader (often too abstract, or empirically generalized, in cognitive discussions); and via an exploration of intercultural reading experiences, he sheds some new light on empathy—another topic that looms especially large in cognitive literary studies. Similarly, Bart Keunen makes progress towards a historicizing cognitive perspective upon narrative by insisting upon the relation between action models and moral paradigms of causality in character-oriented folk psychology—distinguishing broadly between minimalist and maximalist models, but providing a suggestive cue for more elaborated and ideologically grounded accounts.

The editors' introduction to the volume spends some time considering the possible 'threats' or risks associated with cognitive literary studies, among which they foreground reductionist thinking. There are good reasons for this concern, but the invocation of reductionism is itself telling about the continuing challenges of such interdisciplinary work; the term has both a negative humanities sense related to ingrained suspicions of essentialism, and a positive sense in the sciences as one of the foundational principles of scientific method. So is there a realistic prospect of genuine interdisciplinary dialogue here? David Herman's afterword to the volume identifies five open questions for future research, one of which is how to achieve genuine dialogue between narrative scholarship and the mind sciences, rather than the unidirectional borrowing that currently prevails. And he is right; the contributors to this volume, who are predominantly (though not exclusively) from literary backgrounds, cannot claim to be making significant interventions in cognitive science. That is a tall order, though—it cannot really be done unilaterally. A first step towards the reciprocal dialogue required is to open your own disciplinary premises to question; to allow the possibility that cognitive science might fundamentally change your theoretical assumptions, rather than provide a new vocabulary in which to dress them. These essays make some moves in the right direction, but they also provide occasion, I think, for enterprising readers to go much further.

UNIVERSITY OF YORK   RICHARD WALSH

Literary Studies and the Pursuits of Reading. Ed. by ERIC DOWNING, JONATHAN M. HESS, and RICHARD V. BENSON. Rochester, NY: Camden House. 2012. vii+298 pp. £55. ISBN 978-1-57113-431-8.

This anthology is a Festschrift in honour of Clayton Koelb on the occasion of his seventieth birthday. The introduction by the editors takes Koelb's research as a starting-point for the twelve articles, and Koelb's work on the study of reading is referenced throughout the volume. Scholarship on reading, although prospering in literary studies and critical theory since the 1960s, has mostly focused on concepts of an 'ideal reader' and 'ideal reading', rather than addressing the 'embodied reader', as the editors critically remark (p. 3). The book thus joins efforts to 'restore the dignity of the corporeal and emotive (as opposed to the cognitive or interpretive) engagements of reading' (p. 3). Reading, in other words, understood both as a topic of research and as a research technique, calls for a rereading in the light of a cultural turn in literary studies, whereas its scholarly beginnings are rooted in structuralist and poststructuralist settings.

There are mostly two notions of reader/reading research that the volume challenges: first, that the role of the reader 'was primarily a cognitive or interpretive role, fully engaged in extracting the meaning embedded in the text' (p. 2). Second, 'that the meaning he (still not she) aimed to reproduce was a timeless, unchanging one, unaffected by the contingencies of either the text's original historical or cultural context or the reader's historical and cultural position' (p. 2). Instead, the volume aims at three different foci: 'on affective reading, historically and culturally embedded reading, and reading beyond just the printed book' (p. 5).

The contributions are more or less closely related to the editors' agenda. They address reading as an author's practice, a topic of fiction and writing, and, finally, as the act, performed by the very readings in this volume. Unfortunately, all of the articles seem to assume that the various practices of reading they investigate already convey a sufficiently clear notion of what reading *is*—or rather what it is *not*. In turn, the reader might sense a lack of definition of what it actually means to read. The fact that some of the articles extend the notion of 'reading' even into a more general idea of reception, including other media than text, only complicates the matter.

For example, it might be perfectly reasonable to conceive of visual perceptions—such as observation of the constellations or the determination of bodily symptoms—as 'readings' (see Eric Downing's and Alice Kuszniar's essays). Nevertheless, there are significant—and critical—differences between 'reading proper' and the plenitude of cultural techniques concerning all sorts of observation and comprehension. Friedrich Schlegel and Friedrich Schleiermacher knew this very well, when they considered 'divinatory reading' (i.e. a 'magic reading' in Downing's sense) to be the consummation of hermeneutics—however, one that *transcends* the actual terms of a 'grammatical' and 'psychological' reading. At times, the latter can also make a magical reading unnecessary and prevent the reader from misreading. Hence, the famous words 'Was nie geschrieben wurde, lesen' ('Read what was never written') might prove to be a quotation by Hugo von Hofmannsthal and not a coinage by Benjamin, who only cites the former (p. 189).

Yet such selective criticism cannot do justice to the volume in general. Most of the essays are original and thorough, and certainly deserve close attention. Among them, Christopher Wild's close reading of literary and autobiographical conversion episodes and their relation to the reading of codices as well as Kathryn Starkey's explorations of medieval manuscript reading stand out.

VANDERBILT UNIVERSITY   JOHANNES ENDRES

The Emblematics of the Self: Ekphrasis and Identity in Renaissance Imitations of Greek Romance. By ELIZABETH B. BEARDEN. Toronto: University of Toronto Press. 2012. xiv+258 pp. $65. ISBN 978-0-4426-4346-8.

Recent scholarship on Renaissance romance has emphasized the crucial influence of the late classical or 'Greek' romances after their rediscovery and circulation throughout Europe in the sixteenth century. The rich literary sophistication of these works, especially Heliodorus's *Aethiopica*, Achilles Tatius's *Leucippe and Clitophon*, and Longus's *Daphnis and Chloe*, has made them favourite texts for scholars of early modern English romancers from Sidney to Greene to Mary Wroth, and also of their Continental peers, including Cervantes. In her contribution to this growing conversation, Elizabeth Bearden's erudite and acute study makes a powerful argument about why these texts should have been so influential during this period. Building her reading on the tradition of ekphrasis deployed in these texts, Bearden suggests that ekphrastic description provides the authors of romance with a mechanism to explore subjectivity and change in response to external pressures. Thus the appearance of an ekphrastic object—her first example is the lengthy description of a painting of the rape of Europa, which opens *Leucippe and Clitophon*—allows authors to build narratives of subjective mobility. Bearden names this capacity 'passibility', a term she adapts from ancient theology, humoral theory, and early modern theology (p. 4), but which clearly also engages with ideas of racial and cultural difference. In Bearden's model, Greek romance's structure of ekphrastically induced passibility generates a literary form that can embrace, and even welcome, diversity and change.

Bearden argues convincingly that this literary innovation found fertile soil in sixteenth- and seventeenth-century European romances because of the 'increasingly global [nature of] early modernity' (p. 17). Building through ekphrasis and passibility a 'new, critical assessment of romance characterization' (p. 11), she moves beyond the familiar models of Bahktin, Frye, and Vinaver to argue for the lasting force of 'romance's particular constructions of early modern cultural identity' (p. 11). More valuable to her than these traditional approaches is Fredric Jameson's observation in *The Political Unconscious: Narrative as a Socially Symbolic Act* (London: Routledge, 2002), which argues that 'romance is precisely that form in which the worldliness of the world reveals or manifests itself' (p. 198). What is abstract in Jameson becomes very specific for Bearden: her study explores how Greek romance created a genre of Renaissance romance that could respond to the cultural desire for 'verisimilitude' in the face of an increasingly global world. In a very strong first chapter, Bearden demonstrates that the models of Heliodorus, Achilles Tatius, and Longus displaced those of chivalric fictions because the Greek texts helped model a greater capacity to make sense of global variety.

The case studies that follow will each be eagerly read by scholars concerned with these authors, and cumulatively they build a case for romance as an important genre for the understanding of early modern expansion. One important gesture in this study elevates Achilles Tatius to a position of prominence that many previous studies gave only to Heliodorus. Exploring Alonso de Reinoso's Spanish translation as well as other editions of Achilles Tatius leads to a striking claim about the text's elusive narrator—Bearden argues that the tale may be told from the point of view of the cross-dressed Melite (pp. 50–51)—and clear evidence of the international nature of the transmission of romance tropes. A very strong chapter on flexible gender identity in Sidney's *Arcadia* follows, and the argument is noteworthy for finding the influence of Tatius where so many earlier critics had emphasized Heliodorus alone. Perhaps the most striking chapter explores Cervantes's *Persiles and Sigismunda* through attention to New World visual arts and their transmission to Europe. Bearden argues that Cervantes's depiction of American *lienzos* (painted canvases) 'uses *ekphrasis* explicitly to render shifts in foreign identities, providing a space for countercultural discourse and acceptance of cultural difference' (p. 101). This reading of romance as a fantasy of cultural bridging also informs her reading of John Barclay's *Argenis*, in which case the imagined fantasy is an Afro-European alliance (p. 157). Finally, her reading of *Urania*, with its broken marriages and failed alliances, suggests that Mary Wroth refuses or qualifies her faith in romance's ability to integrate identity and difference on both the personal and the political levels.

A tantalizing conclusion argues for the continuing role of ekphrastic conventions in attempts to assimilate difference in novels influenced by Renaissance and Greek romances. Bearden argues that, unlike Achilles's shield in the *Iliad*, ekphrasis in Greek and Renaissance romance becomes 'polyglot' (p. 197); it functions as both an example and a symbol of bringing different things into harmony with each other. The genre thus anticipates the global visions of such novels as *Oronooko*, *Moby-Dick*, and *The Crying of Lot 49*, as well as the strategies of postcolonial critics and writers. This final gesture towards the long tail of romance suggests that Bearden's paradigm of global interconnection and ekphrastic passibility may extend its influence beyond, as well as inside, early modern studies.

ST JOHN'S UNIVERSITY, NEW YORK   STEVEN MENTZ

Contes en réseaux: l'émergence du conte sur la scène littéraire européenne. By PATRICIA EICHEL-LOJKINE. (Les Seuils de la Modernité, 16) Geneva: Droz. 2013. 457 pp. SwF 74.01. ISBN 978-2-600-01615-5.

Patricia Eichel-Lojkine's latest book is an invitation to consider well-known French fairy tales in a new light. Without denying the innovative nature of the art of Charles Perrault or Madame d'Aulnoy, she proposes to explore the interaction of these texts with earlier works (Italian *novelle*, medieval romances, Yiddish narratives, etc.). She brings to light cycles of dissemination and 'recycling' of written texts, and plays down the part played by oral transmission in the circulation of stories, reducing it to one of many links in the dissemination of fairy matter. The emphasis is on the idea of variability, or rather *variance*, at the heart of the transformation of one single tale into many oral and written versions. In her view, although unique as an event, the fairy tale is above all an utterance open to repetition, transformation, and reactivation.

Foucault's concept of *rémanence* dominates the first section of the volume, devoted to a study of the 'networks' of texts that acted as bridges between oriental and Mediterranean civilizations and Western cultures. Eichel-Lojkine begins by sketching a 'prehistory' of the written tale, turning her attention in the first instance to medieval texts, highlighting three major phases, characterized by the parts played successively by edifying fables, homilies, and finally poetry and romances. Once freed from its medieval roots, fairy matter is said to have passed into the sixteenth- and seventeenth-century Italian collections of Straparola and Basile, which were more clearly meant for entertainment. In the process, fairy matter underwent a number of thematic, structural, ideological, and aesthetic reconfigurations, one of which led to its pedagogical takeover at the end of the seventeenth century, as typified by the tableau of the old woman and the listening child. For Eichel-Lojkine, the parallel emphasis on situations of orality at the time goes to show that although its birth marked a break with the oral tradition of the folk tale, the fairy tale took shape by analogy with the folk tale in a blurring of codes that gave rise to the persistent myth of the oral transmission of tales.

The second and third sections of the work are devoted to case studies, in this instance the cycles of Puss-in-Boots and Fair Goldilocks, ultimately made famous by the narratives of Perrault and Madame d'Aulnoy. The discussion of the different versions enables Eichel-Lojkine not only to analyse in great detail the modulations of narrative formulae such as the dynamics of the gift exchange (or help versus debt) in the Puss-in Boots cycle or the decentring in favour of the feminine in the Fair Goldilocks cycle, but also to explore the process of transposition at work in the tales, by bringing to light the multilayered readings of the Perrault story. The work concludes with an analysis of the motif of the animal helper present in both cycles, as an example of the way in which different legacies from different parts of the world combined over the centuries to give rise to some of the better-known fairy tales in the Western canon.

Contes en réseaux is a clear, well-thought-out, and deeply learned book. Both scholarly and accessible to a wider public interested in fairy tales, who will find the innovative readings of the tales offered by Eichel-Lojkine particularly appealing, it leads the reader to reconsider the genesis of the European literary fairy tale, notably in bringing to light the circulation of narratives between Jewish and Christian cultures. It should definitively alter the common perception of the fairy tale as a timeless object and help to counterbalance the excesses of universalist theories of the genre.

GOLDSMITHS, UNIVERSITY OF LONDON   MARIE-CLAUDE CANOVA-GREEN

Coleridge and Kantian Ideas in England, 1796–1817: Coleridge's Responses to German Philosophy. By MONIKA CLASS. London and New York: Bloomsbury. 2012. 245 pp. £18.99. ISBN 978-1-4411-8075-9.

In letter of 1820 to James Gooden, Coleridge presents Kantianism and Platonism as the only schools of 'true' philosophy. He recommends solely the study of Kant, because '[i]n him is contained all that can be *learnt*'—but declares himself a disciple of Plato (Crabb Robinson Collection, Correspondence 1809–17, Letter 101 (misplaced under 1814), Dr Williams's Library, London). This informal distinction-in-oneness does not belittle—in fact, it validates—what Monika Class has done: she skilfully disentangles the manifold 'genealogy' of Kantian ideas within the intricate historical network of learned sociability where Coleridge's 'ability to adopt, to transform, to apply and above all to spread and disseminate' came to pass (pp. 5, 6). Pivotal to Class's argument is Friedrich August Nitsch (a former student of Kant at Königsberg), his 1796 *General and Introductory View of Professor Kant's Principles*, and his 1794–97 London lectures. Nitsch's Idealist idiosyncrasies and syncretisms in discerning a 'pathway for Kantianism into English culture through associationism' (p. 43) present a compelling link not only for Coleridge's first encounter with Kant, but also for his early awareness of Kantianism's speculative possibilities.

The first of Class's seven chapters illuminates the dissenting and radical ferment of 1790s London and Bristol, arguing that here the first transmissions of Kant, due to their call for social reform, gained a stronger foothold than hitherto acknowledged. Chapter 2 then places Coleridge in his 1795 Bristol network, focusing on 'his attempts [. . .] to ground freedom ontologically' and refute philosophical determinism (p. 65). The third chapter combines these two strands in the claim that Nitsch's work constitutes the source of a 1795/96 entry in Coleridge's notebooks echoing the Categorical Imperative—Kant's assertion of a universal moral law whose disinterestedness is transcendent, forgoes 'Hobbesian calculation and self-interest' (p. 73), and which is, thus, constitutive to Being. Class makes the crucial observation that Coleridge's refusal to 'leave the affections outside the sphere of ethical discussion' (p. 75) generates unease with Kant's stoicism, and she claims persuasively that Nitsch's presentation of the highest good—the blending of virtue and happiness—may account for this deviation.

In Chapter 4 Class makes a strong case against Coleridge's political escapism around the turn of the century, and for Nature, 'the great artist' (p. 119), functioning as a progressive 'corrective' to vice in 'France: An Ode' and Kant's *Perpetual Peace* (p. 110). Chapter 5 elucidates the *Anti-Jacobin*'s (justified) charges of republicanism against Kant, how the journal's defamations of Coleridge on these grounds fed into a climate of increasing Germanophobia, and the need for Coleridge therefore to engage with Kant secretly after his return from Germany in 1799. Whereas Coleridge smuggled some unacknowledged results of these studies into his 1808 lectures, the post-Waterloo *Biographia Literaria* professed Kantianism openly—albeit now, ironically, renouncing his own former republicanism by disclaiming Kant's. This is the topic of Chapter 6, in which Nitsch's un-Kantian postulation of the importance of the affections for the moral law and the communal act of becoming aware of this law emerge as lasting influences on Coleridge, despite his departure from Nitsch's (and Kant's) egalitarianism.

'What counted for Coleridge', Class sums up in Chapter 7, 'was that Reason possessed constitutive power'—and that Nitsch 'had introduced Kant's *first critique* in such broad terms' (p. 185). In the Gooden letter Coleridge distinguished between regulative and constitutive ideas, making the latter vital—literally, since constitutiveness gives ideas a 'living potency' (James Vigus, *Platonic Coleridge* (London: Legenda, 2009), p. 48)—for his preference in 1820 of Plato over Kant. Nitsch, it emerges from Class's superb study, may be just as vital for Coleridge's Idealism.

QUEEN MARY UNIVERSITY OF LONDON   PHILIPP HUNNEKUHL

Wonder in Shakespeare. By ADAM MAX COHEN. Basingstoke: Palgrave Macmillan. 2012. x+226 pp. £48. ISBN 978–0–230–10541–6.

This book was, in part, published to mark the untimely death of its author, Adam Max Cohen. After his passing, fellow critics and family members decided to use the draft of Cohen's work on wonder in Shakespeare as the main focus of a monograph, so that his final work could be brought to light in a critical environment. Thus, this book is unusual in layout, being divided into two parts, both of which work very well together. Part I is the actual text of Cohen's work on wonder in the drama of Shakespeare, with seven short chapters across just over a hundred pages looking at a generic mix of plays, the texts read alongside the contexts of early modern society and, in particular, the period's approaches to the various discourses of wonder. The second part of the book features six responses to Cohen's ideas by a range of literary critics through various plays and themes. In actuality, then, we have a short monograph by Cohen and a set of critical responses to his important and thought-provoking ideas.

In his excellent study, Cohen argues that Shakespearian texts can be read for their fascination with the idea of wonder in the early modern period. Importantly for the author, wonder in Shakespeare is not limited by genre because, as he admits, 'wonder' is a rather ambivalent term. Indeed, the book views wonder as a very open-ended and varied topic in itself. But Cohen's excellent point is partly that 'homologies existed between Shakespearean wonder and the wonder traditions—both religious and secular—that influenced his culture' (p. 9). Taking this thesis forward, Part I traces the different types of wonder in Shakespearian drama, including a discussion of amazement and surprise in the numerous wonders of *The Tempest*, as well as a chapter on 'resurrections of the living dead' (which includes fascinating research on resurrection via discussion of Samuel Gardiner's sermon, alongside the famous statue scene in *The Winter's Tale*) (p. vii). Then the monograph tackles types of what Cohen terms 'emphatic wonder', a section illuminated by his detailed close readings of several plays (p. vii). The idea of prodigious birth is likewise the necessary focus of two sections; one includes work on Richard III and his dramatic presentation, while the second moves through a wide-ranging number of texts. Indeed, a particular strength of the research is the way in which Cohen is able to link plays together and manages to trace continuities in a large number of texts. Cohen's sixth chapter, on 'cabinets of curiosity', involves an acute analysis of the apothecary in *Romeo and Juliet* and other early modern contexts in the light of religion and awe (p. vii), while his last section looks at Shakespearian aesthetics, including the odd reference to Giulio Romano in *The Winter's Tale*, a piece which should be of much interest to art historians as well as literary critics of the period.

The book's second part, a series of responses from a range of impressive names in literary criticism, manages to engage with Cohen's ideas directly while at the same time taking some of the concepts in new and interesting directions. The critics (Maura Tarnoff, Janna Segal, M. G. Aune, Rebecca Steinberger, Kristin Keating, Bryan Reynolds, and Joshua B. Fisher) all share Cohen's sense of wonder as a flexible topic for research of both early modern contexts and plays, as the responses engage quite directly with the monograph's approach. Taken together, both parts of the book, but especially the research of Cohen, contribute to a highly valuable and readable study of the multiple senses of wonder in Shakespeare.

DE MONTFORT UNIVERSITY   PETER SILLITOE

Early African American Print Culture. Ed by LARA LANGER COHEN and JORDAN ALEXANDER STEIN. Philadelphia: University of Pennsylvania Press. 2012. vii+422 pp. $55; £36. ISBN 978-0-8122-4425-0.

Dear Reader, if you were not there, allow me to tell you where you should have been on 18–20 March 2010: the Early African American Print Culture in Theory and Practice conference at the University of Pennsylvania. If, like me, you missed the initial conference, you can assuage your guilt by reading the volume of collected essays that grew out of that day. In it, editors Lara Langer Cohen and Jordan Alexander Stein bring together compelling essays that explore the multivalent, complex, and intriguing uses of print in early African America. This is a large, but deliberately not definitive, book that brings together two heretofore generally separate bodies of intellectual enquiry: early African American literary studies and scholarship on the history of the book. Featuring the work of both eminent and younger scholars, the volume examines and theorizes the production and circulation of early black texts, such as the first edition of Phillis Wheatley's *Poems on Various Subjects, Religion and Moral* (1773), black newspapers published west of the Mississippi River during the nineteenth century, and visual images printed in the vast number of texts published by the American Anti-Slavery Society.

As the book's editors outline, the volume presents three main 'insights': firstly, that 'these essays mount a collective challenge to the presumed universality of what we might call the print-capitalism thesis' (p. 13); secondly, that 'the essays in this volume provide an alternative paradigm to the study of "black authorship" that has for so long been the only significant paradigm by which to estimate African American print culture, and African American literature more generally' (p. 14); and, thirdly, that the volume presents 'an optimistic take on the importance of *not* being original' (p. 15). These three central insights can give one a concise overview of the book, but the essays gathered within generate even more nuanced, sophisticated, and surprising analyses of the variety of early black print forms. Thus, a few individual essays merit comment here. Joseph Rezek's 'The Print Atlantic' helps us understand how the material 'heft' of both Phillis Wheatley's and Ignatius Sancho's physical books—constituting what Rezek calls 'the print Atlantic' (p. 22)—helped influence what readers thought about a single text's ability to represent a race *and* about the institution of slavery. Eric Gardner builds upon his field-influencing *Unexpected Places: Relocating Nineteenth-Century African American Literature* (Jackson: University Press of Mississippi, 2009), a book that called our attention to the large number of early black texts published in surprising places such as Indianapolis, St Louis, and California. His essay continues that effort, significantly expanding the archive and theorizing how we might approach it. Derrick

R. Spires challenges us to read print documents such as the *Proceedings of the Black State Conventions* not just as political documents but also '*as* texts, as performative speech acts that seek to manufacture the very citizenship practices from which the delegates had been excluded' (p. 274). I could go on, but suffice it to say that the book, illustrated by engrossing and, at times, disconcerting visual images, productively brings together the work of established critical figures such as Joanna Brooks, Meredith McGill, and Elizabeth Maddock Dillon with fresh analyses from newer scholars, many of which cross-reference one another.

In short, this edition excites me. I learnt fascinating facts from it: that William Wells Brown lugged around the stereotype plates of his narrative with him when he travelled (Jonathan Senchyne's 'Bottles of Ink and Reams of Paper' (p. 141)) and that John Marrant was part of a larger 'Charlestonian music culture' that featured talented French horn players (Elizabeth Maddox Dillon's 'John Marrant Blows the French Horn' (p. 328)). Furthermore, it incites me to ask more questions, such as: how can we continue to problematize pat notions we might have of African American 'authorship'? What critical models can we continue to develop that will help us analyse these myriad forms of African American print culture? What else does the history of the book have to learn from looking to the early African American archive? Indeed, this volume in many ways calls into being this area of enquiry and makes possible future work of this kind. Thus, to close, Dear Reader, because this book excites me and incites me, I think you should read it. I bet it would do the same for you.

UNIVERSITY OF TENNESSEE   KATY L. CHILES

The Literary Imagination from Erasmus Darwin to H. G. Wells: Science, Evolution, and Ecology. By MICHAEL R. PAGE. Farnham: Ashgate. 2012. viii+224 pp. £55. ISBN 978-1-4094-3869-4 (ebk 978-1-4094-3870-0).

According to this accessible new study, Erasmus Darwin's intention to 'enlist the imagination under the banner of science' initiated a dialogue with profound effects on literature (p. 6). This interaction, triangulated around evolution, ecology, and technological invention, gathered momentum through the Romantic and Victorian eras. Darwin's verse discourses in *The Botanic Garden* (1792) undermined Creationism's neat cosmology by intimating that dynamic physical forces drove processes of geo-biological transformation humans might fathom and harness. Mary Shelley's electrically inspired *Frankenstein* is consequently science fiction's 'ür-text' [*sic*] (p. 7). There seems nothing particularly radical about this claim (rogue umlauts aside), but Michael Page extends it more controversially: proposing that SF is thus the defining genre of the Romantic literary imagination, and in turn relocating Romanticism at the heart of scientific romance (as the genre was known in Wells's time). Whether fully convincing or not, as a working hypothesis it illuminates characteristic trends of nineteenth-century writing in thought-provoking ways.

As a response to a sudden and unprecedented magnification of space and time, industrialism, and understandings of the natural world, society, and selfhood, Page argues, there is a fundamental connection between Romanticism's 'literature of change', specifically through its intimations of the evolutionary paradigm, and its simultaneous role as SF's aesthetic matrix (p. 12). The genre would by definition remain subject to the same preoccupation with natural and technological transformation and, consequently, the nature and boundaries of being human. Poets such as Wordsworth, Coleridge, and P. B. Shelley may not immediately spring to mind as progenitors of futuristic themes and practices, but they were nonetheless intensely engaged with scientific perspectives in their sublime and utopian visions of times before, above, or beyond the civilization they rebelled against. As Page acknowledges, recent studies such as Richard Holmes's *The Age of Wonder: How the Romantic Generation Discovered the Beauty and Terror of Science* (London: HarperPress, 2009) historicize this extensively. Moreover, Romantic writings profoundly affected scientific outlooks and public imagination in turn. At their nucleus, Mary Shelley speculated about inventions and future outcomes, simultaneously critiquing patriarchal models of creativity and knowledge. *Frankenstein* and *The Last Man* (1826) expressed visionary ambivalence: passionate endorsement for science as Promethean force, alongside forebodings about artificial post-humanism or even species extinction.

After Erasmus's grandson's *The Origin of Species* (1859) released the full force of evolutionary theory, this topical process accelerated. Mid-Victorians confronted its social implications, notably Charles Kingsley, Edward Bulwer-Lytton, Samuel Butler, Richard Jefferies, and W. H. Hudson. Their fantasies of alternative and future races deployed Darwinian tropes and motifs for critiquing current conditions or imagining humanity evolving otherwise (for good or bad) under radically different ones. Contradictory applications of Charles Darwin's ideas simultaneously boosted and undermined Victorian notions of human perfectibility and automatic social progress. This climaxed at the *fin de siècle* in H. G. Wells's scientific romances, and Page addresses the relative neglect of Wells in Gillian Beer's expanded study (*Darwin's Plots: Evolutionary Narrative in Darwin, George Eliot and Nineteenth-Century Fiction*, 3rd edn (Cambridge: Cambridge University Press, 2009)). This student of 'Darwin's bulldog', T. H. Huxley, became modern science's 'poetic' visionary and thus inheritor of Romanticism's imaginative legacy. This is epitomized by early dystopias focused on the dilemma of tempering effects of the indifferent cosmic process on the species. Exercising an alternative 'ethical process' (T. H. Huxley, *Evolution and Ethics* (1896; repr. London: Pilot Press, 1947), p. 8) might prevent subhuman regression into animalistic economy (see Wells's Eloi and Morlock symbiosis in *The Time Machine* (1895)), post-human mutation into un-empathic intellectuality and genocidal imperialism (see his cyborgian, cephalopod Martians in *The War of the Worlds*), or self-extinction through war or over-consumption. Instead of elitist 'survival of the fittest' (as in Herbert Spencer's Social Darwinist heresy), Wells went on to envision collective social and mental advancement for the species in dynamic balance with instinct and environment, though acutely aware that evolutionism was no guarantor of automatic progress and that human history was 'a race between education and catastrophe' (H. G. Wells, *The Outline of History*, II: *The Roman Empire to the Great War* (London: Newnes, 1920), p. 758).

In spanning a century's dialogue between science and imaginative literature from Darwin's grandfather to *The Time Machine*, *The Island of Doctor Moreau* (1896), and *The War of the Worlds*, Page also detects suggestive affinities between so-called Green Romanticism and trends in post-Wellsian eco-critical themes, further raising the SF genre's cultural stock while reassessing the Romantic canon.

UNIVERSITY OF DUNDEE   KEITH WILLIAMS

Victorian Bloomsbury. By ROSEMARY ASHTON. New Haven: Yale University Press. 2012. xiii+380 pp. £25. ISBN 978-0-300-15447-4.

The relocation of the young Stephens, including Virginia (later Woolf) and Vanessa (later Bell), to 46 Gordon Square in 1904 did not spark a cultural revolution in that quarter of London; rather, the Stephens moved to Bloomsbury precisely because the district was already established as the cultural and intellectual heart of the metropolis. This is the premiss on which Rosemary Ashton's vibrant and colourful book, *Victorian Bloomsbury*, is based. Although we know much about the literary and artistic activity of the famous 'Bloomsbury Group', we know much less about the development of Bloomsbury in the preceding century—an evolution, Ashton argues, which occurred predominantly during the reign of Queen Victoria (1837–1901), when earlier construction projects had transformed the fields of the Bedford Estate into largely genteel city streets, and fledgling establishments, such as the British Museum and the University of London, had encouraged new talent to take residence and the foundation of new institutions.

Ashton rightly cautions readers not to apply the benefits of hindsight to this evolution and see it as inevitable. The ebb and flow of metropolitan life over long periods of time makes it difficult to apply particular characteristics with certainty to any district. Even if nineteenth-century Bloomsbury is unique (as this book shows), Ashton alerts us to the reality that 'in any one part of the area such changes might not have occurred, or might have been reversed' (p. 8). This defiance of inevitability is apparent in the structure of the book. An account of the contribution made by the British Museum comes relatively late, after chapters on the foundation of the University of London and the proliferation of medical institutions, even though the establishment of the British Museum in Montagu House on Great Russell Street in 1759, and designs for its reconstruction during the early nineteenth century, pre-dated these other developments. In fact, Ashton tells us that the proximity of the University of London to the British Museum was 'a piece of luck' (p. 14). Similarly, she makes us aware of the fluidity of the boundaries of Bloomsbury, especially of the way in which much of the intellectual and cultural activity associated with this district spilled out across London, or even further afield. Many key individuals had other, equally significant, geographical reference-points, and while some institutions relocated to Bloomsbury, others established in Bloomsbury found good reasons to move elsewhere.

But, on the whole, there is a tidy structure to this book. Chapters on developments in higher education, the foundation of medical institutions, new churches, collegiate experiments, and the education of particular social groups, including women, the working classes, and young children, not only highlight the ways in which the physical area was transformed but also draw attention to the innovative character of intellectual activity in Bloomsbury. As these chapters are roughly arranged in chronological order, a clear sense is conveyed that many later initiatives (such as the education of the broadly disenfranchised) were built upon a firm base established by earlier efforts (namely the University of London and medical institutions), though Ashton is mostly careful to acknowledge that some initiatives also took their inspiration from broader movements in operation elsewhere (for example, the foundation of Christian settlements in working-class neighbourhoods). Similarly, while Ashton identifies some links between movements and institutions, typically through common individuals, she does not force connections and risk making this evolution artificial. At the same time, these largely self-contained chapters, several of which expose rich institutional archives, focus attention on activity within a growing number of specific buildings, and often remain silent on the space in between. For example, this book tells us relatively little about the way in which burgeoning intellectual activity changed the nature of everyday life in Bloomsbury, especially for its more ordinary residents. This leads Ashton to present readers with a narrative of accomplishment, a celebration of Victorian Bloomsbury; even those institutions which were short-lived have been assessed in terms of their positive contribution to a great purpose, the increasing concentration of intellectual endeavour within this quarter of London. In short, *Victorian Bloomsbury* is a lively introduction which will inspire others, especially in the context of the 'spatial turn' in the humanities, to look more closely at a key location too often taken for granted.

THE OPEN UNIVERSITY   ROSALIND CRONE

Science in Modern Poetry: New Directions. Ed. by JOHN HOLMES. Liverpool: Liverpool University Press. 2012. xi+237 pp. £65. ISBN 978-1-84631-809-2.

In the poem 'Relativity' D. H. Lawrence begins: 'I like relativity and quantum theories | because I don't understand them' (*Pansies* (London: Secker, 1929), p. 116). This stance might be said to represent the ambivalent relationships between poetry and science, poets and scientists, science and literary criticism—which is at once a kind of pseudo-science and a set of disciplines which see themselves, and are seen, as both inferior to and above empirical enquiry. These relationships are the subject of *Science in Modern Poetry*.

This book builds upon the work of the Society for Literature and Science, founded in 2006, and is the fruit of many of its conferences; it also forms part of

Liverpool University Press's 'Poetry & ...' series. It offers chapters which explore, and in some cases debunk, these ambivalences, touching upon the spectre of the Two Cultures argument and its converse, the trendiness of certain kinds of science: here biology and ecology trump physics, although the metaphorical possibilities of quantum mechanics are still apparent. Despite providing a very helpful overview of much of the existing literature in his introduction, the editor reminds us that it is a 'collection of essays [. . .] and not a critical companion' (p. 10). Although usefully sectioned, this does mean that some of the implied coherence is a little strained, and in those parts dealing with specific poets there is arguably an over-concentration on the early part of the twentieth century. The extent to which Hardy can be seen as modern is debatable; but there are here persuasive and surprising new readings of Yeats by Ronan McDonald, Empson by Katy Price, and Pound by Ian F. A. Bell. Bell's rereading of Vorticism in general, and 'In a Station of the Metro' in particular, in relation to speculative physics at the beginning of the twentieth century is impressive, as is McDonald's argument that Yeats might be seen as Darwinian. Price highlights, as does Tim Armstrong on inter-war poetry, the little-investigated significance in poetry of popular science texts of the day.

The readings of more contemporary poets, and poet-scientists, here are more expected but no less valuable. There are investigations of the essential ambivalence to the claims of poetry by the poet-scientists (or possibly scientist-poets) Holub and Hoffmann by Helen Small, and Ammons by John Barnie; of the presence of Darwin, again, in the work of Elizabeth Bishop by Jonathan Ellis, and Judith Wright by the collection's editor, John Holmes; and of the relationship between Language Poetry and contemporary genetics by Peter Middleton. What emerges are not only nuanced understandings of the poets concerned, but a new Darwin: Darwin the 'proto-poet' (p. 192). Yet, such claims might say as much about the position of the critic as they do about the poet or scientist.

This concern is picked up in different ways by the remaining two essays in the collection. From his own practical experience in projects which bring actual scientists together with living poets, Robert Crawford sees potential in the kind of dialogue imagined above, and both the opportunity and threat to poets in the modern university which employs pseudo-empirical measures of value for all its activities. And in a survey of the use of scientific language in twentieth-century poetry, Michael Whitworth revisits, among a series of fundamental questions about the topic of this book, the ambivalence implicit in D. H. Lawrence's relative position vis-à-vis science—what Middleton calls 'the limits of analogy' (p. 51)—and the extent to which creative and critical practice, including this collection, might be said to perpetuate it. We both like and hate science, use and resist its language and underlying ideologies, even as we accept that we do not and cannot understand it.

TRINITY SAINT DAVID, UNIVERSITY OF WALES   PAUL WRIGHT

Modern Realism in English-Canadian Fiction. By COLIN HILL. Toronto: University of Toronto Press. 2012. 286 pp. $50. ISBN 978-1-4426-4056-6.

Colin Hill's *Modern Realism in English-Canadian Fiction* aims to tell the story of Canada's modern-realist movement, looking closely both at the writers who, he argues, modernized Canadian fiction and at the historical context in which the movement took place. He provides a clear definition of modern realism, citing narrative objectivity and the use of contemporary language as essential to its style; a concern to represent human consciousness, and a need to explore moral relativism, modern technology, industrialization, and urbanization, as its driving forces. Hill places the literature in his study on a continuum with European and American models of high modernism, while arguing that these phenomena were not imported from outside, but rather born of an inherent impulse to respond creatively to modernity. In his words, modern realism 'was brought to life through the deliberate and painstaking efforts of writers and critics who were responding to the cultural conditions of the twentieth-century world in their groundbreaking stories, manifestos, book reviews, letters, critical articles, and public statement' (p. 24). The book is ambitious in scope, and presents us with highly detailed case studies, as well as glimpses into the works of a wealth of authors who have received little critical attention, making it a thoughtful contribution to the study of Canadian literature.

Hill's methodology includes tracking down close to four hundred novels of the period, then broadening the scope of his source material to include periodicals and the critical discussions of literature that took place on their pages, as well as archival documents on the writers he deems most significant to modern realist fiction. His critical analysis begins with a fascinating overview comparison of the periodicals *The Canadian Forum* and *The Canadian Bookman*, sussing out the critical context in which authors worked, and showing that 'the originators and early advocates of modern realism in the 1920s were a diverse group of writers and critics, from all parts of Canada, both form conservators and literary innovators, both celebrators of all things Canadian and imitators of foreign modes and models' (p. 53). He goes on to interleave case studies of key writers (Raymond Knister, Frederick Philip Grove, and Morley Callaghan) with chapters that re-evaluate the two subdivisions of realism (prairie, urban/social), touching on a wide range of writers and editors as he does so. For example, Hill's chapter on urban and social realism looks at how periodicals such as *New Frontier* and *Masses* addressed contemporary issues, and reflects on the experimental techniques adopted by writers in order to articulate modernity. He explores, for instance, Hugh MacLennan's fusion of 'stream-of-consciousness passages and detached objectivist passages' in *Man Should Rejoice* (p. 154) and the 'direct reportage' employed by Irene Baird (p. 175), assessing both the innovative qualities and the limitations of different techniques.

There is a notable absence of in-depth study of writers who were not white and male, leaving the reader to wonder if this is because modern realist fiction was an innately masculine and white enterprise. It is an idea that risks returning us to the traditional canon of the high modernists which much recent scholarship has questioned, altered, and extended. The book therefore begs the question: what might the case for modern realism look like if authors such as Martha Ostenso, Madge MacBeth, or Ethel Wilson (all mentioned briefly, and all arguably worthy of receiving the same treatment as Knister, Grove, or Callaghan) had been included more fully? It is a question that points the way towards further study that will build on the insightful new understanding that *Modern Realism in English-Canadian Fiction* provides.

UNIVERSITY OF STRATHCLYDE   MICHELLE SMITH

Night Thoughts: The Surreal Life of the Poet David Gascoyne. By ROBERT FRASER. Oxford: Oxford University Press. 2012. xx+469 pp. £30. ISBN 978-0-19-955814-8.

David Gascoyne left school at fifteen (the Polytechnic Secondary School in Upper Regent Street, to which he had descended from the Salisbury Cathedral School when the family fortunes were sunk by his father's nervous breakdown). At sixteen he published his first collection of poetry, at seventeen his first novel. At the same age he made his first visit to Paris, where he met Max Ernst, and on his return was appointed art editor of Orage's *New English Weekly* and wrote the *First English Surrealist Manifesto*. By eighteen he was corresponding with Paul Éluard and, in Robert Fraser's words, 'knew as much about evolving artistic culture in France as anybody in England' (p. 80). He returned to Paris with a contract to write a book about Surrealism and plunged into the literary and artistic culture of the city, becoming an intimate of Éluard, Breton, Dalí, and Pierre Jean Jouve, writing a tribute to Ernst that was translated by Éluard, being chosen by Breton as his own translator, and being recommended by Éluard to perform the same service for Dalí.

Gascoyne's self-invention as the leading English Surrealist, still in his teens and after such a broken and curtailed education, is extraordinary. It is the foundation of his claim to be considered the most European English poet of the twentieth century, yet it also cast a blight on his reputation. He was very adept at composing the strings of arbitrary images that passed for Surrealist poetry, but he had abandoned this practice, and the label Surrealist, by the time he was twenty. But the label stuck: the half-page devoted to him in Andrew Sanders's *Short Oxford History of English Literature* (Oxford: Oxford University Press, 1994) focuses on poetry written in his teens, acknowledging only that he later 'deviates into a certain kind of logical sense' (p. 572).

Fraser's thoroughly researched and judicious biography teems with the cultural life, especially French, of the mid-twentieth century. The names come so thick and fast that it is sometimes difficult to follow, but this is perhaps a necessary price to pay for an appreciation of Gascoyne's profound engagement with that world. At the same time, though gradually, a more intimate and painful story emerges. He was almost entirely homosexual, but failed to find happiness in sexual relations with men, except for one affair that he may later have idealized because his lover was a victim of the Nazis. He was surrounded by older women as a boy, and they remained his source of emotional and financial security throughout his life. The end of his life was as remarkable as its beginning: the homosexual man who had never had his own home, regular income, or regular partner, who was a latter-day incarnation of the *flâneur*, found happiness in a probably sexless marriage with an intelligent and literary but decidedly wifely woman on the Isle of Wight.

Surrealism was a training ground for Gascoyne, a way of opening up an inner world and individual vision that characterize his really distinguished poetry, from the late thirties on, when the poet had become a Christian. But he was not in flight to the conservative reassurance of the Church, like Eliot and Auden. Like many others, he had experimented with combining Surrealism and Communism, and though he rejected both he never lost the radical vision that had drawn him to those movements. If not the greatest Christian poet of the century, he is perhaps the most humane, decidedly unchurchy, centred on the image of the suffering Christ as a symbol of suffering humanity—most notably in his sequence 'Miserere'.

But there was another more sinister influence on Gascoyne's *dérèglement de tous les sens*. In the late thirties he started taking Benzedrine for toothache and other physical pains. He soon became an addict, and one of the symptoms was psychosis. Always, in Fraser's words, 'manic depressive by temperament' (p. 76), he suffered regular minor breakdowns, but his psychiatric problems reached their climax in the sixties. In 1964 he climbed into the courtyard of the Élysée Palace and announced 'that he was a messenger from the Messiah and wished to speak with the French President concerning the imminent Apocalypse' (p. 299). After a period in a psychiatric hospital and an apparent recovery, he repeated the escapade in 1969 at Buckingham Palace.

He retreated to his parents' home on the Isle of Wight and, when they died, sank into deep depression, resulting in yet another hospitalization. A visitor from MIND, Judy Lewis, came to read poetry to the patients, and when she read 'September Sun: 1947', a 'tall and disconsolate man in a state of deep dejection' said 'I wrote that poem'. Judy's first reaction was a patronizing 'Yes, dear', but this was the start of a relationship that salvaged Gascoyne's later years (pp. 354–55). These were also years of revived recognition, but his reputation is still not, perhaps, secured. Fraser's fine biography should go some way to achieving that; a new *Collected Poems* would do still more.

UNIVERSITY OF SHEFFIELD   NEIL ROBERTS

The Oxford Handbook of Modern and Contemporary American Poetry. Ed. by CARY NELSON. Oxford: Oxford University Press. 2012. xiv+716 pp. £95. ISBN 978-0-19-539877-9.

For his overview in twenty-six chapters of American poetry of the twentieth and twenty-first centuries, Cary Nelson has assembled many of its top critics. Best known for his extraordinary efforts to recover the lost political poetry of the 1930s, Nelson has guided his authors especially towards poetry's social and political functions. This accounts for the appearance herein of a variety of cultural and materialist studies and a salutary attention to ethnic poetries. In the limited space available to me, I would like to pay particular attention to what is new or unexpected among the range of generally excellent essays.

Near the beginning, Robert Dale Parker discusses the virtually unknown archive of poetry housed in his anthology *Changing Is Not Vanishing: A Collection of American Indian Poetry to 1930* (Philadelphia: University of Pennsylvania Press, 2011). Parker establishes how Indian writers, both male and female, staked out an entire spectrum of attitudes towards colonialism, religion, nationhood, and the prospects for adapting to oppression. Focusing on the same period, Melissa Girard and Linda Kinnahan shed new light on a number of women poets. Girard places Edna St Vincent Millay, Elinor Wylie, Louise Bogan, and Genevieve Taggard in a distinct position between nineteenth-century sentimentalism and an emerging modernism, arguing for a degree of literary sophistication in these poets that has thus far not been acknowledged. Kinnahan shows how Mina Loy, Lola Ridge, and Marianne Moore respond to clashing economic theories in the early part of the century, each one siding with a provisioning economy based upon needs, as against the predominant neoclassical economics of consumption.

Another complementary pairing stages new perspectives on central modernist issues of form and rhetoric. Peter Nicholls contends that because rhetoric is an unavoidable aspect of communicative language, it cannot be suppressed altogether in modern poetry. It slips into Pound's usage through his high valuation of the musical aspects of poetry and also through his didacticism. Nicholls discusses how the suspicion of rhetoric has in turn been converted to rhetorical purposes by poets such as George Oppen, Susan Howe, the Language poets, and the conceptual poets. Using the influence of painting instead of the aversion to rhetoric, Charles Altieri argues that Cézanne's term 'realization' best conveys the formal struggles of modern painting and poetry to render the objective world in new ways. Both writers address how poetry seeks to move beyond subjectivity to achieve forms that reveal the world, and yet both recognize that the poet's grappling with materials is a subjective activity in the service of an objective form.

It is not surprising that Pound and Eliot appear as touchstones; more remarkable, though, is the invocation of Langston Hughes with nearly the same frequency. On the evidence of this book, Hughes has emerged as one of the giants of American poetry. Taking Hughes as his starting-point, Edward Brunner traces the impact of blues and jazz on poetry across the entire century. He notes that the flexibility of blues as a lyric form has made it a kind of American sonnet, available for appropriation across every kind of social barrier. In contrast, jazz in modern poetry has a complicated history, having emerged as a central site of racial interchange. John Timmerman Newcomb calls for 'work that refutes the domineering disciplinary assumption that modern American poetry was or should be defined by its antagonism to mass culture' (p. 251), and finds evidence for his view in the incorporation of films in John Gould Fletcher and Vachel Lindsay, African American music in Langston Hughes and Sterling A. Brown, sports in Louis Untermeyer and William Carlos Williams, advertising signs in Muriel Rukeyser and Williams, and in a dialectical relationship to mass culture itself in Kenneth Fearing.

Susan Rosenbaum refutes the commonplace that surrealism had little influence on American poetry by analysing the little magazines of the 1920s through the 1950s. This allows her to disclose how American poets adapted and extended many surrealist ideas and methods, as when she quotes John Ashbery saying, '[w]e have absorbed the lesson [of the Surrealist Revolution] to the extent that we have almost forgotten it, but that is not the lesson's fault, but one of its virtues' (p. 287). Mike Chasar uncovers 'communications circuits' of another sort, tracing how poetry travelled within a mass readership during the first half of the century (p. 304). This is a fine-grained materialist study, concerned especially with clipped or postcard poems carried in wallets (mainly by men) and similar poems collaged into scrapbooks (mainly by women). Jahan Ramazani illustrates the dialogic nature of American poetry by situating it intergenerically between journalism and prayer. He observes how American poets adapt the most ephemeral and local materials to make their poetry 'news that stays news' (Pound), while likewise (and sometimes simultaneously) employing ancient liturgical forms to invoke the resonance of addressing 'eternity' (p. 482).

Locating his analysis in 1960 on the cusp of the transition from 'modern' to 'contemporary', Al Filreis counters received pieties about generational affiliation by noting that poets associated with both eras can be found at this moment contesting the liberal consensus inscribed in Daniel Bell's 1960 classic *The End of Ideology*. Filreis demonstrates how 'modern' Marianne Moore and 'contemporary' William Burroughs signal the end of 'the end of ideology' by partaking of collage writing as a democratizing technique (p. 526). The year 1960 is also the date of Donald Allen's anthology *The New American Poetry*, which provides the backdrop to Lytle Shaw's exploration of the implications of Charles Olson's place-based, anthropologically informed poetry for Gary Snyder and Amiri Baraka. He sees these poets 'as imagining almost symmetrically opposite rural and urban afterlives for Olson's model of the poet as fieldworker' (p. 543), allying it respectively with the social discourses of ecopoetics and Black Nationalism. Lynn Keller undertakes ecopoetic readings of poets who complicate the classic American equation of nature with beauty, the sublime, and individual transcendence. She analyses how the systemic issues of experimentally oriented poetry can be used to investigate systemic issues at the heart of ecology.

James Smethurst maintains that hip hop owes its aesthetics to the connections between poetry, politics, and performance forged by the Black Arts Movement. Since hip hop's advent in the late 1970s, all poets have been writing, he contends, within a popular culture dominated by it: 'In short, hip hop is [. . .] a sort of poetic ocean in which the poet-fish must swim either with or against the current' (p. 651). Adalaide Morris considers the current of new media poetics by examining 'poetry situated at the machine–human interface' from Emerson and Whitman to the present (p. 656). She aligns modern and contemporary poetry, especially Objectivist poetry of the 1930s and the more recent forms of cybertext, computational poetry, and codework, 'with the labor conditions, economics, politics, science, and technology that saturate and sustain it' (p. 657).

Assembling thought-provoking essays that encompass a vast range of poetry and poetics, *The Oxford Handbook* succeeds admirably at offering readers some of the best current approaches to reading modern and contemporary American poetry. The somewhat perfunctory nature of a mere handful of the twenty-six essays helps to emphasize how well conceived, cogent, and imaginative the majority is. It is hard to envision a volume that would better take account of the present state of criticism and scholarship of American poetry.

UNIVERSITY OF NOTRE DAME   STEPHEN FREDMAN

Live Poetry: An Integrated Approach to Poetry in Performance. By JULIA NOVAK. (Internationale Forschungen zur Allgemeinen und Vergleichenden Literaturwissenschaft, 153) Amsterdam: Rodopi. 2011. 271 pp. €26. ISBN 978-90-420-3405-1.

Live Poetry proceeds from the observation that poetry 'is experiencing a renaissance through the spoken word', which academics and critics 'have barely taken notice of' (p. 11). In Julia Novak's opening chapter, this continued privileging of the written word prompts a broader discussion of orality and literacy: for example, in interrogating the 'evolutionist notion of linear progress from speech to writing', Novak suggests how neglect of the spoken word enforces a binary of primitive versus civilized cultures. Her second chapter then works 'Towards a Definition of Live Poetry', locating performance at one extreme of a spectrum of media in which poetry may be created (print; digital media; video; audio; live performance (p. 50)). She also unpicks some of the existing vocabulary in which poems are discussed. Particularly compelling here is the dissection of critical terminology that appears to engage with poetry as sound while implicitly upholding the primacy of the written text. Thus, Novak highlights how the vocabulary used in commanding that we '"*hear* the *voice* of the *speaker*" neither refers to an actual act of hearing [. . .] nor to an actual voice [. . .], and certainly not to a real-life speaker' (p. 53). Though strikingly obvious, such observations locate, at a fundamental level in academic practice, a 'one-sidedness [. . .] grounded in the idea that sound, as a quality inherent to the written word, can be found on the page' (p. 52).

Thankfully, Novak goes beyond the mere recognition of this blind spot by dividing her book into two distinct halves. While the first defines and theorizes live poetry and its apparent neglect, the second establishes the 'systematic approach' and 'analytical "toolkit"' necessary to address the lamented situation (p. 11). The book's largest chapter begins from Charles Bernstein's notion of the 'audiotext', which helps position spoken poems as equal counterparts to written poems, responsive to similar kinds of close 'reading' (p. 75). Novak provides methods by which such readings may be achieved, focusing on aural features such as pitch, accent, non-verbal sound, volume, and timbre. Each subsection maintains a degree of theoretical rigour, but Novak's focus is chiefly on establishing a practical methodology. Regrettably, her comparison of varying methods of notating aural features (describing them; typographically reflecting them; plotting them using musical conventions; depicting them in amplitude graphs) is made midway through the chapter; placing this at the beginning might have helped readers to follow Novak's use of these methods in her own argument. In particular, her attempts to typographically reflect verbal features seem at times unclear and might have been prefixed with the disclaimer that '[a] weakness of integrated verbal notation is its imprecision' (p. 128). Nevertheless, Novak convincingly covers a lot of ground here, before focusing on forms of meaning created extratextually, with chapters on 'Body Communication' and 'Contextualising the Performance'. The book closes with a 'Sample Analysis'—in which Novak's full critical repertoire is applied to one performance—and, finally, a short checklist for future researchers to use *in situ*.

The main failing of *Live Poetry* is its limited range of poets. The majority of performances analysed were delivered at a handful of similar poetry events, with the same performances being frequently revisited. This suggests a narrow frame of reference, though it does allow the full interpretation of a performance to be gradually built, and reflects Novak's commitment 'to engage with the actual workings of a flourishing live literature scene' (p. 13). Perhaps this commitment undermines the desire to rectify live poetry's neglect, which might have been better achieved by demonstrating that the analysis of live readings is a fruitful approach to poetry already on the academic radar. Novak mentions in passing numerous poets who might potentially have been analysed, including cris cheek, Bob Cobbing, Allen Fisher, Tony Harrison, Paul Muldoon, and others; of course, this would have involved using recordings as well as truly live performances, but Novak already does this in the case of Wendy Cope (p. 107). As it stands, the book may leave readers questioning whether Novak's interpretative procedures can productively be applied outside the confines of 'performance poetry'. The answer to that question must nonetheless be affirmative: Novak provides the motivation and means for fresh engagement not only with a neglected 'live literature scene', but also with the vocal practices of a far wider range of poets.

BANGOR UNIVERSITY SAMUEL ROGERS

The Song of Roland. Trans. by JOHN DUVAL. Intro. by DAVID STAINES. Indianapolis: Hackett. 2012. xxiv+239 pp. £8.95. ISBN 978-1-60384-850-3.

This new verse translation of the Oxford *Chanson de Roland* has the ambitious aim of recreating in modern English the assonance of the Anglo-Norman original. This has mostly been achieved while providing stark, powerful, and convincing lines, such as 'Roland hammers the hard stone with his blade, | Which does not even nick, though the steel wails, | And when at last he knows it will not break, | 'Ah Durendal, my valiant,' he complains' (ll. 2275–78). The Translator's Introduction rightly speaks of doing justice to the 'unadorned and straightforward' syntax (p. xxi) and compressed immediacy of the *Roland*. I am less convinced by the somewhat watery references to the 'poetry' that lies in 'the magic of the storytelling' (p. xxi). In addition, the rendering into English is insecurely based, using no single edition. Rather, the translator has 'consulted' (p. xxiii) those of Joseph Bédier, William Calin, T. A. Jenkins, and Frederick Whitehead, but, curiously, neither of the current scholarly touchstone editions by Cesare Segre and Ian Short. The volume provides access to the medieval text, but in yet another version—deriving from an online incarnation of Raoul Mortier's edition—and sadly even this appears not in facing-page arrangement but as an appendix, a supplement, it seems, to the English translation. At this price, the publication is clearly intended to serve as a teaching text. Aside from the inadequacies already discussed, the Introduction would certainly make me hesitate to recommend this. Oddly repetitive, it seems to have been written in complete ignorance of decades of criticism on the *Roland*, and is occasionally even inaccurate in its portrayal of the text itself. Reference to the 'glorious past of the French nation' (p. x) makes me wonder whether the author realized that this is the Anglo-Norman version of the poem. This becomes more puzzling still when only the Oxford and Venice manuscripts are mentioned in the bibliography. Moreover, Roland apparently 'laments his own end' (p. xiii), whereas scholars have long pointed to his troubling suicidal impulses. Unevidenced assertions such as 'there had been no women in earlier medieval audiences for the male-oriented stories of the heroic past' (p. xv)—and I could cite others—round off a piece that would mislead students and which certainly lets down an interesting and original translation.

DURHAM UNIVERSITY   LUKE SUNDERLAND

The Hagiographical Works: The 'Conception Nostre Dame' and the Lives of St Margaret and St Nicholas. By WACE. Ed. and trans. by JEAN BLACKER, GLYN S. BURGESS, and AMY V. OGDEN. (Studies in Medieval and Reformation Traditions, 169) Leiden: Brill. 2013. 400 pp. €131. ISBN 978-90-04-24705-5.

The three surviving hagiographical works by the twelfth-century Master Wace have traditionally been overshadowed by his pioneering chronicles of Britain and Normandy. While modern English renderings of the *Brut* and the *Rou* and Françoise Le Saux's *Companion to Wace* (Woodbridge: Brewer, 2005) have introduced Wace to new cohorts of readers in recent years, the devotional works remain comparatively neglected. With this anthology of original texts and translations, Jean Blacker, Glyn S. Burgess, and Amy V. Ogden not only make Wace's Lives of Mary, Margaret, and Nicholas accessible to a wider public, but usefully reassess the relationship of the hagiographies to the histories. Following a general introduction that pieces together Wace's fragmentary biography, the three hagiographical works—the *Conception Nostre Dame* and the Lives of Saints Margaret and Nicholas—are presented in turn. In each case a previous edition of the Old French is reprinted, with a new facing-page, line-by-line translation by Burgess, and accompanying explanatory notes. Each text is prefaced by discussion of its manuscript tradition (arguably a little on the brief side), modern editions, circumstances of composition, structure, sources, historical context, key themes, and style. The volume is aptly rounded off with a general conclusion by Blacker, a handy family tree for the Virgin Mary and her multiple namesakes (as per Wace's *Conception*), a sensibly divided bibliography, and indexes (including lists of names and manuscripts).

This volume is well within the grasp of the undergraduate student. Burgess's translations adroitly balance fidelity to the Old French with readability. The notes assume zero knowledge of biblical culture (we are, for instance, treated to a précis of Jonah and the Whale, p. 146) or of rhetorical terminology ('anaphora' is defined on more than one occasion). A prose summary of each text, meanwhile, is swiftly followed by more or less the same information in easily digestible tabulated form.

There is much here, however, to interest scholars of all stripes. Particularly strong is the way in which the authors situate the hagiographical works in their historical and literary contexts, not only tracing the development of the cults of Mary, Margaret, and Nicholas, for example, but indicating how Wace's works shaped that development. The *Conception* argues in favour of the feast of that name becoming a permanent fixture, flirting with some particularly thorny theology in the process, such as Mary's immaculate conception and her corporeal assumption. For the first time in vernacular writing, the virginal Margaret is presented as the patroness of women in labour, forging the way for a powerful association that would endure for centuries. St Nicholas, finally, is portrayed not as an inimitable model of clerical holiness but as a compassionate man of the world whose story is highly relevant to layfolk. The significance of Wace's hagiographies (and indeed the need for the present volume) comes to the fore in Blacker's general conclusion. These texts may be collected under the banner of hagiography, but they testify to Wace's remarkably diverse output, here ranging from *enfances* and other biographical forms to a martyrdom narrative and miracle tales. Though they may not be peppered with as many of Wace's trademark rhetorical devices as are found in the *Brut* or the *Rou*, the difference, the authors conclude, may be as much a generic one as a temporal one: the *Conception* and the Life of St Margaret were no doubt composed before the celebrated chronicles, but they certainly bear Wace's stylistic imprint and should not be dismissed as his immature œuvre. This volume will surely prove a valuable teaching resource, and the case it makes for introducing Wace's hagiographical works to a broader audience is a highly persuasive one.

UNIVERSITY OF CAMBRIDGE   HUW GRANGE

Les Paroles Salomun. Ed. by Tony Hunt. (Anglo-Norman Text Society, 70) Manchester: Anglo-Norman Text Society. 2012. ix+242 pp. £37.50 ISBN 978-0-90547-456-2.

The text edited here is one of two prose translation-commentaries of the Book of Proverbs written in Anglo-Norman in the thirteenth century, while a third verse treatment was composed by Sanson de Nantuil in the previous century. The *Paroles Salomun* is preserved in a single copy (Paris, BnF, MS fr. 24862, accessible on the Library's Gallica website), which Hunt describes in some detail (pp. 2–5). Since the manuscript begins imperfectly (at Proverbs 1. 26), the prologue (if there was one) is lacking and with it any evidence as to the identity of the commentator and his patron. The anonymous commentator of the *Paroles Salomun* included the Latin text of the Proverbs, a few verses at a time, which he then translated and expounded by giving first the literal and then the allegorical meaning. His major source for the commentary was Bede's *Super Parabolas Salomonis allegorica expositio*, but some portions, unless they were derived from a source as yet unidentified, were due to the commentator's invention.

In the Introduction Hunt characterizes all three of the commentaries (pp. 5–14), with special attention to the second prose text, which survives in several manuscripts, including the understudied Madrid, Bibl. Nac. MS 18523, from which he publishes some extracts. This discussion is useful in helping the reader judge the differences among them. The discussion of the language of the text (pp. 20–25) highlights the most pervasive features of the orthography, morphology, and syntax, with frequent references to Ian Short's *Manual of Anglo-Norman* (London: Anglo-Norman Text Society, 2007). The section on Lexis reveals relatively few novelties and the learned forms are not unexpected.

The editor has used typographical conventions (boldface and quotation marks) to distinguish the biblical text from its Anglo-Norman translation and from the commentary. Latin quotations within the commentary are set in italics and identified in brackets. Those found in the source are further marked with an asterisk. Hunt has thus made as clear as possible the relationship among the different parts of the text, and facilitated tracing the parts not found in the commentator's principal source.

The Notes report a number of instances where the scribe has miscopied the Latin text even though the translation preserves the correct reading of the Vulgate (e.g. nn. 2479–2512, 2872–91, 2892–2918, 3574–3600). However, the majority of the notes record the passages from Bede's *Expositio* that underlie the editor's punctuation and interpretation of the text. The edition has a very full Glossary (only familiar words whose function and form are clear are omitted); it is further supplemented by an Index of Proper Names and a Conspectus of Scriptural Quotations (both in Latin and in Anglo-Norman).

The editor has done his work well, and produced an accurate text, clearly laid out. Although there is no consideration of the possible audience or readership of the work or its surviving manuscript, the edition is a valuable contribution to

Anglo-Norman studies, and makes an important contribution to the picture of vernacular exegesis.

UNIVERSITY OF NOTRE DAME   MAUREEN BOULTON

Texte et contre-texte pour la période pré-moderne. Ed. by NELLY LABÈRE. (Scripta Mediaevalia, 23) Bordeaux: Ausonius. 2013. 256 pp. €25. ISBN 978-2-35613-087-7.

Texte et contre-texte pour la période pré-moderne is a collective volume of conference proceedings. All contributions are in French. The scope of this volume is impressively ambitious, covering a rich spread of material written in the French vernacular from the fourteenth to the sixteenth century. As the title suggests, the guiding theme is the complex relationship of the text with that which runs counter to it. This is an orthodox quarry of poststructuralist criticism. The linchpin theorist is the medievalist Pierre Bec, whose important study *Burlesque et obscénité chez les troubadours: pour une approche du contre-texte médiéval* ([Paris]: Stock, 1984) reflects specifically on the text/counter-text dynamic in Occitan poetry from its outset. Inspired by Bec's work on the literature of the *langue d'oc*, the objective of the present volume is to investigate text and counter-text in the literature of the *langue d'oïl*: virgin research territory, according to editor Nelly Labère (p. 11). Unsurprisingly, the main focus is not so much the *texte* as the *contre-texte* in all its dimensions (material, literary, socio-cultural). In her largely convincing introduction Labère insists that, in pre-modern French, *contre* implies not only hostility and antagonism, but also a more neutral sense of comparison and dialogue. Hence the *contre-texte* is not always negatively and externally opposed to the *texte*; it may constitute an inbuilt contrasting perspective on the latter, glimpsed only through a nuanced process of interpretation. To unlock the subtleties of textual/counter-textual oppositions in the pre-modern literature of the *langue d'oïl*, the present volume draws on a broad base of literary, historical, and philological expertise.

The most persuasive contributions are those which focus on the counter-text as a genre. As a comic genre which patently interpolates excerpts of serious sermons, the medieval *sermon joyeux* convincingly bears out the symbiotic relationship of text and counter-text under investigation by Labère et al. Margarida Madureira's study of *Le Sermon joyeux de la Choppinerie* is a fine example. Madureira further illuminates this jubilant medieval parody through the lens of Patricia Eichel-Lojkine's concept of *excentricité*: ideological critique combined with a formal undermining of literary codes. Turning to sixteenth-century material, Nathalie Dauvois offers a compelling analysis of the *blasons* and *contreblasons* traded back and forth between Clément Marot and his adversary François Sagon. Here two subgenres of *contre-texte* are exposed: judicial, *ad hominem* writing, aiming to attack and refute; and less direct epideictic arraignment, based on the principle of varied poetic style. Marot, argues Dauvois, surpassed his adversaries by originally combining both.

The *contre-texte* also emerges over time as a parodic motif, as demonstrated notably by Jean-Claude Mühlethaler on pear imagery in *Cligès* texts. Mühlethaler's dense piece shows how representation of sex in the pear tree functions as an ambivalent, almost amoral image in Chrétien de Troyes; yet through several centuries of generic permutation, the same motif begins to assume a more salacious character. By the time it reaches the fifteenth-century Burgundian court, it appeals more to a transgressive sense of humour, and thus invites a new counter-perspective on its original context in Chrétien's writing.

Overall, there is much to commend this book. The main shortcoming is that the concept of *contre-texte* is sometimes overstretched to the point where it loses much of its explanatory power. For instance, when the counter-text is defined as *all* spaces which frame the literary text (p. 25) one wonders if 'paratext' would be more appropriate. Some studies do not articulate the notion of *contre-text* with great clarity, but are in their own right rewarding pieces of scholarship: Adrian Armstrong's sensitive reading of the epitaphs of Jean Molinet is a case in point.

ST HUGH'S COLLEGE, OXFORD   JONATHAN PATTERSON

Procès de Jacques d'Armagnac: édition critique du ms. 2000 de la Bibliothèque Sainte-Geneviève. Ed. by JOËL BLANCHARD. (Travaux d'Humanisme et Renaissance, 510) Geneva: Droz. 2012. cxxv+969 pp. €109.95. ISBN 978-2-600-01695-7.

Joël Blanchard has previously edited the *Mémoires* and *Letters* of Philippe de Commynes (1447–1511). His monumental edition of the trial of Jacques d'Armagnac (1476–77) arose from his interest in Louis XI's judicial policy and gives new tools for studying it. He uses Bibliothèque Sainte-Geneviève, MS 2000, an exceptional source whose diffusion had previously been ensured only by a seventeenth-century copy. In addition to the edition of BSG, MS 2000, Blanchard provides useful reading aids, including tables explaining the text's structure, a detailed chronology focusing particularly on the years 1463–76, rich historical notes, a glossary, and an index allowing the reader to navigate the forest of characters involved in the trial.

The introduction gives background and context regarding the life of Jacques d'Armagnac, count of la Marche and duke of Nemours (1433–1477), and the political and legal aspects of his trial. Closely connected to the royal house of Valois, Jacques d'Armagnac was initially a favourite of the young Louis XI, who granted him titles, possessions, and benefits at the beginning of his reign. But the royal policy of using administrators of low birth rather than counsellors from the higher French nobility led in 1464–65 to an aristocratic rebellion supported by the duke of Burgundy, Philip the Good. After several unsuccessful plots against Louis XI, Jacques d'Armagnac was finally besieged at Carlat by the King's envoys and imprisoned in 1476, before being tried and sentenced to death in 1477.

The editor shows how political trials, the most prominent being those of the dukes of Saint-Pol and Nemours, were characteristic of the government and policy of Louis XI and intensified in the 1470s. This administrative and legal frenzy, and the effort of the King to control the exercise of justice, was a reaction against the feudal rebellion.

The criminal file starts with the opening of the trial, previous enquiries, and royal letters designating commissionaires. It proceeds to the interrogation of witnesses and of Nemours himself, the enquiry regarding the fact that Nemours became a cleric during his detention, and the rejection of the appeal based on this new status. It ends with the final judgment and condemnation. The manuscript is not chronological, rather it is a carefully structured reconstruction composed of heterogeneous pieces selected by the chancellor Oriole, and focuses on the conspiracy against the King.

According to the editor, BSG, MS 2000 provides a judicial memoir for the King and his closest counsellors, rather than for the public record. In a pragmatic way, it gathers evidence against the rebels to delegitimize their action. The trial of Jacques d'Armagnac is also a piece of political justice led by Louis XI and takes place under his close control. The procedure is ambiguous, as it provides legal and judicial evidence against Jacques d'Armagnac, but the uniqueness of the procedure and of the memoir suggests it is a legal construction aimed at justifying the King's policy. The duke of Armagnac was primarily accused of treason and *lèse-majesté*, but the administration also defended the exercise of royal prerogatives in his lands, particularly in Auvergne and la Marche, contributing to the affirmation of the King's sovereignty.

Finally, the duke of Armagnac was suspected of necromancy through his Franciscan confessor, Guy Brianson, an adept of geomancy and divination, and Antoine de la Fons, a reputed necromancer. This allegation was tightly related to political concerns, as the duke was accused of using prophetical texts to attack the legitimacy of Louis XI and justify his replacement on the French throne.

Overall, this edition of major judicial documents provides important materials for the understanding of late medieval France and of Louis XI's government and exercise of justice from a historical, juridical, political, but also literary and linguistic perspective. The analysis is rich and encompassing, providing an interdisciplinary perspective on a wide-ranging source. Among the questions raised in the introduction, the reader might have welcomed further investigations of the accusations of 'anglicherie' in the context of the relations between France, England, and the Low Countries following the Hundred Years War.

UNIVERSITY OF READING   IRÈNE FABRY-TEHRANCHI

Philippe de Commynes: Memory, Betrayal, Text. By IRIT RUTH KLEIMAN. Toronto: University of Toronto Press. 2013. viii+296 pp. $65. ISBN 978-1-44264-562-2.

In this fresh look at the career and *Mémoires* of Philippe de Commynes, Irit Ruth Kleiman subjects Commynes's text to an intensive reading in its own right and in the light of other sources. The focus is on the portion of the text dealing with Commynes's relationship with Louis XI. This inevitably privileges one part of the *Mémoires*—and one period of composition—over another: almost nothing is said about Books VII and VIII of the *Mémoires* or about Commynes's career in Italy. Indeed, at the end of this volume Kleiman seems to suggests that Louis's death is the end of Commynes's narrative, forming the second of '[t]wo edges [which] bound Commynes's narration' (p. 206). This is regrettable, for Kleiman's analysis is compelling and occasionally surprising, and it would have been interesting to read her analysis of the final chapters. However, her concentration on Commynes's relationship with Louis allows a very close and productive examination of the three elements in her subtitle, and most especially the central one: betrayal. Kleiman tells the story of two betrayals, of Commynes's supposed betrayal of the last Valois duke of Burgundy, Charles the Bold, and of Louis's deathbed betrayal of Commynes. Without coming to firm conclusions on many of the questions she raises, Kleiman engages with the text in what she calls 'reading with empathy'. It is a reading sensitive to the human side of Commynes's narrative and to the significance of those things that he does not say but which emerge in other contemporary documents. The stories that Kleiman tells are fascinating, aided by copious quotations from the *Mémoires*, deftly translated and analysed. The translation here is as much an aid to the analysis as it is to the reader unfamiliar with the French of the fifteenth century. Occasionally, though, it privileges one interpretation over other possibilities, as, for example, when 'aneau' is translated as 'lamb', allowing Kleiman to read a piece of jewellery as depicting the '*enseigne* of the Order of the Golden Fleece' (p. 61). This points to something that is at once a strength and a weakness of the work: a methodology which aims to 'take risks with the limits of knowledge and interpretation' (p. 64) is always going to be a very personal and subjective reading. Kleiman is aware of this, and her first chapter provides an overview of previous readings of the meeting between Charles the Bold and Louis at Péronne, and the attitudes that critics have taken to Commynes's involvement. Such attitudes are shaped by the critic's subjectivity, as well as Commynes's text. Kleiman's analysis is not perhaps as much of a departure from that of other scholars as one might suppose, but it is stimulating and offers a perspective on questions that are at the heart of Commynes's *Mémoires* and of debates about those *Mémoires*.

NATIONAL UNIVERSITY OF IRELAND, GALWAY   CATHERINE EMERSON

Corneille, Molière, Racine: Four French Plays. 'Cinna', 'The Misanthrope', 'Andromache', 'Phaedra'. Trans. by JOHN EDMUNDS. Intro. by JOSEPH HARRIS. London: Penguin. 2013. xlvi+281 pp. £10.99. ISBN 978-0-141-39208-0.

There could be few better summaries of the current position occupied by French classical theatre in the English-speaking world than the celebrated Prologue to L. P. Hartley's *The Go-Between*: 'The past is a foreign country: they do things differently there'. Between Corneille, Molière, Racine and us, the countless separations of time and place, of human perception and behaviour, seem to generate a sense of cultural remoteness, of 'untranslatability', that is almost unbridgeable.

It is some testimony to the power of John Edmunds's new verse translations of four central plays in the French classical canon that the very notion of untranslatability is severely challenged, if not entirely defeated. With an eye (and ear) firmly focused upon the living performance of the texts, rather than upon silent reading, Edmunds has produced versions that are both speakable and actable, and sustained by a rhythmic energy that is consistently persuasive. Three decisions, among a number of others, enhance the effectiveness of the translation. First, he judiciously avoids the pitfalls of seeking to imitate either the couplet rhyming scheme or the relatively extended line length of the original French. For reasons ranging from over-emphatic sound patterns to rhythmic ponderousness, neither rhyming couplets nor the Alexandrine have ever made for a natural, unforced idiom in English drama; and Edmunds tellingly opts for the impetus and colloquial vigour of Shakespearian blank verse. Second, the pace and breathing patterns of the original plays, their allegros and rallentandos, crescendos and diminuendos, are effectively captured in a line-by-line rendering that neither loosens nor condenses the dramatic speed of the French. Most of all, perhaps, Edmunds's choice of diction allows both the formality and the elevation of the originals to be maintained, but without artificiality or needless rhetoric. As he argues, the choice of a language that is both 'dignified and timeless' (p. xli) enhances the universality of utterance to which the plays give voice.

The four plays are prefaced by an illuminating introduction by Joseph Harris, who helpfully places them in a broader theatrical and cultural context, stressing their resistance to 'reductive explanation or account' (p. xxxvi). And the inclusion of Corneille's *Critique* and Racine's *Prefaces*, as well as sections on Chronology and Further Reading, a genealogical table, and a guide to pronunciation, enhances the sense of comprehensive treatment. It is, though, Edmunds's excellent and sensitive translations that properly remain at the centre of the book. I can think of few versions from the last fifty years that surpass them, and for this reason alone they can be recommended unreservedly.

BRIGHTON   TIM CHILCOTT

Versailles, ordre et chaos. By MICHEL JEANNERET. Paris: Gallimard. 2012. 372 pp. €38. ISBN 978-2-07-013638-4.

Les Fêtes de Versailles. By ANDRÉ FÉLIBIEN. Ed. by MICHEL JEANNERET. Paris: Gallimard. 2012. 177 pp. €17.90. ISBN 978-2-07-013832-6.

In *Perpetuum Mobile* (Paris: Macula, 1997) Michel Jeanneret embarked on an exploration of the Renaissance fascination with movement, mobility, and change. With *Versailles, ordre et chaos*, he now turns his attention to a study of the tension between the quest for harmony and the recurrent threat of disorder during the seventeenth century. Hence the polemical aspect of an investigation focused on revealing the hidden face of a century often reduced to an ideal of order and harmony by the critics. As Jeanneret explains, 'je voudrais restaurer la face anxieuse de l'art classique, son face-à-face avec la violence et l'animalité, sa symbiose avec des forces sauvages qu'il tente de maîtriser, mais ne refoule pas. La culture classique ne nie pas la nature brute, elle esquisse au contraire un mouvement régressif vers le primitif et le tohu-bohu des origines, elle explore le règne de l'élémentaire, le territoire trouble des passions, des pulsions et des convulsions' (p. 10).

Jeanneret thus offers a panorama of French neo-classical aesthetics, which he sees as unified by the desire of contemporaries to keep these threatening forces at bay and to delude themselves about the nature of the world. Starting with an analysis of the early Versailles gardens with their Ovidian inspiration symptomatic of a fear of a return to primitive ages, he shows to what extent the lavish festivals of the 1660s–1670s, *comédies-ballets*, ballets, and operas included, both duplicated and clarified the message at the heart of the park's design with its monsters and graceful mythological figures. He then goes on to consider the better-known authors of the period, La Fontaine, La Bruyère, La Rochefoucauld, Pascal, Molière, Racine, as well as treatises of physiognomy and clandestine texts such as *Theophrastus Redivivus*, with a view to revealing how they all exposed the same unsettling kinship between man and animal. According to Jeanneret, this was not only symptomatic of a belief in the inherent baseness of man and the barbarism underlying civility, it was also a sign of disillusionment with and contempt for the world shared by the thinking elite of the nation.

Although not comprehensive, this overview of late seventeenth-century works gives its author the opportunity to reflect on the very function of art. In entitling his last section '*la parade*', Jeanneret highlights the apotropaic dimension of French neo-classical art and reveals the defensive gesture beneath the glamour. To mimic the domestication or the defeat of monsters and other baleful agents was, he argues, a way of exorcizing them. Its aim was to restore order in a world threatened by anarchy. The truth of this statement goes well beyond the workings of late seventeenth-century aesthetics. It gets to the heart of propagandistic literature in general.

This splendidly illustrated volume is a remarkable work, elegantly written and insightful. Although some of the analyses are relatively familiar, the thesis is new. Subtle and convincing, it turns on their heads a number of preconceptions of the seventeenth century, while exposing its darker side, so often neglected by critics.

One cannot, however, but be disappointed by Michel Jeanneret's new illustrated edition of Félibien's *Fêtes de Versailles*, previously edited by Martin Meade in 1994 (Paris: Maisonneuve et Larose), as well as surprised that the earlier edition is not even listed in the bibliography appended to the volume. Admittedly this new edition is accompanied by a valuable introduction on Félibien's 'magic realism', in which Jeanneret skilfully dissects Félibien's 'rhétorique de la flatterie' (p. 22), with its insistence on the display of luxury and abundance, the mastery of the elements, and the effects of surprise, brilliantly analysed by Louis Marin in *Le Portrait du roi* (Paris: Minuit, 1981). However, the edition lacks a discussion of the engravings by Chauveau and Le Pautre, reproduced in the volume, the implication being that they are simply illustrations of Félibien's text and have no rhetoric of their own. It is also regrettable that, like the earlier edition, this new edition of *Les Fêtes de Versailles* includes only the 1668 and 1674 festivals and leaves out the 1664 *Plaisirs de l'île enchantée*, whose text, albeit not by Félibien, would have usefully complemented the pages devoted to their analysis in the recently published *Versailles, ordre et chaos*. Despite its undeniable qualities, the volume is a missed opportunity to offer the wider public a complete panorama of the Versailles festivals. One must wonder whether this new edition was at all necessary.

GOLDSMITHS, UNIVERSITY OF LONDON   MARIE-CLAUDE CANOVA-GREEN

Correspondance de Pierre Bayle, vol. X: *Avril 1696–juillet 1697. Lettres 1100–1280*. Ed. by ELISABETH LABROUSSE and ANTONY MCKENNA. Oxford: Voltaire Foundation. 2013. xxx+709 pp. £125. ISBN 978-0-72941-026-7.

Immanuel Kant once pointed out that we cannot think alone: that we need to check what we think by comparing it with what others think, see if our arguments are convincing to others, make sure that we are not too idiosyncratic. This volume may be a monument to that point. If ever there were a philosopher who never even tried to think alone but who compared what he thought with what others thought every day, it was Pierre Bayle. If ever there were a philosopher who throve on interchanges with others and whose work was peppered with quotations and observations from a host of other people, it was Pierre Bayle.

And if ever there were a case for the use of numbers in a review of a book in the history of philosophy, this is it. This critical edition of Bayle's letters covers the sixteen months from April 1696 to July 1697. It contains 1280 letters plus mention of ninety-two lost letters, and of course Bayle may have written or received many more. Bayle corresponds here with fifty-six people. Approximately 2000 names are mentioned, most of them authors or subjects of authors, ranging across the entire course of history. And Bayle was not the only one who has been industrious: in the scholarly notes the editors refer to 296 works published since Bayle's death. A read through these letters confirms the density and breadth of Bayle's network of correspondents. The remarkable thing is that Bayle is not swamped by all of this information. In fact, he uses much of it in his *Dictionnaire historique et critique*, which he was writing in these years.

Bayle and his correspondents exchanged information on a host of topics, ranging widely from books on learned women to accusations against various writers of atheism, Socinianism, and Spinozism. A constant theme is 'the prophet', Bayle's label for his enemy Pierre Jurieu. Many of his correspondents know that Bayle is interested in anything that he can use against the man. And the feeling was mutual. The volume also contains an additional chunk of gold: an appendix with a twenty-five-page pamphlet that Pierre Jurieu published against Bayle. *Jugement du public, et particulièrement de M. l'abbé Renaudot* (1697) includes the judgment of Renaudot which led to the prohibition in France of the *Dictionnaire*, plus comments by Jurieu which make it clear that Renaudot's judgment only scratched the surface of the errors and dangers of Bayle's work. This was surely one of the first published responses, and helped set the tone for the later reception of Bayle as a radical and subversive writer.

This is Volume x of a projected fourteen, so the editors must be seeing the light at the end of the tunnel. The entire project is one of the great scholarly endeavours of our time: a large window opening into the life of the mind in the late seventeenth century and at the beginning of the eighteenth. The drama of episodes and issues among Bayle's many friends and enemies rises and falls as one reads through the volume: it almost rises to the level of an epistolary novel. But this was his real life. For some readers, life will be more interesting than fiction.

UNIVERSITY OF CALIFORNIA, RIVERSIDE   JOHN CHRISTIAN LAURSEN

Sade: Queer Theorist. By WILLIAM F. EDMISTON. Oxford: Voltaire Foundation. 2013. x+244 pp. £60. ISBN 978–0–7294–1064–9.

The title might lead readers to think that this study is a provocative rejection of historicist approaches. William Edmiston himself notes that the title contains an anachronism (p. 6), but it would be wrong to think that his study is aligned with the kind of queer anti-historicism advocated in a much-discussed recent publication by Jonathan Goldberg and Madhavi Menon ('Queering History', *PMLA*, 120 (2005), 1608–17). Scholars with an interest in Sade will be aware that his work has long been the object of unrestrained, indeed militant, anachronism: the Surrealists spoke of the 'divine Marquis' as the first great psychoanalyst. So when Edmiston asks, 'Sade's novels: can we read them as queer? (p. 41), historically minded readers might be forgiven for responding rather tiredly, 'Of course we can, because anything can be read as queer if one sets about it determinedly.' For Goldberg and Menon, the very refusal to read texts in historical context deserves to be understood as a queer interpretative practice. But that is not how Edmiston understands his project. He does apply the queer concept of 'heteronormativity' to the eighteenth century, but he does not suppose it to be unchanging across time. What interests him is how Sade attempts to queer, not all categories of sexuality, but his own culture's binary categories of sex, gender, and sexuality (pp. 25, 38). This is how Edmiston manages to maintain a degree of self-conscious anachronism while at the same time accepting a historicist discipline. The use of anachronistic terms such as 'biological' and 'homosexual' offers what he calls the 'convenience' (pp. 26, 28) of being able to address the work directly to twenty-first-century readers. But Sade is not simply a pretext for a transhistorical reflection on queerness, and it becomes clear that Edmiston is committed to producing substantive propositions that will count in the history of sexuality. He finds in Sade's work, for example, the coexistence of attitudes to sodomy that are declared by Foucault to occur in historical succession (p. 73). More generally, he notes that Sade was writing at a 'turning-point [...] of [...] conceptual models' of sexuality (p. 23). Such observations can be made only in so far as the 'convenience' of translating and transposing Sade's thinking into twenty-first-century terms is resisted at certain points. And

Edmiston rises to that scholarly challenge. Terms such as *antiphysique* that may be quite opaque to modern readers are thus subjected to careful exposition and analysis (p. 32). The very difficulty of dealing with shifting categories and terms is directly addressed in a chapter devoted to *Aline et Valcour* that happens to be Edmiston's most original contribution to the interpretation of Sade's fiction (pp. 141–93). At no point, however, does the study move definitively into historicist mode. The project of addressing Sade's work to modern readers is followed through, sometimes leading to statements that have little analytical or historical value. At those points Edmiston finds himself engaged in apologetic writing. It has to be acknowledged, he says to modern readers sensitized and informed by queer, that Sade fails 'regrettably' (p. 57) to undo such binaries as 'the generic opposition between masculine aggression and feminine docility' (p. 225). 'This undeniable fact', Edmiston avows, 'is of course a huge disappointment for anyone wishing to show the queerness of Sade's texts' (p. 225). Advocacy and enthusiasm are allied here with regret and disappointment. Yet readers with an interest in queer may be puzzled by the almost complete omission of what Sade himself calls 'les goûts cruels', to which sexologists a century later loosely gave the name 'sadism'. There is only one mention of them in passing (p. 205). Are they to be considered so 'regrettable' that even regret cannot be formulated?

In sum, this is a study of good quality. It responds to the double exigency of a history shaped by present concerns, and does so in a conscientious, scholarly manner.

University of Queensland   Peter Cryle

'The Girl with the Golden Eyes' and Other Stories. By Honoré de Balzac. Trans. by Peter Collier. Intro. by Patrick Coleman. Oxford: Oxford University Press. 2012. xxxv+152 pp. £7.99. ISBN 978-0-19-957128-4.

As Tim Farrant points out in his 2002 study *Balzac's Shorter Fictions: Genesis and Genre* (Oxford: Oxford University Press), Balzac was not only a novelist, but a prolific writer of novellas and short stories. Peter Collier's translation of *Sarrasine*, *The Unknown Masterpiece*, and *The Girl with the Golden Eyes* provides readers with a welcome opportunity to rediscover three of the most celebrated short fictions from *La Comédie humaine*. The text is both lively and invigorating, and succeeds in making these stories accessible to an anglophone readership without compromising the register or stylistic subtlety of the originals. This in itself is no small achievement, not least because, as Collier notes in his prefatory remarks, Balzac 'can be by turns tender or violent, mythological or realistic, sarcastic or laconic, decorative or descriptive, emotional or philosophical' (p. xxix). Equally impressive is Patrick Coleman's introduction. Coleman outlines the circumstances behind the composition of the stories, explaining in particular how the newspaper magnate Émile de Girardin helped to establish Balzac's early reputation as the 'roi de la nouvelle' by encouraging his friend to write for the press. Moreover, the introduction relates the stories to the broader aesthetic preoccupations of La Comédie humaine. In posing the question of how the fictional Lanty family amassed its wealth, Sarrasine, for example, illustrates Balzac's fascination with private life, and his stated wish to penetrate the hidden truths of nineteenth-century society. As well as providing the standard critical apparatus that will be especially useful to undergraduate readers, Coleman also allows for some insightful analysis of the texts and the connections between them. Most interestingly, his discussion reflects on the absence of maternal figures in The Girl with the Golden Eyes, and on the way in which Balzac uses the cloak of history to examine the themes of erotic desire and sexual infidelity in The Unknown Masterpiece. Despite some very minor inconsistencies of presentation, the volume is finished to a high standard, with extensive notes and a chronology of Balzac's life and career. A select bibliography takes account of the most recent academic scholarship on the three texts, and helpfully signals which of the stories is addressed in detail by each of the items listed. In summary, this is an elegant and engaging volume, and one that will benefit both students and researchers.

UNIVERSITY OF BIRMINGHAM   ANDREW WATTS

The Fevered Novel from Balzac to Bernanos: Frenetic Catholicism in Crisis, Delirium and Revolution. By FRANCESCO MANZINI. London: Institute of Germanic and Romance Studies. 2011. 264 pp. £25. ISBN 978-0-85457-226-7.

The aim of this study is to chart an alternative history of the modern French novel, 'written over the course of a displaced nineteenth century that began with the collapse of the Restoration and ended with that of Vichy' (p. 15). The premiss here is that there exists a whole series of novels 'written in a fevered style that also foreground the motif of fever' (p. 238). While this fever is made manifest in a multiplicity of corporeal afflictions such as paralysis, tetanus, and even the plague, fever also extends into the mental arena in the form of delirium, hallucinations, and madness. At the same time as being alternately or simultaneously physical and mental, such fevers also represent a social, political, and spiritual malaise which shows the need for regeneration at the level of both the individual and the group: the afflicted individual becomes a kind of often willing, sacrificial victim who embodies not just illness but resistance to illness. Fever is, therefore, associated 'with an ongoing process of virtuous ill-health, related to the mechanism of reversibility' (p. 31)—the process whereby individual suffering can vicariously signal and redeem the ills of a whole society. In this particular case, those ills would appear to result from the errors and the excesses of the Enlightenment and the Revolution, and are perpetuated in the hegemony of bourgeois materialism, scientism, and their at least supposed 'realism'. Given that all of the latter positions are generally instigated and controlled by men, it is the women, particularly the 'pious young woman, just discovering her sexuality' (p. 17), whom these novels portray as quintessentially fevered individuals who thereby become 'the redeemers of their politically and socially broken society' (p. 237).

In the course of the long nineteenth century, the fevered novel assumes a number of guises, from what Manzini calls Frenetic Romanticism to Frenetic Catholicism through to Frenetic Surrealism—or, indeed, combinations of two or more of these varieties. Combining Frenetic Romanticism and Maistrean Catholicism, Balzac's *Ursule Mirouët*, for example, shows a typically martyred young woman, the eponymous Ursule Mirouët, elevating the whole of society through a hallucinatory fever that enables her to inherit her uncle's wealth, offset her illegitimacy, and espouse a thereby restored aristocracy. Barbey d'Aurevilly's *Un prêtre marié* has another young heroine, Calixte Sombreval, cleansing the sins of her apostate father and, simultaneously, unwriting and rewriting *Un prêtre marié*. Zola's *La Faute de l'abbé Mouret* shows another young woman sacrificing herself, to Nature rather than to God. Reneging on Zola's Naturalism in favour of 'Spiritual Naturalism', Huysmans's *En rade* and *Sainte Lydwine de Schiedam* help 'God rebalance the scales of his perfect justice' (p. 172), with further examples of expiatory females 'perfecting their resignation and humility' (p. 169). In Bloy's *Le Désespéré* and *La Femme pauvre* fever, in the form of madness, is shown to be the surest proof of sanctity, while in the novels of Bernanos, 'the last of the Frenetic Catholics' (p. 216), 'accounts of the crisis of fever [. . .] transcend mere literature or even medical case-history and attain the status of prophesy or revelation' (p. 217). If such texts tend to endorse establishment values and gender inequalities, Surrealism's revival of freneticism seems, at least in the work of Artaud, to produce a potentially more liberating 'gratuité frénétique' (p. 233). Although the wealth of quotation (and its translation) sometimes submerges the arguments set out in his book, Manzini's careful charting of the continuities and the discontinuities of the fevered novel constitutes a stimulating, original, and important contribution not just to fiction studies but to a more general understanding of French culture and society.

UNIVERSITY OF BRADFORD   OWEN HEATHCOTE

Taboo: Corporeal Secrets in Nineteenth-Century France. By HANNAH THOMPSON. London: Legenda. 2013. x+157 pp. £45. ISBN 978-1-907975-55-4.

In this short but impressive study, Hannah Thompson explores the darker and hidden aspects of nineteenth-century French literature and reality, namely the taboo body. Using in part theory by the burgeoning and relatively unknown discipline of Disability Studies and the work of David Mitchell (*Disability Studies*, ed. by Sharon L. Snyder and others (New York: Modern Language Association of America, 2002)), the book is concerned with the representation and interpretation of what is hidden in the text rather than what is usually shown.

Nineteenth-century French texts have a particular obsession with being able to know and say everything. The demands of Realist novels dictate that some attempt is made to represent what cannot be represented: the sick body, the monstrous body, or, simply, bodily functions. In the case of the taboo body, literary descriptions frequently stand for something other than themselves, as a means of communicating what cannot be uttered to the reader.

The book is in two main parts, 'The Body' and 'The Reader', that distinguish between bodily taboos on the one hand and the more complex issue of their interpretation by the reader on the other, drawing ingenious parallels between forms and functions. This neat division does not stop the sections from overlapping, but these overlaps give a strong sense of coherence to the study. From the aestheticization of female pleasure in the novels of George Sand and Rachilde, to the depiction of trauma (the trauma of war and defeat after the Franco-Prussian war, which commented on the weakened state of the French nation), in particular the 'unmanning' of the male body; from scenes of torture and suffering containing elements of sadism and masochism in the novels of Octave Mirbeau and the short stories of Barbey d'Aurevilly, to monstrous and marginalized bodies in the novels of Victor Hugo and Émile Zola, the book offers multifaceted readings of the taboo bodies which haunt nineteenth-century French literature.

Thompson shows in rich detail how compelling the spectacle of the disintegrating/marginalized body can be when it becomes a privileged site of meaning. The nineteenth century's morbid attraction to both physical and mental otherness, symbolized, for instance, by the monstrous body of Quasimodo in *Notre-Dame de Paris*, reveals that the shock of physical disfigurement poses problems of representation for the writer as well as problems of interpretation for the reader. The figure of the monster embodies the tension between the difficulty of naming and the necessity of doing so.

The author illuminates the role of the taboo body, at the intersection of the speakable and the unspeakable, and its persistent desire to be heard, even though it can never be fully articulated. It speaks obliquely in ways which are not immediately apparent. For that reason, when the corporeal is displaced away from the body, some scenes depend on the reader's active participation: descriptive passages invite the reader to use the textual clues provided to imagine the excesses of the taboo body. In that respect, the study explores not only the relationship between text, author, and reader, but also what triggers the reader's imagination and how some scenes can be decoded.

One of the principal merits of the book is that it is a study of how the 'unspeakable' manages to find a voice and how taboo excesses can be represented in language. It provides a reflective and stimulating commentary on the ways in which what is not usually talked about signifies and matters.

University of Sydney
Françoise Grauby

La Littérature symboliste et la Langue. Ed. by Olivier Bivort. (Rencontres, 38) Paris: Classiques Garnier. 2012. x+233 pp. €29. ISBN 978-2-8124-0810-6.

In his Foreword Olivier Bivort states that this volume of conference proceedings aims to examine the innovations of late nineteenth-century French literature alongside contemporary developments in linguistics. However, the notion of 'la Langue' inevitably opens itself up to a variety of approaches; in fact, most of the articles engage with the topic through an exploration of the Symbolists' aesthetic theories and practices. This in no sense detracts from the merit of the volume, however. Its breadth is, indeed, its strength, and is evident not only in its methodologies but also in its corpus, which ranges from Baudelaire to Proust. Major figures such as Rimbaud and Mallarmé are considered, and although Verlaine is a notable omission, his work often serves as a reference-point; less-known figures such as Jean Lahor, Max Elskamp, and Charles Guérin also feature. The absence of Symbolist theatre, a relatively minor but nonetheless intriguing aspect of the movement, is regrettable, however.

The volume is dedicated to the memory of Sergio Cigada, whose contribution is undoubtedly one of its highlights, offering an original take on Rimbaud's much-studied aesthetic manifesto, the 'Lettre du voyant'. Although it elides subtle differences between Aristotelian and Baudelairean notions of synthesis, the article's argument that 'Alchimie du verbe' founds the new poetry through its synthesis of self-contradictory elements is compelling. Equally impressive is Henri Scepi and Philippe Bertrand's article on Laforgue's questioning of the limits of language; their assertion that his 'mots-valises' effect a coupling that is pseudo-sexual, yet non-reproductive in its deliberate failure to spawn viable linguistic entities, is particularly insightful.

Mallarmé's work is explored by Jean-Nicolas Illouz and Marco Modenesi, their articles complementing each other well in their considerations of the poet's writings on language, notably *Les Mots anglais*, which Mallarmé himself deemed insignificant, but which recent critics have sought to recuperate. Simonetta Valenti's article on Mauclair is also haunted by Mallarmé, whose influence on the former she acknowledges, while demonstrating that Mauclair's enthusiasm for the idiosyncratic possibilities of *vers libre* distinguished him from his master.

Baudelaire also merits two articles: subtle readings of his reception (André Guyaux) and rhetoric (Mario Richter) are offered, although neither expands on his links with Symbolism 'proper'. At the other end of the reputational scale are Lahor, Elskamp, and Guérin, whose work is examined by Liana Nissim, Christian Berg, and Ida Merello respectively. Their articles are of interest for their analyses of the poets' theories, but none quite succeeds in arguing that the poets' practice contributed significantly to Symbolism's innovation.

Prose's role in the movement was a supporting one; nonetheless, Gilles Philippe's argument that Symbolist prose offered a new model of literary subjectivism is perceptive and original. Marisa Verna, meanwhile, argues that Proust's prose reflects some aspects of Symbolism but ultimately distinguishes itself through its prefiguring of phenomenology.

Verna's forward-looking article is a fitting end to the volume, but the articles at the heart of its project are by Jacques-Philippe Saint-Gérand and Bivort. Saint-Gérand's opening article persuasively argues that contemporary criticism of Symbolism was based more on its resistance to 'le français' as patriotic construct than on its departure from the rules of 'la langue française'. Bivort also considers the ideological dimension of Symbolism in his fascinating article concerning the use of the myth of 'la clarté française' to criticize the movement in both the nineteenth and twentieth centuries.

Although not containing enough consideration of contemporary linguistic theories to attract historians of linguistics, this volume is undoubtedly of interest to scholars of late nineteenth-century literature and to those interested in the period as a crucible of modernist developments. Its contribution to the field lies in its demonstration that the Symbolists not only revolutionized literary language, but did so in a highly self-conscious fashion.

Durham University

Sam Bootle

Understanding Marcel Proust. By Allen Thiher. (Understanding Modern European and Latin American Literature) Columbia: University of South Carolina Press. 2013. xviii+322 pp. $59.95. ISBN 978-1-61117-255-3.

With this volume Marcel Proust has come to join ranks with literary contemporaries (for instance Thomas Mann) and subsequent admirers (such as Samuel Beckett) who have already been the subject of monographs in 'Understanding Modern European and Latin American Literature'. This series has the laudable and expressed aim of making European classics more accessible, especially to a North American audience and to undergraduates and graduates. Allen Thiher has an excellent, detailed knowledge of the whole of Proust's œuvre and thereby proves himself to be a good point of introduction to Proust's life and works. The author spends a pleasing amount of time on Proust's writings prior to the *Recherche*, for which previous introductory studies to Proust have not always had much space, and the account of the complex early volume *Les Plaisirs et les Jours* is especially useful. When discussing *Contre Sainte-Beuve* and *Jean Santeuil*, Thiher does not shy away from difficult questions of editorial choice and necessary intervention; such questions are also attendant on discussions of the publication history of the *Recherche*. In his discussion of the *Recherche* Thiher accounts for wider questions of tense, imagery, and voice in a careful and nuanced manner, although he sometimes tends to veer towards plot summary rather than analysis. His interpretation of *Le Temps retrouvé* in terms of Bakhtin's notion of the 'carnivalesque' is, nonetheless, particularly illuminating and successful. Proust is also well situated among his French predecessors such as Racine, La Rochefoucauld, La Bruyère, or Pascal, as well as alongside more modern novelists (Tolstoy or Flaubert) and poets (notably, Baudelaire and Mallarmé). Details of the changing fate of the aristocracy throughout the nineteenth century and during the Third Republic in particular are provided, such 'class distinctions' not being 'part of the American experience' (p. 141), although other students will no doubt also appreciate this historical contextualization. Thiher's plain speaking can jar a little, with Morel described as a 'rude bumpkin' (p. 226), Brichot as a 'moronic pedant' (p. 236), the protagonist as a 'near psychopath' (p. 172), and Proust's characters in general being considered 'randy animals' (p. 165), but this tactic is part of an attempt to bring Proust closer to his audience, and at other times Thiher's language is much more faithful to Proust's own register. The author's main interpretative contention is that the principal unifying thread through Proust's œuvre is that of fall narratives, or tales of paradise and paradise lost. This is a useful approach to the *Recherche*, as other critics before Thiher have noted; importantly, though, Thiher is resistant to a reading of the final volume as a form of *Paradise Regained*, and remains appropriately ambivalent about vexed concepts of redemption and resurrection in Proust. Much of the bibliography is helpfully glossed to aid readers in selecting editions and relevant critical works for further study if so desired. The coincidental publication date no doubt explains the notable omission of the recent volume of English translations of Proust's poetry edited by Harold Augenbraum (Proust, *The Collected Poems: A Dual-Language Edition with Parallel Text* (New York: Penguin, 2013)), with the author instead tending to rely on Web resources such as the 'Marcel Proust Ephemera Site', which is acknowledged to be 'not entirely accurate' (p. 291, n. 2). Unfortunately, presentational errors including mistakes in French titles and quotations are littered throughout the text, which for the initiated Proustian are distracting and for the uninitiated (Thiher's target audience) risk causing confusion. Such errors mar the otherwise persuasive and thoughtful prose and impede easy reading of this volume.

St John's College, Oxford   Jennifer Rushworth

Le Robinson noir. By Alfred Séguin. Ed. and intro. by Roger Little. Paris: L'Harmattan. 2013. xxxi+212 pp. €25. ISBN 978–2–343–00156–2.

Les Deux Enfants de Saint-Domingue. By Julie Gouraud. *L'Esclave de Saint-Domingue*. By Michel Möring. Ed. and intro. by Roger Little. Paris: L'Harmattan. 2012. xxxii+200 pp. €23. ISBN 978–2–336–00205–7.

The sesquicentenary of France's 1848 abolition of slavery fostered renewed interest in the study of French slavery. After the subsequent Taubira Law of 2001, which declared slavery a crime against humanity, the Committee for the Memory of Slavery was established in 2004, and an important body of work coalesced forcing us to understand Enlightenment, Revolution, and nineteenth-century cultural production in an entirely new light. It is in this context that we should situate two recent editions by Roger Little that republish two novels and a short story by little-known writers from the second half of the nineteenth century.

Originally published in 1877, *Le Robinson noir* tells a black version of Daniel Defoe's *Robinson Crusoe*. It begins with the flogging of its eponymous character, a slave named Charlot, on the orders of his master's son George. At the urging of his mother, Charlot flees on a ship rather than risk attacking George, his milk-brother. En route, the ship encounters a storm, and after the resulting shipwreck Charlot is the sole survivor on a deserted isle, where he is eventually joined by George, himself the victim of a subsequent shipwreck. Helpless in the survivalist mode required in this new environment, George must cease to treat Charlot as his slave and relies on him more as a superior. Upon being taken captive by native Pacific islanders, Charlot discovers that their king is La Gamelle, the very sailor who helped him escape. In the end, both Charlot and George are rescued and return home to Peru.

Julie Gouraud's 1874 novel *Les Deux Enfants de Saint-Domingue* begins with the Haitian slave insurrection of 1791. The Creole Philibert family escapes with the help of a devoted mulatto slave, Guillaume, who sacrifices his life in the process. In the following confusion, the Philiberts' son gets separated from his family and boards the wrong ship, where he is taken in by a British family. Most of the novel, then, consists of narrating the parallel travels and education of brother and sister before they are finally reunited. The same volume includes Michel Möring's 1860 short story *L'Esclave de Saint-Domingue*, the story of a free girl of colour Mika, who sells herself into slavery to save her father from financial ruin. In captivity, Mika befriends her master's daughter and ends up being manumitted. As in Gouraud's novel, the Haitian revolution begins, and Mika is saved along with her young mistress by a heroic slave, whom Mika eventually marries.

Séguin's text is certainly the most abolitionist. Those who have read Olympe de Gouge's 1789 *L'Esclavage des noirs; ou, L'Heureux Naufrage* will find some aspects of Séguin familiar, but will probably prefer Gouge's much more explicit abolitionism and more timely publication. Interestingly, however, by 'blackening' Defoe's protagonist, Séguin must consign the role of Friday to his protagonist's former master. This inversion has important implications for the novel's take on such Enlightenment tropes as the master–slave dialectic, the state of nature, the Noble Savage, cultural relativism, and ingenuity. In the story of La Gamelle's reign over islanders, one might also discern a political allegory in the order of Montesquieu's Troglodytes. Nonetheless, Séguin participates in certain tropes of colonial discourse in his representation of cannibalism and of the native islanders' veneration of their white ruler, to which Gouraud's and Möring's glorification of the benevolent master might be read as parallels. Gouraud's novel, like Möring's short story, valorizes the obedient, devoted slave who puts his/her master's interest above those of other slaves as a class. Furthermore, each presents the Haitian revolution in its most violent light. In Gouraud's case, this representation of revolutionary violence follows the Philibert family to France, which is under the Reign of Terror at the time. In this sense, it may also be characterized as counter-revolutionary. It is nonetheless Rousseauist in its account of its protagonists' education.

While these texts are less satisfying than Doris Y. Kadish and Françoise Massardier-Kenney's work (*Translating Slavery: Gender and Race in French Women's Writing, 1783–1823*; *Translating Slavery: Gender and Race in French Abolitionist Writing, 1780–1830*, rev. edn; *Translating Slavery: 'Ourika' and its Progeny* (Kent, OH: Kent State University Press, 1994, 2009, and 2010 respectively)), they do make accessible a broader corpus of slave literature. Given that they were written for young readers, they make for very teachable texts for undergraduates in the English-speaking world, even reproducing illustrations from the original editions of all three. Given Gouraud's use of Creole, perhaps explained by the fact that her mother was also an escapee from Saint-Domingue, it will additionally be of interest to specialists and students of *créolité*.

UNIVERSITY OF MICHIGAN   JARROD HAYES

Adapting Nineteenth-Century France: Literature in Film, Theatre, Television, Radio and Print. By KATE GRIFFITHS and ANDREW WATTS. Cardiff: University of Wales Press. 2013. x+235 pp. £95. ISBN 978-0-7083-2594-0.

This insightful book not only emphasizes the relevance of nineteenth-century French literature to ongoing discussions around how we think about adaptation, but also the significance of adaptation itself as a lens through which to view that corpus. Much research on adaptation has tended to privilege theatre and cinema, and has done so using a blanket approach. In welcome contrast, Kate Griffiths and Andrew Watts consider a less exclusive range of media so as to look beyond select forms and expand the debates around authorship, especially with regard to questions of originality and borrowing. Importantly, they recognize that such debates are shaped as much by the chosen medium of an adaptation as they are by the individuals involved in the process, from writers and directors to actors and producers. Their shared focus, which is carefully sustained across each of the six chapters, lies on how 'different media adapt differently, their very different aesthetic frameworks and practical requirements authoring adaptations almost as much as the writer penning them and the various creative identities translating them into different forms' (p. 11).

Such an objective prompts a richly detailed, rigorously argued, and repeatedly accessible study of six of the period's most recognizable writers, each of whom are read through different media versions of key works: Émile Zola's *Germinal* and two BBC radio plays; Balzac's *L'Auberge rouge* and *Eugénie Grandet*, dramatized in two films from the silent era; Flaubert's *Madame Bovary* and two literary rewritings; Hugo's *Les Misérables* and musical theatre; a selection of Maupassant's short stories as reimagined in a hugely popular French television series; and Verne's *Le Tour du monde en quatre-vingts jours* in two examples of post-war cinema. Each chapter displays an extensive knowledge of the texts in question and their formal, even surprising, affinities with these adaptive contexts, such as the possibilities afforded by the 'blind' medium of radio to Zola's intimate exploration of human consciousness. What Griffiths and Watts often refer to as the 'artistry' of adaptation becomes delightfully clear, not simply in the different and creative reworkings of nineteenth-century French texts, but also in the design and delivery of those texts themselves. All six writers actively and openly drew upon other texts and sources in the conception of their work, from Balzac's use of popular theatrical melodrama to Flaubert's interest in Romantic fiction.

In effect, a series of comparative readings emerges which draws out the similarities between source and adaptation as intertextual forms, without lapsing into ideas of fidelity or indeed treating the versions in question as derivative copies.

These analyses respect the fluidity of adaptation as an artistic practice, in line with the positions of the writers being explored, and resist the often unhelpful urge to taxonomize that practice, even if at times their understanding of the adaptive act is noticeably broad as a result. The omission of other key writers of adaptive works, such as Alexandre Dumas *père*, and other media such as fan fiction may understandably leave certain areas of coverage open for further investigation, but Griffiths and Watts's book remains a major work of scholarship. They persuasively encourage exciting new directions for how adaptation studies—and how thinking on the reception of nineteenth-century French literature—can move beyond restrictive models of understanding.

UNIVERSITY OF BRISTOL   BRADLEY STEPHENS

Albert Camus au quotidien. Ed. by ANDRÉ BENHAÏM and AYMERIC GLACET. Villeneuve d'Ascq: Presses Universitaires du Septentrion. 2013. 197 pp. €20. ISBN 978-2-7574-0446-1.

The year 2013, which marked the centenary of the birth of Albert Camus, saw a number of events and publications to commemorate the writer's continuing contribution to intellectual debate. The present volume is a welcome addition to this body of work, bringing together ten essays from international scholars under the heading of 'le quotidien', a question which the editors of the collection deem 'primordiale pour Albert Camus' (p. 17). The context for the collection is set out in the book's foreword: 'Celui qui fait face au quotidien, telle est la définition de l'homme. Et tel est [. . .] le thème de ce livre. Albert Camus au quotidien [. . .] dont l'écriture était une écriture au quotidien, dont la discipline était une discipline au quotidien, dont le combat était un combat au quotidien' (p. 12). Accordingly, the essays comprising the volume provide differing perspectives on Camus's relationship with everyday situations and experiences. In 'La Leçon de Tipasa' Michel Onfray provides a useful *mise au point* of Camus's Algerian hedonistic morality on which much of the writer's thinking is based, before Aymeric Glacet proceeds to offer an insightful analysis of the gatekeeper of so many everyday occurrences in Camus's writings, the *concierge*. Staple of everyday life, food in Camus's imaginative writings is examined by Gerald Prince, while David Ellison assesses 'comment Camus, en invoquant la "révolte au jour le jour", cherche dans la vie le bonheur qu'il voyait comme la quête ultime de l'homme' (p. 65). Focusing her attention on images of everyday life in Camus's formative writings, Agnès Spiquel examines the personal emotions and tensions in evidence in the writer's youthful texts, 'à mi-chemin entre l'écriture de l'essai et l'affabulation romanesque' (p. 84). These tensions come into particularly sharp focus, Spiquel observes, in Camus's 'prosaïsme de la pauvreté' (p. 93) evident in the *Voix du quartier pauvre*, where 'le quotidien fonctionne comme revers salutaire enregistré par l'écriture ironique' (p. 97). Ève Morisi examines Camus's early Algerian journalism, particularly 'Misère de la Kabylie', where the young journalist's objective is to 'faire l'anatomie d'une misère quotidienne mortelle' (p. 101). Debarati Sanyal assesses the historical and ethical significance of Camus's representation of nature in his Algerian writings. Algeria, Sanyal argues, is a 'nœud de mémoire' and a 'carrefour identitaire' (p. 126) in the construction of what is deemed an ecology of belonging. Nicolas L'Hermitte offers a reading of *La Chute* 'à mi-chemin entre rhétorique et ontologie' (p. 142) and examines how 'le quotidien' is at the very core of Clamence's identity. Posing the question '[l]e quotidien est-il connaissable?' (p. 159), and with reference to Blanchot's reflections on the subject, Edward Hughes examines the presence of the everyday in the Camus corpus, noting that '[l]es personnages de Camus sont souvent enfermés dans le quotidien' (p. 174). And, examining the relationship between 'l'anecdote et le quotidien' (p. 179), André Benhaïm concludes the volume by highlighting how Camus combines a sense of intimacy with his treatment of everyday situations. Together, the chapters comprising this volume provide a well-informed and useful account of how, in the words of the blurb, 'le quotidien inspire à l'écrivain sa réponse à la brutalité de l'histoire et à l'absurdité du monde'. Both the specialist and non-specialist reader will discover many revealing insights into Camus's depiction of everyday life, insights that have been largely overlooked by critics hitherto.

UNIVERSITY OF CENTRAL LANCASHIRE   MARK ORME

French Crime Fiction and the Second World War: Past Crimes, Present Memories. By CLAIRE GORRARA. Manchester: Manchester University Press. 2012. viii+ 151 pp. £60. ISBN 978-0-7190-8265-8.

France's continuing preoccupation with memories of the Second World War and the German Occupation is hardly new territory. The nation's complex relationship with this period of history is a persistent subject of fascination in literature and film, while cultural critics and historians continue to add to the sum of knowledge and understanding of the *années noires*. What Claire Gorrara succeeds in doing in this book is to turn that critical gaze onto a body of work that has not yet been subjected to sustained analysis—the many works of crime fiction that take the period of Occupation as their focus—and to link this body of work with mainstream memory studies.

The monograph begins with a useful outline of memory studies, emphasizing those theories that characterize memory not simply as a means of recuperating the past but in terms of its contribution to memory work in the present. One of the more radical departures that Gorrara takes from established theories of memories of occupation is in relation to the work of Henry Rousso, whose *Le Syndrome de Vichy: de 1944 à nos jours* (Paris: Seuil 1990) was one of the forerunners in rethinking the ways in which the French remembered the war. While acknowledging the importance of Rousso's work, Gorrara has discovered in the course of her study of an extensive body of crime fiction from the 1940s to the 2000s that his psychoanalytical model of silence, repression, return, and eventual obsession with the realities of occupation is not mirrored in her corpus of crime novels. What she has discovered instead is that the 'waves of reworking the past' are more 'fluid' (p. 9) than Rousso's model allows for. Equally, his model accords insufficient importance to the conceptualization of war across a broad range of cultural production, including popular fiction, and the possibilities such forms offer for rethinking the past.

Crime fiction, as one such popular form, is credited with offering a means of understanding the darker moral conflicts of the Second World War and engaging with those dilemmas much earlier than Rousso acknowledges. The genre is well suited to the task of remembrance through its investigatory structure, allowing for the uncovering of buried memories of war and, in its *noir* embodiments, focusing on ethically ambiguous situations. The study is organized chronologically, moving from the 1940s to the early twenty-first century. Novels from the 1940s and 1950s illustrate early challenges to De Gaulle's heroic narrative of resistance, while novels of the 1950s and 1960s foreground the Jewish wartime experience against a background of public marginalization of Holocaust survivors. Analysis of 1970s and 1980s novels illustrates changing representations of collaborators through depictions of collaboration as a more widespread phenomenon than previously acknowledged. Survivor stories of 1980s and 1990s crime novels are discussed against a background of increased remembrance and of the trials of Vichy officials in France, identifying the contribution that a work such as Daeninckx's *Meurtres pour mémoire* (1984) made to public debates on the legacy of the war. The final chapter brings the study up to the present by exploring children's crime fiction and its construction as a means of imparting civic memory to the young.

This monograph provides an original and well-written overview of crime fiction that tackles the Second World War, not just adding to the understanding of memory processes in relation to that conflict, but also demonstrating the value of crime fiction as a genre that is not simply a form of entertainment but has a key role to play in the construction of memories of the past and in underpinning the impact of those memories in the present.

UNIVERSITY OF HULL   ANGELA KIMYONGÜR

Mortal Subjects: Passions of the Soul in Late Twentieth-Century French Thought. By CHRISTINA HOWELLS. Cambridge: Polity. 2011. x+263 pp. £17.99. ISBN 978-0-7456-5275-7.

Ought an essay on passion, death, and the soul to be beautiful? Is there something of love and death demanding sensitivity of touch and style? Is this what theories miss when they claim to have finally defined, explained, or determined passionate living and the torments of approaching death? It might be impossible to answer these questions, but Christina Howells has given us proof of the precious quality of an art of thinking about human finitude. The achievement is almost perverse, since her material from recent French thought is difficult and abstruse, yet her writing is exceptionally accessible, without ever resorting to commonplace imagery or expectations. This is a rare book. It manages to be companionable and generous on some of the most demanding ordeals and high points of existence, while avoiding the sad simplifications of philosophical consolation that render popular studies useless and damaging.

The heartbeat of her argument is set by a very old problem. How are mind and body related? If they are fully united, then why do love, death, and the passions have a hold on us? If they are separate, how do they work together and then pull apart? What is the soul if it is a vehicle between the two, yet finds its vocation in eternity after death? In charting a path through recent French thought, through its genealogy in Descartes and classical philosophy, alongside literary and artistic sources, and in counterpoint to analytic philosophy and contemporary sciences of the mind, Howells is able to outline a new possibility. The soul is in the body, in its passions and mortality. It is distorting, though, to render her reflections in this bald proposition. Howells offers us variations, in the musical sense, such that her short but scholarly studies of a wide range of thinkers temper the temptation to a simple identity of soul and body, or to a swing back to their independence. The entanglement of subjectivity and flesh leads into discussions of Merleau-Ponty and Beauvoir, then on through religious thinkers, to psychoanalysis and deconstruction.

Despite subtle shifts from problems in one thinker to alternatives in others, Howells's argument is not dialectical. It does not spiral towards better representations of the problem of the soul. Instead, the idea of the passionate situation of the soul in the body grows stronger yet more complicated as the book unfolds. The most intense moment comes with the work of Jean-Luc Nancy, which then reverberates through earlier chapters and views. Nancy allows for the firmest answer to the objection that if the soul is strictly in the body, then body takes full control and we lose the kinds of subjective freedom and directedness making sense of the passions, for instance in dread as posited on our capacity to forestall death. Like the twinning of soul and body, Howells detects a difficult fusion of the subject and death in Nancy's work, so neither can be thought alone.

In its insistence on life as marked by death, as enabled by it too, in its attention to the special freedom of passionate limitedness rather than isolated free will, and in its search to go beyond the seductive but false image of the human as opposed to death, this is a deeply ethical work. It seeks and shares neither solace nor distraction from death, but a new wisdom.

UNIVERSITY OF DUNDEE   JAMES WILLIAMS

Rebelles et criminelles chez les écrivaines d'expression française. Ed. by FRÉDÉRIQUE CHEVILLOT and COLETTE TROUT. (Faux Titre, 386) Amsterdam: Rodopi. 2013. 280 pp. €60. ISBN 978-90-420-3654-3.

The subject of the representation of female violence has developed in the last twenty years, among both women creators and academics working in all disciplines. This collection builds on the pioneering and often cited work of Arlette Farge and Cécile

Dauphin (*De la violence des femmes* (Paris: Albin Michel, 1997)) and Paula Ruth Gilbert (*Violence and the Female Imagination: Quebec's Women Writers Reframe Gender in North American Culture* (Montreal: McGill-Queen's University Press, 2006)), and examines the complex questions they raise, such as whether female violence is different from male violence and, if so, how and why, in relation to the textual representation of rebellious and criminal women in French and francophone works written by women. It is an ambitious project which seeks to explore these issues in works produced from the sixteenth to the twenty-first century, in diverse locations, through a variety of disciplines (history, psychoanalysis, linguistics) and theoretical frameworks (narratology, postcolonialism, trauma studies, and glottophagy).

Following a preface by Paula Ruth Gilbert and an editorial introduction, the book is divided into three parts. Part I explores what is described as the progressive rebellion—here taken in a chronological sense from the sixteenth to the early twentieth centuries—of some fictional women whom the editors consider representative of their contemporaries. It includes five articles on female rebels who expose the tyranny of the patriarchal order in a selection of *nouvelles* from Marguerite de Navarre's *Heptaméron*; plays by Françoise Pascal, Catherine Durand, and the Marquise de Maintenon; works by Madame de Laisse and Madame de Staël; Flora Tristan's *Pérégrinations d'une paria*; and Marcelle Tinayre's *Château en Limousin*.

Part II focuses on more recent texts from various parts of the world which deal with the legacy of French colonialism. It presents five contributions on fictional women in works by Ananda Devi, Sabrina Kherbiche, Leïla Marouane, Marie-Cécile Agnant, Fabienne Kanor, and Calixthe Beyala. These women are shown to be more explicitly violent, against themselves and/or others, in an expression of the after-effects of a double colonization, political and masculine.

Part III focuses on post-Second World War texts and explores how five women writers have created new forms of writing which allow them to inscribe rebellion and violence in the fabrics of their narratives. These narrative and stylistic strategies are explored in the representation of the following textual female rebels: Joyce Mansour's surrealist anti-muse figures; Anne Hébert's 'belle et bête' murderer in *Kamouraska*; Catherine Klein's 'méchantes filles'; Amélie Nothomb's girls and women who love to love 'à mort et à tuer'; and Virginie Despentes's ultra-violent marginalized women.

This wide scope provides an original angle, as the inclusion of temporal and geographical diversity can help to reveal similarities and differences not always discernible when the focus is narrower. However, an editorial presentation of common trends and cultural specificities, and some tentative synthetic interpretations, would have brought more cohesion to this interesting project. More significantly, the undifferentiated and unquestioned, and yet fundamentally distinct, categories of rebels and criminals required justification from the start in order to establish more solid foundations on which to rest all fifteen essays, especially as these do not explore this key distinction.

Readers will undoubtedly find insightful readings of selected works, and in some cases further material for a wider reflection on expressions of female rebellion and/or violence. It is indeed more on the individual rather than the collective level that the strength of the volume lies, although a collection clearly makes a more visible contribution to the field.

SWANSEA UNIVERSITY   NATHALIE MORELLO

Dante and Epicurus: A Dualist Vision of Secular and Spiritual Fulfilment. By GEORGE CORBETT. London: Legenda. 2013. xii+189 pp.; b/w ill. £45. ISBN 978-1-907975-79-0.

This is the first monograph to address Dante's relationship with and reception of Epicurus. George Corbett writes with great clarity and logic, drawing on a wide range of resources from early commentators (among whom he moves with ease) and the whole of Dante's œuvre to a host of modern Dante critics. Points of comparison and continuity rather than of palinodic rewriting are sought between the *Commedia* and the 'minor works', and the author is bold and confident in his challenges to various prevalent critical assumptions. The ambiguities surrounding Epicurus before and during Dante's day are persuasively elucidated, with good, nuanced background on mediators such as Cicero, Augustine, and Albert the Great. Boethius, who is mentioned only in passing, might have merited a little more attention. An important contrast is drawn between Epicurus and the cognate adjective Epicurean; the former is often portrayed as a noble figure, while the latter is more frequently a term of insult equivalent to charges of hedonism or bestiality. Thus it is suggested that Epicurus, although antithetical to Dante's religious beliefs (including, crucially, belief in the immortality of the soul), is worryingly a potential ally for Dante's secular vision of the possibility of fulfilment or happiness in this life through reason, the cardinal virtues, and natural philosophy. Corbett highlights that the popular medieval image of Epicurus is often tarnished by the reputation of his followers, so that against Epicurus as noble philosopher there is also a strand of popular medieval culture (for instance in Isidore of Seville) which revels in the image of the 'pig-Epicurus'. This popular image leads Corbett to discuss Ciacco in the circle of the gluttons (*Inferno* VI), although the decision to include this canto is undermined by the acceptable conclusion that it is not, for Dante, about Epicurus or his followers but only sounds as though it might be. The crucial canto, *Inferno* X, is innovatively considered for its theological rather than political ramifications, bringing the topic of heresy to the fore. The focus is, then, not on Farinata but on Dante-pilgrim's dialogue with Cavalcante. The use of the term 'time-long-sightedness' is helpful even if it amounts to a distance of merely four years. The dense diagram (Figure 2, p. 75) depicting 'The Protagonists' State of Knowledge at the Start of *Inferno* X' is difficult to decipher, and the concept of 'knowledge' therein evoked is seemingly understood in binary terms (one is either knowledgeable or not), rather than with any sense of the possibility of partial knowledge, for instance. This is especially problematic when events that are known include the distant pagan or biblical past. A similar presupposition perhaps lies behind the recurrent invocation of 'the medieval or historically informed/aware reader' (e.g. pp. 20, 32, 79), which seems to imply both that medieval readers were necessarily better informed than modern ones and also that it is possible and desirable, through historical awareness, to get back to a truly medieval understanding of Dante. Issues of how to interpret the famous 'cui' (l. 63) which have consumed Dante critics recently are sidestepped in favour of analysis of the two levels, the literal (earthly) and the spiritual, which collide in the dialogue between Dante-pilgrim and Cavalcante and are enhanced by 'vertical readings' across the three *cantiche*. Dante's *Monarchia* is also helpfully used to differentiate between Dante-pilgrim's accidental and temporary deception of Cavalcante as to Guido's fate and the deliberate, wilful misreading that is characteristic of heresy. Corbett argues that Dante's 'smarrimento' at the end of *Inferno* x arises not from thoughts of exile (which he bears with equanimity elsewhere in Hell), but rather from concerns over the spiritual fate of his first friend and his own uncomfortable closeness to similar charges. Erich Auerbach's analysis of this same canto in *Mimesis: The Representation of Reality in Western Literature* (first published in German in 1946, translated by Willard R. Trask for Princeton University Press in 1953) ought to have been a point of reference. Surprising gaps in bibliography may also be noted in discussions of *Inferno* vi, the resurrection of the body, Virgil and Limbo, *Purgatorio* ii, and liturgical texts in the Valley of the Princes, where pertinent references would have further strengthened Corbett's arguments. Dante's dualistic attitude towards Epicurus (both adulatory from a secular perspective and critical from a spiritual stance) is finally compared with other similar points of dualism in the *Commedia*, such as Limbo, which is considered to be the true 'earthly paradise' alluded to in the *Monarchia*. The Valley of the Princes, though, is a final liminal space which explicitly transforms the site of temporal felicity and natural, rational limitations (located by Corbett in Limbo) into a spiritual arena of exile and sorrow. The balanced dualism proposed by Corbett finally tips in favour of 'spiritual fulfilment', albeit haunted by secular possibilities and precursors.

St John's College, Oxford   Jennifer Rushworth

Idee su Dante: esperimenti danteschi 2012. Atti del Convegno, Milano, 9–10 maggio 2012. Ed. by Carlo Carù. Florence: Società Editrice Fiorentina. 2013. xi+108 pp. £13.89. ISBN 978-88-6032-251-7.

Following the well-received *lecturae Dantis* (*Inferno*, ed. by Simone Invernizzi; *Purgatorio*, ed. by Benedetta Quadrio; *Paradiso*, ed. by Tommaso Montorfano (Milan: Marietti, 2008, 2009, 2010, respectively)), *Idee su Dante* is the latest publication sponsored by Esperimenti Danteschi (www.esperimentidanteschi. it), a remarkably original and lively student-led association based in the State University of Milan, which, from 2005 onwards, has created scholarly links with the most renowned universities in Italy, Europe, the United States, Russia, and Australia. In paraphrasing the archetypal title by Gianfranco Contini (*Un'idea di Dante: saggi danteschi* (Turin: Einaudi, 1976)), the book collects the series of five lectures held at the University of Milan in May 2012, on the most representative 'ideas on Dante' expressed in the last two centuries: those of De Sanctis, Croce, Singleton, Auerbach, and Contini.

The first lecture (Antonio Prete, 'Il Dante di De Sanctis: figure e forme di una drammaturgia poetica') concentrates on the seminal notion of realism as emerging in the pages of the Neapolitan nineteenth-century scholar. De Sanctis's realism means first and foremost the rehabilitation of the 'matter' as opposed to the excesses of abstraction and spiritualism. De Sanctis's Dante is the poet of the earthly world, the poet of the living passions, the poet who—as he would maintain in his *Lezioni*, 'entrando nel regno de' morti si porta dietro tutte le passioni de' vivi, si trae appresso tutta la terra' (p. 10). This hermeneutic approach makes Dante's poetry deeply engaged in his own times and in a historical context that becomes *contemporary* for both ancient and modern readers. 'Il Dante di De Sanctis', writes Prete, 'è fatto contemporaneo, ma secondo una misura direi leopardiana della contemporaneità [. . .], una contemporaneità asintonica, polemica, persino ancora utopica, il che è poi proprio della poesia' (p. 4). Dante's poetry is reborn in De Sanctis's critical pages, and 'il critico da esegeta si fa affabulatore, da lettore drammaturgo egli stesso' (p. 9). We land on the other side of the ocean and in the twentieth century with Rino Caputo's essay, 'Il centro del cerchio: il dantismo di Singleton al di qua e al di là dell'Atlantico'. The mainly theological approach of the American scholar is discussed in the light of Auerbach's figuralism ('nemmeno il termine *figura* è assente dal lessico singletoniano' (p. 17)). The focus on the Christian allegorical meaning, though, does not overshadow the role of realism as the main component of the Dantean world: the *Comedy* is indeed a *Journey to Beatrice*, and 'per Auerbach come per Singleton il realismo dantesco è il riflesso artistico della sua convinzione teologica' (p. 17). A return to the Italian shores is the third essay by Stefano Jossa, 'Rimuovere alquanto l'ingombro dell'ordinaria letteratura dantesca: poesia e polemica nel Dante di Croce'. In order to appreciate the real value of the magisterial teaching of the Abruzzese critic, it is necessary to distance his readings from the vulgate offered by his followers, who, in their attempt to 'crocianizzare Croce' (p. 58) are largely responsible for distinguishing *poesia* from *non poesia* in the body of Dante's poem. Croce's readings permeated the school textbooks for generations, and to this very day they undeniably linger in the common reception of the Italian non-academic readership. In her highly original and thought-provoking essay, Lucia Lazzerini ('Gli studi danteschi di Auerbach e la centralità del concetto di figura') argues for the necessity of completing the seemingly 'percorso incompiuto' (p. 63) by the Jewish German critic by expanding the figural approach to the allegorical interpretation of the whole medieval literary heritage. In the last *lezione*, Uberto Motta's 'Qualcuno arrivato prima di noi: Dante secondo Contini', there is a detailed account and a chronological-statistical analysis supported by bar charts of the prolific activity of the Italian philologist, both as an editor and as a critic of Dante. The greatness of the Continian method, though, was the belief that no method can alone give a full account of the aesthetic value of works of art such as Dante's *Comedy*: 'il risultato è, né più né meno, *un candido omaggio reso in fatto alla fertilità del commentato*, ovvero una verifica oggettiva della sua infinita bellezza' (p. 101).

In sum, the volume offers a valuable assessment and re-evaluation of five of the major *Dantisti* of all times. Common to all of the lectures is the sense of personal engagement of the authors not only with their subject-matter but also with an audience of students who appear enthusiastically—if not heroically—committed to preventing the new 'ordinamento' of the Italian universities from affecting their Dante: 'In un momento in cui il clima sembra segnato dalla delusione e dalla sfiducia, *Esperimenti danteschi* è — crediamo — la documentazione di una curiosità, di un impeto creativo e di un desiderio di condivisione carichi di una promessa di costruzione per tutti' (p. xi).

UNIVERSITY OF BIRMINGHAM   PAOLO DE VENTURA

The Printed Media in Fin-de-Siècle Italy: Publishers, Writers, and Readers. Ed. by ANN HALLAMORE CAESAR, GABRIELLA ROMANI, and JENNIFER BURNS. London: Legenda. 2011. xiii+208 pp. £45. ISBN 978-1-9065-4074-6.

This excellent collection of essays (thirteen in all, five written in Italian, eight in English) focuses on the context in which printed media (books, magazines, newspapers, journals) were shaped and appeared at the end of the nineteenth and the beginning of the twentieth centuries. The text as material object is privileged, while the approach is interdisciplinary. The end result is a different, and more complete, appreciation of the various texts considered here than would be afforded by an analysis confined to content or style. Interestingly, some considerations (modernity versus backwardness, the role of the reader, in reality and as imagined by writers and publishers, gender issues, the importance of the visual aspect of textual production) recur, and prove to be mutually illuminating of publishing phenomena in the period under investigation. The reason for the focus on this period, as Ann Hallamore Caesar and Gabriella Romani note in their introduction to the volume, lies in the fact that it is still relatively neglected, particularly from this critical angle. The collection is divided into four sections, the first dealing with reading publics, the second with cultural productions, the third with publishers and journals, and the last with print and image in the new growth area of children's literature.

The two essays in 'Reading Publics' offer an overview of, respectively, media, markets, and modernity (John Davis) and the politics and poetics of reading in this timeframe (Maria Grazia Lolla). Davis contextualizes, and challenges, the commonly held view of Italy's backwardness in the fields of printing and publishing, noting that prior to Unification, these industries were of high quality; he also offers a nuanced view of the illiteracy question, pointing out that the reach of print media in the new nation was wider than statistics suggest, while illiteracy rates may also have been implicated in a 'precocious' (p. 15) use of illustrations and graphics (this last is touched on by several essays in the collection). Lolla documents, in turn, a strikingly modern recognition of the transformative power of books in post-Unification Italy, which suggests concerns about a shift in the balance of power between writers and readers.

'Cultural Productions' consists of four essays on different kinds of text: Verga's *I Malavoglia* and *Mastro-don Gesualdo*, De Roberto's *L'illusione*, three early twentieth-century Florentine magazines, and Marinetti's literary journal *Poesia*. Joseph Luzzi's essay on Verga explores the topics of language, money, and identity, highlighting a 'questione della lira' running parallel with a 'questione della lingua' at the time of Unification, and is particularly revealing in its analysis of generational conflicts of both economics and language in the novels. Olivia Santovetti focuses on the cliché of the female reader in the literature and iconography of the second half of the nineteenth century, and specifically homes in on De Roberto's strikingly modern meta-reflection on literature and writing in *L'illusione*. Francesca Billiani's study of *Il Regno*, *La Voce*, and *Lacerba* reveals three magazines highly conscious of their readership, keen to extend it in varying degrees, with different ethical and moral missions shaped by a concern with the role of the intellectual at their core. Luca Somigli, in his consideration of *Poesia*, reveals a Marinetti in formation, in the process of changing his relationship with the French poetic milieu and keen to forge an Italian poetic modernity.

'Publishers and Journals' is made up of five essays: on the Sonzogno publishing house, the *Bollettino della Società Geografica Italiana*, the role of Licinio Cappelli in publishing for women readers, the Palermitan magazine *Flirt*, and *Secolo XX*, the Milanese monthly. Silvia Valisa looks at Sonzogno's contribution to journalism, book publishing, and music publishing between 1861 and 1900, revealing both its modernity and its range, and outlines her ongoing project of reconstructing its catalogue (the archive having been destroyed in the 1943 bombings of Milan). Matteo Salvadore is especially interested in the discourse of otherness traceable in the *Bollettino* (particularly in its writings on Ethiopia) between 1867 and 1887, and defines it as a pre-modern discourse, grounded, surprisingly, in religious rather than racial identity. Ombretta Frau traces the evolution of Cappelli from a typographer to a modern editor, focusing primarily on his facilitation of the publication of the work of a body of women writers. Cristina Gragnani's essay on the early period of *Flirt* considers it as a glocal phenomenon, and analyses its visual aspect and its internal contradictions (where the gap between text and image appears emblematic of a sense of crisis). Fiorenza Weinapple, looking at *Secolo XX* between 1902 and 1910, underlines its recourse to a discourse of modernity, and notes its celebratory and nationalist tone in this period, when it was under the control of Achille Tedeschi.

The final section has an essay by Fabio Gadducci and Mirko Tavosanis on the early years of the *Giornale per i Bambini* and a piece by John Welle on the magic lantern in Collodi's work. The first of these highlights the novelty of the *Giornale* and the importance of its illustrations, most of which came from abroad. Interestingly, writers were often asked to produce text for the illustrations, rather than the other way around—though this was not the case for Collodi's *Pinocchio*. Welle's essay notes the intermediality of Collodi's work, especially in his *Giannettino* series, and problematizes his presentation of the magic lantern (Collodi misrepresents the way in which it works—a misrepresentation mirrored in the textual illustrations). Welle suggests that Collodi's texts are 'Janus-faced' (p. 190), as they look towards the future. In that respect, this is an apt essay to close the volume, given the concern around modernity noted in so many of its contributions.

UNIVERSITY COLLEGE DUBLIN   URSULA J. FANNING

After Words: Suicide and Authorship in Twentieth-Century Italy. By ELIZABETH LEAKE. Toronto: Toronto University Press. 2011. 228 pp. $70. ISBN 978-0-8020-9279-3.

Elizabeth Leake's second book is wide-ranging, ambitious, and nuanced. It carries forward many of the compelling qualities and interests of her first monograph, *The Reinvention of Ignazio Silone* (Toronto: University of Toronto Press, 2003), including a focus on complex author–text relations, embedded in a careful awareness of, and set of challenges to, poststructuralist debates over authorship; and also, as with Silone, an interest in instances of moments of sudden revision in our reception of texts and lives. The book is centred on four case studies of twentieth-century Italian writers who committed suicide, and whose work and general reputations were transformed and conditioned by this final act. Each of the four cases is carefully chosen to illustrate a different dynamic of the impact of suicide on texts and on public or critical images. The first is Guido Morselli, who killed himself in 1973 when he was almost entirely unknown, only for a rich body of unpublished experimental fiction to be discovered and launched into the world posthumously. The second is Amelia Rosselli, a trilingual poet championed in the 1960s by Pasolini among others, who strongly identified with Sylvia Plath as well as being haunted by her family history, especially that of her father and uncle, the anti-Fascist Rosselli brothers murdered by Mussolini's thugs in France in 1937. Rosselli killed herself on the anniversary of Plath's own suicide in 1996. The third is the major mid-century novelist, poet, and diarist Cesare Pavese, whose suicide in 1950 is most often put down to problems in his relations with women and with an American lover in particular. The final case is Primo Levi, the famously lucid and forensic Holocaust survivor-writer, who astonished the world with his suicide in 1987 (although some deny it was in fact a suicide). Leake is intent upon acknowledging and then disrupting the retrospective teleology of readings of suicide—the tracing of foretellings of death in the work that then overturns or distorts all our knowledge of that work, or the clustering of suicides together as evidence of a particular kind of writer (Plath and Rosselli, for example). What is offered instead of this teleology is the use of suicide as a tool to reread the circular relationship between text and author ('corpus' and 'corpse', as Derrida has it), as between these and the reader: suicide should not determine readings of a work, but it cannot help but 'loom' over it, as Leake puts it. Each chapter surveys the critical reception of the author and sees in that form of public discourse symptoms of the looming suicide. The chapters then move into a mode of close textual analysis, looking for a middle ground between teleology and some formalist attempts to ignore the suicide altogether. In each case, also, Leake ties in the author in question with an eclectic cluster of connected works of philosophy or literature, as a means of levering open her 'suicidal' rereadings: thus, Morselli is linked with Rensi and Monod, Rosselli with Plath and Kofman, Pavese with Vattimo and Severino, Levi with Agamben and Margalit.

After Words is a rich, beguiling, at times moving and sophisticated piece of work, which is on occasion hard to grasp in all its subtlety. It is written with confidence, and it takes on and marshals an impressive range of primary and supportive material. If the starting-point of its theoretical reflections feels, by now, perhaps a little tired—Barthes's *Death of the Author* and related work by Foucault and Derrida—the book moves on to much more unexpected and fruitful territory in its varied oblique engagements, such as those as listed above. There is possibly the risk of excessive eclecticism there, but the strong central topic is more than enough to hold all these many threads together. The close readings are well chosen, again not always the obvious ones, and are used to excellent effect to recover textuality after the impossible-to-ignore suicide. At times I was a little less convinced by the shape and uses of the surveys of critical reception of each author, in part because, at least in the cases of Pavese and Levi, these needed to be supplemented by a looser and broader public reputation and response to the suicide. Thus, Pavese existed as a sort of myth for a certain generation of (male) young Italians, his suicide included, making him a model of heroic failure. While this is reflected in some of the biographies (Lajolo, Fernandez) and criticism, it is not quite of the same order as literary-critical reception, and this perhaps needed some probing. On occasion also, the book's reflections on suicide might apply as much to any sudden or violent death (perhaps any death), and the analysis would have benefited from clearer lines of distinction from, or indeed a merging with, that potentially universal dimension. How, say, does the case of Morselli differ, in terms of how we read, from another posthumous discovery such as Lampedusa (mentioned in passing)? Or again, does Pasolini's murder not function in precisely analogous ways to suicide in reshaping all our visions and understandings of his life and work? (Indeed, Pasolini famously theorized himself that 'death' operates a sort of editing job on our lives, so that the arc of a life is only readable retrospectively.) These questions are, however, posed as the products of a hugely stimulating book of quite some ambition and sophistication.

UNIVERSITY OF CAMBRIDGE ROBERT S. C. GORDON

Giraffes in the Garden of Italian Literature: Modernist Embodiment in Italo Svevo, Federigo Tozzi and Carlo Emilio Gadda. By DEBORAH AMBERSON. London: Legenda. 2012. 175 pp. £45. ISBN 978-1-907975-26-4.

'Like a giraffe or a kangaroo in your beautiful garden': this is how C. E. Gadda describes himself (writing in 1926 to Bonaventura Tecchi, his good friend and former companion in the prison camp of Celle Lager), and it provides the starting-point of Deborah Amberson's study of three among the most significant Italian narrators of the twentieth century. Gadda's comparison is striking not only for the radical difference it asserts in relation to the landscape of contemporary Italian letters, but also for the way in which it does so: by choosing the realm of the visible, physical shape as the metaphorical field in which to state his own alterity (to the extent of assigning himself to a different *species*), Gadda implicitly but clearly points our attention to the dimension and the experience of the external, spatialized, finite, living matter—that is, the body.

This is, for Amberson, neither accidental nor insignificant, since it paves the way for pursuing one of the fundamental aims of her own effort: the subsuming of three apparently disparate and not easily classifiable writers under one single and transnational label, that of modernism, which, she writes, 'notwithstanding its great variety [. . .] might be understood as a stylistically self-conscious engagement with the experience of human embodiment in the face of a social and technological revolution felt on, by, and in the body, modifying not only the rhythms of its daily movements, practices and interactions, but also its epistemological and ethical status' (p. 7).

It is, indeed, in the critical negotiation of the role played by the *body* (examined in a variety of perspectives: from Svevo's limping, technologically enhanced but doomed human organism, to Tozzi's hypersensitive and convulsed 'bodies of emotion', to the gendered bodies of Gadda's female victims) that the specific function of these three writers is best assessed within the context of modernity, and in relation to the crucial connection between *body* and *style* that their peculiar versions of European modernism highlights.

The work is well written and strongly structured (a short introduction, a more extensive review of theoretical and literary references, one chapter each for our three writers, followed by a brief conclusion); and arguments are lucidly presented throughout, with the right balance of textual analysis, citation from secondary sources, and theoretical elaboration. The usage made of (among others) Weininger, Bergson, Levinas, and William James is very effective in opening up new and stimulating critical perspectives.

My main reservation, at the theoretical level, concerns the definition of the term 'embodiment' itself, which is very extensively used and underpins most of the author's conceptual edifice: in contrast with the considerable care taken in setting out and discussing other critical categories (chiefly that of 'modernism', notoriously contentious in Italy), the complex history and precise meaning of this concept seem to be taken for granted. In Chapter 1, which is specifically devoted to the interrogation of 'Modern and Modernist Embodiment'—and which undoubtedly provides a wealth of relevant contextual information—the reader is at pains to locate a frontal discussion, leading to the elucidation of the way in which the term is understood and used by the author herself. Consequently, the constant reference to 'embodiment, both in its ontological and historical dimensions' (p. 76) remains somewhat hazy.

It is also notable that, despite referring to Bouchard's interpretation of Gadda as a kind of experimentalist precursor of postmodernism, and to Magris's proposal to read Svevo in a similarly postmodernist way, Amberson does not address more systematically this alternative possibility of transnational contextualization.

Amberson does not use the whole corpus of the writings of each author, and inevitably this deprives her discussion of some interesting, additional angles. However, the selection of primary texts is sufficiently ample to be convincingly representative. In analysing those texts she also draws from a large body of critical literature, but goes well beyond existing scholarship by placing the three writers concerned within a strong and varied theoretical framework, supported by references to thinkers ranging from Deleuze and Guattari to Agamben. In so doing, she escapes the danger of homogenization, by consistently paying attention to the stylistic and ideological specificity of each writer, but at the same time manages to make a fairly convincing case for a reappraisal in the light of a broader modernist context, within which it becomes possible to find evidence of links and parallels among apparently very diverse positions and styles, on both a national and an international level.

In conclusion, this is a very interesting book, which not only brings together three exceptional authors, but also focuses on original and stimulating perspectives. The work makes a very valid critical contribution, by dealing with a fascinating topic in a manner which is original and insightful.

UNIVERSITY OF OXFORD   GIUSEPPE STELLARDI

J. G. Schottelius's 'Ausführliche Arbeit von der Teutschen HaubtSprache' (1663) and its Place in Early Modern European Vernacular Language Study. By NICOLA MCLELLAND. (Publications of the Philological Society, 44) Oxford: Wiley-Blackwell. 2011. iv+419 pp. £27.60. ISBN 978-1-4443-3961-1.

Nicola McLelland's study of J. G. Schottelius's *Ausführliche Arbeit* (*AA*) is a masterly exploration of an important milestone in the history of German grammar. The *AA* is, of course, far more than a grammar book. However, Schottelius, whose magnum opus was published in 1663, subsuming and refining most of his earlier work, has drawn forth differing scholarly assessments of his place and importance. His work has frequently been overlooked outside Germany, while among Germanists its importance and influence have been judged at all points on a scale from very significant, via significant in parts, to hardly significant at all. McLelland pursues three aims in her well-written, clearly structured monograph: first, 'to demonstrate the lasting contribution of [...] Schottelius [...] to European thought'; second, 'to provide a comprehensive analysis of Schottelius's *Ausführliche Arbeit*'; and third, 'to attempt an evaluation of Schottelius's contribution to the standardization of the German language' (p. 1). The author's objectives are considerable and her industry no less so: she devotes 297 pages to the nine chapters of her main text, plus a further 121 to various tables and indexes, including a bibliography of some twenty-two pages.

Although the almost 1500 pages of Schottelius's work might appear at first sight to be overly daunting and the task of investigating the entirety in a scholarly monograph almost excessive, one should bear in mind that Schottelius seized the opportunity to augment his text with copious lists, examples, appendices, and references, *inter alia*, drawing on the resources of the largest and best library in Europe, in Wolfenbüttel. Perhaps the most salient example of this is the 181-page list of over 10,000 root words or *Stammwörter* (*AA*, pp. 1269-1450), intended to form the basis of a German dictionary.

McLelland's research has opened up practical and theoretical vistas on Schottelius's work and significance in both a German and a European context that were much less apparent before. She argues convincingly for the importance of the *AA* in the wider European context, and draws attention in particular to its dependence on Dutch and Flemish sources, as well as its influence not only on the German grammars which succeeded it, but also on Danish, Swedish, Dutch, and Russian exemplars. One of the strengths of McLelland's study is its own exhaustiveness: unlike many others who have investigated only specific aspects of Schottelius's work, McLelland strives to survey and evaluate the whole of the *AA*. From this virtue, however, stems one of the potential shortcomings of the study—some of the most important aspects of the *AA* cannot be treated in the detail that they warrant.

Much of the introductory Chapter 1 (pp. 1-31) is devoted to explaining and evaluating the book's 'paratextual material'—that is, the engravings and their symbolism. McLelland shows how they not only support the linguistic endeavours of the *AA*, but are also significant in the wider context of Schottelius's (linguistic) patriotism and the upholding of Christian morality, themes which recur throughout the work. By virtue of its significant contribution to Schottelius scholarship, Chapter 2 warrants special attention here. It examines Schottelius's 'concept of language' and delves into the complexities of his principles for determining the correct form. There are aspects of this where one would have liked to see more detail and emphasis. The concept of a *HaubtSprache*, or supraregional form of German above the dialects, superior to any individual dialect, the 'true' form of High German in an evaluative as well as geographical sense, is adumbrated on page 34. McLelland quotes a poignant reference to this in the *AA*, which also exemplifies Schottelius's German-Latin 'Mischsprache': 'Die Hochteutsche Sprache aber/ davon wir handelen und worauff dieses Buch zielet/ ist nicht ein Dialectus eigentlich/ sondern Lingua ipsa Germanica' (*AA*, p. 174). The truncation of this quotation by the author, however, not only conceals part of its importance, but also obscures Schottelius's subtle appeal to his learned readers' prejudices—by flattering their learning and the part they play in establishing the standard—while addressing them in Latin: 'Die Hochteutsche Sprache [. . .] ist [. . .] Lingua ipsa Germanica, sicut viri docti, sapientes et periti eam tandem receperunt et usurpant' (ibid.).

Schottelius's insistence that, despite the claims that could be made for Low German and other Germanic dialects, the true essence of German was to be found only in High German is further scrutinized by McLelland (pp. 34–38). In this, as in other places, Schottelius shows himself to be a man of his time, still very much influenced by humanist thought. McLelland's investigation shows how confusing and confused Schottelius could be in his attempts to reconcile biblical, historical, patriotic, and scientific matters, especially with regard to the ancestry of German (pp. 38–42). Not only is Germanic conflated or confused with Celtic, but Schottelius even draws upon 'Gothic' letters (supposedly those invented by Wulfila, possibly also confused with 'Fraktur') to demonstrate the prime antiquity of the German *HaubtSprache* and its direct descent from the confusion of tongues at Babel and transmission to Germany by Ascenas. Quaint and charming as this mythologizing may be, it has the effect of obfuscating much of the incipient 'scientific' approach to language (to be realized a century and a half later by Jacob Grimm) that constituted one of Schottelius's major scholarly achievements. He was beginning to show with reference to historical criteria how linguistic change occurred, even though overall his explanations were flawed. As McLelland observes, he was 'on the cusp of a change in thinking about language' (p. 44).

Chapter 2 further investigates the inherent meaning of words in their sound, which Schottelius believed was uniquely well preserved in German and in defence of which he cited a number of onomatopoeic and mainly sibilant words which suggested a link between sound and meaning (pp. 46–48). McLelland investigates the concepts of the *Sprachbaum* (banyan tree) and rootwords, as also that of language as a building (pp. 49–57). She further evaluates Schottelius's concept of *Grundrichtigkeit* and its relationship to his principle of analogy (pp. 55–57), and, although she returns to it in the following chapter, this is one of the areas where more detailed scrutiny would have borne fruit, as it again exemplifies aspects of Schottelius's more modern thinking, in particular his insistence on looking at the historical development of the language in order to determine correct usage, by *discovering* its natural laws.

Chapter 3 investigates 'Intersecting Discourse Traditions' in the *AA*, observing *inter alia* the use of legal terminology and other significant influences on Schottelius's work, including the work of Dutch and Flemish scholars. There is much valuable material here that has not often been examined by scholars treating the *AA*. Chapter 4 investigates the genres of the *AA*, including the orations (*Lobreden*) and treatise on poetics. Chapter 5 deals with the *Sprachkunst*, or grammatical section proper, including etymology, and a useful account of Schottelius's principles of spelling is given (pp. 171–75). There is, however, little analysis of Schottelius's etymologies or more importantly of his penetrating logical criticisms of humanist etymologies. Chapter 6, entitled 'Intertextuality, Authorities and Evidence in the *AA*', offers a valuable insight, especially by means of detailed tables, into Schottelius's sources and influences. Chapter 7, 'The Legacy of the *AA*', offers some useful discussion of the basis for determining correct German, including the refutation of Misnian and other dialect areas. More could have been made of this important aspect of Schottelius's work—his desire for a standardized form of German, based on an eclectic language of men of letters. Chapter 8 looks at 'Prescription and Practice' and offers some truly original research, where Schottelius's usage and prescriptions are compared with the evidence of a number of contemporary corpora. The various different approaches of the grammarian to usage, including his prescription, on occasions, of forms that had never been current, are clearly presented and evaluated in this very useful chapter. A concluding ninth chapter briefly sums up the findings of the preceding work (pp. 296–97).

Our overall assessment of this book is one of positive admiration, despite its shortcomings, especially with regard to the standardization of German. McLelland has succeeded in demonstrating the importance of this seventeenth-century grammarian and linguist in different contexts and from different angles: 'Schottelius championed the task of studying German with such verve and vividness that he showed once and for all that studying the German language is important, relevant, challenging, and fascinating' (p. 297).

KING'S COLLEGE LONDON/UNIVERSITY OF CAMBRIDGE   DAVID N. YEANDLE

German Images of the Self and the Other: Nationalist, Colonialist and Anti-Semitic Discourse, 1871–1918. By FELICITY RASH. Basingstoke: Palgrave Macmillan. 2012. xii+222 pp. £50. ISBN 978-0-230-28265-0.

Felicity Rash's volume is divided into four substantive analytical chapters, three on the issues identified in the title and one on the continuation and culmination of the respective discourses during the First World War. Each chapter concentrates on one key author's central text and several additional literary and non-literary examples, which illustrate that the features identified were widespread and the individual voices part of a pervasive discourse. Houston Stewart Chamberlain's *Grundlagen des neunzehnten Jahrhunderts* (1899) and several ancillary writings form the basis of the discussion of racist and anti-Semitic discourse; Paul Rohrbach's *Deutschland unter den Weltvölkern* (1903) and *Der deutsche Gedanke in der Welt* (1912) are used as examples of colonialist writing. The chapter on the war revisits the same authors and thus affords an insight into how historical circumstances influenced— radicalized or tempered—these authors' positions. The treatment of material that has not been discussed extensively, such as Max Dautendey's anti-Russian rant *Der Geist meines Vaters* (1912), Carl Busse's anti-Polonic story *Das Gymnasium zu Lengowo* (1907), Carl Hauptmann's investigation of Zigano-German miscegenation in *Einhard der Lächler* (1907), Hans Osman's *Buschklatsch* (1905), Gustav Frenssen's *Peter Moors Fahrt nach Südwest* (1906), as well as articles from the *Windhuker Nachrichten*, books and pamphlets by Heinrich Claß, Wilhelm Marr, Adolf Stoecker, Heinrich von Treitschke, Dühring, Fritsch, and other anti-Semites, and by Friedrich Fabri, Carl Peters, and others on the German mission overseas, is both welcome and meaningful. A mention of Theodor Mommsen's anti-Treitschke writings and Theodor Ziegler's *Die geistigen und sozialen Strömungen des 19. Jahrhunderts* (1899) illustrates that the racist and anti-Semitic slant did not remain unchallenged. The findings of the investigations are concrete, though predictable: nationalist discourse did indeed emphasize German supremacy vis-à-vis all perceived 'Others', i.e. minorities, the racially and culturally different, colonial rivals, and colonial subjects. One of the strengths of the study is that it provides evidence in abundance by highlighting the pertinent terminology and by clearly illustrating the dichotomy in the world-view conveyed by these writings, including the literary ones.

On the other hand, the study contains several contentions, some derived from secondary literature, with which one must take issue, such as the claim that the notion of the *Kulturnation* is based on 'common ethnicity' (p. 35), or that anti-Semitism is based on 'opinions [. . .] unthinkingly handed down from generation to generation' (p. 84, citing Wolfgang Benz)—a position that suppresses the fact that, with the advent of racialist thought, anti-Semitism is consciously and deliberately infused with a radicalism and intransigence that was unprecedented in earlier generations. Some typos and mistakes remain, several too severe for comfort. To identify 'der alte Fritz' as Frederick the Great (p. 118) might be an oversight; to treat Wilhelm Raabe's *Frau Salome* (1875) as in any way ambivalent in its depiction of Jews and to date his *Hungerpastor* (1864) to 1908 (p. 123) is quite inexcusable (it would be a different proposition to claim that this controversial text only achieved its greatest impact at the beginning of the twentieth century, but that is not the argument made here). It is also regrettable that Artur Dinter's *Die Sünde wider das Blut* (1917) is chosen as the major representative of the period's anti-Semitic fiction when, as is well documented in secondary literature, it was quite an exceptional diatribe.

The analytical chapters are preceded by a clear and instructive introduction to the various branches of linguistic discourse analysis (critical discourse analysis, discourse historical approach, historical discourse semantics, critical metaphor analysis, and computer-assisted discourse analysis). This approach has, in the last two decades or so, gained currency not only because of the availability of technology that facilitates quantitative surveys, but also because it seeks to integrate qualitative elements of traditional humanities research with quantitative methods. It is slightly disappointing, then, that the quantitative searches for key lexemes and selected collocates in the chosen corpora (i.e. those of the texts available in digital form) largely result in word lists (pp. 58, 87–88, 96, 104, 156–57; slightly more elaborately on pp. 147–50), the evaluations of which, it is claimed, 'would require a monograph of their own' (p. 58). The question arises as to what additional insights, specific to the chosen methodology, linguistic discourse analysis actually affords. The theoretical sources are analysed here for their motifs, persuasive strategies, and key concepts, the literary sources also for imagery, suggestive plot elements, and character configurations. The results are interesting and informative, but not radically new; and some dimensions which would help to contextualize the concrete findings do not come into focus. Questions such as H. S. Chamberlain's appeal even among non-anti-Semites (such as the Viennese Jew and later proponent of Zionism Felix Salten), the mechanisms of demarcation and positioning inside the crowded cultural field of supremacist nationalism (nuances and attempts at outdoing one another abound), or the function of such polemics in a political and cultural environment that changed so radically over the almost fifty years covered here remain unaddressed. At first sight, the clarity of explanation ('What is race?'; 'What is racism?'; etc.) and the straightforwardness of the findings would well suit an advanced undergraduate or early postgraduate readership. Yet while expert readers will be able to integrate the specific findings of the study into their knowledge of the issues, other readership groups would require a degree of additional guidance.

NATIONAL UNIVERSITY OF IRELAND MAYNOOTH   FLORIAN KROBB

Lyrisches Gespür: Vom geheimen Sensorium moderner Poesie. By BURKHARD MEYER-SICKENDIEK. Munich: Fink. 2012. 571 pp. €68. ISBN 978-3-7705-5146-0.

Throughout the ages, poetry has owed much of its appeal to its ability to verbalize emotions. This verbalization generates specific lyrical forms that have remained objects of variation and transformation, sometimes hybridization, but rarely of genuine innovation. Even slam poetry, with its emphasis on rhyme, alliteration, and rhythm, can be traced back to medieval forms of lyrical expression. Its 'newness' arises mainly from its performative quality. In terms of poetic theory, the lyrical verbalization of emotions has attracted considerable attention in recent years. Its origins can, however, be traced to René Descartes's *Traité des passions de l'âme* (1649), to Jean de la Bruyère's character studies of speech, and to the rhetorical doctrine of the affects.

One of the most important recent scholarly initiatives in this field was the major interdisciplinary project 'Languages of Emotions', a 'Centre of Excellence' at Freie Universität Berlin. Burkhard Meyer-Sickendiek's landmark study on 'Lyrisches Gespür' is one of the truly remarkable achievements to have emerged from this endeavour. It offers a fresh approach to the phenomenology relating to the auratic effect of poems by suggesting six categories of 'Gespür': the 'magic' or auratic sense; existential dispositions; empathy or social feeling; atmospheric aspects; and the feeling of temporality.

In his extended theoretical Introduction Meyer-Sickendiek reviews relevant poetological and philosophical material, including current discourses on 'Stimmungen', partly defined as 'background emotions', partly as 'existential feelings' and spatial atmospheres. The author properly situates the existential dimension of 'Stimmungen' in Martin Heidegger's *Sein und Zeit* but also in the first major study by Otto Friedrich Bollnow in *Das Wesen der Stimmungen* (Frankfurt a.M.: Klostermann, 1956). Strangely, the otherwise comprehensive bibliography omits

Hans-Ulrich Gumbrecht, *Stimmungen lesen: Über eine verdeckte Wirklichkeit der Literatur* (Munich: Hanser, 2011; English translation *Atmosphere, Mood, Stimmung: On a Hidden Potential of Literature* by Erik Butler (Stanford: Stanford University Press, 2012), reviewed in *MLR*, 109 (2014), 231–33) and fails to include Stefan Hajduk's contributions as well as the seminal studies in *Zur historischen Semantik des deutschen Gefühlswortschatzes*, ed. by Ludwig Jäger (Aachen: Rader, 1988).

It is no coincidence that the attention given to 'Stimmung' and 'Gespür' by German scholars remains unmatched in the anglophone world, for there is no direct equivalent for these words in English. In fact there is a strong argument for using them as technical terms in English since 'feeling for', or 'sense of' cannot capture the existential meaning of the two concepts. On the other hand the English verb 'to sense' enables the user to implicitly connect feeling with the senses; German does not offer this option, though it can associate reflection with a sensual act in the verb 'sinnen' or, slightly more strongly, 'nachsinnen'. Meyer-Sickendiek's key achievement lies in having established 'Gespür' in poetic theory. With reference to Michael Polanyi he helpfully identifies it as 'implicit' or 'tacit' knowledge contained in poetry. Hence the subtitle of his study—'Vom geheimen Sensorium moderner Poesie'—is unfortunate, for there is nothing 'secret' about 'Gespür', at least not if understood in the context of neo-phenomenology.

That said, the author's ability to connect his thematic objective with a multitude of poetological strands ranging from Eduard von Hartmann and Theodor Lipps to David Wellbery, and from Roman Jakobson to Gernot Böhme's aesthetics of perception, is impressive. However, Meyer-Sickendiek's occasional over-reliance on Hermann Schmitz's conceptions of subjectivity and, in particular, 'new phenomenology' can give the impression of the poems under discussion being mere illustrations of a philosophical theory. In line with 'new phenomenology', which Meyer-Sickendiek fails to probe in sufficient critical depth, he identifies all 'Stimmungen' as 'situations', or rather 'situative Phänomene' (p. 118). This leads him to assume, somewhat problematically, that all poems are, or represent, nothing but 'situations'.

Even though the author can support this view with reference to Eduard von Hartmann, who first introduced the concept of 'Situationslyrik', the reader is not offered a critical appraisal of this concept. Instead, Meyer-Sickendiek suggests that Schmitz's understanding of poetry as a 'schonende Explikation von Situationen' (p. 107) derived directly from Hartmann's aesthetics. The problem with this approach is that it eclipses one major mediator between phenomenology and modern poetry, namely Käte Hamburger's influential work *Die Logik der Dichtung* (Stuttgart: Klett, 1957) and her subsequent study of Rilke. Moreover, Meyer-Sickendiek's opening chapters on poetic theory in relation to 'lyrisches Gespür' have a tendency to repetitiousness, notably in the citing of quotations (e.g. pages 20 and 107, 39 and 108). More crucially, a central question is not addressed: to what extent does 'Spüren' or 'Gespür' depend on knowledge and/or experience? He informs us later (p. 110) that 'Spüren' itself can be a 'magische Form der Erfahrung', but he does not make it clear whether 'Spüren' requires a certain disposition, or simply training in perception, in order for the poem, or the 'lyrisches Ich', to gain a higher degree of intensity. In this context, reference to the following source would have been helpful: Erich Kleinschmidt, *Die Entdeckung der Intensität: Geschichte einer Denkfigur im 18. Jahrhundert* (Göttingen: Wallstein, 2004).

Arguably the most valuable part of Meyer-Sickendiek's study is his exploration of poetic expressions of 'Gespür' with reference to six categories, and his analysis of the significance of the concept for an understanding of the impact of the poems. The range of work discussed is commendable and includes less-known poets such as Emanuel Geibel, Max Dauthendey, Berthold Viertel, Ricarda Huch, Hedwig Lachmann, and Heinz Piontek. Moreover, he is able to demonstrate the increased significance of 'lyrisches Gespür' in German poetry of the last two decades. The author here 'secretly' suggests that poetic experience precedes theoretical reflection. Major poetry often gives aesthetically challenging expression to a specific 'Gespür' or 'Ahnung' (divination) which theoretical reflection subsequently confirms as integral to the respective *Zeitgeist*. Perhaps this is indeed the essence of a great poem's irrepressible attraction.

QUEEN MARY UNIVERSITY OF LONDON   RÜDIGER GÖRNER

Zum Ende der Komödie: Eine Theoriegeschichte des Happyends. By STEPHAN KRAFT. Göttingen: Wallstein. 2011. 455 pp. €46.90. ISBN 978-3-8353-0945-6.

Whatever else about comedy has been debated or challenged, one certainty seems to have remained: comedies must have a happy ending. Stephan Kraft's *Theoriegeschichte des Happyends* explores the various shapes and functions of what he calls the 'finale rule' (p. 13) in discourses of comedy from ancient times to the post-war period. Narrow though this thematic approach may seem, it proves to be extremely productive in presenting a far-reaching web of literary, aesthetic, and philosophical concepts to which the discussion of comedy's traditional happy ending contributes. The title already hints at this interplay: a study of comedy's endings is also a study of the end of comedy, a notion charged with philosophical ramifications.

Although the historical scope is extremely broad, the monograph succeeds in doing justice to all the phases of the history of happy endings that it covers. The chapter on 'traditional poetics' discusses ancient, medieval, and early modern models up to Gottsched's *Versuch einer critischen Dichtkunst*, including the European tradition represented by Dante, Scaliger, Corneille, and Dryden, to name only a few. The second part then focuses on Diderot and Lessing as two authors who developed theories of the happy ending in close connection with their own comedies and critical writings. The section on *Sturm und Drang* (Lenz and Herder) and Weimar Classicism (Schiller) describes a development in which the theory of comedy lost contact with the practice of comedy on the stage and thus grew increasingly radical until theorists of German Romanticism and Idealism (such as the Schlegel brothers) argued in favour of the end of comedy itself, which is eventually seen as an index for the end of art (Hegel) and of history (Marx). The chapter on models around 1900 reads the theory of happy ending as a 'Praxiskommentar' (p. 323) in which modernist playwrights (Hauptmann, Sternheim, Hofmannsthal) use the endings of their comedies to represent both the world's functionality and its dysfunctionality. A final section on the post-war years (Hacks, Dürrenmatt, Benigni) highlights comedy as a 'model of avoiding or replacing tragedy' (p. 380).

By integrating the specific issue of comedy's ending into much broader literary, aesthetic, and philosophical developments, Kraft demonstrates the persistence of this particular quality (which distinguishes it from the *Ständeklausel* and the dramatic unities) while also revealing its lasting significance in contexts where at first sight it may seem less obvious. Kraft's thoughtful discussion of his chosen sources enables him to identify important historical developments and connections—such as Masen's 'gaudium et spes' as comedy's equivalent of Aristotle's *eleos kai phobos* (pp. 67–68)—and it even highlights neglected aspects in otherwise well-researched areas, such as Lessing's discussion of Romanus's *Brüder* in the *Hamburg Dramaturgy*, for instance, and Herder's thoughts on comedy in his late journal *Adrastea* (1801–04). As the study focuses on the discussion of one particular feature of comedy rather than wanting to offer a history of the genre in general, it omits authors one might have expected to see feature in the framework of comedy. Nevertheless, the theory of the happy ending proves to be a promising landmark in the vast field of comedy, and Kraft's study certainly succeeds in navigating this area with great profit.

DURHAM UNIVERSITY   THOMAS MARTINEC

Grenzen im Raum — Grenzen in der Literatur. Ed. by EVA GEULEN and STEPHAN KRAFT. (*Zeitschrift für deutsche Philologie*, 129 suppl.) Berlin: Erich Schmidt. 2010. 332 pp. €46. ISBN 978–3–503–12251–6.

'Border' and 'frontier', 'boundary' and 'limit'—common translations of 'Grenze'—are terms much used in a variety of current critical discourses, in a great variety of ways: mostly metaphorically, referring to all kinds of abstract dichotomies and conceptual differences. Countering such inflationary de-anchoring, the editors of this special issue called for articles on representations in German-language literature of concrete, spatial, topographical, geographical, and socio-economically and politically constituted and contested borders. Their brief Introduction notes the curious disparity between the wealth of criticism on abstract border notions and the paucity on actual borders. There would be more to say on why the latter have become interesting now. The eighteen articles collected, ranging from medieval to contemporary literature, naturally also thematize borders between genres, languages, discourses, genders, states of being, and so on, but always in connection with in some sense more concrete borders. Most focus on canonical works, the nineteenth and twentieth centuries being best represented. All are in German save Michael White's on Fontane and Charlton Payne's on Kleist. It goes without saying, with this journal, that each article impressively articulates current theoretically informed debates about and sensitive close readings of chosen primary works. A sense of coherence might have been provided by a common theoretical framework and some dialogue among the contributors. Even those writing about the same œuvre do not cross-refer. The overall impression is of the rich diversity or, put less kindly, the disheartening atomization of endeavour in *Germanistik*.

The articles are organized in six sections. The first offers two historical-conceptual overviews, and both exceed the volume's mandate in productive ways: Andreas Rutz outlines shifting concepts of borders as realized in local community boundary-marking practices from the early modern period to the present; Jörg Kreienbrock explores competing concepts of border as linear demarcation or as spatial zone in works by Jacob Grimm, Friedrich Ratzel, and Carl Schmitt. In the second section, on the poetics of borders, Christian Moser casts an even wider net, surveying representations of the geo-mythical 'world's end' from the *Epic of Gilgamesh* to *Frankenstein*, an undertaking which is nicely complemented by Christine Weder's account of representations (including maps and other images) of the ways of entering *Schlaraffenland* (the Land of Cockagne). Brigitte Kaute and Michael White provide nuanced close readings of E. T. A. Hoffmann's 'Der Goldene Topf' and Fontane's novel *Unwiederbringlich* respectively. The third section focuses on state borders and border-crossings, with papers on the German–German border in works by Arno Schmidt (Stephan Kraft), and on that and other international borders in works by Emine Sevgi Özdamar and Leïla Sebbars (Kate Roy—the only comparativist paper in the volume), and by Terézia Mora and Yoko Tawada (Brigit Lang and Johan Schimanski). The editors note that while Berlin looms large in this section, an initially planned article on the Wall remains a 'painful gap'. The fourth section turns to war, when borders tend to be unstable and contested. Thomas Gann writes about the front in Ernst Jünger; Alexander Honold tackles Peter Handke's Balkan landscapes of war; Andrea Schütte discusses how Saša Stanišić satirizes wartime boundary-drawing in the novel translated as *How the Soldier Repairs the Gramophone*. The fifth section, on external/internal boundaries, brings together Charlton Payne's analysis of Kleist's 'Verlobung in St. Domingo' in terms of state-decreed and internalized rules of hospitality, state borders, and domestic thresholds; Eva Geulen's exploration of the emergence and dissolution of property boundaries in Gottfried Keller's 'Romeo und Julia auf dem Dorfe', in relation to the Roman legal concept *rex nullius*; and Michael Neumann's analysis of Gustav Freytag's *Soll und Haben* as a legitimation of imperialistic violence. Finally, the sixth section focuses on language. Three finely wrought articles rise to the challenge of exceptionally cunning writers. Thomas Schestag deconstructs language-crossings between German, French, and Alemannic (plus Plato's Greek) in Johann Peter Hebel's story 'Der Wegweiser'; Daniel Eschkötter unpacks the metaphorics of rivers, flows of speech, and acts of naming in Heinrich von Kleist's *Penthesilea* and *Hermannsschlacht*; Lars Friedrich pursues the politics of translation or pseudo-translation, self-editing, scriptural rewriting and wartime commentary in Franz Kafka's texts from 1916–17 set in China, or rather in his

'China-phantasmagoria of the oldest empire on earth, of endless extent' (p. 329). The volume thus aptly ends beyond borders.

SWANSEA UNIVERSITY   TOM CHEESMAN

Sadness and Melancholy in German-Language Literature and Culture. Ed. by MARY COSGROVE and ANNA RICHARDS. (Edinburgh German Yearbook, 6) Rochester, NY: Camden House. 2012. 192 pp. £55. ISBN 978-1-57113-528-5.

Sadness and melancholy provide a fertile ground for literary production. Defining and differentiating between the two is no easy task, as these emotions, moods, or states of mind are both human constants and elusive categories. Mary Cosgrove's Introduction provides a solid foundation for the subsequent chapters, delineating our developing understanding of the terms in the light of literary, medical, psychological, aesthetic, and cultural discourses.

It has long been recognized that the connection of sadness and melancholy with artistic and intellectual creativity—at times a Romantic affectation—is a two-edged sword. While the creative process may provide an outlet for individual suffering and despondency, it can also fan the flames of a pathological state that has led many promising writers into the dark night of depression and despair.

The objective of the volume is to explore how writers and intellectuals have learnt to live with and make productive their (or their protagonists') unhappy disposition. The nine chapters offer case studies from the seventeenth century to the present day, covering Pietism, Goethe's early *Singspiele*, the poetics of *Weltschmerz*, Georg Trakl, Robert Walser, Thomas Mann's *Doktor Faustus*, Wilhelm Genazino, and post-1990 East German texts. The chronological structure helps to demonstrate the shifting meaning of sadness and melancholy, from what was once perceived as a sign of spiritual sloth, via association with Romantic genius and irrational anti-Enlightenment tendencies, to diagnoses of pathological states and beyond.

Cosgrove suggests that the personal is political, in that what is experienced by the individual is a reflection of wider events and global influences. She leaves it at that, though the reader may wonder why the editors have chosen the topic at the present time. 9/11 and its subsequent 'sadness without end' or the global economic crisis may play a role here, though the back cover text refers to a different motive, namely that sadness and melancholy have become the 'embarrassing other of a Western civilization that prizes happiness as the mark of successful modern living'. This assertion would have required further discussion as it is precisely in literary texts that the facile precepts of the modern happiness industry are challenged.

On the other hand, Cosgrove's contention that sadness and melancholy can be seen as entirely rational responses to a 'world out of joint' is persuasive, as is her conclusion, following Julia Kristeva, that melancholy contemplation sits at the heart of cultural production. One may ask, though, to what extent an enlightened individual's decision to indulge in sadness/melancholy is then inescapable.

The chapters are interesting and well edited. The reader benefits from the wide range of viewpoints on offer. Inevitably, there are omissions. One would have wished for a more determined exploration of the role of individuation in literary representations of sadness and melancholy. There is also a tantalizing reference to the 'excessive sadness' displayed by Mignon in Goethe's *Wilhelm Meister*; while W. G. Sebald, 'the preeminent anatomist of melancholy' (Helen Finch in a recent blog, alluding to *The Anatomist of Melancholy: Essays in Memory of W. G. Sebald*, ed. by Rüdiger Görner (Munich: iudicium, 2003)), barely gets a mention, even though Cosgrove has previously written on this theme.

Karin Wozonig explores the notion that sadness and melancholy can be understood as a reaction to the processes of modernity, as the individual struggles with the realization of its existential loneliness. *Traurigkeit, Trübsinn, Schwermut*, and *Weltschmerz* stake out a semantic field that can be employed productively, but it can also lead to depression, for example in response to the (traumatic) experience of losing one's familiar world. In such cases, as Stephen Joy demonstrates, 'the ego becomes the archive of a sadness that is at once dissociated from and constitutively bound to the lost object' (p. 142). Svenja Frank tackles this contradiction inherent in the modern experience of sadness head-on: Genazino's characters discover that the whole world is melancholy and all their struggles are but futile attempts to escape this realization.

This rich collection makes a strong case for the continuing relevance of literature as a space that allows us to project and explore emotional states, but also as a source of *Identifizierungsangebote* for our own (sad?) lives. Readers of a less than sanguine disposition may want to approach it with caution, and remain mindful of Goethe's exhortation: 'Gedenke zu leben!'

UNIVERSITY OF LEEDS INGO CORNILS

Werke, vol. I: *Selbstbiographie, Verdeutschter Bethlemitischer Kinder-Mord, Gelegenheitsgedichte, Aufsätze*. By BARTHOLD HEINRICH BROCKES. Ed. by JÜRGEN RATHJE. Göttingen: Wallstein. 2012. ix+792 pp. €69. ISBN 978-3-8353-0982-1.

Students of eighteenth-century German literature have reason to be grateful to the Wallstein Verlag for recent editions of works and letters by Hölty, Merck, Lichtenberg, Goeckingk, Rabener, and other so-called 'lesser' figures of the period. It has now embarked on a complete edition of the works of Barthold Heinrich Brockes, edited by Jürgen Rathje. The bulk of the edition will of course be taken up by Brockes's opus magnum, the nine volumes of *Irdisches Vergnügen in Gott* (1721–48). This first volume, meanwhile, gives us the prose of Brockes's short autobiography and his contributions to the Hamburg moral weekly *Der Patriot*, and the verse of his first major publication, containing his translation of Giambattista Marino's *Strage degl'innocenti* (1632), augmented by a sizeable number of his own poems. Two essays on the German language from Christian Friedrich

Weichmann's anthology *Poesie der Nieder-Sachsen* (1723-26) and some scattered occasional poems round off the volume.

A facsimile reprint of the *Irdisches Vergnügen in Gott* was published in 1970, but there is no modern complete edition of Brockes's works. This edition is designed to fill the gap. It sets out to be an 'allgemein zugängliche Leseausgabe' (p. vii) rather than a full-scale critical edition. The works are published according to the last editions published in Brockes's lifetime. Paratexts by other authors—a significant feature of his publications—are omitted, as is the parallel text of works Brockes is translating (thus in this volume, Marino's original is not reproduced alongside the *Bethlemitischer Kinder-Mord*). The various print sizes and fonts that characterize the originals have been normalized. The more notable variants are given (the *Kinder-Mord* went through five editions between 1715 and 1742) and there are over a hundred pages of commentary elucidating the many names and literary works referred to or quoted by Brockes. Despite the editor's modest claims and the compromises he has made, this is a substantial edition which will serve the needs of all but the most dedicated Brockes specialists.

The present volume shows Brockes's range, from *Der Patriot*'s moralizing prose to the *marinismo* of the *Kinder-Mord*, from oratorios to Knittelvers, and from pieces in Hamburg *Platt* to poems in Italian and French. This catholic range, embracing both local and European traditions, reflects the generous outlook of his intellectual circle. The engraving on the title-page of *Der Patriot* showed the two sides of a medallion: Socrates on one side, with the inscription 'Cosmopolites', the embracing figures of Minerva and Amalthea (goddess of plenty) on the other, with the inscription 'Civium felicitati patriota Hamb[urgensis]' ('the Hamburg patriot for the benefit of her citizens'). Hamburg and the world came together in Brockes's life and poetic work. His autobiography, begun when he was forty-three, looks back to his Grand Tour to Italy, Switzerland, France, and the Low Countries, but also to his years of public service to his native city. He could be disarmingly frank about what was to her advantage: 'Sorget ein vernünftiger und redlicher Haus-Vater, daß er seinen Kindern etwas nachlassen möge; so kann ja keine Sorge billiger und nothwendiger seyn, als unsern Kindern, unter Göttlichem Segen, einen Ort zu hinterlassen, worin sie nächst GOTT Geld erwerben können' (*Der Patriot*, 84 (1725); here p. 469). But he also wanted intellectual riches to adorn his city and nation, and saw his literary work as a contribution to that end.

That by his writing and translating he was also accumulating and displaying his own cultural capital, and thus cementing his place in Hamburg's elite, was a welcome by-product of his patriotic endeavours. A number of the poems in the present volume are occasional pieces, marking significant moments in the political life of the city as well as ceremonial events in the private lives of its most eminent citizens. Poetry in this period was a thoroughly social activity, a marker of status and the currency of exchanges within political, social, and personal networks. The often elaborate titles tell the story: 'Als Se. Königl. Hoheit, der Durchleuchtigste Fürst und Herr, Herr Carol Friedrich, Erbe zu Norwegen, regierender Herzog zu Schleswig-Holstein [...], etc. bey musicalischer Aufführung des Gedichtes von der

Vergnügung des Gehörs, des Herrn Verfassers Garten mit Dero höchsten Gegenwart beehrten, bezeugte ihre unterthänigste Freude HAMMONIA' (p. 299). This is a nice example of how personal and civic interests could be advanced in the medium of verse.

Religion, however, always came first. His autobiography is a conscientious account of the blessings he has received from God, and his addresses to his compatriots, whether in prose or verse, often seek to remind them of the similar blessings their city has enjoyed. The deepest impulse of his writing came from his desire to make his readers open their eyes to the beauties of a world a loving God had given them for their delectation. There are a number of pieces in this volume that anticipate and echo the themes of *Irdisches Vergnügen in Gott*. The remaining volumes of this welcome new edition are something to look forward to.

St Peter's College, Oxford   K. F. Hilliard

Moral und Ironie bei Gottlieb Wilhelm Rabener: Paratext und Palimpsest in den Satyrischen Schriften. By Nadja Reinhard. Göttingen: Wallstein. 2013. 349 pp. €29.20. ISBN 978-3-8353-1169-5.

The satirist Gottlieb Wilhelm Rabener (1714–1771) is having his moment. Hard on the heels of the same publisher's edition of his letters and other documents (reviewed in *MLR*, 109 (2014), 540–43) comes this substantial monograph on his work. Both are encouraging signs that the study of the eighteenth century before 1770 is a flourishing enterprise. Where the editor of the letters, E. Theodor Voss, relies on editorial philology to lead the way, Nadja Reinhard draws upon literary theory to give a fresh impetus to our understanding of the period.

Reinhard's book is emphatically an attempt to rescue Rabener's reputation from neglect and the condescension of posterity. Famous in his own lifetime, he has never recovered from the faint praise bestowed on him by Goethe, in Book II of *Dichtung und Wahrheit*, and Schiller, in *Über naive und sentimentalische Dichtung*. His satires were pleasing, his style agreeable, and his sentiments unimpeachable: he was, in other words, shallow and dull. Literary historiography since then has merely embroidered this verdict. Now, in Reinhard, he has found a champion eager to make a fresh case for his literary merits and his historical importance.

She succeeds better at the former than the latter. The first sections strain too hard to persuade us of Rabener's modernity. She would have us believe that his satires fulfil 'das Paradigma der Moderne, einer selbstreflexiven Literatur als *heautonome Autopoiesis* im Sinne der Autonomieästhetik' (p. 50), and anticipate the Kantian and Schillerian theory of poetic autonomy by fifty years (pp. 54–58). Not content with this, she argues that the same applies to his friend and literary ally Gellert. Gellert's image of the poet as a bee gathering nectar from many flowers, from his fable 'Die Biene und die Henne', is adduced as a symbol of an 'auf Schiller vorausdeutende Autonomie des schöpferischen Dichters' (p. 27). This misreads the fable, and ignores both the image's significance as a defence and praise of imitation—of being derivative rather than creative—and its own aptly derivative nature (it comes from Plato and Horace, and was a commonplace in humanist poetics). Without evident sense of contradiction, Reinhard also notes how important the aims of *prodesse et delectare* were for Gellert and Rabener (p. 28): the postulates, in other words, of traditional 'Wirkungs-', not modern 'Autonomieästhetik', if one must use these rather constricting terms. Reinhard would have done better to cast off this conceptual straitjacket and avoid the teleological thinking so pervasive in German literary scholarship of the earlier eighteenth century, which means that nothing in it can be allowed to be significant unless it paves the way for one of the great figures of its latter third. The belittling judgement passed on Rabener's works by Goethe and Schiller makes this choice of perspective especially odd.

For as Reinhard is able to show in the longer and better part of the book, Goethe, Schiller, and many other readers since have seriously underestimated the interest and depth of Rabener's writing. Her demonstration of its para- and intertextual complexity and ingenuity is valuable, without that complexity having to do duty as a proxy for the elusive ideal of poetic autonomy. Admirers of Juvenal, Horace, Lucian, Rabelais, Cervantes, Pope, and Swift will not be surprised to learn that satirical writing is particularly adept at irony and para- and intertextual play; what will please them is that a similar observation can be made about Rabener, without worrying too much to what extent the work of any of these writers satisfies the requirement of 'heautonome Autopoiesis'.

Reinhard in any case abandons the argument about poetic autonomy after the first chapter. Her conclusion, more sensibly, places Rabener's ethical satire in the context of Shaftesbury's thought. In between, she has substantial chapters on ideas of satire before Rabener; on Rabener's own explicit theory of satire; on his para- and intertextual techniques (where she uses Gérard Genette's discriminations to good effect); and on two detailed case studies which convincingly demonstrate the subtle effects Rabener's best work achieves by applying these techniques. A particularly valuable point she makes is that the meaning of allusions to and quotations from other, preceding works (which she, following Genette, calls 'hypotexts') is not exhausted by a superficial reading of the immediate passage cited; rather, the educated reader is invited to recall its broader context, and only then will grasp the deeper points being made. The discussion of passages from Horace, Virgil, and Lucretius referred to in the 'Antrittsrede von der wahren Beschaffenheit eines vernünftigen Bürgers' is a particularly fine example of close reading to illustrate this argument.

Reinhard's detailed study of Rabener's writing has a merit that does not depend on the wider historical and aesthetic argument she builds around it. It can be recommended to anyone interested in satire in the eighteenth century; and it gives readers a strong incentive to dust off their Rabener and read him with heightened awareness of his literary talent.

St Peter's College, Oxford   K. F. Hilliard

Literatur und Komik: Zur Theorie literarischer Komik und zur deutschen Komödie im 18. Jahrhundert. By Tom Kindt. Berlin: Akademie Verlag. 2011. 281 pp. €89.90. ISBN 978-3-05-005152-9.

In recent years a number of disciplines have paid significant attention to the comic. These range from philosophy, psychology, and linguistics to evolutionary biology, neurosciences, and cognition theory. Tom Kindt's *Literatur und Komik* draws on various approaches to the comic in order to develop a theory that focuses both on literature in general and more particularly on German comedies (in theory and practice) in the second half of the eighteenth century. Thus the book embarks on a highly productive dialogue between humour studies and literary studies.

The first part outlines a multifaceted theory of the literary comic. A critical investigation of contextualist concepts, which rely on the recipient's individual mood, is succeeded by an outline of universalist models identifying comic features of a given object. On the basis of these models the author then discusses elements that constitute the 'textual comic' (p. 30), meaning 'those features which texts must have in order to be able to appear comic at all' (p. 113). Kindt's theory of the textual comic is based on concepts of incongruity, which find the origin of the comic in the perception of a discrepancy, such as that between an idea and real objects that have been perceived through this idea (Schopenhauer, p. 41). Above all it relies on Victor Raskin's and Salvatore Attardo's 'General Theory of Verbal Humour', which classifies a text as funny if it is 'compatible' with two 'scripts' that are opposed to each other (p. 70). Using stimulating analyses of various short texts, Kindt supplements their 'General Theory of Verbal Humour' with the requirement for harmlessness ('Harmlosigkeitsbedingung', p. 96) in order to distinguish incongruities that appear comic from those that appear threatening. The first part closes with a theory of the textual comic in literature in general, built upon the distinction between comic as representation itself ('Komik der Darbietung') and comic as what is represented ('Komik des Dargebotenen', p. 146).

The second part explores four models of comedy and four comedies by German authors in the second half of the eighteenth century: Lessing, Lenz, Kotzebue, and Tieck. At this point Kindt's previous explorations of the literary comic prove to be fruitful in two respects: they serve as an analytical basis for the discussion of comedies that could hardly be more diverse, and they help to shed new light on texts that have already been extensively treated by scholarship. *Minna von Barnhelm*, for instance, is read as an exploration of the conditions that determine 'whether an inconsistency is to be classified as ridiculous' (p. 184), and Lenz's reflections on comedy are shown to feature the 'possibility of a comedy without the comic' (p. 199). In Kotzebue's *Die Indianer in England*, Kindt identifies an instance of comedy's 'being excused from moralizing tasks' (p. 223), and, compared with Lessing's *Minna*, Tieck's *Der gestiefelte Kater* appears as an attempt to replace an increased awareness of moral judgement ('Urteils*vorsicht*') with a general abandonment of moral judgement altogether ('Urteils*verzicht*', p. 238)

Although the theoretical part, which is almost twice as long as the discussion of comedy, succeeds in combining a literary interest in the comic with humour studies in general, it does feature what one might call a theoretical surplus that cannot be fully applied to the analyses in the second part. Nevertheless, it helps to sensitize the reader to some aspects of the chosen comedies that have hitherto been neglected. Therefore it is to be hoped that the theory of the literary comic developed here will be used for further discussions of the comic in various genres at various times. Kindt's exploration of German comedy in the second half of the eighteenth century demonstrates just how productive such an interplay can be.

DURHAM UNIVERSITY   THOMAS MARTINEC

Die 'Don-Quijote'-Rezeption Friedrich Schlegels und Heinrich Heines im Kontext des europäischen Kulturtransfers: Ein Narr als Angelpunkt transnationaler Denkansätze. By YVONNE JOERES. (Beiträge zur neueren Literaturgeschichte, 305) Heidelberg: Winter. 2012. 404 pp. €62. ISBN 978-3-8253-6060-3.

Goethe emphasized the formative influence of Spain on German literature between 1790 and 1800, and the Romantics characterized the period between 1800 and 1810 as the 'Spanish decade'. German interest in Spain at this time, in its medieval past, its Arab legacy, and last but not least in its revolt against the Napoleonic forces, was striking. Against this colourful and historically complex backdrop, Yvonne Joeres's monograph traces the productive reception of Cervantes's *Don Quijote* in early German Romanticism (with, as the title indicates, a particular focus on Friedrich Schlegel) and in the work of Heinrich Heine. Joeres spends a sizeable part of her book laying out the intricate premisses of the *leyenda negra* and its repercussions in Germany: the importance of European travel accounts, and of burgeoning Hispanophilia, among other factors, facilitated by Wilhelm von Humboldt's research, Friedrich Justin Bertuch's *Magazin der Spanischen und Portugiesischen Literatur*, but also by Johann Gottfried Herder's reflections on Spanish romances as an expression of the national character. An additional brief exploration of the specifically literary reception in the eighteenth century (for example in Musäus's *Grandison der Zweite* and Wieland's *Don Sylvio von Rosalva*) might have been helpful here to understand the significant changes subsequently undergone by the treatment of this motif.

With its specific blend of styles and genres, *Don Quijote* was perceived as a poetological paradigm by the Romantics and famously featured as a commendable prototype for Romantic writing in Friedrich Schlegel's preface to *Lucinde*. Joeres argues that Friedrich Schlegel's reading of *Don Quijote* is a crucial point in the history of reception, as it connects the interpretation of the novel as an expression of national culture with Heine's cosmopolitan interpretation and appropriation of it in the *Vormärz* era. Heine in turn directed his attention to the protagonist, and in so doing accentuated readings of Quixote as both kindred spirit and figure of fun. Heine's 'Donquichottismus' in his life and works is reflected in his permanent wish to improve the social and political conditions in the Metternich era. However, his simultaneous recognition of the futile, utopian dimension of this aspiration created a self-aware 'Donquichottismus', as Joeres concludes, substantially in agreement with previous findings. With his politicized adaptation of *Don Quijote*, Heine went beyond Schlegel's aesthetic programme. Joeres arrives at the conclusion that for Heine the pairing of Don Quixote and Sancho Panza represented the fragmentation of the world that could only be overcome aesthetically (i.e. in Cervantes's novel). As a transnational symbol, Quixote became the topical enthusiastic and good-willed hero whose mission is foiled by an unrelenting reality.

Joeres draws on concepts of cultural transfer and transnationalism that diverge from comparative literary studies in their effort to highlight the emergence and analysis of hybrids rather than to describe differences and commonalities of literary texts. She presents a meticulously researched history of influence which reframes interpretations by other scholars in a transnational context. In doing so, she also collates various previous strands of research and offers a broad survey of changing perspectives on Spain and Cervantes's influence over German writers.

DURHAM UNIVERSITY   CLAUDIA NITSCHKE

Wissenskunst: Adalbert Stifter und Naturforscher auf Weltreise. By CHRISTIAN VAN DER STEEG. (Medienwandel — Medienwechsel — Medienwissen, 22) Zurich: Chronos. 2011. 228 pp. €29. ISBN 978-3-0340-1022-1.

It is possible to finish Christian van der Steeg's book having read it with attention and benefit but without being quite sure what it was about. Paradoxically this is the effect of its concentration on communication. With admirably detailed historical scholarship (the book was a doctoral dissertation, but does not read like one), van der Steeg dissolves Stifter's writing into the shifting discourses and media of scientific reflection and research in the nineteenth century. The context is the long, hesitant co-operation between the aesthetic and the scientific paradigms (in which entire systems of value and assumption were implicit) underlying modes of recording, reporting, and representation in this period. Van der Steeg's extensive bibliography attests to the interest in recent years in this area (for instance, the many studies of the writings of such men as Alexander von Humboldt or Charles Darwin). The poorly travelled Stifter (who did not see the sea until he was over fifty) might seem a surprising figure to consider alongside the titanic traveller-explorer-scientists of the nineteenth century. However, van der Steeg's original contribution is to focus, after such thinkers as Friedrich Kittler and Albrecht Koschorke, upon the medial aspects of the important relation between art and science in Stifter's writings (about which relation itself a fair amount has already been written).

Van der Steeg dedicates the first and last chapters to writing and reading in order to tie the medial analysis to Stifter's pre-eminent medium. These chapters explore some contexts in which he found himself addressing the links between creative writing as he understood and practised it and the objective importance and status of empirical science, for which he had great reverence. His view that Upper Austria did not require a university (since it would generate surplus doctors and lawyers who would then become writers and cause nothing but trouble) throws a shaft of light into the history of values, and van der Steeg's reading of the different versions of *Der Condor* within the context he creates provides an insight into the fine detail of how Stifter saw scientific knowledge and aesthetic reception in relation to one another. The other chapters are broader in their approach to media, beginning with one on images of exotic landscapes (and literary description), continuing with a chapter on the medial dynamics surrounding one particular scientific focus, namely what was called *Pflanzengeographie* (whose English equivalent is 'phytogeography'), and then a particularly good one on the construction of the mind as a place in which these different determinations—wonderment, creativity, information, scientific regularity, photographic records—mix and blend to produce different medial effects. Van der Steeg's style is that irritating mixture of precision and indirectness beloved of some historians ('Am 15. April lief in Rio de Janeiro die Northumbria aus...' (p. 29); '1804 kehrte Alexander von Humboldt von seiner Reise in die neue Welt zurück' (p. 39)—in other words, endless narrative inceptions, but no story), but on the whole this is preferable to the very dry academic style one often finds in German dissertations published as books. The author is an intelligent and insightful reader as well as being a meticulous and well-informed historian, and his book is worth reading for what we learn about Stifter and media history. Given the topic, some carefully chosen illustrations would have been a huge help. The lack of an index is hard to excuse.

Jesus College, Cambridge   Michael Minden

The Truth of Realism: A Reassessment of the German Novel 1830–1900. By John Walker. London: Legenda. 2011. 213 pp. £45. ISBN 978-1-906540-90-6.

Cultural studies, systems theory, postcolonial studies, gender studies, media history, and a number of other more recent approaches have given new impetus to research into nineteenth-century Realism and initiated a reassessment of German Realism within the overarching European development from Romanticism to Modernism. Walker's study of a small number of selected novels by Keller, Raabe, and Fontane makes an interesting contribution to this reassessment by arguing that 'the distinguishing capacity of German narrative realism, and the source of that realism's unique contribution to the European tradition' is the critique of internalized ideology; the novels show 'how the power of society works most effectively through its psychological representation in the consciousness of its members' (p. 2) and expose 'as ideology' the idealist discourse of subjective authenticity and its conception of 'cultural self-knowledge' as defined as 'the enemy of integral moral life in society' (pp. 14, 86). Walker claims that the 'German realist novel is heir to the critical spirit of Heine and Büchner at least as much as it is to the idealist tradition to which they respond' (p. 29), and that 'German narrative realism works primarily as a realism of discourse' (p. 8). The fruits of this approach are detailed and often perceptive critical readings of Keller's *Der grüne Heinrich*, Raabe's *Der Hungerpastor*, *Pfisters Mühle*, and *Die Akten des Vogelsangs*, and Fontane's *Irrungen, Wirrungen*, *Effi Briest*, *Vor dem Sturm*, and *Der Stechlin*, readings that succeed in illustrating how advanced realism 'challenge[s] the culture it represents by the mode, indeed the fact, of its representation' (p. 202).

Whether the book actually 'offer[s] a decisively new approach' (p. 14), however, is more debatable. The thesis that there is a linear 'development of the German novel from the shadow of the romantic *Bildungsroman* to a mature realism which points the way to the beginnings of German modernism' (p. 4) is clearly a construction that significant recent research has successfully challenged along with the notion of a German Realism in the singular. Walker's argument focuses on the *Bildungsroman* tradition and the legacy of idealism to the point of ignoring other, competing and often more relevant, literary and cultural traditions even within his small corpus of canonical novels, let alone in the wider field of realist narrative (e.g. the social novel, the *Zeitroman*, and the novella), which is not taken into account. The reader is left to wonder how Auerbach, Gutzkow, Spielhagen, Stifter, Storm, Ebner-Eschenbach, and so many others might fit into this linear argument. There is also rather limited engagement with German-language research. For example, Walker develops his analysis of Keller's literary critique in *Der grüne Heinrich* 'of social experience through a critical examination of the cultural discourses' (the novel's 'Diskursebene', pp. 33 and 45) without any reference to Wolfgang Rohe's pioneering study of precisely this interpretation (*Roman aus Diskursen: Gottfried Keller, 'Der grüne Heinrich' (erste Fassung, 1854/55)* (Munich: Fink, 1993)). Schopenhauer's relevance for Raabe is discussed without considering Søren Fauth's standard book on the theme (*Der metaphysische Realist: Zur Schopenhauer-Rezeption in Wilhelm Raabes Spätwerk* (Göttingen: Wallstein, 2007)); the entire approach of reading Raabe's and Fontane's realism as a partial continuation of, and partial departure from, idealist aesthetics and Hegel, as well as the focus on 'the divorce between representation and life' (p. 110) in advanced realism, follow effectively in the footsteps of Hubert Ohl's influential study *Bild und Wirklichkeit: Studien zur Romankunst Raabes und Fontanes* (Heidelberg: Stiehm, 1968), which is never acknowledged. Although Walker argues quite rightly that German Realism has more to say on society and modernity than Erich Auerbach and others conceded, there is also no consideration of recent research into German Realism's engagement with modernization and modern realities. Fuller consideration of relevant research would have made the proposed reassessment more convincing.

University of Nottingham   Dirk Göttsche

The Foundation of the Unconscious: Schelling, Freud and the Birth of the Modern Psyche. By Matt ffytche. Cambridge: Cambridge University Press. 2012. 310 pp. £60. ISBN 978-0-521-76649-4.

In his introduction Matt ffytche claims that there has been surprisingly little work done on the Romantic and idealist notions of the psyche and the unconscious (p. 4)

and sets out to correct this deficit with a special focus on the works of Johann Gottlieb Fichte and Friedrich W. J. Schelling. But this statement needs further clarification. Though the author is undoubtedly right to say that for decades Lancelot Law Whyte's *The Unconscious before Freud* (London: Tavistock, 1967) and Henri F. Ellenberger's magisterial monograph *The Discovery of the Unconscious* (New York: Basic, 1970) set the standard for the historical research, as did the investigations by Odo Maquard (*Tranzendentaler Idealismus, romantische Naturphilosophie, Psychoanalyse* (Cologne: Dinter, 1987)) and Ludger Lütkehaus (*Diese wahre innere Afrika: Texte zur Entstehung des Unbewussten vor Freud* (Frankfurt a.M.: Fischer, 1995)) for the philosophical context, there has been an enormous surge in academic interest in the conceptual history of the unconscious during the last decade. The three-volume project on *Das Unbewusste* (Gießen: Psychosozialverlag, 2005–06), edited by Günter Gödde and Michael Buchholz, has demonstrated a new discursive approach to this concept, which played such a central role in the thinking of the nineteenth century. Such an approach acknowledges that throughout this period the concept of the unconscious was dispersed into many different strands of thinking, from philosophy to occultism, from physiology to psychiatry, from science to theology, from literature to politics. Understanding of the concept thus varied according to the academic or non-academic environments and traditions in which it appeared. The breadth and complexity of the concept can only be accommodated through a wider discourse including different disciplines such as the history of medicine, the history of psychiatry and psychology, the history of philosophy, and the history of Western esotericism. The last years have seen a steady increase in publications on the unconscious in all of these disciplines.

ffytche's study is a most valuable contribution to this important debate, but its wish to exceed the discursive framework of conceptual history is almost too ambitious. According to ffytche, increasing knowledge about the historical emergence of the psychic unconscious reveals 'unrecognised historical implications of the psychoanalytic project itself' (p. 15). Though there is no doubt that the disturbance of the roots of psychoanalytic historiography will allow new perspectives to emerge, such an approach also raises the question of how far an approach like ffytche's reads the philosophy of German idealism through the *telos* of Freud's psychoanalysis and twentieth-century psychology. There is a further methodological problem, since ffytche's study vacillates between historical research on Schelling's philosophy and twentieth-century philosophical and conceptual debates on German idealism.

In accordance with his teleological reading of Schelling's late philosophy—which asks what Schelling's late works mean for the emergence of Freud's psychoanalysis—ffytche dedicates the entire third part of his study to an attempt to find out what exactly Freud's theory owes to the idealist and Romantic traditions and where it differs from them. According to ffytche, Freud avoided posing the question of a self, in contrast to C. G. Jung or Otto Rank, and the lack of a definition of individuality would—each time that it becomes necessary to situate the origins of a trauma within the historical-sociological and cultural-ideological realms—destabilize psychoanalysis right up to the present day. Whereas Fichte and Schelling were precisely concerned with the question of self-autonomy and freedom, which—as ffytche demonstrates convincingly—led Schelling to introduce the notion of the unconscious in the first place, ffytche draws a line from Fichte's I, via Schelling's psyche, to Freud's psychic apparatus, describing this development as 'the gradual detachment of the ontology of the individual from the absolute and metaphysical claims regarding the unity of the world' (p. 280).

This thought-provoking monograph most certainly deserves careful study. Taken together with research by Andrew Bowie (*Schelling and Modern German Philosophy: An Introduction* (Abingdon and New York: Routledge, 1993)), Angus Nicholls and Martin Liebscher (*Thinking the Unconscious: Nineteenth-Century German Thought* (Cambridge: Cambridge University Press, 2010)), and Elke Völmicke (*Das Unbewusste im deutschen Idealismus* (Würzburg: Königshausen & Neumann, 2005)), it provides an increasingly detailed account of the unconscious in German idealist philosophy and thus helps to add further facets to our understanding of the kaleidoscopic differentiation of the concept of the unconscious in nineteenth-century German thought.

UNIVERSITY COLLEGE LONDON   MARTIN LIEBSCHER

Todlob: Feldtagebuchgedichte 1915/16. By FRANZ RICHARD BEHRENS. Ed. by MICHAEL LENTZ. (Werkausgabe, 3) Munich: text+kritik. 2012. 122 pp. €24. ISBN 978-3-8-6916-166-2.

Mein bester Freund — Hamlet: Drehbücher, Kinotexte, Filmkritiken. By FRANZ RICHARD BEHRENS. Ed. by GERHARD RÜHM and MONIKA LICHTENFELD. (Werkausgabe, 4) Munich: text+kritik. 2012. 488 pp. €40. ISBN 978-3-8-6916-167-9.

The collected edition of the works of Franz Richard Behrens, which appears in the admirable series Frühe Texte der Moderne, confirms his status as one of the most interesting experimental poets writing in German in the early twentieth century. The edition has already presented some of Behrens's finest work and breaks new ground with the latest volumes. Volume 3, to which the editor has given the appropriately succinct title *Todlob*, contains the text of a hitherto unknown collection of poems. The manuscript was written in the First World War between March 1915 and August 1916. It comprises 116 poems, of which a grand total of ninety-three are published here for the first time.The twenty-three previously published poems first appeared either in Herwarth Walden's journal *Der Sturm* or in Behrens's only book of poems, *Blutblüte* (1917), and some appeared in both; all were included in the first volume of this edition, *Blutblüte: Die gesammelten Gedichte* (1979). Some of the poems now published for the first time belong to the best that Behrens produced, such as the Stramm-like 'Fühlen': 'Alles ist Kugel und alles ist zwei | Hälfte ist Leben | Durch Schanzen | Tanzen' (p. 52). Many poems relate directly to the war, such as 'Trommel Kanonade' (p. 46) and 'Todlob' itself (p. 68). Others evoke cultural icons, notably 'Goethe' (p. 42) and 'Schiller' (p. 53), or masters of the avant-garde, such as 'Vincent Van Gogh' (p. 53) and 'Emil Nolde' (p. 55). Yet others are dedicated to friends and family, including poems to Behrens's father (pp. 49 and 61) and his brother, Herbert (p. 80). This makes for a highly varied collection. As with the poetry of *Der Sturm* in general, linguistic innovation is at a premium, and the final compound word in the poem on Goethe, 'Urmenschenkraft', perfectly sums up the originality on display throughout this powerful collection.

Volume 4 of the collected works gathers together all Behrens's writings connected with the cinema, revealing a largely unknown side of his creativity. The editors have divided the material into four sections. The first, headed 'Drehbücher und Filmerzählungen', comprises seven texts, including *Hamlet* (pp. 7–69) and *Lady Hamilton* (pp. 71–121); the second is headed 'Allgemeines zum Film' and contains seventeen texts, including 'Bekenntnis' (p. 285), 'Beginn der Filmdichtung' (p. 292), and 'Filmmusik' (p. 315); the third contains Behrens's *Filmkritiken*, numbering sixty-eight in all and covering seventy-nine films, including such classics as *Ben Hur* (p. 335), *Metropolis* (p. 337), *Der blaue Engel* (p. 354), *Im Westen nichts Neues* (p. 363), and *Kuhle Wampe* (p. 383); and to conclude, the fourth section, 'Kurzporträts und Interviews', contains eleven items, among them a 'Liebeserklärung an Charlie' (p. 395) and an 'Interview mit Buster Keaton' (p. 398). Behrens's career as a screenwriter began after his return from the front in the First World War and shows him adapting to the new literary circumstances imposed by the need to earn a living. His most successful film by far was *Hamlet* (1920) with Asta Nielsen, the celebrated leading lady, in the title role. It need hardly be said that Behrens's choice of a female Hamlet lent a new dimension to the play. Whereas the *New York Tribune* gave the film a rave review, other papers were puzzled. Behrens's note in self-defence gives a good idea of his method: 'Ich schrieb Hamlet für den Film. [. . .] Nicht durch Nachempfindung ist das Hamletdrama aufzuerwecken, sondern [. . .] durch Umgestaltung ins Bildliche' (p. 455). As a critic, however, Behrens was not always so astute, as is evident from his somewhat bland review of *Metropolis*. There is much else to discover in this fascinating volume, which will be indispensable for anyone interested in the intersection of literary and cinema history. Both volumes are edited and produced to the usual standards of this excellent series.

KING'S COLLEGE LONDON   JEREMY ADLER

The World as Metaphor in Robert Musil's 'The Man without Qualities': Possibility as Reality. By GENESE GRILL. Rochester, NY: Camden House. 2012. 204 pp. £50. ISBN 978–1–57113–538–4.

The cover of Genese Grill's book on Musil's *The Man without Qualities* consists of a drawing by the author entitled 'Word-Maker, World-Maker'. It shows Musil with a somewhat sceptical, mildly tortured, concentrated look on his face, pen in hand and stooped over one of his notebooks, out of which pages covered with writing spiral and engulf the writer. Together with Grill's motto, taken from Musil's posthumous papers and discussed in the second of four chapters, the drawing gives a good indication of the central motif of the book. It is worth quoting at some length from Grill's commentary on this motto, whose second line—'Gleichnisse gehen mehr an als Wirklichkeit'—is rendered as 'Metaphors are more meaningful than reality'. According to Grill,

> The idea of 'metaphoric value' [*Gleichniswert*], a little like the concept of the 'value' of colours, emphasises the idea that beneath these metaphors there is something essential—an 'inner necessity' or idea that can be illustrated or approached in an infinite number of ways, corresponding via many different hues. The core of this idea may be, fundamentally, that the world of concepts and forms dissolves itself into 'breath' as soon as we try to approach it too directly or to pin it down to an absolute and enduring value. 'Metaphor is more important than reality' because whatever is essential can be approached only obliquely and contingently; only temporarily or extratemporally. (p. 78)

Grill's interpretative approach is encapsulated in these shifts from simile to metaphor, and from being more engaging, or of more concern ('mehr angehen'), to being more meaningful, and finally more important than reality. The subtle balance in Musil, as a psychologist of epistemology and an epistemologist of human psychology, between the invention and application of images and the striving for conceptual clarity, is clearly tipped towards the side of shifting configurations.

In four chapters, on 'Circles', 'Repeatability and Crime', 'Word Magic', and 'Still Life: (Not) Doing What Isn't Done', Grill plays out variations on the theme of 'fixed concepts/categories' versus metaphoric inventions and shifts, firmly siding with the latter. We are given an inspired and textually knowledgeable, yet lopsided, characterization of Musil, one in which precision is ultimately secondary to infinite openness, making him, as the conclusion suggests, yet another postmodern thinker *avant la lettre*. However, at the same time he is also presented as a staple modernist, and compared to Proust (in particular) in his search for elusive reality. Add to this the observation that Musil 'did not depict the duration of these moments of exceptional experience', because, 'real essences', in a post-Einsteinian universe, are neither solid nor consistent: real essences are in flux (p. 178), and Grill's claim that failure (to complete the novel) was the only possible success for Musil may seem plausible. And yet, Grill's conclusion insists that the 'Other Condition' was the lifelong centrepiece of Musil's aesthetics, even if it may have receded into the background at times, owing to the metaphoric fluctuations in the process of living—experiencing—creating—writing.

Grill's book offers a spirited and enthusiastic defence of the creative literary act as a kind of utopian 'révolution permanente', without programme or goal to be achieved, forever avoiding closure: 'The aesthetic experience of the Other Condition [...] simultaneously provides the key to the enigma, suggesting answers to the question of whether or not there can be meaning, while continuously ensuring the indigestibility of the work of art' (p. 179). What Grill does not make clear, however, is how this stance is meant to allow Musil to 'stand firm on a number of central questions', and cause us to take 'seriously his role as author in helping to shape social and ethical values' (p. 4). At this point, Grill's deliberations encounter the barrier between word- and world-making. Ultimately, the reader is not taken to a place beyond the conundrums set up eloquently in Nietzsche's essay 'Über Wahrheit und Lüge im außermoralischen Sinne', to which Grill repeatedly refers, placing Musil firmly in the tradition of a radically perspectival Nietzsche. The reader is led through a rich textual landscape, from quotation to quotation (including material from the Klagenfurt electronic edition, though no systematic use is made of this), but the overall impression thus generated is of a self-referential and secular artistic universe that is loaded with theological expectations—something that would surely have made Musil smile.

University of Brighton   Daniel Steuer

Kafka, Prag und der Erste Weltkrieg/Kafka, Prague and the First World War. Ed. by Manfred Engel and Ritchie Robertson. (Oxford Kafka Studies, 2) Würzburg: Königshausen & Neumann. 2012. 279 pp. €48. ISBN 978-3-8260-4849-4.

Kafka und Prag: Literatur-, kultur-, sozial- und sprachhistorische Kontexte. Ed. by Peter Becher, Steffen Höhne, and Marek Nekula. (Intellektuelles Prag im 19. und 20. Jahrhundert, 3) Cologne: Böhlau. 2012. 364 pp. €49.90. ISBN 978-3-412-20777-9.

Few writers are as closely connected with a city as Kafka is with Prague. Notwithstanding the popularity of this topic with critics and biographers, the thirty-four essays in the two volumes under review find many new subjects and angles to discuss. Altogether, these collections represent a major contribution to knowledge, and given the uniformly high standard of the contributions, it would be invidious to single out individual articles for special praise. Most scholars will wish to consult both volumes and treat them as a pair.

As its title suggests and as the editors elaborate in their introduction, the volume edited by Manfred Engel and Ritchie Robertson, *Kafka, Prag und der Erste Weltkrieg*, centres on the largely neglected topic of Kafka's relation to the First World War. Their collection contains fifteen essays in three sections. The first section, 'Historischer Kontext', begins with Johannes Birgfeld's 'Der erste Weltkrieg im *Prager Tagblatt*: Zur Präsenz des Krieges als Kommunikationsereignis im Umfeld Kafkas', which considers the limited possibilities open to newspapers when it came to reporting the war. The section continues with Mark Cornwall's 'The Wartime Bohemia of Franz Kafka: The Social and National Crisis', which offers an impressively detailed historical account of Kafka in the context of the social and national crises that shook the Austro-Hungarian Empire in the First World War. The next two essays deal with the under-researched subject of Zionism and the First World War, Andreas B. Kilcher's 'Zionistischer Kriegsdiskurs im Ersten Weltkrieg' showing how the conflict had a dramatic impact on Jewish life in Europe and the Middle East. Key statements of Buber's stand out as of general significance, such as 'Dieser

Krieg wird für die Menschen den ungeheuren Segen haben, dass er gezeigt hat, was wirklich ist' (p. 65). A concluding section of the essay looks at Kafka and the concept of *Gemeinschaft*. Related stances are on display in Eva Edelmann's closely argued essay on 'Geschichtstheologische Strategien zionistischer Gegenwartsdeutung in der Prager jüdischen Wochenschrift *Selbstwehr* (1914–1918)', and here too one finds generally significant views: 'Es ist fast wie eine ungeheure Reinigung, was jetzt mit der Menschheit geschieht; die Reinigung durch die Katastrophe' (p. 74).

The second section, called 'Tschechen und Deutsche', opens with Claire E. Nolte's 'Inter arma silent musae? Culture in Wartime Prague', which treats a broad span: wartime literary trends, music and art in the war, popular entertainment, and the film industry. This is followed by Rajendra A. Chitnis's wide-ranging 'Putting *Granny* in a Home: Czech Writers and the Village in Kafka's Lifetime', which concludes by finding affinities with *Das Schloß*: 'The Czech village writers [were looking for] a paradigm of healing. [...] their story is [...] the story of K.' (p. 125). Next, Peter Zusi's 'States of Shock: Kafka and Richard Weiner' opens by introducing Freud and Benjamin to the discussion of Kafka before focusing on a Czech writer, Richard Weiner, who shows marked affinities with Kafka's work. The section concludes with Ritchie Robertson's timely revaluation, 'Max Brod's Novel *Tycho Brahes Weg zu Gott*: A Tale of Two Astronomers', which offers the first full and always subtle study of what is arguably Brod's best novel. The third section treats 'Kafkas Schriften aus der Zeit des Ersten Weltkriegs', opening with Reiner Stach's sharply focused biographical study of Kafka's life in Prague during the war, 'Franz Kafka, Kriegsgefangen', which is succeeded by Thomas Anz's perceptive 'Motive des militärischen in Kafkas Erzähltexten seit August 1914', arguing that the war had a significant impact on Kafka's development. By contrast Juliane Blank's 'Historische Konkretisierung und Verallgemeinerung in den "*Gruftwächter*"-Aufzeichnungen (1916/17)' offers a differentiated account of a specific text-complex, claiming that Kafka both depends on concrete historical realities and significantly departs from them. This topic is developed in W. J. Dodd's sophisticated reading of 'Kafka's Russia and Images of War in 1912 and 1914', which shows that *Der Process* was largely unaffected by the war, though the war is echoed in shorter texts such as 'In der Strafkolonie'. This is succeeded by Manfred Engel's summational study 'Entwürfe symbolischer Weltordnungen: China und China Revisited. Das China-Complex in Kafkas Werk 1917–1920', according to which Kafka's China is not an image but a countercultural image of Austria-Hungary. The last two articles treat linguistic matters. Marek Nekula examines 'Kafkas "organische" Sprache: Sprachdiskurs als Kampfdiskurs', in which the metaphor of the struggle is shown to have significance far beyond the First World War; and Benno Wagner provides a welcome treatment of 'Fürsprache — Widerstreit — Dialog: Karl Kraus, Franz Kafka und das Schreiben gegen den Krieg' to show how Kafka's idea of an enemy (*Feindbild*) opposes the standard views of his age.

The volume *Kafka und Prag* is similarly divided into three sections, beginning with 'Franz Kafkas böhmische Kontexte'. Vaclav Petrbok's essay on 'Josef Wenzig und die (Selbst-)Wahrnehmung seiner politischen und literarischen Tätigkeit in den 60er Jahren des 19. Jahrhunderts' adds some essential Czech background to Kafka's Prague, as does Steffen Höhne's 'Nachdenken über kulturelle Zugehörigkeit: Neobohemistische Traditionen und nationale Desintegration in der Kafka-Zeit' regarding the Austro-Hungarian context. Next, Ludger Udoph deals with a single hitherto neglected Czech text, Pavel Eisner's *Milenky*, in '"Tschechische Weiblichkeit" als Erlösung des "deutschen Mannes"'. This is followed by Jörg Krappmann's welcome revaluation 'Der Prager deutsche Philosoph Max Steiner und die Kantforschung zu Beginn des 20. Jahrhunderts', which contextualizes Steiner in Prague modernism.

'Franz Kafkas Lebenswelten' begins with Kateřina Čapková's helpful essay '"Ich akzeptiere den Komplex, der ich bin": Zionisten um Franz Kafka' and continues with Carsten Schmidt's useful discussion, 'Zwei Freunde des Kafka-Kleeblatts: Die Ur-Prager Felix Weltsch und Max Brod'. Next, Karl Braun's theoretically oriented article helpfully revisits the biographical scenery in '"Liebster Vater" oder: Franz Kafkas Befreiung aus dem Ehezwang', focusing on psychoanalysis, the letter to Kafka's father, and the planned marriage to Julie Wohryzek. Taking an empirical line, Josef Čermák treats Kafka's heartbreaking last weeks in 'Nachrichten vom Krankenbett: Franz Kafkas letzte Jahre'. Christoph Boyer's brief 'Die Arbeitunfallversicherungsanstalt — ein *Schloß*?' concludes that the AUVA cannot be identified with the novel *Das Schloß*. Next Kaspar Krolop's highly detailed study 'Das Bild des Juristen im Werk von Kafka: Historische Selbsterfahrung oder zeitlose Charakterisierung?' breaks new ground regarding Kafka and the law. Continuing with this theme of Kafka's professional engagement, Simona Švingrová's archival study 'Die Rolle der sprachlichen Qualifikation bei der Karriere eines (k.k.) Beamten: Franz Kafka und seine Kollegen bei der AUVA' adduces new facts regarding the linguistic context of Kafka's profession. This leads naturally to Ingrid Stöhr's statistically sophisticated article on 'Franz Kafkas deutsch-tschechische Zweisprachigkeit im Prager schulischen Kontext'.

The third and final section of the collection, 'Verortungen Franz Kafkas', opens with Boris Blahak's 'Der Schreiber als Seismograph einer Zeitenwende: Reflexe einer mitteleuropäischen Endzeitstimmung in Franz Kafkas Romanfragment *Der Verschollene*', which argues that Kafka's writing shows a greater absorption of world-historical events than is sometimes thought. Next, Klaus Schenk's '"[...] aber kleine Unterschiede waren doch gleich zu merken": Zur imaginären Fremdwahrnehmung bei Franz Kafka' uses sociological theory to examine *Der Verschollene* and *Das Schloß*. Modernity also looms large in Hans-Gerd Koch's brief but stimulating 'Franz Kafka und die Veränderung der Wahrnehmung von Raum, Zeit und Bewegung'. Among other topics, Volker Rühle's extensive piece on 'Zeit der Geschichte und Zeit des Gerichts: Zur Spannung von geschichtlicher und schöpferischer Erfahrung im Werk Kafkas' includes some insightful comparisons between Kafka and Mandel'stam. Pursuing the comparatist mode, Manfred Weinberg offers an informative study entitled 'Franz Kafkas *Das Stadtwappen* mit Libuše Moníková gelesen'. Another single work forms the subject of Hans Kruschwitz's interesting 'Affenwahrheit und Menschenfreiheit: Sprachreflexion in Kafkas *Ein Bericht für eine Akademie*', and finally Hans Dieter Zimmermann's informative 'Richard Weiner: Ein tschechischer Kafka? Eine biographische Skizze' also provides a valuable comparatist reading. The editing of both volumes is immaculate.

KING'S COLLEGE LONDON   JEREMY ADLER

Hermann Broch und die Moderne: Roman, Menschenrecht, Biografie. By PAUL MICHAEL LÜTZELER. Munich: Fink. 2011. 237 pp. €29.90. ISBN 978-3-7705-5101-9.

In his introduction, provocatively entitled 'Broch lesen — wozu?', Paul Michael Lützeler recounts that as a visiting student in Vienna during the early 1970s, while working on a dissertation about Hermann Broch's trilogy *Die Schlafwandler* (1928–32), he interviewed some of the writer's old friends and relatives. His memories of these encounters are compelling in their vivid evocation of Broch's character and appearance—the daughter of a cousin, for example, recalls, 'Als Kind sei ihr Broch wie ein großer Vogel, ein riesiger Rabe vorgekommen und sein Blick habe sie das Fürchten gelehrt' (p. 26). They also anticipate some recurring themes in the author's appreciation of his subject, such as Broch's ability to inspire feelings of admiration and devotion in his friends, his difficult relationship with some of his fellow writers (especially Musil and Thomas Mann), his profound but conflicted dedication to literature, his restlessness and self-questioning as mirrors of a fundamental ambivalence between, on the one hand, social and cultural pessimism and, on the other, a strong desire to instigate change.

Lützeler's dissertation was published in 1973, and his *Hermann Broch: Eine Biographie* followed in 1985. As well as curating the critical edition of Broch's collected writings and correspondence, he published many articles on various aspects of the writer's life and work. This book, whose publication marks the 125th anniversary of Broch's birth and the sixtieth of his death, is a collection of essays written between 1999 and 2010. Here they are arranged within a carefully divided structure that allows each piece to become part of a coherent and exhaustive whole. The introduction is followed by three major sections, each comprising three essays devoted to the main aspects of Broch's activity as a writer: fiction (with a particular focus on *Die Schlafwandler* and on the comedy *Aus der Luft gegriffen*, 1934), non-fiction (Lützeler discusses Broch's literary and autobiographical essays, including an illuminating chapter on his attitude to modern painting), and the letters (those to his son, as well as the ones written to friends and colleagues at the time of his American exile).

In the first section of the book the author's close reading of fictional texts focuses on Broch's treatment of some typically modernist themes. His perceptive discussion of the poetics of spaces in the urban world of Broch's novels prepares the way for a chapter comparing *Die Schlafwandler* and Thomas Mann's *Der Zauberberg* (1924). The similarities and differences between the two works reveal that, in Broch's case, a shared cultural pessimism is alleviated by a cyclical view of history which allows for the possibility of a new beginning. In the following three chapters Lützeler develops this idea by presenting the distinctive traits of Broch's attitude to modernism as characterized by an acute awareness of the loss of a spiritual and ethical system of beliefs coupled with the need to explore new values in troubled and uncertain times. Interestingly, the first essay in this section is entitled 'Zweifel als Grundimpuls der Moderne', but from the piece on Broch's *Psychische Selbstbiographie* (1942–43) we also learn that he saw himself as a 'Fachmann im Hoffen', a 'Hoffnungsspezialist' (p. 154). In the third section of the book the complexity of Broch's relationship with Thomas Mann is convincingly explored from a biographical perspective. In his final chapter Lützeler illustrates the significance of their association at the time of their exile in Princeton between 1938 and 1941, when they collaborated on an international project about democracy and human rights (*The City of Man*, 1940). The extent of Broch's humanitarian engagement and his endearing altruism and simplicity make a distinctive impression in these pages (Lützeler shows Broch squeezing his tall frame into a tiny room while Thomas Mann resided in a luxurious villa). One of the merits of this volume is to have shown the continued relevance of Hermann Broch's work today. Lützeler provides plenty of answers to the title of his introduction. The reader closes this book with a renewed sense of Broch's prime place in the pantheon of literary modernism and of his important contribution to the cultural and political sphere of the world in which we live.

LONDON   DARIA SANTINI

Fictions from an Orphan State: Literary Reflections between Habsburg and Hitler. By ANDREW BARKER. Rochester, NY: Camden House. 2012. 205 pp. £50. ISBN 978-1-57113-531-5.

Andrew Barker brings a lifetime of scholarly experience and discernment to this collection of essays on literary writers from the erstwhile Habsburg Empire. He has chosen not to focus on the authors about whom we most commonly read in the critical literature: Broch, Canetti, Hofmannsthal, Horváth, Kafka, Musil, and Rilke. Instead, he provides English-speaking readers with some engaging studies of works by other writers than these, which, in combination, convey something of the particular flavour of the socio-cultural mix of Austria after the demise of the Empire.

Schnitzler's *Fräulein Else*, of course, can scarcely be counted among the neglected texts of modernist literature, and since it was published in 1924, but is set in the 1890s, it can easily appear to be a throwback to a bygone age. Barker, however, draws attention to the historical and cultural resonances in the text that should prompt us to more careful consideration of the social world it depicts. He also places it alongside two other narratives from the 1920s, Werfel's *Der Tod des Kleinbürgers* and Joseph Roth's *Zipper und sein Vater*, which poignantly expose the mentalities of the Austrian lower classes of the time.

Joseph Roth, Ernst Weiß, and Heimito von Doderer have all attracted a great deal of scholarly interest in the last few decades, but it is fair to say that they number among the central European authors whose works are less widely known in the English-speaking world, and Barker provides helpful sketches of the careers of each of them. Alongside Weiß's harrowing early story *Franta Zlin*, he also reminds us of the writings of Andreas Latzko, who charted the degradation and destruction of human beings in the First World War long before the spectacular wave of war novels that appeared at the end of the 1920s. And he sets the literary career of the Nazi Bruno Brehm against that of the Galician Jewish writer Soma Morgenstern, who opposed nationalism of any sort and fled from Europe to New York in 1941.

Most interestingly perhaps, he explores the treatment of the Austrian Republic's collapse into authoritarianism under Dollfuß in 1934, and of the failed Socialist insurrection against that regime, in the form of a documentary drama by Friedrich Wolf (*Floridsdorf*, 1936) and a searching social and psychological novel by Anna Seghers (*Der Weg durch den Februar*, 1935). Here Barker frames his analysis with, first, a discussion of why Karl Kraus chose to side with Dollfuß as a last bastion against Hitlerism rather than with the campaign of the Social Democrats against Fascism, and secondly with the proletarian author Alois Vogel's novel *Schlagschatten* (1977), the publication history of which illustrates quite how difficult it remained after 1945 to bring the events of 1934 to the attention of the Austrian reading public, even in a balanced historical perspective.

In each chapter Barker makes connections to well-known German works of the period that enable his reader to situate the selected texts in a broader context. Occasionally one might wish for a sharper analysis of the relation between texts than Barker offers. The war novels of Arnold Zweig and Erich Maria Remarque may have been marketed as 'finally telling the truth about the war', but there is much more that might be said about what they show us and how they do so; and Barker's account of the relation between Weiß's *Franta Zlin* and Freud's (exactly contemporaneous) theory of the 'Todestrieb' is misleading. Joseph Roth's synopsis of Weiß's story, which Barker quotes, speaks of Franta's crippled sexuality turning him into a murderer, whereas Freud introduced the 'Todestrieb' as a putative explanation for phenomena that could *not* be accounted for in terms of his erotic theory. But overall the volume is an attractive and thought-provoking guide to the authors discussed.

St John's College, Cambridge   David Midgley

The German Joyce. By Robert K. Weninger. (The Florida James Joyce Series) Gainsville: University Press of Florida. 2012. 257 pp. £64.50. ISBN 978-0-8130-4166-7.

The 'German Joyce' is primarily, of course, the German translation of *Ulysses*—initially in the version by Georg Goyert, first published in 1927 and subsequently improved (apparently with the author's assistance) for a second edition in 1930. Only much later did it appear in the version by Hans Wollschläger, which was assiduously prepared with the help of scholarly advisers and hailed as an outstanding achievement in literary translation when it appeared in 1975. The Goyert version, which did much to establish the reputation of Ulysses in the German-speaking world as an 'unreadable' text, was preceded by a translation of *A Portrait of the Artist as a Young Man* in 1926 and followed by *Dubliners* in 1928. Notwithstanding the extraordinarily enterprising efforts of Dieter Stündel and a host of others, *Finnegans Wake* has retained its reputation as an utterly untranslatable text and therefore an inaccessible one to readers who lack a near-native competence in English. In a salutary reminder for those who imagine that educated Germans are bound to have excellent English, Robert Weninger points out that German writers and intellectuals of the early twentieth century, who had received their education in *humanistische Gymnasien*, were exceedingly well schooled in Latin, Greek, and French but not in English, and were therefore dependent on translations for their appreciation of Joyce's art.

Weninger provides a very clear and accessible account of the reception of Joyce's writings in the German-speaking world, which began with the singularly unsuccessful production of the play *Exiles* in Munich in 1919. Following in the wake of more sensational plays by Ibsen, Wedekind, and Shaw, *Exiles* failed to impress the public with its more subdued depiction of marital tensions, while critics who were expecting more overtly political content in a play about Irish exiles were equally disappointed. In addition to discussing the precise senses in which works by Hans Henny Jahnn, Alfred Döblin, Hermann Broch, Thomas Mann, and a range of post-1945 authors show signs of having been influenced by *Ulysses*, Weninger explores the relation in which Joyce's experimental narratives stand to texts produced by the Dada movement. Here and elsewhere he is able to correct some of the impressions of Joyce's connections with the German-speaking world conveyed by Richard Ellmann's seminal biography *James Joyce* (London: Oxford University Press, 1966): there was no personal contact between Joyce and the Dadaists in Zurich during the First World War, for example, despite the affinities that early reviewers of *Ulysses* noted and Tom Stoppard later exploited in his play *Travesties*. Weninger is also precise and informative on the significance of Joyce's writings for the German debates of the 1960s about the 'crisis of the novel'. It is somewhat curious that he devotes his final chapter to an expansive presentation of the 'Expressionism Debate' among German Marxists in the 1930s, particularly since his conclusion is that the participants could not see beyond their rather rigid sense of a dichotomy between modernism and realism (p. 201). Perhaps the passion to document this dimension of Joyce reception along with the others should be seen as part of Weninger's riposte to the dehistoricizing effects of poststructuralist approaches to literary texts, which he robustly challenges in his introduction. He complements his own historical survey of responses to Joyce with some fascinating readings of texts by Rilke (*Die Aufzeichnungen des Malte Laurids Brigge*) and Goethe (*Wilhelm Meisters Lehrjahre*) alongside Joyce's, notably bringing out the palpable intertextual relationship in which the narratives of both Goethe and Joyce stand to Shakespeare and Homer.

The German Joyce is the sort of multifaceted work that can only be achieved through patient, long-term scholarly investigation. Weninger is to be congratulated on the richness of what he has to show us here about the importance of Joyce as a reference-point for the understanding of modern German literary culture. The University Press of Florida has made his text into a handsome book.

ST JOHN'S COLLEGE, CAMBRIDGE   DAVID MIDGLEY

Funktion und Bedeutung von Erinnerung im erzählerischen Werk Johannes Urzidils. By ANJA BISCHOF. (Hamburger Beiträge zur Germanistik, 53) Frankfurt a.M.: Peter Lang. 2012. 202 pp. €39.80. ISBN 978-3-631-63344-1.

Johannes Urzidil (1896–1970) is among those authors who went into exile, remained abroad, but continued to write in German, like Jenny Aloni (1917–1993) in Israel and H. G. Adler (1910–1988) in Britain, and have therefore—at least till very recently—been neglected by *Germanistik*. Although Urzidil published a large body of mostly short fiction, he is probably best known for his attractive reminiscences of his friend Kafka, *Da geht Kafka* (1965), and his substantial contribution to Goethe scholarship, *Goethe in Böhmen* (1932). An engaging account of Urzidil can be found in Jürgen Serke's *Böhmische Dörfer: Wanderungen durch eine vergessene literarische Landschaft* (Vienna: Zsolnay, 1987), pp. 182–201. A few academic monographs on his work have appeared, the most significant being *Die Prosa Johannes Urzidils* (Bern: Herbert Lang, 1967) by Gerhard Trapp, who has since published many shorter studies on Urzidil.

A professional journalist and a member of the Prague Circle around Max Brod, Urzidil fled with his wife in 1939 to Britain and in 1941 to New York, where for many years they endured poverty and anxiety. Urzidil showed great resilience, however: as he recounts in his essay 'Handwerkliches aus New York' (1969), he learnt bookbinding, and soon scraped a modest living from this trade. Unlike many exiles, he was keenly interested both in America's brash modernity and in its older culture. Another essay describes a literary tour of Massachusetts, where Urzidil visited the houses of Nathaniel Hawthorne and Henry David Thoreau; in the latter writer he discovered a counterpart to his beloved Stifter. He returned to Europe only for short visits.

Anja Bischof provides an unpretentious, factual overview of Urzidil's life and works, which is the more useful since much of his fiction is now hard to obtain. He published seventy-five stories and one novel, *Das Große Halleluja* (1959), which is set in America and, according to Bischof's plot summary, brings an innocent American country girl into contact with New York high society and criminal gangs. Almost half the stories are set in Bohemia, many in Prague itself. In my judgement, the best-known volume, *Prager Triptychon* (1960), well illustrates Urzidil's distinctive qualities. Its longest story, 'Weißenstein Karl', recounted posthumously by an eccentric misfit, modulates from picaresque incidents into a sombre narrative of guilt and ineffectual atonement, while 'Vermächtnis eines Jünglings', closely based on the Prague Circle, displays Urzidil's combination of grotesquely inventive humour with a pervasive sadness that recalls another underrated Prague novelist, Ernst Weiss.

Urzidil's imaginative revisiting of Prague justifies Bischof's selection of memory as a focus for her study. The book is somewhat fragmented. An early chapter briskly surveying recent developments in memory studies is followed by a thirty-page 'Werkübersicht', and that in turn by interesting reflections on how Urzidil contrasts the traditional 'Dingwelt' of agrarian Europe with the glass-and-concrete modernity of America. Only two-thirds of the way through the book do we return to memory, which according to Bischof's view serves two functions in Urzidil's fiction: preserving the past and coming to terms with recollected guilt. There are two oddities: the author's repeated use of the strange compound 'Erzählungenband' instead of the usual 'Erzählband', and her statement (p. 103) that *Das Große Halleluja* ends with the first moon landing, something hardly possible for a novel published in 1959. Otherwise, Bischof's study can be recommended as a handy guide to Urzidil and his major themes, with a comprehensive bibliography of previous secondary literature.

THE QUEEN'S COLLEGE, OXFORD   RITCHIE ROBERTSON

'Man will werden, nicht gewesen sein': Zur Aktualität Max Frischs. Ed. by DANIEL MÜLLER NIELABA, YVES SCHUMACHER, and CHRISTOPH STEIER. Zurich: Chronos. 2012. 272 pp. €31. ISBN 978–3–0340–1153–2.

This study is based on twelve public lectures given to mark the centenary of Frisch's birth in 2011, the majority by Germanists from the two Zurich universities. It aims to reawaken interest in this author, especially among scholars of modern German literature. The 'received' image paints Frisch as a 'modernist' committed to the tradition of the Enlightenment, a view analysed in the first four chapters on Frisch as a political orator (Thomas Strässle), as a figure in Swiss and German public affairs (Michel Mettler), his attitude to the 1968 student movement in Paris (Christine Weder), and his lifelong interest in the Zurich Schauspielhaus (Ursula Amrein). The last of these has a particular focus on the input of German emigrants of the 1930s, Frisch's changing political attitude during the 1940s, and his introduction of new playwrights to the German-speaking theatre (Sartre, Claudel, Lorca, Steinbeck, Wilder). Here Frisch is viewed in the context of 'modernists' such as Sartre, Brecht, Grass, Bachmann, and Uwe Johnson, but is perceived also as an author who seeks to involve his audience, playing the role of the 'dialogisch Fragender', using a form of Socratic method, while at the same time anxious not to sacrifice his aesthetic principles to the demands of the day.

The remaining eight essays can be subsumed under the broad heading of aesthetics. Frisch's early career as an architect is explored by Hans-Georg von Arburg, who shows how Frisch soon came to reject the 'pictorial' and three-dimensional art in favour of the 'word', which embraced diversity, uncertainty, and the exploration of new social concepts. The chapter 'Bilderangst und Fabulierkunst' by Andreas

Kilcher explores this subject further, although the lengthy discussion of Frisch and the 'Laocoön problem' is not entirely convincing, especially when related to Sartre's existentialism. More interesting are references to Frisch's use of intertexuality, which obscures the author's subjectivity behind a palimpsest of texts. His characters deceive themselves as well as their readers; his portrayal of life through literature does not aim to posit the self as an aspect of reality, but 'deconstructs' it as a potentiality. Such attempts to place Frisch in the vanguard of postmodernism may go too far, since this can also be found in earlier literary traditions. The three essays on Frisch's novels take this into consideration. They are discussed in the context of the modernist crisis of the narrative, with references to similarities in the works of Mann, Benn, and Hesse, as well as to Goethe's *Wahlverwandtschaften* (Wolfram Groddeck). Interpretations of *Montauk* (Daniel Müller Nielaba) and *Gantenbein* (Barbara Naumann) explore this further, and Sabine Schneider's discussion of *Der Mann erscheint im Holozän* not only refers to Barthes's death of the author but also to that of the novel's protagonist, suggesting that the artistic subject relinquishes its dominion within its own work.

Only one article refers to Frisch's dramatic œuvre, that by Peter Schnyder, concentrating on the early and late editions of *Biographie*, rather than his more popular plays. The final contribution by Karl Wagner considers Frisch's *Tagebücher*. They feature as 'autobiografiction', portraying Frisch's involvement with the *Zeitgeist*, though in a distanced, fictional form. Together with Adorno's *Minima Moralia* and T. S. Eliot's essays, they were the first books published by Suhrkamp and have today lost nothing of their topicality.

OXFORD   HANS J. HAHN

Still Songs: Music in and around the Poetry of Paul Celan. By AXEL ENGLUND. Farnham: Ashgate. 2012. 239 pp. £55. ISBN 978-1-4094-2262-4.

This study examines the intersection between music and poetry in Paul Celan's work and explores the prominence of Celan's poetry for the music of late modernism. Notwithstanding conflicting statements by Celan, for Axel Englund music and musicality constitute a key principle of, and meta-reflective mirror for, the poetry of the Jewish Shoah survivor. Celan's encounters with music have in fact proved to be very fruitful and serve an equally meta-reflective function for the musical avant-garde of the late twentieth century. Alongside interpretations of Celan's poems, Englund offers close readings of musical settings by ten composers, including Tilo Medek, Harrison Birtwistle, Aribert Reimann, György Kurtág, Wolfgang Rihm, and Peter Ruzicka.

Methodically, musical compositions based on poetic texts can either be approached in their singularity, without taking the interpretation of the poetic text into account, or they can be read against the hermeneutic horizon of the poems. However, reading the musical piece through the filter of the textual interpretation might conceal significant aspects present only in musical works. Englund combines his perspectives as a musicologist and literary scholar in multiple ways either by prioritizing references to music or the foregrounding of acoustic structure in his close readings of Celan's poems, or by projecting textual interpretations 'upon the surface of the musical structure' (p. 16). In some cases he puts emphasis on the interpretation of the compositions, which are, in turn, used as a guide to attain a more comprehensive understanding of the structure of the poems.

The study explores 'the metaphorical interplay between words and music' (pp. 163–64), drawing on Paul Ricœur's theory of metaphor. It is important to note that Englund's readings of Celan's poems are not mere interpretations of the texts themselves, but rather set out to analyse the mutual exchange between music and poetry as a metaphorical dynamic. The argument hence remains in the area of literary-aesthetic experience by focusing on key moments of Celan's encounter with music. It does not provide a deeper theoretical discussion of Ricœur's theory, intermedial relations, or meta-referentiality (as proposed by Werner Wolf, or Gruber and Gier). Englund addresses the process within which music and poetry become 'hermeneutic agencies [. . .] actively commenting and reinterpreting each other' (p. 17) from multiple perspectives.

Having interpreted the thematization of music and musicality in both Celan's poems and their musical settings, Englund insists that Celan's poems, even his controversially debated 'Todesfuge', do not aesthetisize the Shoah but call traditional notions of music and musicality into question by reflecting on their conditions of existence. The study reveals that musical compositions can be used as aids for textual interpretations of Celan's poems. Even though Englund uses the somewhat simplistic metaphor of reading Celan's poems through the filter of musical compositions—failing to take account of the fact that references are usually fractured in Celan's poetry and cannot be treated as analogies—his approach convincingly shows that musical adaptations of Celan's poetry, their sonic strata, texture, and pitch, often uncover the interrelations and hierarchies between different meanings and readings of a poem.

The strength of the study lies in its broadly based examination of poems and musical compositions from every phase of Celan's work. It thereby highlights the development of the musico-literary interplay in Celan's poems, extending from the emphasis on acoustic structure via a positive presence of music in the poem 'Fadensonnen' to 'a negative attitude towards poetic musicality' (p. 19) in conjunction with notions of German and Jewish music-making in Celan's late poetry.

UNIVERSITY OF CAMBRIDGE   ANNJA NEUMANN

Letzte Menschen: Postapokalyptische Narrative und Identitäten in der Neueren Literatur nach 1945. By JUDITH SCHOSSBÖCK. (Post-Apocalyptic Studies, 2) Bochum: Projektverlag. 2012. 177 pp. €17.80. ISBN 978-3-89733-261-4.

The apocalypse and the post-apocalypse are upon us—hardly a day passes without some item of news, cultural, political, religious, philosophical, or medical, reminding us of the fragility and tenuousness of our human condition, whether it be our exposure to previously unknown viruses, a possible nuclear holocaust, the earth's impending collision with some errant comet or asteroid, or any number of ever looming natural disasters such as a man-made eco-breakdown or a volcanic Super-GAU, or even—in the imagination of some—our annihilation through aliens. Humankind's death is the stuff that keeps Hollywood alive. And literature lags not far behind. Indeed, the apocalypse and post-apocalypse have become such a hot topic in recent literary and cultural studies, it seems, that Christian Hoffstadt (Tübingen University) and Stefan Höltgen (HU Berlin) have recently seen fit to dedicate a new series to their study, the first volume of which was their own *This is the End...: Mediale Visionen vom Untergang der Menschheit* (Bochum: Projektverlag, 2011). The series' second volume is Judith Schossböck's monograph on narratives about last men and last women.

The subject of Schossböck's book is primarily post-1945 German literature, with the focus being on texts by—in chronological order—Arno Schmidt (*Schwarze Spiegel*, 1951), Marlen Haushofer (*Die Wand*, 1963), Herbert Rosendorfer (*Großes Solo für Anton*, 1976), and Thomas Glavinic (*Die Arbeit der Nacht*, 2006), with occasional further reference to Yorck Kronenberg's *Welt unter* (2001), Domian Jürgen's *Der Tag, an dem die Sonne verschwand* (2008), and the German-Czech writer Iva Procházková's 'Jugendbuch' *Wir treffen uns wieder, wenn alle weg sind* (2007). Schossböck also allows herself forays into American and Italian literature, specifically Cormac McCarthy's *The Road* (2006) and Guido Morselli's *Dissipatio humanis generis* (1977). And this is where I felt some of the problems begin, and where the volume betrays its roots in the 2009 *Diplomarbeit* at the University of Vienna, as which it was submitted. Before I continue, let me state that, for the purposes of an MA-level *Diplomarbeit*, this is an outstanding piece of scholarship and a remarkable achievement to boot for a budding scholar. Schossböck's theoretical survey of, and introduction to, the burgeoning field of (literary) apocalypse and post-apocalypse studies in the opening sections of the monograph are well researched, informative, and useful. Naturally, and appropriately so for this topic, the focus lies on German secondary publications. While an impressive range of English-language material is also cited (Brian Aldiss, Mike Alsford, Norman Cohn, Frank Kermode, David Seed, Susan Sontag, and more) alongside works by French theoreticians Baudrillard, Blanchot, Derrida, and Foucault, the field is obviously far too extensive for any sole scholar in this area to achieve exhaustive coverage, regardless of how much time is spent on researching it—although I would have been curious to see such important studies on futuristic fiction as those by Paul Alkon and W. Warren Wagar as well as some of the illuminating essays in *The End of the World*, ed. by Eric S. Rabkin and others (Carbondale: Southern Illinois University Press, 1983), used as additional props to the arguments presented.

My qualms lie elsewhere. First, the volume suffers from a peculiar imbalance; although the stated goal is to offer an analysis of the primary texts listed above, it is the introductory theoretical survey that in the end comes to occupy the bulk of the book's argument, namely seven of its nine sections. The single remaining analytical section ('8. Motivanalyse'), in which the theory is put into analytical practice, and the three-page closing argument ('9. Ausblick') occupy a mere third of the total page count. For lack of space and attention to textual detail, the analyses themselves have remained rather sketchy and cursory; there is so much more that could have been done if space and time had permitted. Second, we encounter frequent references to a purported apocalypse vogue in the 1980s, only for us to be reminded over and over again that we will *not* find any texts from that decade discussed ('Neben gelegentlichen Verweisen auf englische Science-Fiction-Vorlagen beschränke ich mich auf deutsche Romane nach 1945. Es liegt an den beschriebenen Auswahlkriterien, dass Romane der 1980er Jahre bewusst nicht herangezogen wurden' (p. 103)): so why this stress on the 1980s in the first place? And why then so prominently include McCarthy's American novel *The Road* and Morselli's Italian *Dissipatio humanis generis* and not just stick to the German primary sources? If McCarthy, why not also Atwood, Lessing, Markson, or Miller? In short, the cast of subsidiary or supporting texts struck me as rather arbitrary. And finally, in the crucial eighth chapter itself, I did not feel too comfortable with the analytical approach taken: the characters (such as the 'Ich-Erzählerin' in Haushofer's *Die Wand* or Jonas in Glavinic's *Die Arbeit der Nacht*) were invariably discussed as 'real' people rather than fictional constructs. The authors themselves figured only marginally in the analyses. Thus we read: '[Jonas'] Hauptmotivation seiner Bewaffnung ist nicht eine wirkliche Gefahr, sondern eine psychische Bedrohung' (p. 130), or 'Jonas scheitert gerade deshalb, weil die Speicherung des Wissens nicht mit seiner eigenen Wahrnehmung korrespondiert' (p. 147), or 'Die Protagonistinnen schreiben daher insbesondere gegen den Verlust ihrer Erinnerung' (p. 146). Yes, I agree in all instances. But what do these forms of characterization of the protagonists tell us about the authors' reasons for portraying them in this way? We are continually told what the fictitious characters in their unreal (and sometimes surreal) worlds think and believe, and why they do things; but only occasionally are we told why the authors are doing these things with their characters and what their perspectivizations might convey about the shifting ideologies of apocalyptic thinking in the authors' real worlds.

In short, I would have preferred this project, and particularly its practical text-analytical section, to have been given more time to mellow before publication. As it stands, the volume has some merit as an introductory theoretical survey, and readers new to the field will find it valuable; but it will not satisfy the more advanced reader looking for mature and detailed analyses of Schmidt's or Haushofer's mesmerizing works, not to mention the later primary texts discussed in this volume.

KING'S COLLEGE LONDON   ROBERT WENINGER

A New History of German Cinema. Ed. by JENNIFER M. KAPCZYNSKI and MICHAEL D. RICHARDSON. (Screen Cultures: German Film and the Visual) Rochester, NY: Camden House. 2012. xvii+673 pp. £60. ISBN 978-1-57113-490-5.

Recent accounts of German film history generally adopt one of two approaches—they either focus on one of the seven Germanies witnessed and recorded by

German-language cinema (Imperial, Weimar, National Socialist, occupied, East, West, reunified) or, as in Stephen Brockmann's *Critical History of German Film* (Columbia, SC: Camden House, 2010), proceed on a film-by-film basis, selecting 'representative' classics to exemplify the aforementioned Germanies (and, more recently, Austria). Standard works on German cinema also tend to fall into one or other of these categories: Kracauer on Weimar, Elsaesser on the New German Cinema, Berghahn on DEFA, Rentschler on literary adaptations.

Jennifer M. Kapczynski and Michael D. Richardson's edited volume *A New History of German Cinema* adopts a different approach, though its title is somewhat misleading. The history it recounts is not quite as challenging to 'unidirectional narratives' or quite as 'new' as is claimed—the introduction, epilogue, and seven linking chapters, all written by the editors to contextualize the short essays that make up the body of the volume, are informative and thorough, but traditional in their chronological retelling of political, social, and cultural history. The editors of the new volume themselves refer to the book's approach as 'eventalization' (a term which betrays the volume's strong US bias). The result is not so much a history as a subjective 'chronicle', and therein lie both its considerable strengths and certain weaknesses. Each of the eighty-eight essays (of around five pages, accompanied by useful cross-references) concentrates on a specific date, beginning with 1 November 1895, the day on which the Skladanowsky brothers first showed their attractions in Berlin, and ending on 11 February 2008, when Ulrike Ottinger's documentary *Prater* won the German Critics' Award for best documentary. These bookends amply demonstrate the volume's 'highways and byways' methodology, which makes for a read that is both stimulating and a little frustrating. Many entries—and there are almost as many as there are authors—are enlightening, lively, and scholarly mini-essays shedding light on less-known aspects of film history. Deniz Göktürk on the 1913 disaster movie *Atlantis*, Tobias Nagl on Chinese students demonstrating against racism on film in 1920, Daniel H. Magilow on Jewish identity in popular Weimar Cinema, and Marc Silberman on Brecht's *Threepenny Opera* lawsuit are outstanding examples in the pre-1933 sections. There are fascinating insights into the ideology of Third Reich cinema, not least Jaimey Fisher on melodrama and Total War, and many stimulating discussions of post-1945 cinema, including fine commentaries by Hester Baer on Ilse Kubaschewski and her Gloria film distribution company, and Kapczynski on Sirk's *A Time to Love and a Time to Die*. The latter further highlights the aforementioned US focus of a volume which includes detailed studies of the Hollywood work of Dieterle, Lang, and Preminger. Revealing as these essays are, their prevalence skews the volume's perspective. Moreover, although there are excellent essays on Wenders (Brad Prager), Fassbinder (Brigitte Peucker), and post-reunification film (Roger F. Cook on *Ostalgie*, Randall Halle on von Praunheim), there are some notable lacunae: Schroeter, Schlöndorff, Syberberg, Schlingensief, Böttcher, and, regrettably, women's film of the 1970s and 1980s (no von Trotta, Sander, or Sanders-Brahms) despite a passionate celebration of the journal *Frauen und Film* by its editor Annette Brauerhoch. Moreover, although Austrian cinema is included (albeit on occasion referred to as 'German'), Swiss cinema is not. In summary, this event-centred volume offers myriad insights into the 'unknown stories' and, to a lesser extent, the mainstream of German-language cinema. It is ambitious, highly informative, and meticulously compiled (some lamentably poor-quality DVD captures, a few passages of purple prose, and a mistitled collection of Brecht poetry notwithstanding) and it is a welcome addition to the growing corpus of ambitious work on German-language cinema. It should, however, be read alongside some of those other, 'unidirectional' histories that it sets out to challenge.

KING'S COLLEGE LONDON   MARTIN BRADY

We Modern People: Science Fiction and the Making of Russian Modernity. By ANINDITA BANERJEE. Middletown, CT: Wesleyan University Press. 2012. viii+206 pp. $24.95. ISBN 978-0-8195-7334-6.

In *We Modern People* Anindita Banerjee argues that Russian science fiction from the 1890s to the 1920s helped to form a unique vision of modernity. Each of four chapters focuses on a different but interrelated intersection of science and science fiction. In the first chapter, 'Conquering Space', Banerjee describes how technologies such as the railway, the aeroplane, and the telescope were used by science fiction writers to create a new vision of Russia and its relationship with the world. The building of the trans-Siberian railway led to depictions of Russia as Eurasian, an image strengthened by scientific work proving that Russia was not ecologically separate from Asia. Siberia became an antidote to Western infection, an unexplored place where 'the prehistoric past merges with Promethean future not tainted by modernity' (p. 39). In the concluding part of this chapter Banerjee discusses how the invention of the aeroplane shaped a vision of the earth as a harmonious whole and how Fyodorov's and Tsiolkovskii's influential theories of a unified universe extended this map.

'Transcending Time' discusses how new technologies and scientific discoveries affected the representation of time in Russian science fiction, among them the locomotive, the telegraph, and the escalator, the technological manipulations enabled by the phonograph and cinema, and the influence of philosophers such as Nietzsche and Bergson and scientists such as Einstein and Maxwell.

'Generating Power' extends its discussion much further back in time to trace the image of electricity from the writings of Lomonosov and Radishchev to the early nineteenth-century obsession with Galvani's experiments to the depiction of electricity in Odoevskii's *The Year 4338*. This interest in electricity concludes with the fascination with the lightbulb during the 1890s as a symbol of modernity, the motif of lighting the countryside in Russian science fiction, and the Bolshevik electrification campaign. Banerjee concludes this chapter by discussing the influence of Nikolai Fedorov on early twentieth-century science fiction, where electricity became the stuff of physical immortality and psychic transfiguration.

The final chapter, 'Creating the Human', examines Russian science fiction of the first two decades of the twentieth century as attempting to resolve mind–body duality through physiological psychology and monistic evolutionary theory. The various theories of physical, psychological, and parapsychological energy from both Europe and Russia led to Tsiolkovskii's vision of 'pan-psychism', in which animate and inanimate are part of a universal whole, and Bogdanov's blood transfusion theory, an attempt to create an 'immortal collective organism' (p. 142) on his fictional Mars through the exchange of blood.

Bannerjee's book examines an astounding variety of texts to weave together analysis of science, popular culture, and science fiction into a fascinating vision of Russian modernity. Her study surprises the reader at every turn with fresh insights and a fast-paced overhead view of a world where the boundaries on traditionally drawn literary maps are no longer visible. Banerjee's highly entertaining and meticulously researched book explores the intimate connections between science and literature during this period of rapid technological and scientific change, and with luck will give a much-needed push to the study of Russian and Soviet science fiction. Most important (for me at least) is the fun of reading Banerjee's book. Her highly readable narrative combines science, literary theory, and textual analysis into a book that is entertaining as well as informative and thought-provoking.

UNIVERSITY OF UTAH   ERIC LAURSEN

The Readers of 'Novyi mir': Coming to Terms with the Stalinist Past. By DENIS KOZLOV. Cambridge, MA and London: Harvard University Press. 2013. 442 pp. $55. ISBN 978-0-674-07287-9.

Denis Kozlov's *The Readers of 'Novyi mir'* is a hard book to classify. Part institutional history, part literary analysis, and part biography, Kozlov's work examines the debates surrounding the quintessential Soviet 'thick journal', *Novyi mir*, during the years of the post-Stalinist 'Thaw'. Beginning with Vladimir Pomerantsev's game-changing article 'On Sincerity and Literature' in 1954, and ending with the ousting of *Novyi mir*'s reforming editor Aleksandr Tvardovskii in 1970, Kozlov takes the reader through the major literary events of the Thaw era, including the publication of Aleksandr Solzhenitsyn's *One Day in the Life of Ivan Denisovich*, Boris Pasternak's awarding, and subsequent rejection, of the Nobel Prize for literature, and the trial of the authors Andrei Siniavskii and Iulii Daniel. Much of this story is familiar, but viewing these scandals through their reception by the *Novyi mir* readership sheds new light on old controversies, and Kozlov weaves these individual cases into a much bigger story about the evolution of literature and the memory of Stalinism. The work hinges on the discussion of Solzhenitsyn's *One Day*, which, according to Kozlov, 'set the ethical framework for verbalizing the human experiences of the twentieth century's mass violence' (p. 209). Alongside his close readings of significant literary moments, Kozlov includes numerous digressions on the major ideological debates of the era, including the nature of literary truth, the limits of language, and the issue of belief and complicity in the face of terror.

Kozlov is hardly the first to write about Soviet cultures of reading, or indeed to use readers' letters as a source, and his work is often in provocative dialogue with that of Miriam Dobson, Aleksei Yurchak, and Orlando Figes, among others. Yet in the sheer scope of his thematic reach, and his careful close reading of the dialogue between readers, writers, and the *Novyi mir* editorship, Kozlov reveals a nuanced and multidimensional picture of Soviet cultural practices during the Thaw that reaches beyond its immediate subject-matter to contribute to key debates about Soviet power, subjectivity, and ideology. Kozlov rejects the picture of Soviet culture as a 'top-down', regulated sphere, arguing that 'Soviet reading and intellectual history were diverse and nonlinear, reflecting the wide variety of perceptions that existed in that multifaceted and sophisticated culture' (p. 20). These letters show the degree to which the meaning of Soviet classics was created by their readership, who filtered these works through their own memories and experiences, and reveals widespread questioning on the part of both readers and editors about what could and could not be said. At the same time, this book is less a retracing of the boundaries of the permissible during the Thaw, and more an exploration of the nature of memory and the problem of language in approaching the Stalinist past. His work documents the rupture with the traditional 'language and ethos of the Soviet media' (p. 208), and a search for new forms of expression. This book foregrounds Soviet readers' voices, creating a tangible—and indeed emotional—picture of how people began to read and talk about the terror, as well as a sense of the acute topicality and meaning of literature for ordinary Soviet citizens. One might perhaps question his bold claim that this explosion of discussion marked 'the *unmaking* of Soviet subjectivity' (p. 9) in the Thaw years, which seems to sit slightly at odds with much new scholarship on the explosion of grass-roots activity and the 'relaunch' of the Soviet ideological project under Khrushchev. Yet the sheer power of these letters, alongside Kozlov's thought-provoking examination of their thematic and stylistic significance, contributes much to our understanding of the nature of Soviet individuals' engagement with politics and the past.

UNIVERSITY OF BRISTOL   CLAIRE SHAW

ABSTRACTS

'Simplicité, clarté et précision': Grammars of Italian 'pour les Dames' and Other Learners in Eighteenth- and Early Nineteenth-Century France   by Helena Sanson

Across eighteenth-century Europe, a number of authors composed **grammars**, of their own language or of foreign languages, 'for the Ladies', '**pour les Dames**', 'per le Dame', 'für die Damen'/'für Frauenzimmer'. These texts, meant also more generally for **non-Latinate** readers and **beginners**, claimed they offered **easy**, engaging, and innovative study methods. In **France** one of the languages that feature most among works of this type is **Italian**. Parisian ladies wanted to learn it to dazzle in society and there was no shortage of **Italian teachers** keen to assist them in their enterprise with their grammars.

Filming the Silent (Br)Other: Levinasian Ethics and Aesthetic Faith in Patrick Drevet's *Les Gardiens des pierres* and Philip Gröning's *Die große Stille*   by Erin Tremblay Ponnou-Delaffon

This paper investigates the relationship between **ethics** and **aesthetics** by comparing how **Patrick Drevet**'s novel *Les Gardiens des pierres* and **Philip Gröning**'s documentary *Die große Stille* (*Into Great Silence*)—two intimate portrayals of cinematic encounters with cloistered monks—depict what **Emmanuel Levinas** has called the asymmetrical self-**Other** relationship. Self-reflectively struggling against the limits of **representation**, these works paradoxically reveal their authors' fragile **faith** in art's communicative potential. In so doing, they perform non-reductive approaches to **alterity**, suggest possible aesthetic and ethical encounters in *and* with a work of **art**, and shed new light on Levinasian-inspired approaches to literature and cinema.

An Unthinkable *History of King Richard the Third*: Thomas More's Fragment and his Answer to Lucian's *Tyrannicide*   by Jürgen Meyer

This article establishes two **intertexts** for Thomas More's historiographical fragment about Richard III. One of More's Lucianic *controversiae* focuses on legal problems similar to those dealt with in the *History*, refuting the claims of a fictional tyrant's assassin demanding his reward. **Fortescue**'s *On the Governance of England* distinguishes between **tyranny** and **regality**, and thus relates to certain power issues in the *History*. It is argued that More's struggle with his own text had its cause less in the need to represent a ruthless tyrant than in the constitutional obligation to present his successor as a providential saviour of the commonwealth.

Lord Byron: Paratext and Poetics   by Ourania Chatsiou

This article seeks to shed new light on Byronic or **Romantic irony** by approaching it from a fresh paratextual perspective, focusing on footnotes, endnotes, and **annotation**. It suggests that the digressive structure of *Don Juan* develops out of the paratextual play of the Oriental tales, where **Byron**'s diverting notes construct a hybrid narrative that interweaves fiction and 'fact'. *Don Juan* is thus an assimilation of paratextual commentary that characterized Byron's poetics ever since *English Bards and Scotch Reviewers*, revealing that **paratext** has been integral all along to the **reading process** and **writing practice** of a totalized, hybrid text.

'Why don't you write a play?' Kipling the Poet in Full   by John Batchelor

The Cambridge Edition of the Poems of Rudyard Kipling is an impressive and invaluable scholarly achievement. The editor presents a remarkable number of poems which were hitherto **unpublished**, including 'The Press', a strikingly angry attack on **intrusive journalists**. He also presents a rich haul of poems which had never hitherto been **collected**. The three volumes of this edition bring Kipling back into serious consideration as a **major poet**. With his masterful **ballads**, such as '**Danny Deever**' (praised unreservedly by **T. S. Eliot**), Kipling explored an **English working-class voice** which had never been heard previously.

Narratives of Child Sexual Abuse in Cristina Comencini's Novel *La bestia nel cuore* by Luciano Parisi

Italian novelists, playwrights and poets have told interesting but understudied **stories of child sexual abuse**. This type of abuse has been found to be more widespread in Italy than previously thought, and contemporary authors such as **Maraini** and **Comencini** have denounced it as an example of violence against women in a patriarchal society. I analyse Comencini's novel *La bestia nel cuore*, published in 2004, and show that more narratives may be needed, and are in the making, as over-reliance on a single narrative may lead to a loss of critical reflexivity.

Vallejo and González Prada: A Note on *Trilce* XIX by Dominic Moran

The principal aim of this article is to demonstrate the profound indebtedness, in terms of both subject matter and expression, of Poem XIX of **César Vallejo**'s *Trilce* (1922) to the work of Peruvian thinker and poet **Manuel González Prada** (1844–1918). It goes on to argue more broadly that González Prada's thinking about **religion, science**, and **poetry** provided Vallejo with both a thematic and a formal template for a revolutionary and specifically **Americanist poetics**, the roots of which have generally been located by critics in the **European avant-garde**.

'Die Juden schießen!' Translations by Hermann Adler and Wolf Biermann of Yitzhak Katzenelson's Epic Poem of the Warsaw Ghetto by Peter Davies

This article discusses **German translations** by **Hermann Adler** (1951) and **Wolf Biermann** (1994) of **Yitzhak Katzenelson**'s **Yiddish** narrative poem about the **Warsaw Ghetto Uprising**, *Dos lid funm oysgehargetn yidishn folk* (*The Song of the Exterminated Jewish People*, written 1944). It explores the difficulties of **translating the victim's viewpoint** into the 'language of the perpetrators' and the way that these two **German Jewish writers** have conceptualized the relationship between Yiddish and German, showing that they have both used Katzenelson's text in order to perform interventions in the discussion of **victim–perpetrator reconciliation**.

Writers' Linguistic Observations and Creating Myths about Languages: Czesław Miłosz and Joseph Brodsky in Search of the 'Slavonic Genius of Language' by Shamil Khairov

The article deals with evaluative **judgements about languages** made by Czesław Miłosz and Joseph Brodsky. Both authors follow and build upon the **language myths** according to which Polish and Russian are contrasted with 'Western' languages as representatives of the respective **national psyches**, although they focus on different linguistic features. Miłosz's statements tend towards the technical, while those of Brodsky are more ethical and metaphysical. As to their statements on Russian and Polish respectively, the differences tend to lose any systemic linguistic basis, but instead relate mainly to the history of Polish–Russian relations and the writers' individual experiences and exile strategies.

Freedom and Captivity in the Works of Vladimir Sorokin and Vladimir Tuchkov by Nicolas Dreyer

This article analyses the 'prison camp' mentality of **post-Soviet man** as represented by **Vladimir Sorokin** and **Vladimir Tuchkov**. The works under discussion explore the relationship between the individual and power in Russia past and present, and depict people as being theoretically free but imprisoned mentally and ideologically. The texts are analysed with reference to writers including **Dostoevskii, Turgenev, Zamiatin**, and **Solzhenitsyn**, as well as to concepts developed by **Kant, Freud**, and **Rancour-Laferriere**, and are approached in terms of **humour, irony**, the **grotesque**, and **satire**.

www.ingramcontent.com/pod-product-compliance
Lightning Source LLC
Chambersburg PA
CBHW052112010526
44111CB00036B/1829